CENTRAL AMERICA AND THE UNITED STATES

The Clients and the Colossus

TWAYNE'S INTERNATIONAL HISTORY SERIES

Akira Iriye, editor
Harvard University

CENTRAL AMERICA AND THE UNITED STATES

The Clients and the Colossus

WITHDRAWI

John H. Coatsworth
Harvard University

TWAYNE PUBLISHERS • NEW YORK
MAXWELL MACMILLAN CANADA • TORONTO
MAXWELL MACMILLAN INTERNATIONAL • NEW YORK OXFORD SINGAPORE SYDNEY

Twayne Publishers
Macmillan Publishing Company
866 Third Avenue
New York, New York 10022

Maxwell Macmillan Canada, Inc.
1200 Eglinton Avenue East
Suite 200
Don Mills, Ontario M3C 3N1

Twayne's International History Series, No. 12

Library of Congress Cataloging-in-Publication Data

Coatsworth, John H., 1940– .
    Central America and the United States : the clients and the colossus.
        p.   cm. — (Twayne's international history series ; 12)
    Includes bibliographical references and index.
    ISBN 0-8057-7901-9 — ISBN 0-8057-9210-4 (pbk.)
    1. Central America—Foreign relations—United States. 2. United States—Foreign relations—Central America. 3. United States—Foreign relations—1945– . I. Title. II. Series.
    F1438.8.U6C63 1994
    327.730728—dc20   93-29998
                                                                                              CIP

The paper used in this publication meets the minimum requirements of American National Standard for Information Sciences—Permanence of Paper for Printed Library Materials. ANSI Z39.48-1984. ⊗™

10 9 8 7 6 5 4 3 2 1 (alk. paper)

10 9 8 7 6 5 4 3 2 1 (pbk.: alk. paper)

Printed and bound in the United States of America.

To Janet Whedon Bell Barr and Irving Barr
and to
Anna Karabin Sopiak and Metro Sopiak
with love

CONTENTS

FOREWORD

Twayne's International History Series seeks to publish reliable and readable accounts of post–World War II international affairs. Today, nearly 50 years after the end of the war, the time seems opportune to undertake a critical assessment of world affairs in the second half of the twentieth century. What themes and trends have characterized international relations since 1945? How have they evolved and changed? What connections have developed between international and domestic affairs? How have states and peoples defined and pursued their objectives and what have they contributed to the world at large? How have conceptions of warfare and visions of peace changed?

These questions must be addressed if one is to arrive at an understanding of the contemporary world that is both international—with an awareness of the linkages among different parts of the world—and historical—with a keen sense of what the immediate past has brought to human civilization. Hence Twayne's International History Series. It is to be hoped that the volumes in this series will help the reader to explore important events and decisions since 1945 and to develop a global awareness and historical sensitivity with which to confront today's problems.

The first volumes in the series examine the United States' relations with other countries, groups of countries, or regions. The focus on the United States is justified in part because of the nation's predominant position in postwar international relations, and also because far more extensive documentation is available on American foreign affairs than is the case with other countries. The series addresses not only those interested in international relations but also those studying America's and other countries' histories, who will find here useful guides and fresh insights into the recent past. Now more than ever it is imperative to understand the complex ties between national and international history.

This volume offers a fascinating, up-to-date account of the United States' involvement in Central America since the war. John Coatsworth, who has written extensively on U.S.-Mexican economic relations and on other aspects of Latin American history, shows that while the Central American republics have often been viewed as "client" states dependent on the United States for their peace and well-being, they have not hesitated to manipulate the latter to serve their own ends. Moreover, the United States' freedom of action has often been limited by regional and global considerations. As the post–cold war world faces the prospect of regionalization, with various economic and cultural groupings defining themselves in various parts of the globe, it is particularly fitting to have a reliable, detailed story of the United States' complex relationship with Central America.

Akira Iriye

PREFACE

This book surveys U.S. foreign policy in Central America, focusing primarily on the post–World War II era. Ronald Reagan and Akira Iriye provoked me to write it—Reagan by pursuing a particularly destructive and eventually self-defeating foreign policy in Central America and Iriye by inviting me to contribute a volume to the Twayne series just as the full dimensions of the disaster, including the Iran-contra scandal, were unfolding.

Though essentially a narrative history of U.S.–Central American relations over the past half-century, this book assesses the success or failure of U.S. policy in its own terms and tries to come to grips with the impact of such policy on the six isthmian countries. I have not attempted to explicate or summarize what U.S. and Central American foreign policy makers believed they were up to or claimed to be doing, though I have referred to major foreign policy doctrines and occasionally to policy debates directly related to U.S. activity in Central America. In part, my preference for summarizing patterns of foreign policy activity or behavior rather than discourse about it stems from the common bias among students of modern international relations that actions speak louder than words. It also arises from the fact that, until recently, few of the great articulators of U.S. foreign policy goals in the postwar era paid any attention to Central America. And when they did, particularly in the 1980s, official discourse tended to obscure or distort rather than illuminate.

I have also resisted the temptation to discuss systematically the evolution of U.S.–Central American economic relations, the role of private institutions such as U.S. corporations, or the origins and structure of the poverty and inequality that beset the region. The publication of a number of well-researched, analytically sophisticated works on Central American economic, social, and environmental problems in the past decade made this an easy decision and helped keep this book closer to its projected length.

Since I came only recently to the study of U.S.–Central American relations, I have relied much on the work of other scholars, many of whom are cited in the Bibliographic Essay. The controversies surrounding U.S. policy in Central America during the 1980s inspired a veritable explosion of new work on the region and its external relations, without which this book could not have been written. I am especially indebted to Anna and Patricia Coatsworth, Akira Iriye, Friedrich Katz, Terry Karl, Steven Mange, and Thomas Passananti, who read all or part of the manuscript and helped immeasurably to improve it. Francisco Forest Martin, Michael Gambone, Peter Guardino, Thomas Passananti, and the late Joan Nicklin provided invaluable research assistance. Support for research and writing was provided by the Social Science Divisional Research Fund of the University of Chicago and the Faculty of Arts and Sciences at Harvard University and is gratefully acknowledged. None of the above should be responsible for errors or misjudgments that remain despite their efforts.

chapter 1

THE CLIENTS AND THE COLOSSUS

CENTRAL AMERICA

Historically, Central America consists of the five states that gained their independence from Spain in 1821 and formed a single country, called the Central American Federation, until 1838. They include (from north to south) Guatemala, Honduras, El Salvador, Nicaragua, and Costa Rica. The creation of Panama in 1903 added a sixth country at the foot of the Central American isthmus. This book is about the history of U.S. relations with these six countries since World War II.[1]

A seventh Central American country emerged in 1981, when Great Britain granted independence to Belize (formerly British Honduras). Guatemala insists that Belize is part of its own territory, though it has done nothing in modern times to recover its "lost province" beyond issuing occasional threats and protests. This book leaves out Belize for three reasons. First, as a British colony, Belize had no formal diplomatic relations with the United States until its independence in 1981. Second, U.S. policy toward Belize since 1981 has differed from U.S. policy toward the other countries of Central America. For example, the United States did not seek to embroil Belize in the conflicts affecting the other Central American nations in the 1980s, and Belize made no effort to become involved.[2] Third, Belize's history as a British outpost has endowed the country with unique cultural and political traditions, even though it shares in the poverty that afflicts its neighbors.

Panama, however, shares more than its poverty with the rest of Central America. Like the other Central American republics, Panama formed part of Spain's New World empire until 1821. During the nineteenth century it experienced the cultural continuity, political cleavages, and foreign interventions that shaped its northern neighbors, though it experienced them as a provincial backwater in a much larger polity. In the twentieth century Panama's birth as a nominally sovereign and independent nation coincided with its incorporation into a system of client states dominated by the United States, like the rest of the small states of Central America and the Caribbean. The creation of the Panama Canal Zone turned an important part of Panama into a virtual colony of the United States until it was returned to Panama under terms of the 1978 Panama Canal Treaty. Although the other five republics never turned over territory in this way, the United States forced all of them, like Panama, to subordinate their domestic and foreign policies to U.S. interests early in the twentieth century. Finally, Panama played a major role in the political and military conflicts that erupted on the isthmus beginning in the 1970s, unlike Belize or the other U.S. clients in the Caribbean.

The Central American republics range in size from El Salvador's 8,260 square miles (smaller than Vermont) to Nicaragua's 50,180 square miles (about the size of Alabama). All of Central America would fit comfortably within the state of Texas. At the beginning of the twentieth century, only Guatemala had a population larger than 1 million; today Guatemala's 9 million inhabitants make it the most populous of the Central American countries. Panama, with a little over 2 million people, has the smallest population in the region. California has more people than all the Central American republics combined (see Table 1.1).

Most Central Americans are poor. Annual income per capita in 1990 ranged from $600 in Nicaragua to $1,740 in Panama—between 3.2 and 9.3 percent of the 1990 U.S. per capita income of nearly $19,000. A tiny minority in each country has controlled most of the wealth and earned the bulk of the income for centuries. Costa Rica's peculiar history and impressive educational and social programs have made it less unequal than its neighbors. In Nicaragua the Sandinista revolution of 1979 brought about a significant redistribution of landed wealth, while Sandinista social and economic policies in the early 1980s increased the income share of the poorer strata of the population. After 1983, however, U.S. hostility to the Sandinista regime (the contra war, trade embargo, and the like) contributed to a sharp decline in overall living standards while inflation induced by the war and by economic policy errors reconcentrated income. Poverty and inequality dominate life in most of the region.

In addition to their small size, the poverty of their citizens, and the rampant inequalities of their social systems, most of the Central American republics are politically unstable and militarily weak. Since 1948 only Costa Rica has managed to avoid the military coups, guerrilla movements, and massive social protests that have erupted repeatedly throughout the region. Nicaragua, Guatemala, and El Salvador experienced large-scale civil warfare in the 1970s and 1980s. Military institutions in the region play a major role

Table 1.1. Population and Territory of Central America
and the United States

	Population (1,000s of inhabitants)			Territory (square miles)
	ca. 1900	*1950*	*1990*	
United States	76,212	150,697	251,400	3,540,939
Central America [1]	3,270	8,919	28,900	193,172
Guatemala	1,365	2,787	9,200	42,042
Nicaragua	505	1,053	3,900	50,180
Honduras	399	1,505	5,100	43,277
Costa Rica	243	801	3,000	19,652
El Salvador	758	1,859	5,300	8,260
Panama[2]		801	2,400	29,761

[1]Five original Central American states plus Panama.
[2]Excluded from 1900 population.

Sources: For population estimates ca. 1900 see Ciro F. S. Cardoso, "Central America: The Liberal Era, ca. 1870–1930," in *The Cambridge History of Latin America,* vol. 5, ed. Leslie Bethel (Cambridge: Cambridge University Press, 1984–88), 199. For 1950 population see *Hammond's New Supreme World Atlas* (Garden City, N.J.: Garden City Books, 1952), 1–3. For 1990 population and territory see *Information Please Almanac, 1991* (Boston: Houghton Mifflin, 1991).

in domestic political life, except in Costa Rica, which dismantled its weak armed forces after its 1948 national revolution. None of the Central American republics possesses a military force capable of waging a modern war or of influencing the regional, let alone the global, strategic balance.[3]

Early in the twentieth century the United States succeeded in its drive to secure unilateral strategic, political, and economic dominance in the Caribbean, including the Central American republics. None of the states in the region could have hoped to offer effective resistance to the United States, and all were induced to accept severe de facto limitations on their sovereignty and independence. Except for its colonies and former colonies (such as Puerto Rico and the Philippines), the United States has dominated the small states of the Caribbean more completely and for a longer time than it has any other part of the globe. Although U.S. policy makers and their closest collaborators in the region have argued that this unequal "partnership" has been mutually beneficial, the evidence to support such claims is at best contradictory. Compared with the rest of Latin America since World War II, for example, Central American economic development has lagged, poverty and inequality are more widespread, and, in proportion to its small population, political violence has claimed a far greater number of victims.

U.S. dominance has not protected Central America from these scourges. Indeed, social and political upheaval in the Western Hemisphere in this century has concentrated disproportionately in precisely those countries where U.S. power and influence has been greatest—from the Mexican Revolution of 1910 and the Guatemalan, Cuban, and Dominican upheavals of the 1950s and 1960s to the Central American wars and revolutions of the late 1970s and 1980s.

A SYSTEM OF CLIENT STATES

The vastly superior economic and military might of the United States has shaped U.S. relations with the six predominantly Spanish-speaking Central American republics since the end of the nineteenth century. Beginning with the Spanish-American War in 1898, when the United States seized Cuba and Puerto Rico as well as the Philippines from Spain, the United States deployed its disproportionate power first to create, and then to maintain, a system of client states in the Caribbean basin. The only modern parallels to this system have been the interwar network of British protectorates in the Middle East, which collapsed after World War II, and the Soviet buffer-state system in Eastern Europe, which was created just as its British counterpart began to fall apart.[4]

Client-state systems have arisen and disintegrated for thousands of years. The Chinese and Roman empires, for example, forced the small polities located on their peripheries to pay tribute, respect imperial emissaries and merchants, and provide mercenaries for new conquests. The trading-post empires established by the Dutch and Portuguese in Africa and the Indian Ocean in the fifteenth to seventeenth centuries often led to efforts to control local governments. Many of the formal colonies of Britain, France, Germany, Belgium, and the Netherlands in Asia, Africa, and the Middle East began as client states. In each of these cases the more powerful nation forced nominally independent local rulers to alter their internal and foreign policies to serve imperial interests.

Client states that formalize their subordination to a superior power in exchange for protection from the designs of other states (or, in some cases, from internal rebellion) are called "protectorates." Usually, a formal treaty establishes the right or obligation of the great power to use military force to protect the "sovereignty" of the weaker state. In exchange, the protectorate surrenders some degree of control over important aspects of its foreign and domestic policy to its "protector." For example, protectorates have always ceded control over foreign relations that involve potential external threats to which the great power must respond, but great power has often included partial or total control of military and police forces, and even of broad areas of internal policy making. The protectorate retains nominal independence and continues to govern internally, but usually under imperial supervision, or subject to an imperial veto over major policy and personnel decisions.[5]

Client states retain greater formal autonomy than protectorates, but they submit to similar constraints by routinely accepting the advice of the great power's ambassador on major personnel and policy decisions, by subordinating national armed forces to a military alliance dominated by the great power, and by tailoring domestic fiscal and social policies to meet the requirements of foreign economic interests and aid programs as well as the great power's political biases and preferences. In addition, direct supervision of key government agencies by administrators or advisers from the dominant power often occurs in such cases.

Clientalism can also be described as a particularly intense form of what has been called neocolonialism or external dependence. Most former European and U.S. colonies in the third world soon discovered that political independence did not free them from dependence on foreign trade, investment, technology, and aid. External economic ties determined the shape and pace of these countries' economic development and made their governments vulnerable to political pressures from well-organized foreign business interests and governments. The vastly disproportionate economic power of the major industrial nations such as the United States gives them immense political leverage in most third-world regions. In many of the weakest third-world countries, U.S., European, or Japanese diplomats, together with banks and multinational companies from their home countries, are major actors in domestic economic and political life. In these extreme cases of neocolonialism, foreign interests come to form part of what local leaders perceive as their national interest and thus help to shape the foreign policies of third-world states from "within." The weakest of the smaller states lack even the capacity to formulate independent national policy objectives.

The economic gap between the great industrial powers and the poorer nations makes it possible for the developed countries to exert economic pressure on third-world countries at little cost or risk. For example, when the United States imposed economic sanctions on Nicaragua and Panama in the 1980s, those countries suffered sharp reductions in trade and gross national product (GNP). In the United States, however, these measures had no visible effect on economic life. Occasionally, a third-world country or group of countries finds itself in possession of a scarce resource critical for the application of advanced industrial (or military) technology in the developed world. In rare circumstances third-world nations have combined to create an artificial scarcity of a major commodity (such as petroleum) in order to raise or stabilize prices. For the most part, however, the economic leverage of third-world producers has been negligible in comparison to that of the major industrial countries.

The Central American nations share their economic weaknesses and political vulnerabilities with much of the third world. For a number of reasons, however, the subordination of the Central American countries to the United States has been more complete, multifaceted, and continuous than is characteristic of neocolonial relations in most other regions of the globe. The Central American economies depend on a small number of agricultural exports (mainly bananas, coffee, and cotton). Their trade, investment, and technology flows are dominated by the United States and by U.S. companies. Central American landowners, businesspeople, bankers, politicians, military officers, and members of some occupational groups (managers, foreign-trained professionals, and some white-collar employees) often have close ties to U.S. private businesses or government agencies. Tastes in consumer goods, entertainment, and education often follow U.S. trends, especially among the wealthy, who can afford them, and the middle classes, who try to keep up. Central American news media depend largely on U.S. wire services. Many depend on advertising by U.S. companies. Their reporters, editors, and publishers often receive subsidies from U.S. government agencies and, in exchange, slant the news and publish items prepared by U.S. embassy or intelligence personnel. Central American political leaders, including those in the police and military establishments, cooperate with U.S. authorities who possess the power to remove them or to destabilize their governments. Key government personnel in Central American countries have on occasion supplemented their incomes with salaries or fee-for-service payments from U.S. institutions, including U.S. intelligence agencies.

The dominance of the United States in Central America is enhanced by social, political, ideological, and cultural conflicts within each country, and by rivalries and animosities that at times have erupted into open warfare. Moreover, for most of the twentieth century, no great power other than the United States has shown much interest in the region, so Central American governments have had little success in turning competition in the international arena to any lasting advantage.

Despite its overwhelming power, the United States has resisted the temptation to formalize its control by subjecting the small states of the Caribbean to formal colonial rule. Puerto Rico, which became a U.S. colony in 1898, had never been independent: when the United States seized the island it still belonged to Spain. Even during periods of prolonged occupation by U.S. military forces—which has occurred in Cuba, the Dominican Republic, Haiti, and Nicaragua—U.S. policy makers rejected proposals to turn these countries into colonial possessions administered directly from Washington. Although hotly debated in the United States in the pre–World War I era— when European powers were scrambling to take over vast areas of Africa and to carve up among themselves other portions of the third world they had neglected to subjugate earlier—this decision proved to be a durable one for many reasons. The anticolonial origins of U.S. independence made overt colonialism unpopular in the United States. Perhaps more to the point, U.S. policy makers soon learned that they could achieve their main strategic, political, and economic aims in the region without assuming the costs, both political and financial, that colonial rule would have entailed.

The client-state system in Central America forms part of the larger system of U.S. relations with the nations of the Western Hemisphere. The United States developed four distinct patterns of relations in this region over the course of the twentieth century. First, there are the relations with the U.S. clients, which include the Central American republics as well as the small island states: Cuba until 1959, the Dominican Republic, and Haiti. In these cases direct U.S. military intervention, including prolonged periods of military occupation, led to more or less complete subordination to the United States between 1898 and World War I. U.S. relations with Central America thus developed as part of a larger system of U.S. dominance in the Caribbean.

Second, there is the pattern of U.S. relations with the Caribbean colonies and the former colonies of the European powers in the Caribbean, principally those of Britain. Since the British proved willing to accede to U.S. power elsewhere in the Caribbean beginning in the 1890s, the United States reciprocated by leaving the British colonies alone. U.S. trade, investments, and tourism gradually moved the British island economies closer to the United States. Britain began granting independence to its Caribbean colonies in the 1960s. Britain's reluctance or inability to exercise sufficient (for the United States) informal control over its former colonies has led the United States to incorporate them into its own system of clients. By the 1970s most of the former British dependencies had become economically and politically subordinate to the United States, despite their continuing ties to the British Commonwealth. In 1983 the United States ignored formal British protests against its occupation of Grenada and received support from the governments of most of the former British colonies. Similar assertions of U.S. power have affected the former Dutch colony of Suriname, though the United States has had little to do with the remaining colonies of the Netherlands Antilles. French possessions in the Caribbean, which include the islands of Guadeloupe and Martinique and the mainland territory of French Guiana, remain colonies. Unlike Britain and the Netherlands, France has successfully resisted pressures both for independence and for incorporation of these territories within the U.S. sphere.[6]

Third, there are the unique bilateral relationships the United States has established with the two states with which it shares long common borders, Canada and Mexico. U.S. relations with Canada have proved the easier to manage. Canada and the United States have common cultural and linguistic roots, parallel legal traditions and political systems, and comparable economies that provide nearly equal living standards. Relations between the two countries have benefited from an early and amicable settlement that defined their common border and a history that brought them into close military alliance during the two world wars. In 1988, however, the Canadian and U.S. governments ratified a free-trade agreement that seems to have evoked latent Canadian fears of subordination to the United States.

With Mexico, U.S. relations have been far less easy. In the Mexican War (1846–48), the United States invaded Mexico, occupied most of the country, and forced it to give up half its national territory, which included what are now the U.S. states of Texas, California, New Mexico, Colorado, and Arizona, along with parts of Oklahoma, Utah, and Nevada. During the Mexican revolution of 1910–17, U.S. military forces invaded Mexico three times, and U.S. political and business leaders threatened to invade even more often. The economic gap between the two countries has produced sharp and irreducible conflicts of national interest, while differences in language, customs, and culture have created multiple sources of friction. However, Mexico's political stability since the late 1920s, its remarkable record of continuous rapid economic growth from the 1930s to 1982, and the skill and caution with which its modern leaders have managed their relations with the United States have all helped to keep relations stable, even during periods of stress. On the U.S. side, the temptation to deploy U.S. power has been held in check by the costs of direct intervention (Mexico is much larger and more populous than any of the U.S. clients) and by the potential spillover effects of social and political instability so close to the United States. In their dealings with Mexico, U.S. policy makers have employed indirect and nonmilitary methods of exerting influence since the second decade of the century.

Fourth, and finally, there is the pattern of U.S. relations with South America. As with Mexico, the United States has developed and used a variety of indirect and nonmilitary mechanisms for exerting influence because the costs of imposing a more thoroughgoing clientage would be much higher than in the Caribbean. As in the case of Mexico since the 1910–17 revolution, the absence of direct U.S. intervention in the affairs of these states has facilitated the development of ruling classes less reliant on U.S. support to stay in power. Unlike Mexico, however, the South American states have no history of direct confrontation with the United States. With the exception of Argentina (which attempted to compete with the United States for hemispheric leadership until the 1950s), the South American republics have not made defense against U.S. pressures a cardinal point of their foreign policies.

AN AMERICAN LAKE

For nearly one hundred years, generations of U.S. policy makers have found turning the Caribbean Sea into an "American lake," and keeping it one, to be both irresistible and easy to accomplish. No sooner had the United States founded its twentieth-century foreign policy on the Open

Door doctrine than U.S. policy makers set about closing the door on the Caribbean in general and on Central America in particular. In the rest of the third world the Open Door doctrine (and its corollaries and successors) has militated against open colonialism and formal spheres of influence—systems that the European powers (and later Japan) used to exclude international political and economic competition from the regions they dominated. In World War II the United States proclaimed its commitment to an open world in which ideas and commodities as well as people could move freely from place to place without the political constraints the Axis powers had imposed on the areas they had conquered. After World War II this doctrine formed the basis for verbal attacks by U.S. leaders on Soviet policy in Eastern Europe. In the Caribbean, however, the United States pursued a different policy, one more akin to those its leaders criticized elsewhere.

At the end of the nineteenth century, when the United States set out to dominate the Caribbean, four motives loomed large in the strategic thinking of its leaders. First, a diverse array of interest groups had been clamoring for an interoceanic canal since early in the nineteenth century; the clamor increased after the United States seized the northern half of Mexico in the Mexican War and the California gold rush began in 1848. A trans-isthmian canal was needed to facilitate trade between the east and west coasts of the United States and thus strengthen national unity (still a preoccupation, with the 1861–65 Civil War fresh in the memory of many). The potential economic benefits of a trans-isthmian canal dovetailed with fashionable theories about the importance of sea power in terms of both protecting and extending overseas commerce and providing for national defense.[7]

Second, there was the experience of the great depression of the mid-1890s, which many interpreted as a crisis of overproduction. The United States needed foreign markets for its products to avoid or mitigate periodic crises at home. Traditionally export-conscious farmers found allies among industrialists and bankers, and a diverse array of interest groups lobbied for more aggressive foreign economic policies to break down barriers to U.S. exports throughout the third world, including the colonial empires of the European powers.[8] U.S. trade with the Caribbean basin increased rapidly in the late nineteenth century; the Central American countries began exporting large quantities of coffee to the United States and Europe and later became major exporters of bananas to the United States. U.S. companies began buying land and building railroads in the region, first in Mexico and then in Central America, the Dominican Republic, and Cuba. By the end of the century U.S. policy in the Caribbean had become important both as a symbol of the U.S. government's commitment to promoting overseas trade and investment more aggressively throughout the world and as an aid to a growing number of producers and investors seeking profits in the area.

Third, U.S. leaders discovered that they could persuade the European powers (particularly Britain) or force them (as in the case of Spain) to accept

U.S. dominance in the Caribbean at very little cost in blood or treasure. The Spanish-American War (1898) proved to be a lark; Cuba and Puerto Rico fell to U.S. invaders in a matter of weeks. Britain, increasingly anxious for U.S. support against its European rivals, retreated at each assertion of U.S. power. The British received repeated assurances that the United States had no designs on the British possessions, so long as Britain would recognize U.S. preeminence in the rest of the area. The Caribbean was important to the United States but of marginal importance to Britain in terms of that nation's economic interests and military strategy.

Fourth, as the British gave way, calculating correctly that they would thus be in a better position to enlist U.S. support in case of a European conflict, U.S. policy makers were already convinced of the potential strategic importance of the area. U.S. military occupations of the Dominican Republic, Haiti, and Nicaragua all began within two years of the outbreak of World War I in Europe in 1914 (though the United States did not enter the war until 1917). Both to defend its neutrality against attacks on U.S. shipping and to deny bases to enemies in case of war, the United States sought to dominate the region in military, and thus also in political and economic, terms.

As U.S. leaders came to define the Caribbean as central to the security of the U.S. mainland, they began to see the region as different from the rest of the world. This had two consequences. First, it meant that the Open Door policy would not suffice. Content to demand no more than equal access for U.S. trade and investment elsewhere in the world, the U.S. government sought to create an exclusive sphere of influence in the Caribbean. No other great power could be permitted to exercise significant political influence there; as Assistant Secretary of State Robert Olds wrote in 1927, "There is no room for any outside influence than ours in this region."[9] Second, U.S. security concerns produced a growing disjuncture between the limited significance of U.S. economic ties to the region and the importance of the Caribbean basin for U.S. diplomacy. Though U.S. trade and investment in the Central American republics were never large, U.S. policy makers supported U.S. businesspeople and bankers in their efforts to compete with British and other European interests, because closer economic ties strengthened U.S. political influence and reduced that of potential rivals. Sometimes, of course, U.S. policy makers refused to support a private U.S. bank or company when doing so could have undermined their larger strategy of making the Caribbean into an "American lake." For the most part, however, U.S. economic and strategic concerns coincided.

The creation of a client-state system in the Caribbean depended on an unusual set of international and local circumstances, including the clamor for a trans-isthmian canal, the increasingly global ambitions and interests of the United States (which made control of the Caribbean a logical step in the effort to project U.S. interests abroad), the absence of any rival power willing and able to confront the United States in the region, the development of a U.S. policy that defined the Caribbean as critical to U.S. military security, and the weakness and vulnerability of the Caribbean states (which kept down the costs of controlling the region).

THE STRATEGIES OF THE CLIENT STATES

In the face of the United States' efforts to assert and maintain its dominance, Central American governments have tried, even in the most unfavorable circumstances, to preserve and expand their freedom of action. U.S. and Central American interests have never coincided completely and have often directly conflicted. Central American political leaders have thus sought means to assert and defend their countries' interests (however they defined them) against those of the United States. Over the past century they have pursued five different but occasionally overlapping strategies to reduce U.S. constraints on their sovereignty.

International competition has provided the occasion for the first of these strategies. Central Americans have repeatedly sought to counterbalance the overwhelming power of the United States by attracting the interest or enlisting the support of other countries, especially competing great powers.[10] From the late nineteenth century to World War I, Central Americans attempted to use the British (and occasionally the Germans) in this way. For a brief period in the 1930s some Central Americans hoped that Nazi Germany could be induced to counterbalance U.S. dominance, but World War II put an end to that prospect. In the postwar era, various Central American governments looked to Western Europe or the Soviet bloc. More recently they have expanded their ties to Japan; to the larger states in the Caribbean, such as Mexico, Colombia, and Venezuela; to the rest of South America; and to the third world. Some have also sought support from multilateral organizations, such as the European Community, the Nonaligned Movement, and the United Nations, or appealed to international law and legal institutions, such as the International Court of Justice in the Hague, to restrain the United States.

Second, some Central American governments have attempted to mobilize domestic political resources to reduce U.S. constraints. This strategy has usually entailed high risks, both domestic and international. Domestically, the mobilization of popular support to free policy makers from U.S. pressures has usually required a populist, center-left, or left-wing program of social and economic reforms. Nationalist or anti-U.S. rhetoric without some promise of beneficial social change does not move the masses. But reform programs usually challenge entrenched economic and political interests. Thus, while reformism has sometimes helped to strengthen governments in their dealings with the United States by mobilizing popular support, this strategy has also provoked internal conflicts and divisions for the United States to exploit. At times reformism has also facilitated U.S. efforts to isolate a

Central American government pursuing it; it has also made it easier, especially after World War II, for U.S. policy makers to appeal to anticommunist sentiment in the U.S. electorate in order to gain support for intervention in the region.

Third, Central American governments have sporadically combined to pursue common policies in the face of U.S. interests and pressures. This strategy has occasionally produced some short-term advantage but has usually been undermined, either by rivalries and divisions within the region or by the capacity of the United States to use its leverage to persuade one or more of the governments to defect. The Central American Common Market (CACM), for example, never managed to develop common policies that might have affected U.S. interests in the region, and fell apart after Honduras and El Salvador fought the brief but bitter "Soccer War" in 1969. In 1987, however, the Central American nations, led by Costa Rica, signed a regional peace agreement—opposed by the United States—designed to reduce conflicts in the region.

Fourth, Central Americans have attempted to influence U.S. political processes and politicians in a variety of ways. The pioneers of this strategy were Rafael Leónidas Trujillo, dictator of the Dominican Republic from 1930 to 1961, and Anastasio Somoza García, founder of the Somoza clan that ruled Nicaragua from 1936 until the Sandinista Revolution of 1979. Both men assiduously cultivated U.S. officials, entertained congressmen and senators, charmed ambassadors, granted valuable concessions to influential U.S. businesspeople, and employed public relations experts and lobbyists to help them. Salvadoran president José Napoleón Duarte provided a more recent and more effective example of this strategy in the 1980s when he successfully lobbied Congress for U.S. aid. All these leaders, however, sought mainly to improve their positions within the framework of a basic accommodation to U.S. power. This strategy was also used in the 1980s by the Salvadoran opposition and the Sandinista movement of Nicaragua in support of more independent postures; it included efforts to shape public opinion as well as to influence high U.S. officials.

The fifth and most common strategy employed by Central American governments may be described as bargaining from a position of weakness.[11] Since the early twentieth century most of these governments have found it convenient to accept U.S. dominance and to seek concessions within the framework of a basic accommodation to U.S. power. While the benefits of this strategy have varied over time and have often seemed minimal to many Central Americans, the risks to anyone in power have usually been smaller than those associated with any of the alternatives. Accommodating governments avoided provoking the lethal combination of U.S. pressure and elite opposition that often forced less-cooperative regimes from power.

In the long run, however, this strategy of accommodation to the United States has tended to make Central American governments more brittle and repressive than they might otherwise have been. Social reforms or nationalist economic projects requiring active government intervention in economic affairs have usually met with suspicion in Washington. Although such measures might have been crucial to establishing the legitimacy and responsiveness of Central American governments, they have often been blocked by elite opposition supported by the United States. Right-wing political parties and military establishments in Central America often found U.S. diplomatic personnel and policy makers sympathetic to their ambitions because such groups were reliably pro-U.S. and anticommunist and opposed reforms that might have affected U.S. economic interests adversely. Except for brief episodes, such as the early Kennedy and Carter years, U.S. influence has tended to strengthen elite resistance to social change, and U.S. aid has provided local military establishments with the means to repress demands for it.

At times Central American politicians and political parties have competed with each other for U.S. approval, each seeking to "outbid" the other. Evidence of U.S. support can make or end political careers in much of Central America. In most Central American countries this created a political dynamic with two characteristics that contributed to instability. First, conservative and right-wing Central American leaders, competing to demonstrate their anticommunism, forged repressive political cultures intolerant of opposition. Second, because these leaders' political destinies at critical junctures usually depended to an important degree on the support they could muster in Washington, their legitimacy as national leaders suffered. Criticism of their subservience to Washington, interpreted as pro-communist sentiment, then justified further repression.

While the benefits of accommodation often seemed irresistibly high to Central American political leaders and economic elites, the risks increased over time. The two major risks, symbolized by the parallel tragedies of Nicaragua and El Salvador in the 1980s, are revolution and intervention. Accommodation to the United States and the domestic repression it often entailed raised the level of violence required to effect political and social change in both countries. In Nicaragua the Sandinista revolution in 1979 cost political and military leaders their power and the economic elite much of its wealth. In El Salvador, when a short-lived reformist experiment failed in late 1979 and revolutionary movements could not be controlled without massive U.S. aid, the United States gave the needed assistance but in exchange took virtual control of the country's political destiny. Political and military leaders were forced to accept close U.S. supervision of their activities, and some lost power to politicians and officers preferred by Washington. The economic elite temporarily lost control of economic policy and some of its members lost property to a series of reforms intended by U.S. officials to reduce support for antigovernment insurgents.

From the standpoint of U.S. dominance, governments that simultaneously pursue the first two strategies—external support and popular mobilization—present the greatest danger to U.S. dominance. It was this potentially threatening combination that provoked the two major confrontations between U.S. policy makers and Central American governments in the twentieth century: in Guatemala in the early 1950s and in Nicaragua in the 1980s. The third strategy—that of seeking unity among the Central American nations—has seldom posed a substantial threat to U.S. policy, because it generally failed in the face of U.S. pressure and the historic rivalries and disputes among the Central Americans themselves.[12] Efforts to exert influence within the United States—the fourth strategy—occasionaly proved helpful, but it did so generally as a complement to one or a combination of the other strategies. For most of the twentieth century the Central American republics have pursued the fifth strategy of accommodation to U.S. interests.

THE COMPLEX RELATIONS BETWEEN PUBLIC AND PRIVATE POWER

The United States and Central America, despite their vast differences, are capitalist societies in which productive property is privately owned by individuals, institutions, and businesses. Economic conditions as well as government finances (tax revenues, interest rates on government debt, and the like) depend on the decisions made by private entrepreneurs. In Central America government officials can inform themselves about the perceived needs and demands of domestic capitalists in direct conversations with leading private magnates. In some cases consulting with "private-sector leaders" is merely a matter of checking with relatives and friends. To interpret the needs of foreign investors, Central Americans either consult them directly or rely on the advice of U.S. ambassadors or private contacts among U.S. bankers and company executives. After World War II, as the Central American economies became more complex and governments made efforts to understand trends in the crucial foreign markets that absorbed most of their exports, conversations sometimes proved inadequate. Central American leaders began to employ economists and other technicians to interpret the mountains of data on prices and production that the behavior of capitalists (and consumers) generates. In this, the Central American governments merely followed the conventions established earlier by the United States and the other industrialized countries. Whatever the means employed to understand foreign market trends, and whatever the political coloration of the regime in power, private-sector opinion on public business continuously shapes the behavior of governments in Central America, as it does in more complex ways in the United States.

In strictly economic terms, the concentration of wealth and income has been greater in the Central American countries than in the United States for at least the past half century. In political terms, members of elite families usually enjoy direct and unmediated access to the highest government officials. The United States, in contrast, has a more complex economy spread over an immense territory and has developed a larger and more autonomous set of governmental agencies to manage relations between the state and the private sector. Effective and direct access to presidents, cabinet members, key members of Congress, and even the "subcabinet" of middle-range policy-making officials is limited to a handful of private-sector leaders and major lobbying groups in the United States. Constraints on the access and influence of popular or grass-roots organizations such as trade unions, farm organizations, environmental groups, and other voluntary or civic associations are usually greater in Central America than in the United States. In most Central American countries such organizations have been outlawed, severely repressed, or subjected to direct government controls for long periods of time, often in response to pressures from both foreign and domestic private interests or from the U.S. government. In the United States, however, such organizations now enjoy sufficient legal protection and institutional stability to enable them to exert influence commensurate with their support among the electorate or their financial resources. In this sense the relative openness of the U.S. political system serves to redress imbalances in economic power. In Central America this sort of balancing has seldom occurred, except in Costa Rica and since 1979 in Nicaragua.

In the making of foreign policy, the U.S. government has traditionally recruited policy-making personnel from the private sector and from a small number of major universities and "think tanks." Policy-making posts in the Department of State often go to individuals from large corporations, commercial banks, and corporate law firms whose business activities include overseas operations. Career foreign-service officers who advance to policy-making positions generally share the conservative, business-oriented views of their colleagues. Even when avoiding direct conflicts of interest, U.S. officials have traditionally sought to defend and promote U.S. private interests abroad. The priority given to efforts on behalf of individual firms or industries has varied with the circumstances of each case, with the political resources of the interested parties, and with the private tastes and ambitions of the officials involved. Overriding diplomatic or strategic concerns occasionally force policy makers to discount the needs of particular special-interest groups. For the most part, however, the foreign policy of the United States has reflected the high priority given by policy makers to advancing the economic interests of private businesses, particularly export-producing industries and major corporations and banks with foreign investments.

In regard to Central America, three special circumstances have shaped the relations between private business and U.S. policy. First, U.S. policy makers believe that U.S. economic penetration serves strategic objectives, and vice versa. The strategic significance of the Caribbean to U.S. policy makers originated in part from private-sector pressure for government aid in building and protecting the Panama Canal and in securing and defending overseas economic gains. This, together with concern for the military and naval defense of the United States, gave rise to the policy objective of creating an "American lake" and promoted close cooperation between public officials and private companies earlier and more thoroughly than in other parts of the world. Throughout the region, U.S. diplomats routinely pressured the Central American governments to grant concessions and contracts to U.S. firms rather than to British (or other European, and now Japanese) companies. The identification of U.S. diplomacy with the interests of such U.S. businesses as the United Fruit Company (UFCO) and the Chase Manhattan Bank between 1900 and the 1950s symbolized this policy.

The second special circumstance involves the attention paid by U.S. officials to the way Central American governments treat U.S. business on the isthmus. Most U.S. diplomats and policy makers responsible for the region have viewed this as an important indicator of the commitment of Central American governments to their unequal alliance with the United States. U.S. officials became accustomed to treating economic issues in Central America as significant even when the strictly economic or financial stakes of the United States as a whole or of particular U.S. citizens and companies were small. U.S. policy makers continue to believe that if they were to permit unfavorable treatment of minor U.S. economic interests in the Caribbean, where U.S. influence is most powerful, they would have greater difficulties preventing unfavorable treatment in the larger countries, where the U.S. stake is much larger. This concern over the "demonstration effect" of acquiescing to even relatively minor affronts to U.S. private business has reinforced the tendency of the United States to protect its minor economic interests in Central America, particularly when it can do so at no immediately apparent cost to larger U.S. objectives.

The third special circumstance involves the gap between the importance assigned by policy makers to promoting U.S. economic interests in Central America and the low level of U.S. trade and investment in the region. The actual U.S. economic stake in Central America has never been large. The relatively small U.S. interests in Central America, however, belong to important and powerful U.S. banks and corporations. The access and influence of the firms that own small subsidiaries or sell small quantities of goods and services in Central America, rather than the magnitude of their interests, have tended to push U.S. policy makers to give priority to securing small gains and preventing insignificant losses.

The significance the U.S. government attaches to promoting and protecting U.S. business interests has limited its tolerance for reformist economic policies and social legislation in Central America. Occasionally, the United States has even opposed reform legislation in Central America that the Central Americans carefully modeled after similar programs and policies adopted long before in the United States or Western Europe. While the United States has often opposed innovative social and economic policies in other parts of the world—especially policies that could have potentially negative effects on U.S. economic interests—its opposition has carried immeasurably greater weight in the small nations of the Caribbean than anywhere else. The intensity of U.S. opposition to reform has varied over time, however, and in relation to its political and strategic concerns. Thus the United States has not opposed, and at times has even promoted, moderate reforms to reduce support for left-wing political parties or guerrilla movements.

THE LIMITS OF ATTENTION AND POWER

Central American affairs have usually received little attention from top policy makers in the United States. Presidents and secretaries of state have traditionally focused their attention on Western Europe. Since World War II the European theater of the global cold war against the Soviet Union and the geopolitics of East Asia and the Middle East have received high priority. Latin America usually ranked as far less important than these other areas, though it received more attention than North Africa west of Ethiopia and most of sub-Saharan Africa. Many of the African states remain closely tied to their former European mother countries and are thus usually left to European management. Within the Latin American region, Central America has usually received less attention than Mexico and the larger countries of South America.

The low priority usually given to Central America has had two deleterious consequences. First, U.S. ambassadorial and policy-making appointees in Central America have often been of lower quality, and have exerted less influence within U.S. administrations, than their counterparts assigned to other regions. Decision making has tended to be less flexible and more driven by bureaucratic routine. Initiatives originating either in Central America or among staff professionals with Central American experience in Washington have often failed to reach the desks of those who make the important decisions. This pattern of decision making has reinforced the conservative social bias of the policy-making establishment by adding a layer of bureaucratic inertia to the policy process. Second, whenever a crisis has erupted and crucial, high-level decisions must be made in the White House, the key decision makers have usually been those who know little about Central America. The important decisions about Central America have tended to discount Central American conditions and to reflect the preferred global strategies and ideological biases of the decision makers. Ironically, the small nations of the region are so weak, and the United States is so dominant, that even foolish decisions have seldom been costly to the United States. Central America has occasionally proved to be a convenient arena for the application of presidential political preferences and symbolic initiatives, for example, because the consequences of making a mistake have always been lower in this region than anywhere else.

U.S. policy making, whimsical or wise, has had greater impact on the small countries of the Caribbean than anywhere else. In the twentieth century the United States has dominated Central America in the sense that it has successfully used its disproportionate power to shape both particular events and historical trajectories. It has usually sought to exert its dominance unilaterally, by repeatedly and explicitly excluding other actors, both domestic and international, from exercising comparable influence. At critical junctures in the history of each of the Central American countries, the United States has deployed its power—or refrained from doing so—in ways that have altered specific political outcomes and thus larger historical trends.[13]

The gap between the relative insignificance of Central America to the United States and the overwhelming importance of U.S. actions for the Central American nations has led to "asymmetrical" relations of unusual complexity. On the U.S. side, neither security nor economic interests—the twin pillars of conventional international relations theory—reliably accounts for U.S. behavior. This is particularly true for the cold war era, during which Central America developments often acquired importance more for their symbolic implications for the United States' "grand strategy" than for their actual impact on U.S. interests. In Central America, U.S. policies, particularly those adopted in moments of perceived "crisis," often had profound, long-term effects that went far beyond the calculations of policy makers in Washington.

While the United States dominates Central America, it does not control the region. This distinction may seem academic, but it is crucial both for understanding the complexities of U.S.–Central American relations and for interpreting the behavior of political and economic actors in the United States and in Central America. As the dominant external power, the United States has deployed its immense resources to shape or constrain public policies; to promote or undermine key political organizations and personalities; to change or alter governments and regimes; and, less directly, to affect broader social and economic patterns of development. Control, however, implies a capacity to manipulate every significant process or outcome—a costly and perhaps unattainable power that the United States has seldom sought and never acquired. The United States has not proved capable, for example, of preventing the emergence of social and political forces hostile to its interests and policies in the region. Indeed, the persistence and intensity of this opposition is, to a large extent, a byproduct of the persistence and intensity of U.S. dominance in the region.

The economic dependence of the Central American countries on the United States has declined over the past half century. It reached a high point in the period immediately after World War II. As Table 1.2 illustrates, the United States supplied more than three-fourths of the region's imports and bought a similar percentage of its exports in 1948. The recovery of the European and Japanese economies in the 1950s undercut the

Table 1.2.   Percentage of Central American Foreign Trade with the
United States, 1948–1980

Country	Exports 1948	1960	1970	1980	Imports 1948	1960	1970	1980
Costa Rica	78.6	52.3	42.5	34.9	77.7	45.4	34.8	34.5
El Salvador	77.4	35.1	21.4	29.7	73.5	42.9	29.6	25.2
Guatemala	89.0	55.6	28.3	28.7	76.2	46.0	35.3	33.7
Honduras	72.9	57.9	54.6	53.1	78.7	55.9	41.5	42.2
Nicaragua	74.5	40.4	33.2	38.7	83.8	52.7	36.5	27.5
Panama	91.5	96.1	63.4	49.9	75.5	51.5	39.8	33.8

Source: The Yearbook of International Trade Statistics: Trade by Country (New York:
U.N. Department of Economic and Social Affairs, 1954–).

postwar trade dominance of the United States and substantially reduced
the U.S. share of Central America's foreign trade (except in the case of
Panama) by 1960. This trend continued throughout the following decade.
The Central American Common Market (CACM), established in 1958,
stimulated trade among its five member countries (again, excluding
Panama); this further eroded the U.S. share in the 1960s, though exports
produced by branches of U.S. corporations represented a significant portion of the trade between the CACM countries. By 1980 Central
America's trade dependence on the United States had fallen from three-
fourths to approximately one-third.

Trends in foreign investment turned around more slowly and less decisively. Virtually all of the external investment in Central America in the
1940s and early 1950s came from the United States. By the late 1970s
Western Europe, Japan, Canada, the member nations of the Organization of
Petroleum Exporting Countries (OPEC), and Mexico were investing in the
region, often in direct competition with U.S interests. Western European
and Japanese investors began to compete successfully for investment opportunities throughout the region in the early 1960s. Throughout the 1960s and
1970s, as trade dependence on the United States continued to decline, the
U.S. share of direct investment in plants and equipment also fell. The need
for indirect (or portfolio) investment in the form of trade credits and hard-
currency loans to governments and businesses, however, pushed Central
America back toward the United States. In 1973 OPEC raised oil prices by
more than 400 percent. To avoid severe recession or bankruptcy, Central
American governments and businesses borrowed heavily from U.S. commercial banks to pay for the oil they needed. They also sought loans to cover the

increasing cost of importing other inputs and capital goods essential for industrial growth. Thus, while the U.S. share of direct investments declined, U.S. indirect investments rose dramatically—enough to maintain or increase the U.S. share of total capital flows into the 1980s.

These economic and financial trends formed part of the global decline in U.S. economic predominance as the world economy revived after World War II. Having assumed the heavy financial burden implied by its military and strategic leadership of the non-Communist world, the United States experienced rates of economic growth well below those of its cold war allies in Western Europe and East Asia. Even the revival after 1973 of the U.S. share of foreign investments in Central America did not alter this fundamentally negative trajectory. Most of the private "U.S." funds lent to Central America in the 1970s consisted of surplus oil revenues deposited in U.S. banks by the petroleum-producing countries of the Middle East.

The long-term relative decline of U.S. economic dominance in Central America had two major consequences. First, it helped to inspire other countries, principally in Western Europe, to reassess their diplomatic relationships in the Western Hemisphere. For more than two decades after World War II, Western European governments viewed Latin America, and especially the Caribbean and Central America, as off-limits. They were content to leave the region to the United States and to support U.S. policies regarding Latin America.[14] By the late 1960s, however, Western Europe's economic stake in Latin America had become so large that Britain, France, West Germany, and eventually other nations of that region began to formulate their own foreign policy objectives in Latin America and to pursue them with increasing vigor, even when they differed from those of the United States. Public opinion in Western Europe reinforced this trend; there was a widespread perception that the United States had had a hand in the rise to power of a series of repressive authoritarian regimes, beginning in Brazil in 1964.

Second, the development of significant (though friendly) competition with the United States in the international arena encouraged the growth of nationalist and reformist opposition within Central America. Business and political leaders in the region forged new ties to their counterparts in Europe and in other Latin American countries. These ties helped not only to weaken the almost automatic pro-U.S. attachments of elites in Central America but also to create new political spaces for a diverse array of opposition groups. Radical and revolutionary groups, many linked either to the Catholic church or to a variety of Marxist and socialist parties, benefited from this trend; so did more moderate or opportunistic political organizations. Radical Catholics received help from an international network of Christian social activists throughout Latin America, encouraged by the reforms of the Vatican Council in 1962 and the Medellín conference of Latin American bishops in 1968. Marxist and socialist groups received encouragement and aid from their counterparts in Western Europe, Latin America, and a number of radical or Communist countries, including Cuba.

By the 1970s historical conditions appeared to favor a substantial loosening of U.S. dominance in Central America. The international environment had become more competitive, and internal opposition to pro-U.S. military and personal dictatorships was stronger than ever before. The United States did not devote much effort to countering these trends. Republican administrations from 1969 to 1977 paid little attention to Central America; economic competition did not worry them because the stakes were so small, and political and ideological trends did not worry them because none of the opposition organizations and movements had enough strength to challenge incumbent governments. The Carter administration (1977–81), in contrast, devoted a major portion of its foreign policy energies to Central America. It gave priority to negotiating a new Panama Canal treaty and made Central America a focus of a campaign to reduce human rights abuses in the Western Hemisphere. These policies encouraged reformist, nationalist, and even revolutionary organizations to push for social change and democratization because they suggested that the United States would no longer support repressive regimes in the region. This proved to be true in the case of Nicaragua, where the U.S. administration withdrew support from the Somoza regime and accommodated itself to the Sandinista victory.

No significant U.S. economic or security interest was affected by the Sandinista revolution in Nicaragua or by the prospect of a guerrilla victory in the civil war in El Salvador that began in 1980. Moreover, the costs to the United States of intervening effectively in either country appeared to be quite high. Nonetheless, great symbolic weight was attached to the restoration and maintenance of U.S. dominance over the mini-states of the Caribbean and Central America by some U.S. political leaders and a portion of the U.S. electorate. The choice faced by the United States in the 1980s was therefore direct and unequivocal: it could accommodate to the relative decline of its economic and political influence in Central America by adopting a more tolerant pluralism in its relations with countries of the isthmus (as the Carter administration did in Nicaragua), or it could deploy its vast resources—economic as well as military—in an effort to restore its unilateral dominance in Nicaragua and to suppress challenges elsewhere on the isthmus.

The Reagan administration (1981–89) chose the second course and failed. The new administration's main goals in Central America were to secure the forcible overthrow of the Sandinista government in Nicaragua and the military defeat of the Salvadoran guerrillas. Both of these goals proved impossible to attain. The failure owed to public and congressional opposition in the United States, to the widespread support in the region for political forces opposed to U.S. dominance and committed to democracy and social change, and to efforts within Central America and the international community to secure negotiated solutions to the armed conflicts the Reagan administration had initiated or sought to intensify. By the time the new Republican administration of George Bush (1989–93) was in place, it had become clear that the United States would have to accept outcomes in Central America similar to those it could have achieved at much less cost much earlier.

The U.S. failure was both obscured and mitigated by two dramatic events: the U.S. invasion of Panama in December 1989 and the defeat of the Sandinista National Liberation Front (FSLN) in national elections held under international supervision in February 1990. In Panama the United States demonstrated not only its undiminished military power but also its political capacity to act decisively, even when no important economic or security interest was at stake. The circumstances surrounding the invasion of Panama were sufficiently unusual, however, as to make their recurrence unlikely though not impossible. Moreover, the stability of the regime installed by U.S. forces soon came into question as evidence of corruption and ineptitude accumulated.

A military overthrow of the Sandinista regime in Nicaragua would have made it possible to exclude the FSLN from the country's political life, though achieving such a goal would have required widespread violence and repression. Instead, the Sandinistas merely lost an election and emerged, despite their defeat, as the country's largest political party. Moreover, the armed forces remained intact and under the command of a Sandinista defense minister and a largely Sandinista officer corps. The U.S.-backed coalition that won the 1990 election subsequently split. Three years after its electoral defeat, the FSLN returned to government in alliance with President Violeta Chamorro and her supporters. The apparent success achieved by the United States in securing the election of Chamorro and her supporters in 1990 thus proved short-lived.

Similarly, the United States failed during the 1980s to secure the military defeat of the Salvadoran guerrillas, who fought the U.S.-backed Salvadoran armed forces to a stalemate. The Bush administration, facing the threat of a congressional cutoff of military aid to El Salvador, ultimately embraced a negotiated political settlement to the Salvadoran civil war in which the Salvadoran army was purged of all its senior officers, reduced in size to its prewar level, and removed from any tasks involving internal security and policing in exchange for the disarming of the guerrillas. The agreement relied on the United Nations and the Organization of American States, along with several Latin American and European countries, to monitor its implementation—an intrusion into Central American affairs by other international actors that the Reagan administration had fiercely resisted.

The failure of the United States to restore its unilateral dominance in the 1980s coincided with the end of the cold war and the dissolution of the Soviet Union and its system of client states in Eastern Europe. These developments tended to diminish the symbolic importance of Central America in U.S. political discourse, and the election of a new president in 1992 presaged an era of domestic preoccupations. Moreover, the policies of the Reagan administration had such destructive effects on the region that even conservative, pro-U.S. governments and political parties came to embrace a peace process that the Reagan administration had opposed. Thus in the 1990s the United States faces an unprecedented opportunity to develop a new, more constructive relationship with Central America. To do so it will have to escape the burdens of its own history.

chapter 2

CLOSING DOORS: RELATIONS THROUGH WORLD WAR II

THE NINETEENTH CENTURY

On 15 September 1821 the provincial assembly of the Captaincy-General of Central America, meeting in Guatemala City, proclaimed the entire region's independence from Spain. Delegates to the assembly had been sent from each of the Central American provinces the previous year under the terms of the Spanish Constitution of 1812. Panama was not represented, because it formed part of a different Spanish colony, the Viceroyalty of New Granada; until its independence in 1903, Panama remained a province of New Granada, later renamed Colombia. In January 1822—less than four months after declaring independence—a Central American assembly meeting in Guatemala City voted for annexation to the newly proclaimed Mexican empire. When the Mexican general Agustín de Iturbide had himself crowned as emperor five months later, he sent an army to Central America to enforce his authority—particularly in the province of El Salvador, where local notables had voted to seek annexation to the United States and had dispatched a delegation to Washington. Less than a year later, on 19 March 1823, Iturbide was overthrown. When the new Mexican republic ordered its troops to withdraw, the Central American provinces (except for Chiapas) seceded from Mexico and declared their independence again on 1 July 1823. Mexico held on to Chiapas and the northern part of Soconusco (now incorporated into the Mexican state of Chiapas). Mexico's early interest in Central America, and its nineteenth-century border conflicts with Guatemala over Soconusco, created frictions between the two countries that persisted well into the twentieth century.

The assembly that voted to secede from Mexico also voted to create a single Central American nation, first called the Federation of the United Provinces of Central America, then renamed the Federation of Central America in the Constitution of 1824, and often referred to simply as the Central American Federation. Torn by provincial revolts and political conflicts between liberals and conservatives for much of its brief history, the federation collapsed in 1838 to be replaced by the five independent states that remain today. Despite the failure of the federation, Central American unity became part of the region's political culture as an ideal worth struggling to recapture.

Economic life, never brilliant under colonial rule, stagnated after independence. Central America did not possess the large mineral resources that made Mexico and the Andean colonies (which later became Peru and Bolivia) so valuable to the Spanish crown. Indigo, a blue plant dye used by Europe's growing textile industries, became the region's most important export product after cacao declined in the seventeenth century. Production was centered in El Salvador, but until the collapse of the federation, merchants in Guatemala City monopolized export transactions and credit to the planters. The invention of chemical dyes, cheaper and easier to use in cloth manufacture than plant dyes, reduced indigo exports to insignificance by the mid-nineteenth century.

Early U.S. interest in Central America had three components. First, the United States sought, although without great energy or commitment, to negotiate commercial treaties embodying the principle of commercial reciprocity (mutual lowering of tariff duties and other impediments to trade). British diplomats seeking similar treaties often competed with their U.S. counterparts. In Central America as well as elsewhere in the newly independent countries of Spanish America, diplomats from the United States and Britain backed rival political factions and thus exacerbated the political cleavages inherited from the colonial era.

Second, the U.S. government tried, with little success, to block British and other European political and territorial designs on the region while pursuing its own continental expansion at the expense of Spain and, later, Mexico. The economic backwardness, political conflicts, and military weakness of Central America allowed the British to strengthen their hold on Belize and the Mosquito Coast of Nicaragua. By the 1840s British warships patrolled Central American waters on both sides of the isthmus, landing troops to "protect British subjects" allegedly threatened by hostile forces (nearly always those opposed to pro-British factions). British forces also landed to enforce claims to offshore islands belonging to Nicaragua and Honduras and to impose customs receiverships in order to collect debts on behalf of British claimants. Until late in the century the United States did little more than protest these British interventions and occasionally supported them.

Third, and eventually most important, the United States sought to promote the development of an interoceanic canal to enable ships to move between the Atlantic and Pacific oceans without traveling around Cape Horn. This interest took on a new urgency after the U.S.–British Treaty of 1846, which recognized U.S. claims to the Oregon Territory, and the Mexican War (1846–48), in which the United States seized half of Mexico, including what is now California. In less than three years the United States acquired over a thousand miles of Pacific coast. The California gold rush began within a matter of weeks after Mexico signed the Treaty of Guadalupe Hidalgo. Until 1848 the trans-isthmian canal was a foreign policy issue that mainly concerned merchants involved in trade with the Orient (though occasional adventurers from U.S. slave states promoted various annexation schemes). After 1848 the canal became a domestic priority for all those in the United States—politicians and citizens alike—who wished to see the newly enlarged nation united economically as well as politically.

The two areas most affected by the growing U.S. clamor for an interoceanic canal were Colombia's province of Panama and the republic of Nicaragua. Panama had been chosen by Spanish authorities as the sole legal transit route for goods shipped overland between the Caribbean and the Pacific coast of South America. This function disappeared when Spanish rule ended in 1821. Colombia's government was interested in reviving trade across the isthmus but could do little to promote it. Its leaders also worried about the development of separatist sentiments among the Panamanians and vigorously repressed any signs of agitation for independence. In 1846, fearing a British move to seize Panama, the Colombian government signed the Mallarino-Bidlack Treaty with the United States, in which the United States guaranteed Colombian sovereignty over Panama in exchange for Colombia's pledge to allow free transit across the isthmus to U.S. goods and citizens and to grant the United States access to any future canal. In 1849 entrepreneurs from the United States secured from the Colombian government a contract permitting them to develop and operate a transportation system across the isthmus. They initially operated stagecoaches but soon began the construction of a railroad line, which was completed in 1855.

In effect, Colombia had turned one of its provinces into a protectorate of the United States. The U.S. guarantee of Colombian sovereignty over Panama led to conflict with the British government, but the Clayton-Bulwer Treaty of 1850 resolved this problem by providing for joint U.S.–British development of any future canal across Central America. The U.S. guarantee of Colombian sovereignty also placed the United States on the side of the Colombian government against Panamanian efforts to achieve independence. On the basis of the Mallarino-Bidlack Treaty, and with British acquiescence, the United States met its obligation to protect Colombian sovereignty over Panama by stationing warships in Panamanian waters and by landing U.S. marines on occasion to protect U.S. property and to suppress independence movements and other disturbances.

In Nicaragua a similar combination of U.S. private initiatives and official meddling developed with dramatic consequences for the entire region. Throughout most of the nineteenth century Nicaragua was considered the most likely site for an interoceanic canal, but economic backwardness and political turmoil blocked every effort to advance such a project. Even before separating from the Central American Federation in 1838, Nicaragua had been torn by violent conflicts between conservatives based in the colonial capital of Grenada and liberals from León. The British usually supported the conservatives, while the U.S. backed the liberals. Conservatives and liberals in the neighboring republics repeatedly invaded Nicaragua in support of their ideological allies; their Nicaraguan counterparts responded in kind. The United States became deeply involved when William Walker, a San Francisco newspaper editor, politician, and adventurer, organized a military force of unemployed gold rushers and mercenaries to take over the country.

The Walker affair, a major event in Central American history, eventually embroiled all five Central American republics. It began in 1849, when U.S. financier Cornelius Vanderbilt persuaded Nicaragua's conservative government to grant him concessions permitting him to develop a transit route from the Caribbean to the Pacific. The route combined small steamboats, which ran up the San Juan River and across Lake Nicaragua, with stagecoaches (later, a planned railroad) that made the 12-mile run down to the Pacific coast town of San Juan del Sur. The project's big success was ensured in part by help from the U.S. government, which lobbied the Nicaraguan government on behalf of the project and even landed troops in 1853 to protect the company's property in San Juan del Sur from seizure by local officials.

Walker's expedition originated independently of the Vanderbilt project, with an invitation from a leading Nicaraguan liberal, General Francisco Castellón. Castellón signed a contract with Byron Cole, a San Francisco businessman passing through the country on Vanderbilt's transit system. The contract offered land grants and other inducements for the recruitment of a force of 300 U.S. mercenaries to aid the liberal cause. The conservatives had been discredited by their failure to resist a British occupation of San Juan del Sur in 1848. The British had turned the port over to putative representatives of the Miskito Indians (actually an assortment of foreign traders) and given it a new name, Graytown (Nicaragua did not resume control of San Juan del Sur until 1894). The conservatives had also provoked opposition in 1854 by adopting a new constitution that centralized power and severely restricted the franchise. The liberals rebelled but had failed to take power. When Castellón met Cole the country was in the throes of yet another civil war.

Cole contacted Walker on his arrival in San Francisco. Walker, who had failed in a filibustering expedition into Mexico two years earlier, organized an expedition and landed in Nicaragua with 57 soldiers of fortune on 16 June 1855. With reinforcements carried in Vanderbilt's ships from San Francisco, Walker's army eventually grew to over 2,500 men. By October, with more luck than skill, Walker had routed the conservatives' army, negotiated a shaky peace between the warring parties, and installed a conservative, General Patricio Rivas, as a puppet president. The Vanderbilt company immediately loaned money to the new government through its Nicaraguan manager and offered to bring in additional men and weaponry. In June 1856 Walker staged fraudulent elections and had himself inaugurated president. Only the United States recognized the Walker government (though El Salvador had briefly opened diplomatic relations with Rivas). With the country at his feet, Walker issued a series of decrees that legalized slavery, established English as an official language equal to Spanish, and initiated a land-registration scheme that called all existing land titles into question. Walker supporters appealed to slaveowners in the southern United States for aid and colonists, promising generous land grants and other government support.

The international reaction to the Walker episode proved its undoing. Officially, the U.S. government had nothing to do with Walker; unofficially, it gave him considerable help. The success of the Mexican War and the gold rush that followed gave the administration of President Franklin Pierce (1853–57) reason to revive the U.S. desire for a trans-isthmian canal. The Clayton-Bulwer Treaty removed a major obstacle by neutralizing British opposition to this objective. Vanderbilt, whose 1849 concessions from the government of Nicaragua included a contract to build such a canal there, had lobbied successfully for Senate ratification of that treaty. It pledged both sides to seek no colonies or territorial gains on the isthmus—a provision that prevented the Pierce administration from sending military forces to Walker's aid when Central Americans briefly put aside their political differences to throw him out of Nicaragua. Costa Rica declared war on the Walker government on 1 March 1856. Walker responded by invading Costa Rica, where he suffered the first of a series of disastrous defeats. That June a cholera epidemic forced both sides to suspend hostilities, but they resumed fighting in September, when military forces from Costa Rica were joined by Nicaraguan opponents of the Walker regime, as well as by troops from Guatemala, El Salvador, and Honduras.

Walker's position also weakened when he revoked the Vanderbilt concessions and awarded new contracts to a rival group of former Vanderbilt associates, including the transit company's former president, who had been helping Walker all along. Vanderbilt managed to cut off supplies to the Walker forces and used his political influence to keep the U.S. government from coming to Walker's aid. Rescued by a U.S. warship on the brink of defeat in May 1857, Walker returned to a hero's welcome and immediately organized two more expeditions. On the last of these, in 1860, Walker's force landed near Trujillo, on the Honduran coast. The British, who had seized the port and imposed a customs receivership, ordered Walker to surrender. Pursued by Honduran troops, Walker finally surrendered to the British navy. He was promptly turned over to Honduran authorities, tried, and executed on 12 September 1860.

The Walker episode deeply affected Central America. It discredited both the United States and its erstwhile liberal allies in the region. Conservative governments ruled most of the region for the next quarter century, and British influence rose accordingly. The Walker affair also cast a spotlight on the racism not only of Walker and his followers but of U.S. officials in the region as well. Walker included even the local elites as members of the "inferior" races that, he maintained, had been justly condemned to servility by God and Manifest Destiny. As he put it in his best-selling account, *The War in Nicaragua*, "They are but drivellers who speak of establishing fixed relations between the pure white American race, as it exists in the United States, and the mixed, Hispano-Indian race, as it exists in Mexico and Central America, without the employment of force. The history of the world presents no such Utopian vision as that of an inferior race yielding meekly and peacefully to the controlling influence of a superior people. . . . The war in Nicaragua was the first clear and distinct issue made between the races inhabiting the northern and central portions of the continent."[1] U.S. diplomats and policy makers, though usually less candid in expression, generally shared Walker's racial prejudices throughout the nineteenth and well into the twentieth century.[2] The fear and resentment produced by the Walker episode complicated Central American relations with the United States until the promise of economic gain and a new U.S. assertiveness led Central American elites to suspend their suspicions as the nineteenth century came to an end.

Central America's modern economic growth began with the development of coffee. First introduced into Costa Rica in the colonial era, coffee production grew slowly until the 1850s. The California gold rush stimulated Pacific coast shipping, while the completion of the transit route across Panama in 1855 lowered transport costs to Europe and the eastern United States for coffee producers along Central America's Pacific coast, where most of the best coffee lands were located. These developments coincided with growing demand and rising prices. Coffee spread throughout the region—to Guatemala in the 1860s, El Salvador in the 1870s, and Nicaragua and Honduras in the 1880s. The coffee boom affected nearly every aspect of Central American political, social, and economic life.

Costa Rica, the most backward of the colonial provinces, had been settled by Spanish farmers and traders. With no Indian labor force to exploit, most of the colonists worked the land themselves. Much of the best land was concentrated in the temperate plateaus near the Pacific coast. Until coffee, the colonists had produced crops mostly for local consumption; no export product could be found that promised a reasonable return. Only coffee, they discovered, fetched prices high enough to withstand the cost of transportation to the Pacific coast and then across the isthmus through Panama or Nicaragua for shipment to Europe and the United States. Because coffee could be produced efficiently on a small scale, its spread did not destroy Costa Rica's relatively egalitarian distribution of land and income. Landowners with property well suited to coffee and located near transport routes prospered disproportionately, as did processors and merchants. Nonetheless, in contrast to its neighbors, Costa Rica began to modernize in an environment of relative social and economic equality that favored the growth of democratic institutions. When U.S. companies set up banana plantations on the Caribbean coast beginning in the 1880s, the Costa Rican government imposed an export tax and used the revenues to develop public services and infrastructure.

In Guatemala and El Salvador, the spread of coffee production produced quite different social effects. Colonial caste distinctions between Indians, mestizos (people of mixed Indian and European ancestry), and Europeans persisted after independence.[3] The backwardness and poverty of the two countries made the fortunes of even the wealthiest landowner or merchant small by U.S. or European standards, but unlike Costa Rica the rigid social hierarchy inherited from the colonial era limited access to political power and economic opportunity for most of the population. Despite such similarities between Guatemala and El Salvador, however, the effects of the coffee boom were not identical in those countries.

In Guatemala the Indians constituted a majority of the population. The civil strife accompanying independence provoked a number of Indian towns to rebel against Spanish taxes and abuse. In the 1830s Indian leaders from many of the highland towns and villages formed a loose alliance with a local conservative leader, Rafael Carrera, who promised local autonomy, lower taxes, and protection of their communal lands. Their support enabled Carrera to overthrow the Federation government in 1838 and to rule Guatemala until his death in 1865. Nearly all of Guatemala's Indian population lived in the highlands, far from the lowland areas most suited to coffee cultivation. Even after Carrera's death, when liberals took control of the government, the Indians managed to retain possession of their lands because they were not worth the trouble to steal. What the emerging coffee elite needed was not Indian land but Indian labor. So Guatemalan authorities devised legislation empowering local officials to pressure and coerce Indian laborers to migrate down to the sparsely populated coffee areas to work as harvest labor on the new coffee estates. Vagrancy laws authorizing local authorities to send "unemployed" Indians to the lowlands for seasonal labor survived in Guatemala until the revolution of 1944.[4]

In El Salvador, Indians constituted a smaller percentage of the population, but their villages and those of mestizo farmers occupied lands suitable for coffee. In 1879 and 1882 liberal land legislation abolished communal landholding and the protections it enjoyed under Spanish law. The new laws encouraged coffee cultivation by giving coffee planters preferential access to public lands as well as to the privatized landholdings of villages and towns. These liberal land laws thus promoted the concentration of land ownership, particularly in coffee-growing areas. The Indian and mestizo farmers who lost their land came to form a large rural "semiproletariat" of squatters, tenants, and migrant laborers. This rural proletarianization in El Salvador caused the linguistic and cultural differences between Indians and *ladinos* to diminish more rapidly than they did in Guatemala, but the economic distance between landowners and the majority of the rural labor force was greater in El Salvador, as was the potential for violent social confrontation. Protests against land usurpations and poor working conditions on the coffee estates occurred sporadically as coffee cultivation grew. These protests culminated in 1932, when the Salvadoran army, together with armed guards organized by the coffee planters, suppressed a short-lived Indian revolt and then massacred at least 10,000 suspected participants and supporters of the movement. Indian dress and speech virtually disappeared because government troops and private police interpreted any sign of Indian roots as evidence of rebelliousness and grounds for execution.[5]

Nicaragua also joined the ranks of the Central American coffee producers in the late nineteenth century. As in El Salvador, some of the best coffee lands in Nicaragua belonged to Indian or mestizo communities, whose rights were abolished by new land legislation in the 1870s and 1880s. Though the Nicaraguan reforms were initiated by conservative regimes, they were implemented mainly during the long rule of liberal General José Santos Zelaya (1893–1909). Like Costa Rica, however, Nicaragua also produced bananas. The country's development thus moved on two tracks. A new coffee oligarchy emerged in the populous provinces along the Pacific coast, while foreign-owned banana plantations developed in the sparsely populated lowlands facing the Caribbean. For three reasons, Nicaragua did not manage to use banana revenues to develop such public services as education, as Costa Rica had done. First, much of Nicaragua's Atlantic coast was barely governed by Managua; most of the region was a virtual British protectorate until 1894. Second, the coffee oligarchy and its allies preferred to use banana revenues to cover minimal government expenditures and thus free themselves from tax obligations. Finally, the Nicaraguan government, especially under Zelaya, was highly autocratic; pressures for modernization along more democratic lines were absent or repressed. Had it not been for the U.S. occupation (1912–25, 1926–34), Nicaragua would probably have developed a more or less stable governing class of coffee oligarchs, as in El Salvador and Guatemala. Banana revenues, however, would have made it possible to finance less repressive solutions to social problems than in El Salvador, and the isolation of the bulk of the Indian population on the Atlantic coast made it uneconomical to force the Indians into seasonal coffee labor, as in

Guatemala. Nicaragua took a different path than its historic conditions might have determined after the United States intervened.

In Honduras coffee production was insignificant. Export agriculture on a large scale did not develop until U.S. banana companies established plantations there late in the nineteenth century. In Honduras, as in Costa Rica and Nicaragua later on, banana plantations developed on the remote Atlantic coast and initially employed laborers imported from the British West Indies. Except for a small mining industry, bananas came to dominate Honduran exports. Though tax rates on banana exports stayed low, banana tax revenues soon represented the largest source of income for the Honduran government. By the first decade of the twentieth century, U.S. banana companies had become major actors in Honduran politics. The Honduran economic elite, unlike the coffee oligarchies of Guatemala and El Salvador, did not own or produce the country's major export. As banana revenues flowed to the government and quickened the pace of economic life, politics and trade, rather than production, formed the basis of new family fortunes. Immigrant merchants and professionals found it relatively easy to make a respectable fortune and to marry into the best families. With a weak government dependent on foreign banana companies[6] and a heterogeneous commercial elite, Honduras readily succumbed to foreign meddling, both by neighboring Central American republics and by the United States.

Large-scale export production of bananas began along the Caribbean coast of Costa Rica in the 1880s. Unlike Honduras, Costa Rica also produced large quantities of coffee. Therefore the Costa Rican government did not depend so heavily on banana revenues and could insist on better terms from the banana companies and other foreign entrepreneurs. Banana production was first promoted by a North American entrepreneur and adventurer, Minor C. Keith, who hoped to stimulate freight on his railroad. The government had granted him a concession, and generous subsidies, to build a line from San José in the highlands to the Caribbean port of Limón. The government wanted the railroad built to carry coffee. When Keith found that bananas would fetch a good price in New Orleans, he acquired land and ships of his own and formed the Tropical Trading and Transport Company in order to integrate his expanding empire. By manipulating railroad and ocean freight rates to favor bananas produced on his own land, he managed to drive other producers into selling out. Similar stratagems brought even more spectacular success to Lorenzo Jones, whose Boston Trading Company acquired land, railroad concessions, and shipping in Honduras. Jones's bananas went mainly to Boston and other East Coast markets, while Keith supplied New Orleans and the Gulf Coast. The two companies merged in 1899 to form the United Fruit Company (UFCO), headquartered in Boston.

Costa Rica and Honduras became Central America's leading banana exporters. UFCO and its two competitors, the Standard Fruit Company and the Cuyamel Fruit Company (the latter of which was eventually absorbed by

UFCO), established operations in Guatemala, Nicaragua, and Panama as well. Only El Salvador never produced bananas for export. In addition to owning the majority of Central America's banana plantations, UFCO came to dominate both the region's rail network (through its subsidiary, International Railways of Central America) and its steamship connections with the United States (through UFCO's "Great White Fleet").

Guatemala and El Salvador entered the twentieth century with well-established ruling classes whose grip on the two countries had been strengthened by the coffee boom. In Nicaragua a similar development took place under Zelaya but was cut short by the U.S. occupation. Instead of evolving under a securely dominant coffee oligarchy ruling through a succession of stable elite regimes, Nicaragua's political life took shape under U.S. tutelage. The unanticipated consequence of U.S. intervention was the establishment of a highly personalist regime run by the Somoza family and supported by the United States (with occasional expressions of distaste) after 1934.

In Costa Rica the absence of colonial caste distinctions and a less-concentrated pattern of land tenure spread the benefits of export growth more broadly and contributed to the development of democratic institutions. Banana revenues helped to modernize the state apparatus and to finance a precocious expansion of public services, including education.

Honduras remained the most backward of the Central American republics. A largely foreign-born economic elite slowly merged with or replaced local notables, foreign companies controlled the local economy, and the government grew both more corrupt and more autonomous from the domestic elite through tax revenues derived mainly from banana exports.

Like Honduras, Panama never developed an indigenous landowning class capable of dominating political and social life. Panamanians (along with U.S. banana companies) produced export crops, but the health of the economy depended mainly on the movement of foreign goods to foreign destinations long before independence and the construction of the Panama Canal. As in Honduras, the local elite grew rich mainly from trade and transportation. Merchants rather than landed interests shaped local responses to provincial and national issues and dominated the government of the new nation after independence. Unlike Honduras, however, Panama's weak and unstable government shared power not with a foreign company but with a foreign government, whose military forces, civil administrators, foreign workers, and exclusive enterprises and institutions occupied a major part of the national territory. The Panama Canal helped to make Panamanian society and politics exceptionally permeable to U.S. influence.

CREATING THE CLIENT-STATE SYSTEM, 1898–1933

The Central American countries' decline into client states between the 1890s and World War I coincided with a long period of economic growth induced by the success of coffee and bananas. Central American landowners, merchants, and politicians were the principal beneficiaries of this growth, along with foreign (mainly U.S. and British) entrepreneurs and companies. Although some Central Americans resisted incorporation into the new U.S.-dominated system, the United States did not lack for allies. Central American elites often perceived the political and economic subordination of their countries as part and parcel of a process that, on balance, benefited them and their nations. Since most Central Americans were excluded from political decision making, even in countries with parliamentary regimes, the new system took hold with little organized opposition in its early years.

Throughout Central America, naval demonstrations, brief marine landings, the support of U.S. business interests, or a nod from the U.S. ambassador usually proved sufficient to tip the political balance in favor of political groups and personalities willing to accept U.S. conditions (Table 2.1 lists overt U.S. military interventions in Central America between 1900 and 1934). Nicaragua's liberal dictator, General José Santos Zelaya, proved to be the most difficult obstacle, until a U.S.-backed conservative revolt threw him from power in 1909. When the liberals staged a revolt in 1912 against Adolfo Díaz, the conservative president preferred by the United States, U.S. Marines occupied the country to keep him in power. U.S. forces remained in Nicaragua until withdrawn in 1925. The next year they returned to crush another liberal revolt and remained until 1933.

Table 2.1. U.S. Military Interventions in Central America, 1900–1933

1901	Panama	Troops land to maintain order and keep transit lines open; stay two weeks.
1902	Panama	Troops stationed as armed guards on all trains crossing isthmus; stay two months.
1903	Honduras	Troops occupy Puerto Cortés to "protect American consulate and steamship wharf"; stay one week.
1903–14	Panama	Troops land to prevent suppression of independence revolt; remain during canal construction. Additional troops land during disturbances in 1904 and to supervise elections in 1912. (Does not include forces permanently stationed in the canal zone.)
1907	Honduras	Troops are sent to six Honduran ports and towns during war with Nicaragua; activity lasts three months.

Table 2.1. (cont.)

1910	Nicaragua	Separate troop landings at Corinto and Bluefields during revolt.
1911	Honduras	Armed demonstrations during civil strife at various locations; activity lasts two months.
1912	Honduras	Troops land at Puerto Cortés to protect railroad owned by U.S. citizens; are withdrawn after U.S. authorities disapprove.
1912–25	Nicaragua	Troops protect conservative governments, supervise elections, maintain order.
1918–20	Panama	Troops from canal zone enter Chiriquí to maintain order and during election and subsequent unrest.
1919	Honduras	Troops land to create a "neutral zone" during civil strife; stay one week.
1920	Guatemala	Troops land to protect U.S. legation and private property during civil strife; stay three weeks.
1921	Costa Rica, Panama	Naval demonstrations in Atlantic and Pacific to prevent war between these two countries.
1924	Honduras	Troops land twice to protect U.S. citizens and property during civil strife; stay two months.
1925	Honduras	Troops land at La Ceiba to protect foreigners during civil strife.
1925	Panama	Troops land to maintain order during strikes and riots; stay one week.
1926–33	Nicaragua	Troops land to protect government from Sandino revolt; stay to supervise elections, create new army (the National Guard), fight rebels.

Source: Excerpted from "Instances of the Use of United States Armed Forces Abroad, 1792–1945," document presented to a joint hearing of the Armed Forces and Foreign Relations Committees of the U.S. Senate on 17 September 1962: "The Situation in Cuba," presented by Secretary of State Dean Rusk.

The weaknesses and vulnerabilities of the Central American polities served not only to facilitate U.S. dominance in creating the system of client states but to justify it as well. Expanding exports improved each country's creditworthiness. European and U.S. banks extended loans that Central American governments used to pay European and U.S. companies to modernize ports, construct railways, and electrify capital cities, as well as to cover the salaries of bureaucrats and military officers and to build or spruce up public monuments and office buildings. To repay these loans, and to balance budgets swollen with new expenditures, they depended mainly on taxes levied on exports and imports. In good years of expanding trade, all went well. In recession years, when foreign demand fell, Central American governments often found themselves hard-pressed to make timely payments to their foreign creditors. When such years coincided with political unrest, as they often did, the payments stopped altogether, and bankers in the creditor nations appealed for the support of their governments to insist that payments be resumed. In extreme cases the U.S. and European governments dispatched naval forces to threaten retaliation, to blockade or bombard ports, or even to occupy port cities, where they seized customs houses, collected tariff revenues, and remitted the proceeds to their bankers. With political upheavals under way, export earnings down, and credit from abroad cut off, Central American governments were simply unable to resist foreign intervention.

If the Caribbean was to become an "American lake," the United States had to monopolize financial policing. Gradually, beginning in the 1890s, U.S. leaders began taking steps to do so. In 1904 President Theodore Roosevelt announced that thenceforth the United States alone would act as guarantor of the fiscal integrity of the Caribbean nations. To prevent European powers from using debt problems to meddle in the region, he said, the United States would do it for them. U.S. leaders justified Roosevelt's position on the grounds that default invited European intervention, in violation of the Monroe Doctrine.

Formulated in 1823 by Secretary of State John Quincy Adams and proclaimed by President James Monroe, the Monroe Doctrine committed the United States to opposing the reimposition of European colonial rule over the newly independent states of Latin America. Monroe's statement pledged the United States to refrain from meddling in European affairs and to respect European colonial rule where it still existed (in the Spanish, British, Dutch, and French West Indies and in the Guianas). Despite its significance as a foreign policy doctrine for the United States, Monroe's statement amounted to no more than a unilateral proclamation with no basis in international law.

The equally unilateral U.S. assumption of police powers in the Caribbean under the 1904 Roosevelt Corollary also lacked the force of law. The Roosevelt Corollary crystalized U.S. intentions in the Caribbean. Its principal assumption was that European military and naval expeditions to collect debts undermined the sovereignty of the Caribbean countries and thus represented a violation of Monroe's demand that Europe refrain from recolonization efforts in the Western Hemisphere. The objective of the United States, Roosevelt proclaimed, was to protect the independence of the small states in the region. Since none of these countries had requested this assistance, the Roosevelt Corollary amounted to a unilateral declaration of a U.S. protectorate encompassing all of the states in the region.

Disputes among the Central American republics precluded any unified stand against U.S. ambitions at the same time that they provided yet another justification for intervention. The republics' long history of warfare and of meddling in one another's political affairs had begun immediately after they gained independence from Spain in the 1820s. Conservatives sought to create a strong central government, with its capital in Guatemala City, to unify all of Central America. They appointed local officials throughout the region, thus creating a network of conservative politicians and interest groups from one end of the isthmus to the other. Liberals, who initially sought greater local autonomy within the Central American Federation, organized armed rebellions that led to the secession of Costa Rica, El Salvador, Honduras, and Nicaragua and the collapse of the federation in 1838. Liberals, however, often led efforts to restore the federation throughout the nineteenth and into the twentieth century. Occasionally, conservative politicians embraced the federation as a mechanism for dislodging liberals from power. Liberals just as often reconciled themselves to the breakup of the federation and fought for power in the five separate national capitals. Contenders for power in each country enlisted the support of their political counterparts elsewhere in Central America. Exiled conservative politicians sought help from conservative governments in neighboring countries; liberal exiles did likewise. Conservative regimes in Guatemala sought to impose conservative regimes in Honduras and El Salvador. Liberal governments in Nicaragua sought to dislodge conservatives from power in Costa Rica and El Salvador. When interest and ideology proved insufficient cause for belligerence, each of the Central American republics could find ample justification for conflict in the ill-defined borders that generated innumerable territorial disputes among them. By the twentieth century these conflicts had become almost routine; occasionally they escalated into full-scale warfare among the Central American nations.

The United States recognized that it could extend and simultaneously justify its political influence in the region by acting as a peacemaker in regional conflicts. Governments that failed to make peace with their neighbors on terms mediated by the United States were condemned to U.S. hostility as international outlaws. The United States thus exploited conflicts between the Central American states to induce them to acknowledge formally their acceptance of the new U.S. role. The first opportunity to make such a move occurred in 1906, when El Salvador reignited simmering conflicts by giving its support to rebels in Guatemala seeking to overthrow the conservative and pro-U.S. regime of Manuel Estrada Cabrera. When Estrada defeated the rebels and threatened retaliation, Honduras mobilized its forces to aid El Salvador. The U.S. government then persuaded Mexico and Costa Rica to jointly sponsor peace talks aboard the U.S.S. *Marblehead*.

On board the U.S. vessel in July 1906, representatives of all five republics signed an agreement to end hostilities and to refrain from aiding rebels seeking to overthrow other governments in the region. These agreements were confirmed by four of the republics at a meeting in San José, Costa Rica, but Nicaragua's President Zelaya had second thoughts, refused to attend, and accused the United States of meddling. In January 1907 fighting resumed when Honduran troops, claiming to be in hot pursuit of rebels aided by Nicaragua, crossed the Nicaraguan border several times. Nicaraguan rebels in Honduras proclaimed a revolt to overthrow Zelaya, and Honduran troops crossed the border again. Nicaragua then granted diplomatic recognition to a "government" of Honduran exiles and joined them in an invasion of Honduras. Within a few weeks the Honduran government had fallen, and Nicaragua's troops and its small navy had occupied all the major cities and blockaded or occupied the country's ports. By June, Zelaya was supporting rebels in El Salvador and announcing the imminent restoration of the Central American Federation under liberal auspices. El Salvador crushed Zelaya's allies, however, and joined with Guatemala to mount an invasion of Nicaragua. Honduras, by then allied with Nicaragua, loudly refused to permit the two armies to cross its territory for such a purpose. Fortunately, peace came before the Honduran refusal could be tested. Honduras and Nicaragua appealed for negotiations and asked Mexico and the United States to resume mediation. The United States, with Mexico cooperating, invited the five Central American nations to a conference in Washington.

At the Washington conference, which took place between 14 November and 21 December 1907, the five countries signed nine treaties and agreements. Neither Mexico nor the United States signed any of them, but both pledged their support. The two most important agreements were the General Treaty of Peace and Amity (which reaffirmed the elements of the *Marblehead* and San José meetings) and the Convention for the Establishment of a Central American Court of Justice. The court set up shop in Cartago, Costa Rica, but U.S. power gave its decisions what force they had. When the court rendered a verdict in 1912 that challenged the legal basis for U.S. intervention in Nicaragua, the United States decided to ignore that decision (as well as another unfavorable ruling in 1916), thus depriving the court of any claim to legitimacy and effectiveness. The United States continued to impose solutions to disputes among the Central American states after 1912 but abandoned the effort to legitimize its actions juridically. The 1907 convention that created the court expired in 1918. When Nicaragua (at that time controlled by the U.S. Marines and scarcely independent) announced that it would not agree to an extension of the convention, the court died a quiet death.

World War I played a key role in facilitating U.S. dominance in Central America. The war forced all potential European competitors to concentrate their economic and military might on destroying each other. British, French, and German investment virtually ceased; U.S. banks and corporations bought out or took over European interests at bargain-basement prices. Central American trade with Germany ended with the Allied blockade of German ports; trade with Britain and France continued, but by the end of the war the United States had consolidated its unchallenged economic predominance in the region.

The war also removed all potential challenges to U.S. political and strategic dominance in the Caribbean. Except for a brief period in the late 1930s, Germany would never again mount a serious campaign to undermine U.S. influence. For Britain the war confirmed the wisdom of cooperating with U.S. ambitions in the Caribbean—a small price to pay for U.S. support against Germany (though this was by no means the only price exacted by the United States for its entry into the war). None of the other European powers—not even the French, who had once harbored dreams of a "pan-Latin" empire in the region—could have competed with the United States in Central America had they tried, and none did. So complete was U.S. predominance after World War I that the cost-conscious Republican administrations controlling the White House from 1921 to 1933 became increasingly anxious to end the U.S. occupations of Nicaragua, Haiti, and the Dominican Republic. Because the small countries in the region had nowhere else to turn anyway, the U.S. occupations had become unnecessary and anachronistic. The U.S. occupation of the Dominican Republic ended in 1924. In Nicaragua and Haiti, however, the United States continued to station troops for another decade because it could not devise pro-U.S. administrations capable of surviving without Marines protection.

A second Washington conference of Central American states took place after World War I, following another abortive effort in 1921, led by El Salvador, to re-create the Central American Federation. The U.S. government did not openly oppose the project but refused a request to issue a declaration supporting it. The project was muted by a military coup in Guatemala that overthrew the pro-Federation, or Unionist, government of Carlos Herrera on 6 December 1921. As the other republics prepared to intervene, U.S. Secretary of State Charles E. Hughes informed each of them that the United States opposed the use of force. When the backlash from the failed project brought Honduras and Nicaragua to the point of hostilities, their differences were resolved at a meeting on yet another U.S. warship, the U.S.S. *Tacoma*, which had been dispatched to the Gulf of Fonseca. The meeting was also attended by the president of El Salvador and the U.S. ambassadors to the three countries. The three Central American presidents signed the usual pledge to prevent exiles from using their territories to plot against neighboring states and issued a call for a new Washington conference.

The Washington meeting, held between 4 December 1922 and 4 February 1923, concluded with another series of treaties and agreements, drafted in advance by U.S. State Department personnel. A new General Treaty of Peace and Amity reaffirmed most of the provisions of the 1907 version but added stronger language on the nonrecognition of unconstitutional regimes. The nonrecognition provision reinforced the tendency of political parties and actors in Central America to seek accommodation with the U.S. government, since U.S. nonrecognition of new regimes encouraged other factions to revolt. The United States repeatedly employed nonrecognition or the threat of it to manage political conflicts in the ensuing years. The United States refused to recognize, or withdrew recognition of, regimes in Honduras (1924–25), Nicaragua (1926–27), and Guatemala (1930–31), bringing about the fall of incumbents in each case (twice after the by-then routine conferences aboard U.S. warships). Nonrecognition failed, however, in the case of El Salvador in 1931–32, when Costa Rica broke ranks, dispatched an ambassador to San Salvador, and withdrew from the 1923 treaty.

U.S. dominance in Central America did not go unchallenged. Two major irritants developed in the prewar era and continued into the 1920s. The first was U.S. domestic opposition. The phrase "dollar diplomacy" entered the political vocabulary of the Americas. To the prewar anti-imperialist campaigns of U.S. Socialists and their allies were added the voices of many Democratic party politicians and interest groups, including the American Federation of Labor. Isolationists in the Republican party also raised objections. Public opposition to U.S. policy in the Caribbean and Central America frequently affected congressional sentiment. The Senate repeatedly rejected agreements and treaties carefully crafted by U.S. diplomats to advance U.S. control and supervision of governments in the region. In 1911, for example, the Senate rejected proposals for the establishment of new customs receiverships in Nicaragua and Honduras. The Senate also refused to ratify the 1914 Bryan-Chamorro agreement until the administration deleted articles, similar in spirit to Cuba's Platt Amendment, that would have turned Nicaragua into a U.S. protectorate.

Second, growing opposition to U.S. dominance within Central America, especially in the case of the rebellion of Augusto César Sandino against the U.S. occupation of Nicaragua, found support in other Latin American states. After the Mexican revolution of 1910–17, in which the United States intervened repeatedly, Mexico refused further cooperation in Central America; between 1926 and 1933 Mexico sent arms and money to Sandino's rebels. Argentina led diplomatic efforts on behalf of the principle of nonintervention throughout the 1920s and succeeded in attracting a majority of the Latin American countries in the Pan-American Union to the cause.[7] In 1928, at the Sixth Pan-American Conference (held in Havana, Cuba), the hostility produced by U.S. interventions in the Caribbean and Central America led to sharp confrontations between several Latin American countries and the U.S. delegation, led by former Secretary of State Hughes. Even the Central American leaders and political groups who found it convenient or necessary to accommodate U.S. interests maneuvered to elude or subvert U.S. constraints when it served their purposes. In the 1920s Central American opposition to U.S. dominance also began to erupt from new political organizations created by members of the small but growing urban middle classes and from newly organized labor unions and socialist parties just beginning to attract the support of workers. These protests had an economic dimension inasmuch as they served to discredit U.S. motives and interests in the region. Like U.S. domestic protests, they could not be ignored. Yet neither the domestic nor the Latin American opponents of dollar diplomacy had any effective alternative at hand. In the 1920s the United States was as safe from big-power competition in the Caribbean as the Republicans were from competition with the Democrats at home.

DEPRESSION AND THE WAR MAKE "GOOD NEIGHBORS"

The Great Depression produced major changes in both the United States and Central America. In the United States it brought the collapse of Republican dominance, which was not to be rebuilt for a generation. In Central America it abruptly halted the export-led economic prosperity that had helped to cement U.S. dominance and ensure the collaboration of Central American economic and political elites—and with this economic collapse came political repercussions, including violent rebellion, throughout the region.

President Franklin D. Roosevelt (1933–45) proclaimed a new "Good Neighbor" policy for the Western Hemisphere soon after taking office. The Hoover administration had already removed U.S. troops from Nicaragua. Roosevelt's Secretary of State Cordell Hull, confronted by the nearly unanimous condemnation of all of the Latin American republics at the Seventh Pan-American Conference (held in Montevideo, Uruguay, in December 1933), pledged the United States to a policy of nonintervention. For a time it appeared that the United States intended to end its interventions in the Caribbean and to pursue a new policy of respect for the sovereignty of the small states in the region. In fact, no direct U.S. military intervention in the Caribbean occurred in the 30 years between the withdrawal of U.S. troops from Haiti in 1934 and the reoccupation of Santo Domingo, the capital of the Dominican Republic, in 1965.[8]

The Good Neighbor policy rested on the recognition that times had changed. Like its Republican predecessors, the Roosevelt administration could count on the absence of international competition to ensure U.S. predominance in the Caribbean. Even without the constant threat of U.S.

intervention, Central American governments had no choice but to listen carefully to Washington and its ambassadors. In such circumstances the United States could generally rely on finding the allies it needed among local politicians and business groups. This was the lesson the Roosevelt administration learned in Cuba soon after taking office. When a revolutionary government took power after the collapse of the Machado dictatorship in 1933, Roosevelt withheld recognition and dispatched State Department troubleshooter Sumner Welles to Havana. In a matter of weeks Welles managed to induce the new armed forces chief, General Fulgencio Batista, to overthrow the "radicals" and install an acceptably moderate government. With a pro-U.S. government in power, the Roosevelt administration renounced the Platt Amendment, which had been imposed by the United States as a condition for the withdrawal of U.S. troops and U.S. recognition of Cuban independence in 1903. The amendment had formalized Cuba's status as a protectorate of the United States by granting to the U.S. government the right to send troops to Cuba whenever it wished in order to protect U.S. citizens and property, or Cuba's independence, from internal or external threats. By renouncing intervention, the Good Neighbor policy made the Platt Amendment inoperative and obsolete.

Intervention was not only costly and unnecessary (as the Republicans knew) but also, in the view of many New Dealers, essentially corrupt. The use of U.S. military might on behalf of banks and fruit companies (even when plausible strategic interests were also involved) did not square with curbing the greed of the "economic royalists" at home. The Good Neighbor policy became a popular component of the New Deal's reformism.

For most of Central America the Good Neighbor policy required no formal change in relations with the United States. In the case of Panama, however, a new treaty was needed. The original canal treaty had been negotiated in 1903 by Philippe Bunau-Varilla, a French citizen acting on behalf of a Panamanian government that had barely declared its independence and in direct violation of its instructions. In the 1903 treaty the United States had agreed to guarantee Panama's sovereignty (presumably against any attempt by Colombia to recover its lost province). In exchange the United States received the right to build a canal and to control the Panama Canal Zone "as if it were sovereign," as well as the right to send troops into Panama City and the port of Colón to maintain order whenever the United States deemed it necessary. Other provisions limited Panamanian sovereignty still further. In 1936, after two years of negotiations, the two countries signed the Hull-Alfaro Treaty, by which the United States withdrew its guarantee of Panamanian sovereignty and gave up its right to intervene with military force. Although the United States retained control of the canal zone, Panama's status as a formal protectorate ended when the U.S. Senate ratified the Hull-Alfaro Treaty in 1938.

The impact of the Good Neighbor policy in Central America was significant but not entirely positive. The most positive result for the Central Americans was that U.S. ambassadors slowly relinquished their roles as proconsuls. Central American governments were no longer required to seek the approval of the U.S. ambassador on every major question of policy and personnel. As long as each country maintained cordial relations with Washington, respected U.S. property and citizens, and behaved otherwise respectably, Washington no longer demanded day-to-day control. Later it became apparent that the United States would resume closer supervision over governments that violated Washington's requirements and would meddle in local polities whenever it appeared convenient to do so. For the moment, however, the Central American governments were pleased at their elevation from formal or virtual protectorates to dignified clients.

The Good Neighbor policy had important negative repercussions for Central American politics. On the one hand, local governments gained the freedom to manage their domestic affairs with greater flexibility and sensitivity to domestic interests than before. On the other hand, however, the withdrawal of U.S. supervision created a political vacuum at a time when the depression had led to social and political unrest. In Costa Rica this vacuum was filled by a rising tide of popular participation in electoral politics, spurred by the emergence of the labor movement as a major political actor after a successful series of strikes sparked by banana workers in 1933. In the rest of Central America, however, this vacuum was filled by the armed forces. Political leaders and traditional political parties in Guatemala, Honduras, El Salvador, and Nicaragua, discredited by their previous subservience to the United States and by their inability to cope with the collapse of their dependent economies, fell to military regimes that promised order, even if they could not solve economic problems. Most of Central America fell under the heel of a series of "depression dictators." Preoccupied with its own depression (and with keeping clear of costly interventions elsewhere), the United States first acquiesced to, then embraced, the new regimes.

The wisdom of the Good Neighbor policy was confirmed by its utility in blunting a German trade and investment offensive in Latin America. The German National Socialists had taken power in 1933. By the end of 1934 German trade missions throughout Latin America had begun to undermine the efforts of the United States to aid economic recovery by stimulating U.S. exports to Latin America. The United States opposed the spread of German influence in Central America as a threat to its dominant economic position. As war approached, U.S. security concerns also arose. To counter German economic influence, Washington offered reciprocity, embodied in lower tariffs, and trade credits through the new Export-Import Bank. Germany offered much more: barter deals that enabled Latin American countries to exchange their raw materials for German manufactured goods on terms far more favorable than those of free-market exchanges with the United States. "Between 1932 and the late 1930s," Bulmer-Thomas has shown, "Germany trebled its market share of imports in Guatemala, El Salvador, Honduras and Nicaragua and doubled it in Costa Rica."[9]

Guatemala and Costa Rica, with their important populations of German-immigrant coffee growers, now part of the local elite, also provided a significant base for German political aims. Elsewhere Nazi diplomats, military and economic advisers, and political agents grew in number and influence, although they never came close to offering an effective balance to U.S. interests. Washington's response to the German offensive made use of its new policy of nonintervention to deflect criticism of U.S. policy and to argue that closer economic ties to the United States would no longer endanger Latin American sovereignties, not even in the Caribbean. In Guatemala the United States cultivated closer relations with the oppressive dictatorship of Jorge Ubico. A new commercial treaty and other measures succeeded by 1936 in discouraging trade with Germany. Germany's share of Guatemala's exports, which reached a high of 36.9 percent in 1934, dropped to 11.5 percent in 1939. Germany's import share continued to rise until 1938, when it reached a high of 35.1 percent before dropping to 27.0 percent in 1939.[10]

In Costa Rica the United States failed to blunt German trade and political efforts until after 1940. German political and cultural programs grew considerably during the 1930s, nurtured as in Guatemala by influential coffee growers and merchants of German descent. The anti-Semitic and pro-Axis sympathies of President León Cortés (1936–40) were reflected in policies that helped to sustain the German trade offensive. Costa Rica was the only Central American country in which the German share of exports as well as imports increased throughout the 1930s. The United States supported the election of President Rafael Calderón Guardia (1940–44), who had prudently demonstrated his ties to the United States in a preelection trip to Washington. The war in Europe, which began in September 1939, caught Costa Rica ill prepared: the European markets now closed to it had been the intended destination of more than half of its exports—a situation that made the new government particularly vulnerable to U.S. pressure. In addition, Calderón saw that closer ties to the United States could help him to counter ex-President Cortés's continuing political ambitions. As war approached and U.S. pressure became more intense, Calderón moved against the Costa Rican German community. In 1941 and 1942 the Costa Rican government seized the assets of 200 firms and individuals on the U.S. blacklist and apprehended 300 German men, who were turned over to U.S. authorities for transfer to internment camps in the United States.[11]

Calderón's cooperation with the United States against German influence precipitated a major realignment in Costa Rican politics. The government's attacks on the German community alienated a large number of Costa Rica's leading coffee farmers and merchants. To compensate for loss of support among the elite, the Calderón government sought support from the labor movement, which had been organized mainly by Costa Rica's Communist party.[12] The results of this alliance were seen in 1942 and 1943, when the Costa Rican legislature approved major new social legislation, including a social security law and a new labor code.

In Panama, U.S. security concerns predominated once the war in Europe had started. Panamanian irritation over the U.S. delay in ratifying the Hull-Alfaro Treaty of 1936, together with the economic effects of the depression and widespread disgust with the incompetence and venality of the ruling elite, produced an election victory for opposition leader Arnulfo Arias in 1940. Arias, an ardent nationalist, held some pro-Axis views. He apparently saw the European fascist regimes as examples of how strong national leaders could lift their countries out of divisiveness and economic collapse. In Panama the German community was small and lacked influence, trade with Germany had not risen significantly, and Arias had no significant contacts with Axis officials and diplomats. Trouble with the United States arose mainly because Arias's nationalism conflicted with U.S. security interests. He denounced U.S. influence in Panama as excessive and even immoral. When he balked at a U.S. demand that Panama permit the United States to build 134 new military installations both in the canal zone and outside it, the United States used its contacts in the Panamanian National Guard to have him overthrown in 1941.

By the time war broke out in Europe, the U.S. government had already begun to plan for its own involvement in the conflict and moved quickly to create the agencies and institutions that involvement would require. U.S. diplomats in Central America had already spent years working against German and pro-Axis influence. As the U.S. entry into the war approached, these efforts intensified. To ensure Central American support, the United States altered its traditional distrust of political interventions in the marketplace in order to help Western Hemisphere coffee producers adjust to the loss of European markets. The 1940 Inter-American Coffee Agreement set quotas for imports to the United States for all of the hemisphere's coffee producers. The Central American quotas were set high enough to guarantee a market for all of the region's exports. Costa Rica, more dependent than any other Central American country on exports to Germany and England, benefited disproportionately; Calderón's cooperation was amply rewarded.

After the United States entered the war in December 1941, the U.S. government negotiated a series of commodity price-stabilization agreements, in which most of the Latin American countries agreed to supply raw materials and foodstuffs to the United States at negotiated prices (rather than at the much higher market prices, which reflected the vast wartime increase in demand). The Central American countries signed agreements that fixed prices and set production goals for rubber, cinchona bark (for quinine), abacá (hemp), and foodstuffs to provision the vastly increased number of U.S. troops stationed in the Panama Canal Zone.

The U.S. war effort in Central America reversed the hands-off restraints of the Good Neighbor policy. By 1940 U.S. diplomats pressuring for the suppression of pro-Axis political and cultural organizations were joined by military missions looking for air and naval bases, technical experts and aid officials seeking agreements for the production of war matériel and provisions, FBI agents tracking Axis spies, and ships laden with lend-lease military equipment for the cooperative Central American military establishments.

Military cooperation was high on the U.S. list of goals in Central America, but not because the United States expected Central American countries to supply troops for the war (the only Latin American country to do so was Brazil). The United States sought to avoid diverting resources to deal with pro-Axis regimes or movements in the region and, more immediately, needed air and naval bases to protect ships in the Caribbean from German submarines. The United States viewed these war-related goals as more important than domestic political arrangements in the region. The Central American dictators cooperated fully with U.S. war aims. In fact, repressive regimes proved to be convenient because they could respond rapidly to U.S. needs without worrying much about public opinion. In Costa Rica, by contrast, criticism of the terms of the rubber agreement with the United States led the national legislature to reject Calderón's proposal for its renewal in 1943. By that time a new U.S. ambassador had begun to complain about Calderón's alliance with the Communists. When the rubber agreement failed, in part because the Communists voted against it on nationalist grounds, the U.S. retaliated by stopping all work on the Pan-American Highway, a major public works project the United States had agreed to subsidize because of its potential military significance. Work continued on the segments of the highway that ran through neighboring countries with less democratic regimes because there were no legislatures to object to the low prices the U.S. was paying for rubber.[13] Close collaboration between the U.S. and Central American military establishments, begun when the occupying U.S. Marines created the Nicaraguan National Guard a decade before, grew rapidly during World War II. U.S. relations with the depression dictators warmed considerably as all of them cooperated enthusiastically with the U.S. war effort.

CONCLUSIONS

Through an effective combination of private initiative and official policy, the United States created a system of client states in Central America and the Caribbean early in the twentieth century. British competition fell away before World War I. German ambitions, eliminated by the war itself, revived during the 1930s, only to be liquidated again after 1939. Previously British and German warships had backed the claims of foreign investors in the region; by World War I the United States had taken over the region's policing and the external debts that motivated such efforts. When local governments failed to conform to U.S. requirements, the United States saw to their replacement. In the case of Nicaragua this policy led to a prolonged military occupation. Though the Nicaraguan intervention provoked opposition both within the United States and throughout Latin America, it also had a strong demonstration effect on Central America's traditionally fractious political parties and economic elites. By the 1920s direct challenges to U.S. dominance in Central America were attempted only by new political actors and organizations, none yet in a position to take power in the region. Only the Sandino movement in Nicaragua proved effective against U.S. power, and then just temporarily.

The Great Depression and the Good Neighbor policy changed Central America. The depression called into question both the export-led model of economic growth and the political dominance of the export oligarchies. This double crisis was most profound in Guatemala and El Salvador, where coffee exports and coffee barons dominated economic and political life. The military regimes that took power in these two countries were notable for their repression of all challenges to elite interests. However, both the Ubico regime in Guatemala and the Martínez dictatorship in El Salvador represented a distinct move away from past patterns of direct elite rule in two respects. First, in both cases, the military establishment asserted its own institutional and bureaucratic interests, exacting a price in exchange for the stability it imposed through the repression of dissident movements. Military salaries increased, modern weaponry was purchased from abroad, and military officers assumed important positions in civil administration. Second, both regimes strengthened the capacity of the state to intervene in the economy, often by imposing legislation or creating institutions previously opposed by the elite.

The tendencies toward militarism, bureaucratic centralization, and strengthening of state capacities proved to be permanent legacies of the depression in Central America. In Nicaragua the National Guard created by the United States during the occupation became the power base from which Anastasio Somoza imposed himself as president in 1936. Though personalist in style, the Somoza regime gradually institutionalized the role of the guard in diverse aspects of civil administration—a process that simultaneously enhanced the power and the effectiveness of what had previously been a weak presidential system. In Honduras a nominally civilian regime under Tiburcio Carías Andino was no less repressive and centralizing than its military counterparts elsewhere. In Panama the National Guard, also a virtual creature of the United States, seized power in 1941 and again in 1948 but returned the country to chastened civilian rule shortly after each coup.

Panama's military establishment was strengthened by its wartime partnership with the U.S. military, but the civilian governments it installed were less inclined to state intervention than the openly military regimes elsewhere.

Costa Rica was the only country in the region that did not experience a coup d'état during the 1930s. Labor unrest spread from the banana plantations to the towns—especially to San José, the capital city—but the countryside remained calm. The country's relatively egalitarian land-tenure arrangements and functioning electoral system worked to channel discontent along more peaceful lines. The weak Costa Rican military made no attempt to take power, so the state interventionism provoked by the depression took a decidedly populist turn when the United States succeeded in pressuring President Calderón to alienate the elite by moving against the local German community, and the president sought to rebuild his political base by incorporating organized labor.

U.S. security concerns in World War II cemented relations between the Central American military establishments and their U.S. counterparts. Lend-lease military equipment and training programs gave added prestige to local officer corps and provided new weaponry for use against civilian dissidents. The enthusiastic and efficient cooperation of the dictatorships with the United States in providing military bases and promoting the production of war matériel contrasted with the slower and more problematic legislative process through which wartime agreements had to pass in Costa Rica. This may help to explain the skepticism about democratic processes in Central America so frequently expressed by U.S. officials in the postwar era, when new security issues posed by the U.S. confrontation with the Soviet Union came to dominate U.S. policy in the region.

Contrary to the spirit of the Good Neighbor policy, World War II pushed the United States back toward its pre-1933 intrusiveness in Central America's internal political affairs. U.S. diplomats, military officials, FBI agents, technical advisers, and private businesspeople swarmed through the region in unprecedented numbers. The exigencies of war justified rapidly escalating demands for economic cooperation and diplomatic support. Domestic political or social groups deemed hostile or even lukewarm to U.S. war needs were targeted by U.S. agents, and demands were made on every regime in the region to take effective action against them. The 1941 coup in Panama demonstrated how far the United States was prepared to go in enforcing compliance with its demands. U.S. officials combined their big stick with soft talk about postwar economic aid to be awarded in compensation for wartime cooperation. Promises of postwar aid helped secure wartime trade and production agreements. In the postwar era, after a brief interlude during which the United States did little more than renege on these promises of economic aid, U.S. officials began to revive the mechanisms and agencies developed during the war to enforce conformity to U.S. economic and security needs.

chapter 3

CONTAINING CHANGE: THE COLD WAR
IN CENTRAL AMERICA, 1945–1957

THE POSTWAR TRANSITION TO THE COLD WAR

World War II put an end to the last vestiges of great-power competition in the Western Hemisphere. For the next quarter century, Central
America faced an international environment dominated by the unchallenged power of the United States. German economic and political competition ended when the war began in 1939. Commercial ties to Europe closed
down in 1940. By the end of the war an overwhelming proportion of the
region's foreign trade was with the United States. Of all the developed industrial powers, only the United States survived the war without damage to its
economy; thus only the United States could provide the private capital and
foreign aid needed to develop the Central American economies in the postwar era. U.S. military predominance in the Caribbean more than matched
the U.S. economic position. In the postwar era U.S. leaders sought to institutionalize Central America's political and military subordination to the
United States, to include all of Latin America within the new order, and to
do so at the lowest cost possible, in view of the vast resources needed to project U.S. power throughout the rest of the world.

The first step in this direction was taken even before the war had ended.
In January 1945, at the initiative of the United States, an inter-American
meeting was assembled at Chapultepec Castle in Mexico City. Argentina,
the only Latin American country that had failed to declare war on the Axis
powers, was not invited to attend.[1] From the U.S. point of view, the purpose
of the Chapultepec conference was to form a U.S.-led bloc in anticipation of

the June conference in San Francisco, at which the charter of the new United Nations organization would be written. The Latin American representatives brought with them various proposals for U.S. economic aid and concessions, which they hoped to obtain in exchange for their support. The United States rejected or postponed consideration of all economic questions. The Latin Americans were bitterly disappointed, but they had no alternative but to accommodate U.S. interests and wait for more favorable conditions for pressing their agenda.

At the U.N. meeting in San Francisco, the Latin American nations supported U.S. proposals that resulted in the inclusion of Articles 51 to 53 of the U.N. Charter. These articles authorized the creation of regional organizations to which conflicts might be referred prior to action by the full U.N. body. Assistant Secretary of State for American Republic Affairs Nelson Rockefeller and his collaborators saw this as a form of international recognition of the Monroe Doctrine. Disputes in the Western Hemisphere would be referred to a regional organization in which no country outside the Western Hemisphere would have a voice. The United States could readily dominate any such organization and use it to prevent the United Nations from meddling in what amounted to a U.S. sphere of influence. Articles 51 to 53 solved the dilemma of reconciling the U.S. wartime call for an open world with its insistence on a closed hemisphere.

Latin American support for Articles 51 to 53 stemmed from an entirely opposite logic. At a series of Pan-American conferences, beginning in 1928, a large majority of the Latin American republics had demonstrated their commitment to the principle of nonintervention. They reasoned that a regional organization would serve to restrain the United States by forcing the U.S. government to secure Latin American approval for any measures affecting security of the region. Allies of the United States predominated in the full United Nations, and the United States held veto power in the Security Council. Thus in the event that the United States abandoned its adherence to the Good Neighbor policy of nonintervention, the United Nations seemed to offer less protection for the security of Latin American states than would a regional organization.

The Latin American supporters of Articles 51 to 53 failed to take into account the immense power of the United States to affect the decisions of their own governments on security and other issues. In most inter-American meetings of the postwar era, the United States was assured of the support of at least 8 of the 20 Latin American republics—a near majority of states. This bloc included all of the small Caribbean and Central American states except Guatemala: Costa Rica, Cuba, the Dominican Republic, El Salvador, Haiti, Honduras, Nicaragua, and Panama. Guatemala's support became automatic after the U.S.-sponsored coup in 1954. Joseph Stalin complained to Roosevelt at the Yalta Conference in 1945 about the number of Latin American votes the United States would control in the new United Nations (of the United Nations' original 46 member nations, 20 were Latin American). In response Roosevelt agreed to support U.N. seats for the Soviet republics of Byelorussia and the Ukraine. As postwar celebrations gave way to cold war tensions, Stalin's complaint began to seem less and less farfetched.

The subordination of most of the Latin American military establishments to U.S. war aims, coordinated through the Inter-American Defense Board (created in 1942), continued in the postwar era. The U.S. insisted on renewing leases on the military bases constructed in the Caribbean during the war and retained most of its installations. The Truman administration, however, put an end to the lend-lease program and stopped financing arms sales to Latin America. U.S. officials permitted arms sales to most Latin American countries but no longer provided loans or other forms of aid to promote them. Some administration officials expressed concern that large-scale arms shipments would stimulate domestic repression in the region or lead to an arms race, and perhaps even war, among the Latin American countries. Proponents of military aid argued that making U.S.-made weapons standard equipment for the region's military would enhance dependence on the United States and thus increase U.S. influence and leverage.[2] They also argued that the training of Latin American officers, either on site or in U.S. military schools, would improve hemispheric defense and, incidentally, win friends and agents for the United States inside the military establishments of the Latin American countries. In the end this position prevailed. After the outbreak of the Korean War in 1950, the U.S. administration decided to include military aid for Latin America in its 1951 foreign aid request to Congress and to expand training programs for Latin American military officers, which had continued at reduced levels since 1945.

The centerpiece of U.S. postwar security policy in Latin America was the Rio Treaty of 1947—the first fruit of Articles 51–53 of the U.N. Charter. Formally titled the Inter-American Treaty of Mutual Assistance, it bound the United States and the Latin American republics to a military alliance in which each nation agreed to come to the aid of any other that might be threatened by external aggression.

At the insistence of the United States, Article 6 of the Rio Treaty explicitly extended the concept of "collective self-defense" to include cases of "aggression which is not an armed attack" as well as any "extra-continental or intra-continental conflict or any other fact or situation that might endanger the peace of [the] America[s]."[3] Without stating so openly, this language made it possible in later years to claim that allegedly Communist political organizations involved an extracontinental conflict that justified U.S. intervention, even in cases where all the alleged Communists were citizens of the country in which their political activities took place.

U.S. officials understood that the threat of a Soviet attack on the Western Hemisphere was remote, if not nonexistent. This understanding was reflected in the nature of the arms sales authorized prior to 1951 and in the military aid programs that began that year. The weapons shipped to Latin America consisted largely of small arms, light armor, outdated aircraft, and the like, suitable mainly for maintaining domestic order but virtually useless against a real superpower. The significance of the Rio Treaty, therefore, did not lie in its contribution to making the Western Hemisphere safe from the Soviet Union. Rather, it signaled the nearly universal recognition throughout Latin America that the international system no longer offered any viable alternative to collaboration with the United States and the understanding that the United States was prepared to promote stability in the region by arming cooperative governments against their domestic foes.

This kind of collaboration had been imposed on the small Caribbean and Central American countries half a century earlier. Thus their subordination to the United States in security matters was more advanced than that of other Latin American nations. The Nicaraguan armed forces, for example, were created by the United States during the occupation and remained closely tied to the United States: "From 1956 until its dissolution in 1979 the National Guard was commanded by West Point graduates and the cadets of the [Nicaraguan] military academy, founded by the Americans in 1930, spent their fourth year of study in an American school; this was especially true beginning in the 1960s with the establishment of the School of the Americas in the Canal Zone."[4] Relations between the U.S. and Panamanian military establishments were equally close. Elsewhere in Central America, new and stronger ties were forged in the postwar era. Totally dependent on the United States for equipment and advanced training, the Central American military establishments of the 1950s and 1960s operated less as national armies than as "agents of the security interests of the United States."[5]

The political and diplomatic counterpart to the Rio Treaty was established in 1948, when the Organization of American States (OAS) was created at an inter-American meeting in Bogotá, Colombia. The OAS Charter, unlike the Rio Treaty, contained language embodying the principle of nonintervention. Article 15 of the OAS Charter states that "no state or group of States has the right to intervene, directly or indirectly, for any reason whatever, in the internal or external affairs of any other State."[6] This unambiguous language was modified, at the insistence of the United States, by other charter provisions that incorporated the collective self-defense provisions of the Rio Treaty. In the years since, critics of U.S. intervention in Latin America have cited Article 15 of the OAS Charter, whereas proponents of U.S. military action in the region—usually U.S. government officials—have cited the collective security provisions of Article 6 of the Rio Treaty to justify their position.

Economic aid was not part of the Pax Americana in the immediate postwar era. U.S. economic assistance to Central America was confined to small-scale "technical assistance" missions under President Truman's Point Four program, along with infrequent loans, at market rates of interest, through the U.S. Export-Import Bank. Both of these programs had been designed in the 1930s to promote economic recovery by stimulating U.S. exports. During the war technical assistance had been expanded to promote the production of important raw materials and to inspire goodwill toward the United States. After the war U.S. officials repeatedly and pointedly stated that their country's new global responsibilities would not permit large-scale aid programs in the Western Hemisphere. In January 1945 Latin American representatives at the Chapultepec conference in Mexico City called for an inter-American economic conference in June to discuss postwar economic and aid policies. The United States, unwilling to respond to a long list of Latin American proposals on such issues, refused to attend. The Latin American governments postponed the meeting, hoping to secure U.S. participation at a later date. For the next three years the Truman administration found reasons to refuse U.S. participation each time a new date was proposed.[7]

At the Rio de Janeiro and Bogotá meetings, U.S. representatives rejected a long list of Latin American economic proposals. The United States abruptly canceled the wartime price and production agreements by which the Central American countries had supplied raw materials and foodstuffs to the United States at prices well below market levels. U.S. officials dismissed Latin American proposals for new international commodity agreements to stabilize the prices of Latin America's exports and rejected suggestions to enter into agreements that would peg the prices of Latin America's exports to the prices of the manufactured goods the region imported from the United States. The United States also rejected proposals for the creation of an inter-American bank that would offer long-term, low-interest loans for development projects, as well as most other proposals for economic aid.

Instead of proffering development aid and price-fixing agreements, the United States proclaimed the virtues of private enterprise and free trade. To attract private capital, the United States argued, the Latin American countries had to improve the investment climate they offered U.S. firms by eliminating excessive taxes and regulations. They were also urged to abandon the economic nationalism that had led some nations to adopt high tariffs, nationalize local or foreign companies, and create state enterprises in the petroleum, transport, and utility sectors of their economies. U.S. diplomats, technical aid officers, and State Department officials pressured constantly for these changes. At times the fervor of U.S. officials in promoting private U.S. economic interests reached rhetorical heights that managed to appear simultaneously offensive and ridiculous to Latin American (and even U.S.) ears. Spruille Braden, assistant secretary of state for inter-American affairs for two stormy years under Truman, summarized the U.S. government's position as follows: "The institution of private property ranks with those of religion and family as a bulwark of civilization. To tamper with private enterprise will precipitate a disintegration of life and liberty as we conceive and treasure them. The time has come to realize that the United States Treasury is not an inexhaustible reservoir."[8] After 1948 U.S. officials habitually accused individuals and organizations that called for active government intervention in economic life—including the new U.N. Economic Commission for Latin America (ECLA)—of having Communist sympathies because of their alleged hostility to free enterprise.

At the Bogotá meeting and in the Rio Treaty, the United States succeeded in persuading delegates to approve ringing declarations of anticommunist faith. These declarations coincided with a new U.S. effort to pressure Latin American governments to outlaw local Communist parties and to suppress Communist influence in labor movements and other civic organizations. Anticommunism, as an ideology, did not represent a departure from previous expressions of official U.S. social philosophy. From time to time U.S. ambassadors had condemned strikes against U.S. businesses or expressions of opposition to U.S. policy as Communist or inspired by communism. As early as 1926, U.S. officials claimed that Moscow was sending aid through Mexico to Sandino's rebels in Nicaragua and justified the reoccupation of Nicaragua by U.S. Marines on the grounds of a Communist threat to the Western Hemisphere.[9] Although moderated by the wartime U.S. alliance with the Soviet Union, expressions of concern over Communist influence occurred even during World War II, when Communist parties generally supported Allied war efforts.[10] In the postwar era such occasional statements of concern or annoyance gave way to a concerted anticommunist campaign that affected every Latin American country.

In most Latin American countries with functioning electoral systems, Communist parties had been permitted to organize legally during either the 1930s or World War II. By the end of the war Communists played a particularly prominent role (although always in the minority or in the opposition) in Cuba, Guatemala, Costa Rica, Brazil, and Chile. In Cuba and Chile, Communists had served in cabinet positions; in the other countries they had held seats in the national legislatures and led important labor unions and union federations. After the war ended, U.S. officials encouraged Latin American governments to move against Communists and others who shared their sympathy for labor or their enthusiasm for government intervention in the economy. Latin American governments received repeated formal requests to reduce or suppress open expressions of Communist influence, to intensify or develop the capacity of their police and security forces to control or weaken Communist-led or "-tainted" organizations, and to break diplomatic relations with the Soviet Union.

The U.S. effort to purge Latin American labor movements began immediately after the war. The Truman State Department helped the American Federation of Labor (AFL) to organize a new anticommunist confederation of labor unions in the Western Hemisphere. AFL agents, led by AFL official

Serafino Romualdi, worked closely with anticommunist labor groups throughout the region. In most cases conservative Catholic unions were deemed the most suitable allies; noncommunist socialist or liberal groups were also recruited to the cause. Local governments and their police and security services worked with U.S. diplomats and intelligence agents to identify, harass, and even suppress labor organizations alleged to be Communist-led or -influenced. In a number of countries labor and police ministries worked to see to it that left-wing unions lost strikes and that their conservative counterparts won generous contracts from employers. In January 1948 the AFL and conservative labor organizations from all over Latin America joined to form the Inter-American Confederation of Workers (known by its Spanish initials, CIT). Three years later, in January 1951, the CIT was dissolved and replaced by the Inter-American Regional Organization of Workers (ORIT). These organizations were created to compete with older, more established, and more left-wing labor organizations that belonged to the Confederation of Latin American Workers (CTAL), headed by the prestigious Mexican labor leader Vicente Lombardo Toledano. The CTAL belonged to the World Federation of Trade Unions (WFTU), which established its headquarters in Prague, and which the United States saw as Communist-dominated. ORIT became the Western Hemisphere affiliate of the International Confederation of Free Trade Unions (ICFTU), a new global organization formed when the U.S. CIO (Congress of Industrial Organizations, later merged with the AFL) and the British TUC (Trades Union Congress) broke with the WFTU. In Latin America the CTAL unions tended to be more militant and politically independent of local governments, whereas the ORIT affiliates, often much smaller and initially less effective, derived much of their support from the Church and employer associations.[11]

In Central America ORIT made its greatest headway in Costa Rica after the 1948 revolution suppressed the local Communist party. The Church-led Rerum Novarum movement virtually took over most of the old unions, many of whose leaders were now in jail or in exile abroad. In Guatemala, by contrast, the new democratic government refused to cooperate with the AFL efforts; ORIT made headway only after the U.S.-sponsored coup in 1954. ORIT showed little interest in the other Central American countries. In Nicaragua the Communists had been suppressed in 1948 and posed no further threat to the regime; the Somocista federation joined ORIT. In Honduras the AFL and ORIT made no effort to recruit until 1954, when a major strike against U.S. banana companies led U.S. officials to suspect Communist influence. In El Salvador and Panama government support for the AFL efforts met little success. Salvadoran regimes had little influence in the labor organizations they continuously sought to suppress. In Panama, where the AFL had "browbeat[en] the War Department into setting up two scales of pay, one for United States citizens and one for 'foreigners,'"[12] ORIT was viewed by Panama's unionists as tainted by the AFL's endorsement of wage discrimination against Panamanian workers. Eventually, ORIT succeeded in attracting Catholic and company unions, together with unions representing government employees, throughout Central America.

Initially, the U.S. anticommunist effort was poorly coordinated and accorded low priority. As the cold war intensified—beginning in 1947 with the proclamation of the Truman Doctrine and the subsequent U.S. aid to right-wing, pro-U.S. factions in the Greek civil war—anticommunist activities drew more government staff and attention. This trend was reinforced by the recovery of the Republican party in the United States. The Truman administration's alleged lack of commitment to combatting communism was part of "the mess in Washington" that helped Republicans win control of the Congress in 1946 and nearly unseat the president in the 1948 elections. With the Communist victory in China in 1949 and the start of the Korean War in June 1950, anticommunism became the basic organizing principal of U.S. foreign policy.

The U.S.-sponsored campaign against communism in Latin America succeeded for two main reasons. First, the United States offered modest economic aid and other inducements to secure the cooperation of governments that hesitated to join the effort. No other great power was bidding for the support of the Latin American nations—nor was any other power interested in protecting any of them from U.S. hostility, should it be provoked. Second, the end of the war had already led political and economic elites in most countries to accept the need to accommodate their nations' economic and security interests to those of the United States. Many now saw the economic nationalism, social reform, and democratic openings of the depression and war eras as anachronistic. As the postwar economic recovery in the United States helped to restore the international economy, the exceptional conditions that had disrupted the flow of trade, capital, and technology after 1929 came to an end. Left-wing political parties and labor unions had been accepted or tolerated by Latin American elites as a necessary and unavoidable consequence of the depression or of the economic and political pressures unleashed by the war. After 1945, however, elites in most of the Latin American countries happily cooperated with the United States in dividing or suppressing such organizations. To elite-dominated conservative parties and regimes, anticommunism offered domestic political and social dividends, whether the promised U.S. aid materialized or not.

The U.S. postwar anticommunist crusade undermined, and eventually reversed, a trend toward democratization that had acquired momentum throughout Central America during World War II. The war put an end to the depression, and thus to the conditions that had fostered dictatorships in El Salvador, Guatemala, Honduras, and Nicaragua. Wartime inflation fueled social tensions that undermined military rule. Labor movements grew stronger in tighter labor markets in which employers learned to be more flexible. Growing numbers of urban middle-class employees, professionals, and property owners became active in supporting political parties and movements that demanded democracy and reform. The Nazi attack on the Soviet Union turned Communist parties and their left-wing allies into enthusiastic supporters of the war effort. Wartime cooperation between Communists and non-Communists opened political spaces, even under otherwise repressive regimes, and helped to spread visions of social and economic reform. Allied propaganda painted the war effort as a struggle for freedom against militarism and reaction.

Throughout Central America authoritarian regimes began to shake and even to fall. In April 1944 a mass movement, culminating in a general strike, persuaded the Salvadoran armed forces to eject General Maximiliano Hernández Martínez, dictator of El Salvador since 1931. Subsequent regimes were controlled alternately by moderate and right-wing factions within the military, each with its civilian collaborators. For a few months in 1944–45 and again in 1948–49, military regimes loosened controls and enacted modest reforms. Ubico in Guatemala, who had come to power in 1931, fled the country on 1 July 1944, when his army deserted him amid mass protests and strikes. A new constitution and the country's first genuinely free elections brought a moderately reformist government to power, headed by President Juan José Arévalo. In Honduras strongman Carías, elected in 1932, resigned under pressure in 1948. Although Carías was replaced by his own defense minister, Juan Manuel Gálvez, after fraudulent elections, the new government was less repressive. Even the Somoza regime in Nicaragua loosened its grip. In 1947 Somoza temporarily turned over the presidency to a hand-picked successor (whom he later removed), relaxed controls on the opposition, and, on resuming the presidency in 1950, had the compliant Congress pass new (though largely unenforced) social legislation. In Costa Rica President Calderón's alliance with the labor movement and the Communists won a resounding victory (albeit tainted by fraud) in the elections of 1944. Despite U.S. discomfort, the alliance continued under Calderón's successor, Teodoro Picado (1944–48), and the social legislation of 1942 and 1943 remained in force.

Only in Panama did these trends work in reverse, largely because of the United States. Although the National Guard turned over the government to Arias's vice-president after the 1941 coup, it did not relinquish its new U.S.-supported role as the ultimate arbiter of Panamanian political life. After suppressing riots protesting U.S. demands for renewal of the leases on its military installations in 1947, the guard intervened to prevent Arias, the apparent winner of the 1948 elections, from returning to power.

Except in the case of Panama, the U.S. role in the regime changes that occurred at the end of World War II was modest but nonetheless significant. U.S. diplomats, pleased with the cooperation provided by the Ubico and Martínez dictatorships, sought and immediately received assurances from the new democratic authorities that all wartime agreements and understandings would be respected. In both cases U.S. officials found themselves working with virtually the same military and police officials as before. Once reassured, U.S. diplomats welcomed the new governments and resumed their activities on behalf of U.S. war aims. This was true even in those countries—including Costa Rica, Guatemala, Honduras, and Nicaragua—where local Communist parties were active supporters of the movements that led to these democratic trends.

While the United States did not oppose democratization in the region, it did little to encourage it. As the cold war intensified, so did U.S. skepticism about the trend toward democratization. Although some officials of the Truman administration, particularly in the State Department and the diplomatic corps, supported democratization, this support had all but disappeared by the time the Korean War broke out in 1950. Global security concerns once again came to dominate U.S. policy in Latin America, and the United States tied its political interests to the ardent anticommunism of right-wing political parties and military establishments. This shift had disastrous consequences for the smaller countries of the region, where the United States exerted the most influence.

The evolution of U.S. postwar policy in Central America and the ways in which local conditions mediated the impact of U.S. actions are well illustrated by the case of the anticommunist national revolution in Costa Rica in 1948 and by that of its Guatemalan counterpart in 1954. In 1948 the United States cautiously supported a Costa Rican revolt, led by José Figueres, that gave power to an unusual coalition of social reformers and old-line conservatives. The new regime suppressed the Communist party and its affiliated labor unions but also nationalized domestic banks, reaffirmed and extended existing social legislation, and abolished the army. Costa Rican democracy survived and, despite the initial repression, even flourished. This positive outcome owed to both U.S. restraint and favorable local conditions. Six years later, in 1954, the United States intervened more actively to organize the overthrow of the democratic reformist government of President Jacobo Arbenz in Guatemala. In this case no local proponents of democratic government or social reform were willing to take up arms against the incumbent government, so the United States backed the extreme right. The new Guatemalan government of Colonel Carlos Castillo Armas suppressed the Communist party, but the reign of terror his regime launched targeted all individuals and organizations that had supported the previous government. Nearly all the reforms of the decade after the 1944 revolution were swept away, democratic rights and institutions were abolished, and the military, eventually purged of moderate officers, consolidated its position as the country's unchallenged master.[13] The trend toward democratization in Central America, which developed so much momentum after 1944 and survived the 1948 civil war in Costa Rica, was finally destroyed by U.S. support for the violent anticommunism of the Guatemalan coup.

THE UNITED STATES AND THE 1948 COSTA RICAN WAR

In the spring of 1948 a brief but intense civil war in Costa Rica, known as the national revolution, overturned the Picado government, whose electoral and programmatic alliance with the local Communist party had caused the United States to support its opponents. José Figueres, the leader of the insurrection, took power in a deal brokered by the U.S. and Mexican ambassadors and ruled for 18 months. The new government outlawed the Communist party, imprisoned or exiled its leadership and many of its members, suppressed labor unions affiliated with the Communists, closed the Communist party press, and prohibited further Communist activity. Figueres's anticommunism won him the support he needed from the United States. By the time he turned over the government to Otilio Ulate in November 1949 the power of the Costa Rican Communist movement had been reduced dramatically; its influence was confined to the banana workers' union on UFCO plantations and to a dwindling number of working- and middle-class supporters in San José.

Unlike later anticommunist episodes supported by the United States, the Costa Rican national revolution did not lead to military rule, nor did it result in the liquidation of social programs and other reforms legislated by previous governments. Instead, Figueres boldly abolished the weak Costa Rican army (which his rebel militia had already defeated in the spring fighting) on 2 December 1948. Ruling mainly by decree, he nationalized the domestic banking system, imposed a "temporary" income tax of 10 percent on the nation's wealthiest citizens, and initiated an impressive package of social programs insulated from the vagaries of the electoral process because of their administration by new, semi-autonomous "institutes." The abolition of the armed forces and the institutionalization of the social gains of previous administrations established the foundation for the modern Costa Rican electoral system. Without recourse to the military, the Costa Rican right wing had no choice but to compete for electoral support. The left—faced with a labor movement permanently weakened by Figueres's repression, and further fragmented by the collaboration of some unions whose members benefited from the Figueres reforms—lost its capacity to mobilize broad popular support outside the electoral arena.

Before taking power, Figueres was virtually unknown to the United States. He had applied for a visa to visit the United States in 1944, but his application was rejected, apparently because he had criticized the Calderón government's persecution of Nazi sympathizers as unconstitutional in 1942. Figueres spent two years (1942–44) in exile in Guatemala, where he formed a close association with future Guatemalan President Arévalo. Arévalo revived the idea of a Central American Federation after his election in 1945 and linked this objective with the democratic ideology of the 1944 uprising that had overthrown the Ubico dictatorship and brought him to power. In 1947

Arévalo and President Salvador Castañeda of El Salvador signed an agreement to reconstitute the Central American Federation, beginning with their two countries. Figueres lent his support to the revival of the federation, although Costa Rica had previously pursued a studied isolation from the affairs of the other Central American states and had consistently opposed reunification ever since the collapse of the federation in 1838. At the same time, Arévalo began supplying weapons and financial support for a small army, called the Caribbean Legion, whose goal was to overthrow all of the dictatorships in the Caribbean. Figueres became a leader of the legion, which was composed of political exiles from throughout the Caribbean. The legion devoted much of its attention to efforts aimed at overthrowing Trujillo, dictator of the Dominican Republic, and Somoza of Nicaragua. In 1948 the legion, backed by Guatemala, provided arms and men for Figueres's insurrection.

The circumstances that brought Figueres to power had more to do with Costa Rican internal politics than with U.S. policy, though the U.S. role was not negligible. When Picado took office in 1944 he enjoyed more than a year of cordial relations with the United States. The U.S. embassy had supported his electoral opponent, León Cortes, as had Guatemala, El Salvador, and Panama; Picado had enjoyed the support of Nicaragua, Cuba, and Mexico. Nevertheless, U.S. authorities accepted the Picado administration and welcomed its support of the U.S. war effort, as well as its willingness to renew the U.S. military mission and its facilities in 1945 and 1946. U.S. authorities were also pleased when Picado moved to reduce government spending and to impose more order and efficiency in government ministries that had grown rapidly under Calderón, his freewheeling predecessor and patron. When Picado failed to break with Calderón or the Communist party after the war, however, the United States set out to encourage the opposition. The leading opposition candidate for the presidency was Ulate, whom the U.S. embassy cultivated assiduously. In 1946 Ulate traveled to the United States for two months, with all his expenses paid by the State Department. Even the explicit and sometimes vulgar anti-Semitism of Ulate's newspaper was not sufficient to change the U.S. position; Germany had been defeated, and anti-Semitism no longer suggested sympathy for the enemies of the United States. Embassy funds were contributed to Ulate's political party. In August 1947, six months before the February 1948 presidential elections, Ulate's followers staged a nationwide general lockout, known in Costa Rican history as the "Strike of the Downed Arms" (la huelga de los brazos caídos). When Picado allowed Communists and other government supporters to vandalize shops and warehouses owned by supporters of Ulate, the State Department became alarmed. U.S. Ambassador Walter J. Donnelly, who respected Picado and discounted Washington's fears of the local Communists, helped to broker an end to the lockout. He persuaded Picado to reform the Costa Rican election laws to create multiparty commissions to oversee the registration of voters and to manage the elections.

Picado even agreed to give the opposition control of the registration commission.

The election of 8 February 1948 was unusually violent for Costa Rica. Figueres's vigilantes fought against militias organized by the Communist party. The opposition controlled the polling process and excluded many voters seeking to support the government candidate, former president Calderón. The electoral commission declared Ulate the victor after canvassing only one-third of the votes. Picado called the national congress into session and had the election annulled on 2 March. In response Figueres ordered his followers to prepare for an insurrection with arms that had been flowing into the country from Guatemala for several months. The Figueres revolt began on 12 March. After the rebels captured Limón and Cartago on 11 and 12 April, Picado resigned the presidency and fled the country, abandoning the Communist militias that had pledged to defend San José from rebel troops. Figueres negotiated with Communist leader Manuel Mora to ensure a peaceful occupation of the city. He promised amnesty for members of the Communist militias and pledged that he would not outlaw the party. Three months after his "Army of National Liberation" entered the capital unopposed, however, Figueres broke his pledge and unleashed the anticommunist repression that earned him the support of the United States.

The Picado government had known that Figueres was planning a revolt long before the February 1948 elections. Picado had tried to buy arms in the United States to improve the antiquated weaponry of the Costa Rican army. U.S. law required arms manufacturers to obtain U.S. government permission for arms sales to foreign governments. Lend-lease arms shipments to Costa Rica during the war had been minuscule (arms worth a total of $119,181.82, in contrast to lend-lease weaponry worth $300,000 for Nicaragua, more than $1.5 million for El Salvador, and $3 million for Guatemala). When Picado first requested permission for arms purchases in 1946, his request was denied on grounds that the Costa Rican government still owed the United States $63,000 for the lend-lease shipments. This same reason was cited in January 1947, when Picado renewed his request. The United States refused permission for the purchase of five small aircraft, 50 machine guns, and other light arms. Picado received permission to purchase only 25 machine guns, a number too small to make a difference in the fighting that broke out a year later. In August, as the opposition's national lockout turned violent, Picado dispatched agents with urgent orders for arms in Europe. The United States used its influence with the European governments to block any purchases.

Picado's one international ally was the Somoza regime in Nicaragua. The origins of this alliance predated both governments. Since the nineteenth century Nicaraguan governments had consistently backed Costa Rican politicians opposed to a revival of the Central American Federation under Guatemalan leadership, while Guatemala had supported their opposite numbers. Mexico generally supported anti-Guatemalan factions throughout the region, including Costa Rica. Guatemalan governments, worried about their Mexican neighbors, generally sought close relations with the United States. U.S. policy cut across political factions, supporting liberal, anti-British factions in the nineteenth century (whatever their positions on reviving the federation) but imposing pro-U.S. conservative puppet regimes on Nicaragua in the 1910s and 1920s. Throughout the 1930s and 1940s Guatemala supported the Costa Rican opposition, first under Ubico and then under Arévalo. Nicaragua under Somoza had close ties to the Calderón administration in Costa Rica between 1940 and 1944, maintained those ties during the Picado presidency, and supported Calderón's bid for reelection in 1948.

As Picado's relations with the United States soured, especially after the national lockout in August 1947, Somoza maintained his support. In addition to the historic animosity between Nicaragua and Guatemala, Somoza had two other powerful reasons to support the Costa Rican regime. First, there was the Caribbean Legion, supported by Arévalo and Figueres and pledged to overthrow Somoza's government. Guatemala had provided arms to Nicaraguan exiles in Costa Rica and Guatemala as well as to Figueres's insurrectionists. Second, Somoza found himself embroiled in a dispute with the United States in 1947. On 2 February of that year he organized elections that put his handpicked successor, Leonardo Argüello, in the presidency. Argüello's effort to distance himself from his patron led Somoza to stage a coup on 26–27 May that replaced Argüello with a more compliant interim president, Benjamín Lacayo Sacasa. In July Somoza sent a small shipment of arms to Picado to aid the government in controlling Figueres's vigilantes during the national lockout. Then, on 15 August, Somoza had one of his uncles, Victor Román y Reyes, inaugurated to serve out Argüello's term. Costa Rica recognized the Román y Reyes government immediately. The United States, citing the doctrines proclaimed in the 1907 and 1923 Washington treaties (which it had ignored in the past) and annoyed at Somoza's support for Picado, refused to recognize the new Nicaraguan government and pressured the other Latin American governments into excluding Nicaragua from the list of countries invited to the Bogotá conference set for March 1948.

When Figueres began his revolt on 12 March 1948, on the eve of the Bogotá meeting, Somoza sent 60 armed men and two old AT-6 aircraft (with a promise of three more planes) to Picado. Ten days later, on 22 March, he leaked word to the U.S. embassy in Managua that he intended to send 1,000 men to Picado's aid. By the end of that same day, after conversations with the U.S. embassy, Somoza backed down and agreed not to send the aid. A few days later Nicaragua received an invitation to Bogotá. By late March, as the Picado government weakened, Somoza told the U.S. ambassador that he would recognize any government the United States wished to choose for Costa Rica. In May, after the Figueres victory, the United States recognized the Román y Reyes government. Shortly thereafter Nicaragua received new aircraft from the United States and from the Trujillo government in the Dominican Republic.

There remained, however, the animosity between Somoza and Figueres, whose Caribbean Legion was pledged to rid Nicaragua of the Somoza regime. On 17 April, just as Figueres prepared to take power, Nicaragua invaded Costa Rica. Somoza allowed himself to be persuaded by the United States to withdraw, but the warning to Figueres was clear enough. Despite the warning, Figueres allowed the Caribbean Legion, as well as a separate force of anti-Somoza Nicaraguans, to set up camps in Costa Rica, just across the border from Nicaragua. Somoza waited for the United States to pressure Figueres to close them down, but he prepared for war. The U.S. efforts were only partially successful. In October Figueres broke with Guatemala, denounced Arévalo's criticisms of his repression of labor unions and the Costa Rican Communist party, and refused Arévalo's request for the return of arms that Guatemala had loaned to the Figueres movement for the insurrection. On 27 November Figueres bowed to U.S. pressure and disbanded the Caribbean Legion, shutting down its camp and confiscating its weapons. He did not, however, disband the Nicaraguan exiles.

The climax of these events took place in December 1948. On 1 December the U.S. ambassador informed Figueres that Somoza was preparing to launch an invasion, using Costa Rican exile partisans of Calderón and Picado. The U.S. embassy had known of the invasion plans as early as October but had not passed on the information. On 2 December, despite this warning, Figueres issued a decree abolishing the national army. Two days later he ratified the Rio Treaty, the terms of which allowed him to appeal for OAS support against the impending invasion. To go into effect, the Rio Treaty required the ratification of 14 signatories. Costa Rica was the fourteenth nation to ratify. On 10 December the Costa Rican exiles invaded from Nicaragua. Figueres immediately invoked the Rio Treaty, citing Article 6 at the suggestion of the U.S. ambassador. Article 6 refers to aggression by extra- or intracontinental forces. Figueres could have cited Article 3 of the treaty, which refers to aggression by one Latin American state against another. He chose instead to cite Communist support for Calderón and to invoke the article the United States had insisted on including in the treaty—and the one it would thereafter cite as the legal basis for U.S. intervention in the region. Costa Rica's action served U.S. interests by establishing a Latin American precedent for invoking Article 6.

In response to the Costa Rican appeal, the OAS called for a cease-fire and appointed a commission to investigate Costa Rica's charges against Nicaragua. After a brief visit to both countries, the commission acted quickly and, strongly supported by the United States, submitted its report on 24 December. Both countries agreed to its main recommendations. Somoza abandoned the invasion and forced the Calderonista rebels to disarm.

Figueres disbanded the Nicaraguan exiles in Costa Rica, a move that would have been more difficult politically without the OAS action. By the end of January 1949 the drama had come to an end. Somoza had succeeded brilliantly in securing U.S. recognition for his 1947 coup and stimulating U.S. pressure on Costa Rica to dismantle the exile force that threatened him. Figueres gained little from the bargain, save U.S. approval and a convenient escape from an embarrassing issue.

The U.S. role in the Costa Rican national revolution was unique because, as Victor Bulmer-Thomas put it, "for once U.S. security interests and the cause of democracy coincided rather than clashed."[14] This unusual coincidence was the result not of U.S. diplomatic efforts but of Costa Rican history and politics. The United States backed Ulate, a conventional politician allied to the wealthiest coffee planters and merchants. These powerful interests opposed the social and economic legislation promulgated by presidents Calderón and Picado, feared the growing strength and political influence of the labor movement and the Communist party, and wished to install a regime more responsive to business interests. In short, the allies the United States backed in Costa Rica were similar in social composition and ideology to the conservative and right-wing groups with which the United States allied itself elsewhere in Latin America and the third world during the cold war era. In Costa Rica as elsewhere, a regime based solely on such narrow interests and ideas could not have remained democratic for long. Costa Rican democracy survived the 1948 upheaval because, under Figueres's interim rule in 1948–49, the new regime embraced social-democratic domestic reforms (many already promulgated by the preceding administrations) and could thus claim to represent the aspirations of the majority of Costa Ricans who benefited from them.

The Picado government gave up after suffering military defeats at the hands of a rebel movement organized and led by Figueres with arms from the Arévalo government in Guatemala. Neither the United States nor its local allies played a central role in the military collapse of the Picado government. In the spring of 1948 Figueres's army of "national liberation" controlled the country. This made it necessary for Ulate (with U.S. acquiescence) to strike the deal that put Figueres and his followers in power for the crucial first 18 months of the new regime. The Figueres regime and the reform legislation of 1948–49 thus became possible because it was the Figueres movement, not the United States or its allies, that organized and executed the military defeat of the old regime. Since Figueres also used his 18 months to suppress the Costa Rican Communist party and to break most of the Communist-led unions, the United States did not take issue with his moderate social and economic decrees. Figueres, for his part, avoided direct confrontation with U.S. economic interests. Though he was critical of UFCO and other foreign enterprise at times, his efforts to wrest control of the banana workers' union from its elected Communist leadership were well received in both Washington and Boston (UFCO's corporate headquarters).

THE INTENSIFICATION OF THE COLD WAR

The U.S. confrontation with the Soviet Union intensified dramatically between 1947 and 1953. The Truman administration committed itself to providing support to conservative pro-U.S. forces in civil or colonial wars in Greece, China, the Philippines, and Indochina in 1947; by the end of the next year the East-West cold war line in Europe was frozen in place. In January 1948 the first steps were taken toward the formation of the NATO military alliance; in February the local Communist party seized control of Czechoslovakia. On 7 June the Western allies publicly committed themselves to the creation of a rearmed German state in the British, French, and U.S. occupation zones; the Soviets blockaded Berlin two weeks later. The first year of President Truman's second term, 1949, witnessed the culmination of these developments: on 4 April the NATO Treaty was signed; in September the Soviets tested their first atomic bomb; in October the Federal Republic of Germany came into existence; and by the end of the year the Chinese Communists had proclaimed the People's Republic. The next year, on 25 June 1950, the Korean War began.

U.S. domestic politics interacted with these external events. To mobilize political support for massive new military expenditures just as the country was demobilizing after World War II, and to win support for a renewal of universal military conscription and the creation of vast new foreign economic and military aid programs, the Truman administration used the highly charged rhetoric of defense against an external threat. The images and symbols of the World War II struggle against fascism and fascist "fifth columns" were appropriated to the new struggle against communism and Communist influence. Mobilizing the country for a war—even a cold one—brought with it a wide range of officially endorsed efforts to persecute individuals and organizations that failed to display sufficient "loyalty" to the nation. Within government, individuals suspected of left-wing or Communist associations were purged under President Truman's loyalty program; many officials and employees who escaped such treatment found it prudent to either leave government service or alter their opinions.

While the rhetoric of U.S. cold war foreign policy invoked images of defense against external threats, the policies pursued by the United States involved projections of U.S. power into many areas of the globe where the United States had never exerted much influence in the past. The result was the transformation of the international system from the unstable prewar system of multipolarity, in which the United States had acted as one large power among many midsize and large powers, to the postwar system of bipolarity, in which the United States actively sought to assert its hegemony throughout the non-Communist world.

The cumulative impact of these trends was to make the formulation and implementation of U.S. foreign policy more rigidly conservative than it might otherwise have been. In regions where no major U.S. interests were at stake and where local governments had the means to preserve their independence, the U.S. drift to the right did not have profound effects. In Western Europe, for example, the United States found it necessary to treat the peculiarities of each nation's political culture with tact and sensitivity, despite the immense leverage achieved through the Marshall Plan and NATO. The United States did not, for example, insist that the governments of France and Italy take steps to suppress their powerful and prestigious Communist parties. In the third world, however, and especially in small countries with little capacity to resist U.S. pressures, the growing ideological rigidity of U.S. domestic and foreign policies impinged more directly than elsewhere.

In Central America the cold war shift to the right was reflected in the selection of new ambassadors. Neither Nathaniel Davis in Costa Rica (1947–49) nor Richard Patterson in Guatemala (1948–49), for example, had ever served in a Latin American country. Both gave priority to uncovering Communist influence and pressuring for its suppression. Both expressed great hostility toward any individual or organization that sought to undermine U.S. private firms with regulatory, tax, or other burdens, whatever their motivation. Both replaced diplomats of decidedly greater ideological and temperamental flexibility. By 1950 all of the U.S. Central American ambassadors fit this mold.

In Latin America the United States began to rebuild its World War II ties to local military establishments and to intelligence and police agencies. Despite earlier misgivings, military aid for Latin America was added to the administration's foreign aid request for 1951. Whereas as late as 1948 the National Security Council (NSC) had taken the position that communism in Latin America posed no danger to established governments or to the United States, by 1950 it cited the global Soviet "threat" in recommending military aid for the region.[15]

The change of U.S. administrations in 1953 marked an important though temporary watershed in U.S.–Central American relations. The key policy makers of the Eisenhower administration, particularly Secretary of State John Foster Dulles, adopted a decidedly more rigid rhetorical posture on foreign policy issues. The new administration took the view that hemispheric solidarity in the struggle with the Soviet Union was vital to U.S. security. After a gloomy February 1953 briefing by CIA Director Allen Dulles on Communist advances in Latin America, Eisenhower ordered the NSC staff to prepare a special report on the region. Written in less than a month, the NSC paper, known internally as NSC 144/1 and adopted in March 1953, took the view that the main objective of U.S. policy in the region should be to enlist Latin American support for the United States in the global cold war.[16] This meant acting more decisively to eliminate internal Communist "subversion," which could reduce the enthusiasm of the Latin American countries for cooperation with the United States.

U.S. INTERVENTION IN GUATEMALA

The United States had played an active but relatively minor role in the demise of the Picado government in Costa Rica at the beginning of the cold war in 1948; in contrast, it played a major role in the overthrow of a similar center-left coalition government in Guatemala in 1954. The Picado government would probably have fallen even without U.S. political and diplomatic support for Ulate, Figueres, and the rebels. In Guatemala, however, the government of Jacobo Arbenz would not have fallen without a major effort by the United States. In fact, even with U.S. support, the 1954 revolt nearly failed.

Excellent historical accounts of the events of 1954 have appeared in the last decade,[17] all of which begin by showing how relations between Guatemala and the United States changed after the revolution of 1944. While the Arévalo government professed admiration for the United States and cooperated fully with U.S. security and economic needs in the last year of the war, tensions developed over a series of economic and political issues. These tensions escalated after the election of Jacobo Arbenz, who was inaugurated as president early in 1951. The economic issues mainly concerned UFCO and its affiliated companies. The political issues related to the role of Communists and alleged Communists in the Guatemalan government and labor movement. The two sets of issues were closely related. Communists were vocal critics of UFCO operations in Guatemala and were leaders of labor unions at UFCO installations.

UFCO owned approximately 548,000 acres of Guatemalan banana lands, of which a maximum of 139,000 were in production in the early 1950s. The rest were held in reserve. UFCO also controlled the country's major rail lines through its ownership of International Railways of Central America (IRCA), which charged UFCO shipments lower freight rates than others. IRCA's rail link constituted the only means of transportation between Guatemala City and the Atlantic coast. All of the port facilities at Puerto Barrios, Guatemala's only Atlantic port, belonged to UFCO, as did most of the ships engaged in Guatemala's trade with other nations and one of the country's major radio stations. U.S. ambassadors to Guatemala were accustomed to cooperating closely with UFCO officials and to assisting them in obtaining favorable treatment from the Guatemalan government. U.S. officials in Guatemala and in Washington usually perceived evidence of hostility toward UFCO as a reflection of hostility toward the United States.

The first serious tensions in U.S.-Guatemalan relations after the revolution of 1944 involved UFCO. Between 1947 and 1950 unions representing UFCO workers staged a series of strikes and other job actions to press their demands for better wages and working conditions. The unions were encouraged by the passage of a new labor code in 1947, which recognized union rights and imposed new obligations on private employers. Some of the provisions of the new code applied only to firms with more than 500 employees. UFCO protested these provisions as discriminatory, whereupon the Guatemalan government extended its coverage to include all private employers. UFCO also protested the lack of protection afforded the company when the Arévalo government proved unwilling to use police and army units to break strikes.

The most important UFCO union and the labor federation to which it belonged counted Communists among their leaders. The country's major labor federation, the Confederación de Trabajadores de Guatemala (CGT), was headed by Victor Manuel Gutiérrez, a Communist. The CGT refused to join the Inter-American Confederation of Workers (CIT) or the Inter-American Regional Organization of Workers (ORIT) and instead remained a member of the Confederation of Latin American Workers (CTAL) and the World Federation of Trade Unions (WFTU). By 1950 the CGT was the only major labor federation in Central America that had not left the CTAL for ORIT. Its refusal to leave the CTAL was a "major defeat for anti-Communist labor groups in Latin America."[18] The influence of Communists in the Guatemalan labor movement provided UFCO with much of the material for the major propaganda campaign it mounted in the United States to convince journalists and U.S. officials that the Guatemalan government had fallen under Moscow's control.

The issue of "Communist influence" inside the Guatemalan government had also been raised by U.S. businesspeople, UFCO spokespeople, and occasionally by U.S. officials during the Arévalo administration. Arévalo refused to legalize the Communist party, citing a provision of the 1944 Constitution that forbad the organization of political parties and associations with "foreign" ideologies or organizational ties. On two occasions, in 1946 and again in 1950, he closed evening schools for workers that the Communists had set up. When the United States imposed an arms embargo on Guatemala in 1948, it had little to do with communism; instead, it was meant to signal displeasure with Arévalo's open plotting against dictatorial governments in the region (such as those of Trujillo and Somoza). The United States did not protest Arévalo's aid to the Figueres rebels in Costa Rica in 1948 but did pressure Figueres to disband the Costa Rican branch of the Caribbean Legion.

The Communist issue came to dominate relations between the United States and Guatemala only after the appointment of Richard C. Patterson, Jr., as U.S. ambassador at the end of 1948. Patterson was an engineer and businessman with little diplomatic experience, apart from two years as U.S. ambassador to Yugoslavia. He had been recalled from Yugoslavia at the request of Marshal Tito, who found Patterson's confrontational style and constant public criticism of the Yugoslav government undiplomatic. Patterson, who knew even less about Latin America than he did about the Balkans, harassed Guatemalan officials with complaints about the treatment of U.S. business. He constantly denounced Communist influence in the country and in the government. Finally, when he presented Arévalo with a list of 17 officials and demanded they be dismissed because of their Communist affiliations, Arévalo sent his foreign minister, Ismael González-Arévalo, to Washington, where he met with officials of the State Department's Latin American division and requested that Patterson be withdrawn. Although the State Department rejected the Guatemalan complaint, it recalled Patterson to Washington for consultations and never sent him back to Guatemala.[19]

Just as the Patterson affair was heating up, the Arévalo government faced a succession crisis. Arbenz, the defense minister, was going to be the nominee of the official party. Conservatives in and out of government, as well as the U.S. embassy, preferred Army Chief of Staff Colonel Francisco Javier Araña. Araña, convinced that he would lose the election to Arbenz, decided to stage a coup. When he delivered an ultimatum to Arévalo, the president contacted Arbenz, who dispatched armed men in two cars to detain him. In the shootout that ensued on a highway outside Guatemala City on 18 July 1949, Araña was killed, and his supporters in the army attempted a coup against the Arévalo government. For several days fighting raged in the streets of the capital. Loyal army units, together with a hastily assembled militia of urban workers, turned the tide against the plotters.[20]

When Arbenz assumed the presidency 18 months later, he faced the combined opposition of the United States and a large portion of Guatemala's wealthy elite of landowners and capitalists. In order to stay in power and govern effectively, Arbenz moved to strengthen his domestic support by accelerating the reforms begun under Arévalo. As U.S. hostility mounted, he also began looking for external sources of support.

The Communist issue, which obsessed the U.S. government between 1951 and 1954, had two dimensions: a personnel one and a policy one. The personnel dimension was rather straightforward. Guatemala may have had as many as 4,000 Communists in a population of roughly three million in 1954. Of that number, however, those "who could think and organize probably were no more than 40," party leader José Manuel Fortuny told Piero Gleijeses in an interview decades later.[21] A few Communists—members of the Guatemalan Party of Labor (PGT), as it was called—were appointed to low- or mid-level administrative posts, mainly in the agrarian reform agency[22] but also in the ministry of education and the government press office. No cabinet officers or persons in subcabinet positions were

Communists. Out of a total of 56 deputies to the national congress, only four Communists were elected in 1953.

Yet Arbenz legalized the PGT, and its membership was growing. The official government gazette and radio station often praised the Soviet Union. And though the United States did not know it, President Arbenz's closest adviser during his presidency was PGT Secretary-General Fortuny; the president's sympathy for the party was "obvious," according to Gleijeses,[23] and the president himself joined the Communist party in exile in 1957. Neither Arbenz nor Fortuny, however, believed that a Communist regime could be installed in Guatemala. Pragmatic men, the president and the PGT leaders believed that Guatemala was a "semi-feudal country [and] must first pass through a capitalist stage in which the material conditions for socialism would be developed through an agrarian reform that would eventually lead to industrialization and the growth of a proletariat."[24] This outlook matched Guatemalan realities. Radical change would have been impossible, given the constellation of political and social forces opposed to it. Arbenz and the PGT gave priority to a series of modest reforms designed to modernize, but not transform, the country. It did not matter to the United States that Arbenz's policies were moderate, that his PGT allies were known for their honesty and idealism, their ideological convictions tempered by their surroundings, and their reforms indispensable for modernizing the country's economy and social structure. What U.S. policy makers understood was that the country had come to be governed by men it did not trust, by a government whose behavior it could no longer predict with certainty.

The policies that provoked the United States had two aspects. First, in December 1952 Arbenz permitted the PGT to register as a legal political party. This irritated U.S. officials because it flew in the face of U.S. efforts throughout the hemisphere to criminalize Communist parties and to restrict or suppress their activities. For Arbenz, however, the move responded to domestic developments—particularly the unification of the urban labor movement in an expanded labor federation called the Confederación General de Trabajadores de Guatemala (CGTG). The new CGTG was led by Communists, though individual unions were independently led, and many federation officials were not Communists. The CGTG managed to develop close working relations and a common platform of support for reforms with the country's main peasant organization, the Confederación Nacional Campesina de Guatemala (CNCG). Although the CNCG was led by non-Communists, some of its members and local chapter leaders were Communists. Legal registration of the PGT made it easier for the growing labor movement to mobilize electoral support for candidates pledged to support reform; many candidates supported by the PGT were not Communists.

Second, Arbenz adopted reform policies that went beyond the modest achievements of the Arévalo administration. Nearly all of the Arbenz initiatives were cited by U.S. officials and the U.S. media as evidence of

Communist influence in, or even control of, the Guatemalan regime. The most important of these was the agrarian reform law, known as Decree 900, proclaimed on 27 June 1952. The agrarian reform law was moderate in comparison to the earlier Mexican and Bolivian laws. It permitted the government to expropriate only unused lands from large estates and required that compensation be paid. On 5 March 1953 the Guatemalan government expropriated 233,973 acres of unused UFCO land located on the Pacific coast near Tiquisate; nearly a year later, on 24 February 1954, the government took another 172,532 acres of unused UFCO land located near Bananera on the Atlantic coast. In total, 406,505 acres were expropriated. The government offered compensation at the level at which the properties had been assessed for tax purposes—a total of a little over $1 million. UFCO claimed the land was worth over $15 million.

In addition to the agrarian reform, Arbenz took other measures that affected UFCO adversely. He announced plans for the construction of a road from Guatemala City to the Atlantic coast, a direct threat to the IRCA monopoly. He contracted with a U.S. firm to begin construction of a new Atlantic coast port to compete with UFCO's monopoly at Puerto Barrios. In October 1953, when IRCA failed to reach an agreement with its striking workers, the government "intervened" the enterprise—that is, it seized the company's property and appointed a public commission to operate the rail lines until a labor-management contract was signed. Arbenz irritated another powerful U.S. interest when he intervened the U.S.-owned company that supplied electricity to Guatemala City. The facilities were returned when the company finally reached an agreement with its striking workers, but the government announced a five-year plan to develop electric power and created a state company to begin construction of generating plants to compete with the U.S. company.

Arbenz succeeded in consolidating support for his government among organized workers, peasant beneficiaries of the agrarian reform, and many among the urban middle classes who supported both his agrarian policies and the nationalism he displayed in confronting U.S. business interests. The loyalty of the armed forces (in which there were virtually no Communists) to the Arbenz regime remained steady throughout his presidency until the U.S.-backed rebel invasion in 1954 convinced the officer corps that it was facing an imminent U.S. attack. Arbenz even managed to obtain a small shipment of Czech rifles (after the United States and its European allies refused to sell him arms), although this was the only concrete indication of Soviet-bloc interest in Guatemala in the entire period. Thus Arbenz's political strategy worked. He faced elite opposition and the hostility of the United States with political resources that proved sufficient to enable his government to survive. The CIA rated prospects for the success of its plan to overthrow Arbenz at "no more than 20 percent,"[25] although it was unaware of how successful its propaganda had been in demoralizing the army. The counterrevolution of 1954 succeeded, but its success was due entirely to the efforts of the United States, not to internal developments.

The U.S. government first became involved in an effort to overthrow the Arbenz regime in 1952. In April of that year U.S. officials discussed a joint effort to oust Arbenz with Nicaraguan president Somoza, who was visiting Washington. The CIA arranged for a shipment of arms on a UFCO freighter to aid Guatemalan exiles living in Nicaragua. The project was aborted after Secretary of State Dean Acheson learned of it belatedly and persuaded President Truman to stop it, apparently because of advice that suggested the plot would fail without better preparation.[26] When Dwight Eisenhower took office in January 1953, his administration inherited the consensus of the Truman policy makers that efforts to persuade Guatemalan authorities to change their domestic or foreign[27] policies would be fruitless. Richard Immerman believed that the Eisenhower administration made its decision to organize the overthrow of the Arbenz government sometime in the late spring or early summer of 1953; Gleijeses concluded that "Operation PBSUCCESS," the actual plan for Arbenz's ouster, was born in "late summer."[28]

The effort to overthrow Arbenz had three essential components. The first was a diplomatic and propaganda campaign waged by agencies of the U.S. government, with the aid of an expanded UFCO public-relations effort and the cooperation of the U.S. news media. U.S. propaganda portrayed the Guatemalan government as an instrument of international communism and a threat to the peace and security of the Western Hemisphere. At the Tenth Inter-American Conference,[29] held in Caracas, Venezuela, from 1 to 18 March 1954, the United States insisted that the delegates approve a strongly worded declaration aimed at Guatemala (but without mentioning any specific country) that condemned the spread of communism to the Western Hemisphere. The Declaration of Solidarity for the Preservation of the Political Integrity of the American States against International Communism, known as the Caracas Declaration, was approved by a large majority (17) of the delegates. Only Guatemala voted against it, with Mexico and Argentina abstaining. Guatemala's foreign minister, Guillermo Toriello, argued that the resolution had no other purpose than to justify U.S. intervention in his country. Toriello's speech condemning U.S. policy in Latin America was warmly applauded by many of the delegates, much to the chagrin of Secretary of State Dulles. Most of the Latin American countries that supported the resolution stated their opposition to any attack on Guatemala. On his return to Washington, Dulles presented the vote as a triumph for U.S. diplomacy and claimed that it showed support for U.S. policies toward Guatemala, but he privately recognized that the OAS could not be counted on to support any overt action by the United States against the Arbenz government.

The final version of the Caracas resolution deleted U.S. language calling for immediate action and recommended only that the member states meet again at a later time to consider what action, if any, they ought to take. To obtain support even for this watered-down version, Dulles had to make concessions on economic issues, including a pledge to increase Export-Import Bank (Ex-Im Bank, for short) lending to Latin America. In beating back a series of amendments that would have weakened the U.S. resolution even further, Dulles was forced to rely mainly on the votes of dictatorships. Though the meeting ended well enough for U.S. interests, it impressed on Dulles and other U.S. officials the seriousness of the Latin American commitment to the principle of nonintervention and the need for a U.S. policy more responsive to the region's political sensitivities.[30] On the eve of the invasion the United States signed bilateral military-aid pacts with Honduras and Nicaragua, underscoring Guatemala's isolation and suggesting that the United States would become involved if Guatemala were to take action against the armed men training at camps in both countries. Finally, once the Guatemalan coup was under way, U.S. officials worked around the clock to discredit and deflect Guatemalan efforts to enlist international support in the United Nations and elsewhere.

The second component of the U.S. strategy involved the organization of the opposition outside Guatemala. Several groups of plotters vied for U.S. support. The most promising appeared to be the group headed by Carlos Castillo Armas, a former army colonel and leader of a failed coup attempt in 1950. With U.S. support, Castillo Armas had little difficulty in imposing himself as the leader of a hastily unified anti-Arbenz coalition. With CIA help, including funds and weapons, Castillo Armas recruited a "liberation army" of several hundred men who trained at camps in Honduras and Nicaragua. They were supplied with weapons flown in by plane from U.S. bases in the Panama Canal Zone. On 18 June 1954 Castillo Armas and 150 of his followers invaded Guatemala from Honduras, moved about six miles into the country, and stopped. Most of the "fighting" that overthrew Arbenz was done by U.S. citizens employed by the CIA, who flew World War II surplus aircraft over Guatemala City and other towns, provoking panic by dropping bombs, hand grenades, and Molotov cocktails on targets below. Clandestine radio stations set up and operated by the CIA in Honduran territory were even more important to the effort. The stations simulated a continuous stream of communiqués between fictitious units of the invading army, fabricated entire battles (always won by the invaders), and implied that large-scale reinforcements—even U.S. troops—were scheduled for imminent arrival.

The third component of the effort involved Ambassador John Peurifoy and his staff, who sought to undermine support for Arbenz in the military with threats of direct U.S. intervention and demands for Arbenz's resignation. Peurifoy's efforts bore fruit when Arbenz and his allies in the army high command became convinced that the invasion was much larger than it actually was, and many in the officer corps believed Peurifoy's threats of an imminent U.S. invasion. The main two rebel attacks were actually defeated. The first was an assault by sea from Honduras on Puerto Barrios, which was repelled by police and hastily armed civilians. The second was staged by the main invasion force at Guálan and was driven back by a junior officer and a few men, who had lost contact with army headquarters. The main Guatemalan army force sent to meet Castillo Armas, however, encamped at Zacapa and never moved on to engage the enemy. On 25 June Arbenz learned that the Zacapa forces were not fighting and received a demand from their officers to step down; if he refused, the army would march on Guatemala City and depose him. The next day Arbenz resigned and turned over power to a trusted subordinate, Colonel Carlos Enrique Díaz, who promised he would remain loyal to the 1944 revolution and would not negotiate with the rebels. In the next two days Peurifoy maneuvered to force Díaz out. A new bombing attack on the capital turned the tide. On 29 June Díaz resigned from the three-man military junta that had replaced Arbenz, ceding power to Colonel Elfego H. Monzón, whom Peurifoy preferred. Washington, however, wanted Castillo Armas to head a new government; Peurifoy managed, after some additional negotiations, to have the junta appoint Castillo Armas as provisional president on 7 July. Running unopposed in stage-managed elections the following October, Castillo Armas received more than 99 percent of the votes cast.[31]

CENTRAL AMERICAN POLICY AFTER GUATEMALA, 1954–1957

After the fall of Arbenz in June 1954, visible elite or public opposition to U.S. political and economic dominance in Central America virtually disappeared. U.S. officials monitored the internal affairs of all six isthmian republics (ostensibly on the watch for Communists) and used their weight to move events and people to conform to U.S. interests, without encountering major obstacles. Economic growth, driven by the post–World War II recovery and the Korean War, stimulated an export boom and helped to still local complaints. Within the U.S. administration, hard-line conservatives controlled foreign economic and security policy. U.S. officials, led by Dulles and Treasury Secretary George Humphries, turned a deaf ear to occasional clamorings for economic aid, although both welcomed opportunities to institutionalize the region's subordination to U.S. aims through military aid pacts, investment agreements, and other formal arrangements favorable to U.S. security and economic interests.

The Guatemalan affair thus helped to inspire a series of largely symbolic moves designed to impress domestic and international opinion with the U.S. commitment to democracy and the administration's willingness to accommodate the economic concerns of reliably anticommunist regimes in the area. After Arbenz's fall the United States began sending economic aid to Guatemala, coupled with official expressions of U.S. interest in the country's democratic development and social progress. When Nicaragua's Somoza invaded democratic Costa Rica in January 1955 the United States reacted quickly, as it had done in 1948, to stop it. In Honduras the U.S. ambassador opposed the return of strongman Carías to the presidency in 1954 and supported the anticommunist but reformist government of Ramón Villeda Morales, who assumed the presidency in 1957. Finally, on the eve of the Guatemala invasion, the United States suddenly agreed to consider Panamanian demands for revisions in the canal treaty; in 1955 the two governments signed a new accord. These gestures moved the Eisenhower administration back toward the rhetorical posture of the Truman years, but they involved no significant departures from the substance of the Dulles-Humphries hard line.

Having scored a resounding triumph in Guatemala, the administration saw no reason to alter its policies. In Guatemala, however, the uncertainty and disorganization caused by U.S. hostility toward Arbenz, the change in regime, and the subsequent restructuring created an economic crisis. The preservation of U.S. prestige required some convincing gesture of support for the new government. Economic aid was extended on a scale unprecedented in the region. Initially, U.S. officials thought they could turn Guatemala into a showcase of the benefits to be derived from compliance with U.S. political and security requirements. This, however, would have required the new government to return to many of the policies of the Arbenz era, which had antagonized the United States in the first place. This contradiction did not occur to the anonymous author of the administration's *National Intelligence Assessment of the Caribbean Republics*, prepared the summer after Arbenz had fallen; this author concluded, "In the longer view, the success of the new regime . . . will depend on its ability to eliminate Communism without repudiating the objectives and achievements of the Revolution of 1944."[32] But the new government thought otherwise. U.S. aid served mainly to strengthen Castillo Armas and his allies as they set about dismantling the rudimentary social programs of the Arévalo-Arbenz era. When Castillo Armas was assassinated in 1957 and subsequent elections proved to be manifestly fraudulent, the U.S. administration was sufficiently embarrassed to pressure the Guatemalan military to hold a new vote. The new elections in January 1958 were also tainted by fraud and intimidation and still excluded supporters of Arbenz, but they did certify the electoral victory of the leading vote-getter among the right-wing candidates permitted to run. The new president, Miguel Ydígoras Fuentes, formerly a high-ranking official of the Ubico dictatorship, repaid the United States with close and continuous cooperation.[33]

In Honduras the United States had exerted intense pressure on President Juan Manuel Gálvez to permit Castillo Armas and his exiles to use Honduran territory as the base for the invasion of Guatemala. Gálvez insisted to U.S. Ambassador Whiting Willauer that the United States agree to defend Honduras in case the invasion failed and Guatemala, with its larger though ill-equipped army, should retaliate. The State Department proposed that the two countries sign a Military Assistance Agreement, under which the United States would undertake to provide military aid and agree to defend Honduras in case of attack. A similar agreement had already been negotiated with Nicaragua in exchange for Nicaraguan aid, which eventually included two aircraft, to the Guatemalan exiles. Despite the misgivings of the Defense Department, which pointed out that neither Nicaragua nor Honduras had a military establishment capable of contributing to hemispheric defense, the agreement was signed in May 1954, just weeks before the invasion. The Honduran agreement also created a new option for the United States. Under the terms of the agreement, Honduras could have requested direct U.S. military help against any Guatemalan threat, real or manufactured, and the United States could have dispatched its forces, in compliance with the agreement, without the need for OAS approval.[34]

By the time the new military pact was signed, Honduran workers in the northern banana-growing regions had begun a major strike. The strike erupted on 10 April 1954, when dock workers struck UFCO facilities at Tela, on the Atlantic coast, demanding overtime pay for working on Sunday. They were joined by stevedores at Puerto Cortés and by banana workers in the company town of El Progreso—25,000 in all. By mid-May the strike had spread to include workers in Standard Fruit banana fields, factory workers in San Pedro Sula, and miners at Rosario's new El Mochito mine. The economy of the northern provinces came to a standstill. Honduran officials intervened to isolate, arrest, and expel left-wing labor leaders, many of whom sympathized with Guatemala's reformist regime. By July, with Arbenz gone, new strike committees, under moderate leaders whom the Honduran government had encouraged to come forward, won recognition and modest concessions from the U.S. companies. U.S. officials helped by appealing to company executives to recognize the moderate unions. George Meany, president of the AFL-CIO, helped to convince UFCO officials to settle and provided direct aid to the moderate unionists. After the strike grateful Honduran officials organized a new Ministry of Labor, with help from the AFL-CIO and ORIT.

The strike ended just as the Honduran presidential and congressional election campaign was getting under way. The State Department worried that the election would provoke violence and lead to an "emergency" that could be exploited by local Communists. Ambassador Willauer, who had spent the previous year organizing the Guatemalan exiles and then directed the CIA bombings of Guatemala City, recommended that the U.S. Defense Department expedite the delivery of two C-47 transport aircraft to provide the Honduran army with the mobility it might need in the event of disturbances, especially in the north. The planes were not needed.

Willauer also cultivated close relations with all three of the major candidates for the presidency. All were acceptable to the United States, though former president Carías, who ran second, was viewed as too rigid and repressive in his views to be a stabilizing force in Honduras. None of the candidates managed to win a majority in the balloting on 10 October. Therefore, according to the Honduran constitution, the new president had to be chosen by a majority vote in the Congress. Since none of the parties had managed to win a majority of the seats, a stalemate occurred. Willauer worked to persuade two of the candidates, liberal frontrunner Ramón Villeda Morales and "reformist" Abraham Williams Calderón, who finished last, to form a coalition to break the deadlock. When this proved impossible he sought State Department permission to propose that President Gálvez set aside the election and remain in office until a new poll could be taken. Gálvez, in poor health, left the country for rest and medical treatment, putting the government in the hands of the vice-president, Julio Lorenzo. With U.S. support Lorenzo declared himself "chief of state" and announced that he would call new elections for a constituent assembly to write a new constitution. In the ensuing two years Lorenzo took care to maintain close relations with Willauer—so close that the United States came to be identified with his government in Honduran public opinion.

In 1956, with new elections scheduled under the terms of a new constitution, Lorenzo hoped for U.S. support when he maneuvered to ensure his own election through fraud and intimidation of the opposition. On 21 October 1956 the Honduran military deposed Lorenzo and promised to hold honest elections. Willauer, who characterized the military junta as "a group of the finest men in the country,"[35] urged immediate recognition of their regime. Although recognition was announced on 27 October, the State Department's enthusiasm cooled when the junta dispatched 500 troops to lay claim to disputed territory along Honduras's Coco River border with Nicaragua. Willauer was ordered to insist that the troops be withdrawn and to use the threat of a cutoff of U.S. aid to ensure compliance.[36] The Hondurans complied.

One year later the Honduran junta kept its promise by organizing relatively open elections to a constituent assembly, which drafted a new constitution in 1957 and then elected Villeda Morales to the presidency. Although Villeda was well known to the State Department, his reformist social views were not altogether welcome at the U.S. embassy. In the early 1950s he had been a supporter of Arbenz and of Figueres's Caribbean Legion. Though the demands of his political career made him adjust his views on Arbenz in time to win U.S. confidence, he maintained his close ties with Figueres in Costa Rica.

Villeda hoped to work within the constraints of Honduras's close and subordinate relations to the United States to implement a program of moderate reforms. Reliably anticommunist, he won Willauer's praise for cooperating in the effort to exclude Communists from the labor movement and for accepting Lorenzo's continuation in office in 1954 without calling his supporters into the streets. In his first two years in office Villeda secured passage of new labor, social security, and economic reform legislation. These achievements helped to maintain the influence of "nonpolitical" moderates in the labor movement, as Honduran spokesmen repeatedly pointed out. Villeda thus managed to exploit the post-Guatemala flexibility in Washington to achieve modest reforms. He failed, however, to implement a large-scale agrarian reform, one of his main goals. The initial draft of the legislation would have affected UFCO and other U.S. interests. At the insistence of the U.S. embassy, Villeda flew to Miami to meet with UFCO executives. When they threatened to close their Honduran operations, Villeda was forced to back down. He had reached the limits of U.S. tolerance for social change.[37]

The Guatemalan affair also coincided with a renewal of hostilities between Nicaragua and Costa Rica. On 4 April 1954 Nicaraguan dissidents attempted to assassinate Anastasio Somoza as part of an effort to overthrow the Nicaraguan government. The revolt was planned and organized in Costa Rica, where Somoza's nemesis, Figueres, had been elected president in 1953. Somoza mobilized his National Guard and threatened to invade Costa Rica. Having just signed a Military Assistance Agreement with the United States, Somoza looked even more formidable in 1954 than in 1948.

Somoza's threats could not have been better timed to serve U.S. aims. They sent Figueres running to the U.S. embassy for protection. The United States responded by demanding that Figueres abandon his support for Guatemala as the price for its help against Somoza. "It took considerable pressure to induce Figueres to turn against Arbenz," recalled the U.S. ambassador to Costa Rica. Eventually, "Figueres supported the U.S. . . . , but this was at a time when he was deep in difficulties with Nicaragua and desperately needed U.S. arms to bolster his defenses."[38] Although Figueres then announced his support for the United States in its dispute with Guatemala, the United States did not respond immediately to his request for military aid.

Somoza was not impressed with Figueres's tilt toward the United States and may have known of the U.S. embassy's angry complaints about the hospitality afforded former Arbenz officials who fled to Costa Rica after the Guatemalan regime collapsed in June. U.S.–Costa Rican tensions were also due to Figueres's verbal attacks on UFCO and on U.S. economic policy more generally. The U.S. embassy had already begun to orchestrate a campaign of vilification, replete with dirty tricks engineered by the local CIA station, to undermine Figueres's authority. Somoza may well have believed the United States would welcome a change in the Costa Rican government. He certainly had grounds for believing that his own standing in Washington had reached an all-time high because of the support he had provided for the Guatemalan rebels. Some of the rebels had trained on a Somoza family ranch for several months before the invasion. The P-47 bombers loaned to the rebels by the U.S. government took off for bombing runs over Guatemala City from the Managua airport. In January 1955 Somoza launched an attack across the Costa Rican border, apparently intent on bringing down the

Figueres government. The attackers, including Costa Rican followers of ex-President Calderón García (as in the invasion of December 1948), were backed up by air support from the Nicaraguan National Guard. The Calderonistas also received arms from the Venezuelan military regime. Figueres had refused to send a Costa Rican delegate to the Caracas meeting of the OAS in March to protest the repressive character of the Venezuelan government of General Marcos Pérez Jiménez. He had also granted political asylum in Costa Rica to prominent Venezuelan political refugees.

Figueres immediately appealed to the United States and the OAS for aid, as he had done in December 1948 under similar circumstances. Once again the United States sought a quick OAS intervention. To warn off Somoza, the U.S. administration quickly agreed to sell Figueres four F-51 Mustang propeller-driven combat aircraft for one dollar each. As in 1948, Somoza backed off, recalled his forces, and abandoned the Calderonistas. Figueres agreed to disarm and expel Nicaraguan anti-Somocistas in Costa Rica and to persuade leading Venezuelan exiles, including former (and future) President Rómulo Betancourt, to take their plotting elsewhere. The outcome of the 1955 conflict was also similar to that of the 1948 war. Somoza agreed to pull back, but Figueres had to abandon his support for anti-Somoza exiles as well. The affair ended, as in 1948, with Somoza once again secure from attack, Figueres tamed and indebted to the United States, and the U.S. goal of regional stability achieved by decisive action in defense of a democratic regime.

After negotiating a new contract that significantly raised taxes on UFCO's operations in Costa Rica, Figueres changed his mind about the company. Eventually, he secured UFCO and U.S. official support for efforts to undermine the leadership of the banana workers' union, the last redoubt of the Costa Rican Communist movement. By the summer of 1955 Figueres happily acceded to the suggestion of the U.S. ambassador that he use the occasion of a luncheon speech before "200 leading Costa Rican and American businessmen" to praise UFCO's role in Costa Rica. The luncheon was organized in honor of the visit of U.S. Vice-President Richard M. Nixon to Costa Rica.[39]

As in 1948, the rapid U.S. response to the Nicaraguan invasion of Costa Rica was motivated in part by broader diplomatic and strategic objectives. In 1955 the U.S. wanted to forestall a possible U.N. assertion of jurisdiction that might have called into question the role of the OAS, through which the United States exerted its influence without interference from outside the hemisphere. As Secretary of State Dulles explained it on 18 August 1954 (five months before Somoza's attack on Costa Rica),

> During the Guatemalan crisis we insisted that the problem be handled by the OAS rather than the United Nations. We were opposed by Russia and a strong group of our allies, including the United Kingdom, France,

Australia, and Denmark. When [Anthony] Eden visited the United States
. . . I told Eden that the United States considered it imperative that he
countermand instructions under which the United Kingdom delegate was
acting in the United Nations. In view of the Secretary's very firm position,
Eden told his delegate to abstain. France followed suit and, as a result, the
United Nations did not take jurisdiction of the problem, and it was handled
within the OAS.

If a new crisis now arises in Central America, our own allies will agree
with Russia that it was a mistake to let the past problem [Guatemala] be
handled in the OAS and they will side with Russia, thus damaging the prestige of the United States and weakening the OAS.[40]

Thus, explained Dulles, any Nicaraguan action that disturbed
the peace of the region would provoke a swift U.S. response to forestall any
U.N. intervention. Although warned against doing so by U.S. Ambassador
Thomas Whelan, a close friend of the dictator, Somoza went ahead with his
January 1955 attack. The reasons are not difficult to discern. Somoza benefited from the OAS intervention he provoked because it forced Figueres to
cease supporting Somoza's exiled enemies. The two leaders later signed a
Pact of Amity and a Treaty of Conciliation, negotiated through the good
offices of the OAS, in September 1955. For added insurance (against Costa
Rica's new U.S.-supplied air force), Somoza sought to purchase U.S. aircraft
for his small air force. After being rebuffed in Washington, he then bought
25 combat fighters from Sweden. Figueres, suitably chastened, left Somoza
alone and apparently had nothing to do with his assassination in September
1956. After the assassination Figueres carefully refrained from meddling
when Somoza's sons faced internal opposition in asserting their control over
the country.

Reaction to the Guatemalan affair also affected U.S policy in Panama.
After resisting requests from a succession of Panamanian governments for a
renegotiation of the 1903 and 1936 Panama Canal treaties, the Eisenhower
administration suddenly reversed itself in 1954 and opened talks with the
government of President José Remón. As commander of the Panamanian
National Guard, Remón dominated that nation's political scene. In 1948 he
prevented Arnulfo Arias, anathema to the United States, from winning the
presidential election by forcing the elections board to throw out enough
Arias votes to secure the election of a rival candidate. In 1949 Remón staged
another coup that briefly installed Arias as president, and then yet another
that ousted him in 1951. The following year Remón engineered his own
election as president and embarked on a mildly populist program of economic and social reforms, directed against the country's wealthy white oligarchy.

Remón's popularity increased still further when he began to press the
United States to negotiate a new Panama Canal Treaty. He demanded an
increase in the annual payment Panama received from the United States
for its use of the canal zone—from $430,000, which it had been paying

since 1936, to $5 million. The two sides agreed to raise the payment to $1,930,000. The new treaty also included provisions that allowed Panama to tax its citizens working in the zone, returned some lands the United States held outside the zone, and surrendered the U.S. monopoly on railroad and highway construction (although the United States retained a right of veto over future projects). The United States also agreed to give up control over sanitation in Panama City and Colón, to restrict sales in canal zone commissaries to U.S. employees and to Panamanian workers who resided in the zone, and to increase purchases of zone supplies from Panamanian businesses. In exchange for these concessions, Panama granted the United States a new lease on 19,000 acres of land outside the zone, near Río Hato. The United States had acquired the land during World War II and constructed a large military base on the property. A separate agreement, a "Memorandum of Understandings Reached," was also signed by the two governments in 1955. In this memorandum the U.S. government agreed to end racial discrimination in canal zone hiring and to seek congressional approval for a single wage level for all zone employees.[41] The new treaty was approved by the U.S. Senate by an overwhelming vote of 72 to 14, but not until Eisenhower officials gave repeated assurances that none of its provisions undermined U.S. sovereign rights in the zone.

President Remón did not live to see the new treaty ratified. He was assassinated on 2 January 1955 and succeeded by his vice-president, Ricardo Arias. A wealthy scion of the oligarchy, Arias immediately set about repealing the social and economic reforms Remón had initiated. While the conservative tilt of the new government pleased Washington, tensions between the U.S. and Panamanian governments did not end. After ratification of the new treaty, the U.S. government began making the higher payments promptly but delayed implementing the other provisions of the treaty and fulfilling the commitments made in the separate memorandum. The United States did not return the lands specified in the treaty until 1957, and Congress did nothing about equal employment opportunities in the canal zone until it passed a weak provision, subsequently ignored, in 1958.

CONCLUSIONS

After World War II the United States emerged as the world's dominant military and industrial power. Although Communist regimes succeeded in excluding U.S. influence from Eastern Europe and most of mainland East Asia, U.S. dominance in the Western Hemisphere could not be successfully challenged. The United States deepened its dominant position in the Caribbean and incorporated its Caribbean clients into a larger hemispheric political and military alliance under U.S. leadership. Because the Central American countries had no viable alternative to this alliance, the United States managed to achieve this outcome at relatively low cost. The major threat to the U.S. position came not from the Soviet Union but from local political coalitions, forged in the 1930s and 1940s, whose reformist goals brought them into conflict with U.S. business and political interests. In El Salvador, Honduras, Nicaragua, and Panama, where reformist coalitions were weak, political and economic elites welcomed the growing hostility of the United States toward their domestic critics and actively cooperated with U.S. aims. In Costa Rica and Guatemala, however, U.S. aims could be accomplished only through an internal realignment of political power. In Costa Rica this realignment occurred with little direct U.S. intervention, but in Guatemala the United States played a direct and decisive role.

In both cases, armed revolts overthrew governments dominated by uneasy coalitions of moderate and reformist politicians allied with left-wing labor unions and popular organizations in which the local Communist party played a key role. Communists held a small minority of the seats in the two national legislatures, where they usually supported government initiatives. Communists occupied low- and mid-level administrative positions in certain government agencies, although in both countries—especially Guatemala—they enjoyed access to some top policy makers. Communists held some key posts in labor unions, organized electoral support for their own candidates as well as those of the ruling party, and mobilized support for reforms by calling out thousands of citizens to march peacefully through major cities and to swell the crowds at pro-government rallies. In both Costa Rica and Guatemala Communists attempted to organize militias of workers and the poor to defend the governments they supported when armed revolts broke out.

In Costa Rica the Communists allied themselves with conventional politicians whose commitment to social reform came less from conviction than from necessity. With a weak military establishment, a less rigidly stratified society, and a tradition of electoral democracy (however fraudulent the elections were at times), Costa Rica accommodated itself to the anticommunism of the United States at little cost to its traditions of democratic government and progressive social reform. The Arbenz regime in Guatemala, however, traced its origins to the recent past—the 1944 revolution against the Ubico dictatorship. The popularity and legitimacy of the 1944 revolution helped presidents Arévalo and Arbenz withstand numerous coup attempts, some backed by elements of the local elite. Both presidents were personally committed to reforming and modernizing the country, but with a highly stratified and ethnically divided society, a more powerful military, and no traditions of democracy or reform prior to 1944, their prospects for success were far from certain. Accommodation to the United States would have shattered the coalition that made Guatemalan democracy viable. The opposition to Arévalo and Arbenz included few democrats and no reformers and repudiated all that had happened in the country after 1944. When the United States succeeded in breaking the Arbenz government in 1954, it crushed prospects for democracy and reform in Guatemala for more than a generation.

The Costa Rican revolution arose from the domestic political conflict between the Calderón-Picado coalition with the Communists and the alliance Figueres forged between his own group of middle-class technocrats and intellectuals and a large portion of the elite that supported Ulate. This conflict had its roots in Costa Rican society and politics; both sides had widespread popular support within the country. These roots in local soil also helped to ensure that successor regimes would be democratic and reformist. The United States helped by supporting Figueres's allies (though not Figueres himself), by imposing an arms embargo on the Picado government and preventing it from buying arms in Western Europe, by doing nothing to stop the flow of arms to the insurgents from Guatemala, and by keeping Somoza's Nicaragua at bay. The United States did not create the rebel organization or supply arms to the 1948 insurgents. In Guatemala, however, the U.S. role was crucial. Opposition to the Arbenz regime existed within Guatemala, but it was disorganized and demoralized by electoral failures and the popularity of the regime's reforms. The United States organized and equipped the rebels, supplied the technical means to persuade Arbenz and the army that the revolt was much larger than it actually was, and convinced the army officer corps that a U.S. invasion would occur if Arbenz did not resign. The United States could not, however, supply a social base for the new regime beyond the narrow white elite that stood to benefit from a thoroughgoing counterrevolution.

The fall of Picado in 1948 in Costa Rica occurred without any effort by the United States to mobilize international opinion against it. No one in Washington saw Picado as an agent of Moscow. Indeed, Picado enjoyed good relations with the U.S. embassy from the time he took office in 1944 until July 1947, when vandalism against antigovernment businesses during the national lockout persuaded the embassy and the news media that the Costa Rican Communist party was larger and more powerful than previously supposed. Even after the lockout, however, the United States sponsored no overt acts against the government except the arms embargo and provided no covert aid to the rebels. The Picado government supported U.S. postwar policies in Latin America with no more complaint than most other Latin American governments. Its representatives voted with the United States on most issues that came before the United Nations and pledged the country to a military alliance with the United States by supporting the Rio Treaty (although ratification of that treaty did not occur until after Figueres took over). Except for its electoral alliance with the Communist party, whose support it needed at the polls and whose deputies in congress were crucial for passing government programs, the Picado regime usually accommodated itself to U.S. policies and interests without protest.

The Guatemalan case was different. When U.S. pressure increased between 1949 and 1953, the regime moved to enhance its domestic support by pushing through additional reforms. In the last months of the Arbenz government, as U.S. hostility became ever more intense, Arbenz appealed for support from other Latin American countries and the United Nations. He even sought to use his alliance with the local Communist party to appeal for support from the Soviet Union and the Soviet bloc. Arbenz's effort to counterbalance American pressures with domestic support and international aid came closer to succeeding than even Washington acknowledged. Not until the United States organized an invasion by counterrevolutionaries and orchestrated a credible threat to invade the country did army support evaporate. Even then, Arbenz turned over the reins of government to a sympathetic colleague, who pledged to continue his government's reformist policies.

The triumph of the Costa Rican insurrection was not a success for U.S. policy, because U.S. aid was not crucial to its success. Figueres's hostility to the local Communists, whom he correctly saw as competitors for the working-class support he wanted for his own social democratic party, did not come from the U.S. embassy. While he earned U.S. approval for his suppression of the Communists and their union allies, he would have moved against them once in power in any case.[42] Had the United States intervened to assure the success of Figueres's revolt, it would likely have insisted on the immediate inauguration of Ulate and thus prevented Figueres from imposing the social reforms that subsequently formed the basis for Costa Rican democracy.

The triumph of the Guatemalan counterrevolution was not a success for U.S. policy, because it plunged Guatemala into more than 30 years of repressive military rule and thus became a potent symbol to critics of U.S. policies throughout the world.[43] Between 1954 and 1990 more than 140,000 civilians were killed by the Guatemalan armed forces and the death squads associated with the military. While some of these killings occurred in combat between the armed forces and two generations of guerrilla rebels, most were executions of unarmed civilians who maintained dissident political views and associations. Surveying this scene at the end of the 1980s, one U.S. official exclaimed, "What we'd give to have an Arbenz now. We are going to have to invent one, but all the candidates are dead."[44] Had the United States not intervened to overthrow Arbenz, he would have stepped down after new elections in 1957 (the constitution prohibited the reelection of the president) and left behind a far more stable and democratic country than Guatemala has been ever since.

After 1954 a wide-ranging debate took place in the United States and abroad about the significance of the Guatemalan coup. For many years the U.S. State Department maintained that the Arbenz regime had fallen under the control of communism and the Soviet Union and that its overthrow was the product of a popular revolt carried out by the Guatemalan people.

Neither of these assertions was true. The Arbenz government was not controlled by either the Soviet Union or the local Communist party. Though Arbenz collaborated closely with the PGT and joined it in exile later, his domestic policy orientation was moderately populist and nationalist, his government and legislative coalition were dominated by non-Communist parties and politicians, and the army was decidedly anticommunist in outlook. In many respects the Arbenz government was more moderate than the first Figueres administration in Costa Rica or the National Revolutionary Movement (MNR) regime in Bolivia after 1952, both of which were supported by Washington.[45] Moreover, the Arbenz government's foreign policy supported the U.S. position on most international issues, including many on which the United States was opposed by Soviet Union. Arbenz was not overthrown by the Guatemalan people. No more than a thousand individuals were involved in the successful effort to oust the Arbenz government, and nearly all of them were citizens of the United States, in the employ of U.S. government agencies (mainly the CIA), or both.

Historians and analysts have offered several alternatives to the discredited official version of the Guatemalan coup story. Immerman, for example, emphasized the "cold war ethos" of the early 1950s. Because the Guatemalan government was not Communist-controlled and not likely to become Communist for the foreseeable future, U.S. policy makers were literally talking nonsense when they asserted that it was or would be. U.S. policy makers were induced to think and behave in irrational ways because the cold war ethos of the period impaired their faculties. The strength of this interpretation lies in its fidelity to the historical record. Both in private as well as in public, most U.S. policy makers said they were fighting communism in Guatemala.

This interpretation, however, leaves the origin, evolution, and characteristics of the cold war ethos in the United States unexplained. The ethos exists outside of history, a force with no clear relation to social, political, or economic power. But the evidence of the postwar era shows that U.S. policy makers were not passive victims of a mass hysteria that clouded their perception of events in other countries. On the contrary, they nurtured and exploited fears of the Soviet Union to increase domestic and international support for unprecedented and costly projections of U.S. power throughout the globe. The Guatemalan affair allowed Secretary of State Dulles to proclaim a "victory" for his announced strategy of rolling back Communist advances. This "victory," in turn, impressed public opinion in the United States and helped the Eisenhower administration maintain support for its larger foreign policy goals.

The cold war ethos interpretation also tends to confuse political discourse with political reality. U.S. officials loudly proclaimed any indication of opposition to U.S. private or public interests in Guatemala to be evidence of Communist influence. Some may have believed this to be true. Most key policy makers, however—like Secretary of State Dulles—displayed little interest in distinguishing between Communist and non-Communist opponents of the United States in Guatemala. Even if U.S. policy makers had been uncertain of the facts or convinced that the charges of Communist influence were untrue or grossly exaggerated, they had powerful reasons to maintain that communism was a serious threat. U.S. officials charged that Guatemala was falling under Communist influence because that charge helped to polarize Guatemalan politics, intimidate Guatemalan leaders, strengthen Arbenz's domestic opponents, and mobilize both domestic and international support for U.S. efforts to isolate and overthrow the Guatemalan government.

If the Guatemalan government was not Communist or close to it, then what caused the U.S. effort to overthrow it? An alternative interpretation has stressed the role of UFCO, suggesting that the company had extraordinary influence in the U.S. administration. As Table 3.1 shows, nearly all of the key U.S policy makers in the Truman and Eisenhower administrations who participated in the decisions that escalated tensions and finally led to the overthrow of Arbenz in June of 1954 had ties to UFCO. Some were major stockholders; others had worked for the Wall Street legal firm of Sullivan & Cromwell, which represented UFCO in Guatemala and elsewhere; still others were members of the UFCO board of directors or associated with UFCO-related financial institutions (the Old Colony Trust and the First National Bank of Boston). The table lists the most important UFCO-related officials of this period. In the Eisenhower administration the influence of officials with current or former ties to UFCO was pervasive; every U.S. official making policy for Guatemala belonged to this group except for President Eisenhower.[46]

Sympathy for UFCO's plight, even among policy makers without a direct financial interest in the company, was pervasive in the Eisenhower State Department. Cole Blasier is undoubtedly right in pointing out that the initial deterioration in relations between Guatemala and the United States under Arévalo in 1949 was due mainly to U.S. Ambassador Patterson, who spent most of his time defending UFCO and other U.S. private interests, often without specific guidance from Washington.[47] Without UFCO, relations between Guatemala and the United States would not have deteriorated as rapidly or as completely as they did.

Eisenhower and high officials in his administration were concerned about the multiple links between key officials and UFCO, although they worried more about bad publicity than about ethics. High-level discussions took place in 1954 to develop a strategy for deflecting possible charges of corruption and conflict of interest, which Secretary of State Dulles and others were convinced would arise. This worry, together with differences on aid policy in Latin America, led to the resignation of John Moors Cabot, the assistant secretary of state for inter-American affairs, on the eve of the Guatemalan coup.

Table 3.1.   U.S. Officials with Links to UFCO, 1945–1954 (Partial List)

Truman Administration (1945–53)

Spruille Braden	asst. secy. of state, American republic affairs, ambassador to Argentina	later lobbyist for UFCO
Edward Miller	asst. secy. of state, inter-American affairs	ex-partner, Sullivan & Cromwell law firm
Thomas Dudley Cabot	dir., Office of International Security Affairs (State Dept.)	ex-pres., ex-dir. UFCO and First National Bank of Boston

Eisenhower Administration (1953–54)

John Moors Cabot	asst. secy. of state, inter-American affairs, ex-ambassador to Guatemala	major UFCO stockholder (brother of Thomas D. Cabot)
Robert Cutler	spec. asst. to the president for national security affairs	ex-pres., Old Colony Trust
Alan Dulles	dir., CIA	ex-UFCO board; ex-partner, Sullivan & Cromwell; dir., Henry Schroeder Bank (IRCA)[1]
John Foster Dulles	secy. of state	ex-partner, Sullivan & Cromwell
Robert Hill	ambassador to Costa Rica	ex-v.p., W. R. Grace; later dir. UFCO
Henry Cabot Lodge	U.N. ambassador	major UFCO stockholding family
John J. McCloy	pres., World Bank	ex-UFCO dir.
Walter Bedell Smith	undersecy. of state; ex-CIA	became UFCO dir. in 1954
Sinclair Weeks	secy. of commerce	ex-UFCO dir.; dir. of First National Bank of Boston
Ann Whitman	pers. secy. to president	ex-wife of Edward Whitman, UFCO v.p. and dir.

[1]IRCA = International Railways of Central America (controlled by UFCO)

Sources: Richard Immerman, *The CIA in Guatemala: The Foreign Policy of Intervention* (Austin: University of Texas Press, 1982), 122–26; Walter Lafeber, *Inevitable Revolutions: The United States in Central America* (New York: Norton, 1983), 118–19; *Foreign Relations of the United States: 1952–1954* 4: 195.

Such concerns also caused Eisenhower to order Attorney General Herbert Brownell, Jr., to delay the Justice Department's antitrust prosecution against UFCO for a year, on the grounds that it would "appear to justify Arbenz' position completely, and would thus greatly strengthen his hand."[48]

Nonetheless, Fortuny was probably right when he concluded that "they would have overthrown us even if we had grown no bananas."[49] Defending UFCO coincided with other U.S. policy objectives, chief among which was maintaining U.S. dominance over its Caribbean clients. When Arévalo requested the recall of Ambassador Patterson, he signaled an unusual and unwelcome independence from the United States. The hostility that developed at this time pushed Arévalo and his successor, Arbenz, to broaden their domestic political support against U.S. pressure. Their agrarian reforms and other measures, despite their moderation, reinforced the existing hostility and helped to convince U.S. officials to overthrow the Arbenz regime. The reform measures taken under Arbenz were adopted without consulting the United States and adversely affected U.S. private interests. Even if communism was not an imminent danger, independence from U.S. control was clearly threatened. The United States overthrew the government of Guatemala in 1954 because its leaders mobilized domestic political support and sought external assistance to recover a portion of the country's lost sovereignty. As Gleijeses put it, "Eisenhower's Guatemala policy was no aberration; it was derailed neither by UFCO nor by Senator Joe McCarthy. It fit within a deeply held tradition, shared by Democrats and Republicans alike and centered on the intransigent assertion of U.S. hegemony over Central America and the Caribbean."[50]

The fall of Arbenz reinforced the dominance of the United States in Latin America and the Caribbean with a vivid demonstration of the costs of opposition. The fact that U.S. forces were not needed to depose Arbenz impressed politicians throughout the hemisphere because it demonstrated the capacity of the United States to employ local assets to achieve its objectives. The United States thus came to be seen as a powerful actor in local politics. Conservative politicians and organizations, especially in Central America, now competed even more intensely for U.S. support by offering policies and programs attuned to U.S. interests. Nationalist and left-wing critics accused their conservative opponents of pandering to the United States. The U.S. success in Guatemala thus tended to polarize political conflict throughout the region.

The "lessons" Guatemala taught Latin Americans in the 1950s returned to haunt U.S. policy makers five years later in Cuba. Ernesto "Che" Guevara, a medical doctor from Argentina who was working in Guatemala in 1954, witnessed the U.S. pressure on Arbenz, as well as the terror unleashed by Castillo Armas against Arbenz's supporters. In 1959, as a key adviser to Fidel Castro, Guevara urged the Cuban revolutionary to abolish the prerevolutionary army, mobilize popular support through radical urban and agrarian reforms, and prepare for the inevitable U.S. hostility by moving quickly to cement relations with the Soviet Union. Thus the United States failed when it sought to apply the "Guatemalan solution" to Cuba after 1959.

At the time, however, the Guatemalan success helped to convince the Eisenhower administration of the wisdom of its policies in Latin America— referred to by some as "the cheap backyard" because of the relatively low cost of maintaining the region's subordination to U.S. interests. In the single case in which U.S. interests came into conflict with a Latin American govern- ment, the United States managed to expel the offending government at little cost. Thus, from 1955 through 1957, the Eisenhower administration pursued conservative policies in Central America, yielding occasionally to the need for minor symbolic concessions, as in Panama, but maintaining and even consolidating its dominance in the region without any significant conces- sions to domestic or foreign critics. It supported democratic regimes, as in Costa Rica and Honduras, but kept them on a short leash, insisting that they respect U.S. political and economic interests and reining them in effectively when they thought to transgress. It also maintained cordial relations with authoritarian regimes in El Salvador, Nicaragua, and Guatemala and reward- ed them (particularly Guatemala) for their consistent anticommunism and their respect for U.S. business and economic concerns. Most Eisenhower offi- cials, including the president, saw no need to irritate loyal allies like Somoza with comments on their domestic political practices. The Latin American dictators provided the United States with the votes it needed to keep the OAS in line and proved helpful in curbing the tendency of democratic lead- ers to play for votes by criticizing the United States. The U.S. administration saw no need to devote significant resources to costly aid programs in a region so far from the Soviet Union, where the United States faced no discernible strategic threat. Instead of providing aid, administration leaders exhorted Latin America, and especially Central America, to rely on freer trade and to work harder to make their countries attractive to U.S. private investment.

chapter 4

DOLLARS AND DICTATORS:
THE ALLIANCE FOR PROGRESS, 1957–1969

EISENHOWER CHANGES COURSE

For more than a decade, from 1958 until the inauguration of President Richard M. Nixon in January 1969, the United States experimented with a much more actively interventionist policy in Latin America than it had employed in the region since the era of Woodrow Wilson. The major elements of the new policy were developed during the last three years of the Eisenhower presidency, from early 1958 until Eisenhower left office in January 1961. Repackaged and institutionalized under President John F. Kennedy (1961–63) and modified during the presidency of Lyndon B. Johnson (1963–69), the new policy came to be identified with Kennedy's Alliance for Progress. The main components of the Alliance were a rhetorical commitment to democratic regimes and social reform, greater flexibility in U.S. economic policy in response to regional initiatives that coincided with U.S. economic interests, large-scale deployments of U.S. military and intelligence assets to aid in the suppression of political forces deemed hostile to the United States, and sharp increases in U.S. economic and military aid, with a corresponding rise in U.S. efforts to influence policy processes and political outcomes in the region.

The new U.S. policy developed in response to a series of challenges to U.S. power and influence in Latin America. Though none of these challenges originated in Central America, the Central American nations were incorporated within the Alliance framework by virtue of their location in the hemisphere and in order to immunize them from the effects of disturbing developments elsewhere in the Caribbean and South America. Although the focus of this U.S. activism eventually became the hemispheric campaign to isolate Communist Cuba and to prevent further defections from the inter-American system, it began well before the Cuban revolution and lasted long after the successful suppression of pro-Cuban movements in other countries. Before the Cuban revolution turned to the Soviet Union for help and thus became the overriding obsession of U.S. policy makers, the new U.S. activism in Latin America was directed chiefly toward containing and controlling the effects of a wave of democratizations that swept the region in the late 1950s.

Between 1956 and 1960, 10 military rulers were deposed in Latin America, two by assassination.[1] In 1958 alone democratic governments took over from military regimes in three major countries: Argentina, Colombia, and Venezuela.[2] No movement for democratic change in the region could have succeeded without recruiting followers among students, intellectuals, urban workers, marginal slum dwellers, white-collar malcontents, and even portions of the poverty-stricken rural population. And no effort to mobilize members of these groups to risk death and imprisonment for democracy could have succeeded without the promise of social and economic reform to improve their living and working conditions. Organizations already formed to represent these goals, such as reformist (as well as revolutionary) political parties, trade unions, peasant leagues, and slum-dwellers' associations, along with student and cultural organizations, constituted the backbone of the region's democratic movements. The perception that military regimes and dictators favored only the rich and constituted an obstacle to social justice was confirmed by their suppression of such organizations and their relative permissiveness toward elite institutions and organizations. In many cases left-wing activists, including Communists, played notably distinguished or heroic roles in toppling repressive regimes. Thus, the kind of reformist coalition the United States had helped to topple from power in Guatemala in 1954 did not, as the administration hoped, disappear from the scene. Instead, democratization tended to produce similar political challenges throughout the region. Worse yet, many of the resurgent democratic political parties and social movements of the late 1950s accurately perceived the U.S. government as hostile to their reformist (or, in some cases, revolutionary) objectives.

U.S. policy makers viewed these democratic movements as potentially destabilizing and harmful to U.S. interests. While the Eisenhower administration could not oppose democratic movements overtly, it continued to provide aid, including weapons and other forms of military assistance, to most of the dictatorships until the moment of their demise.[3] U.S. officials also scrutinized such movements for evidence of left-wing and Communist participation and used various means, including penetration and disruption via U.S. intelligence agencies, to undermine or eliminate them. Frequently, this required covert collaboration between U.S. agencies and the political police of the authoritarian regimes. Once the dictators were overthrown the U.S.

administration invariably used its influence and leverage to ensure that the more reliably pro-U.S. (and usually more conservative) elements of the democratic movement emerged on top in the ensuing power struggles. The new democratic regimes were then pressured to eliminate left-wing elements from the governing coalition and from the popular organizations supporting it. As the dictators fell, however, problems of political management multiplied. In the absence of adequate political and financial resources to support governments and political organizations friendly to the United States, democratic change in Latin America threatened to produce governments less and less sympathetic to U.S. security and economic interests.

Some Eisenhower officials had been making arguments along these lines since early in the administration; until the dictators began falling, they were ignored or sacked. The political initiative for a new Latin American policy thus came largely from congressional and academic critics of the "cheap backyard" strategy of Dulles and Humphries. With Congress securely in the hands of Democrats, the administration confronted increasingly harsh criticism for its warm relations with dictatorial regimes, its suspicion of and hostility toward noncommunist (and even anticommunist) reformers like Figueres of Costa Rica and Betancourt of Venezuela, its dogmatic promotion of U.S. business interests as the solution for the region's economic ills, and its military aid programs, which did nothing to protect the hemisphere from the Soviet Union but did strengthen Latin America's right-wing military establishments. In May 1958 Vice-President Richard M. Nixon was greeted in Caracas by angry protesters who attacked his motorcade and nearly killed him; the Venezuelans' anger stemmed from U.S. support for the Pérez Jiménez dictatorship, which had just been overthrown.[4] This event came to symbolize the need for rethinking U.S. policies in Latin America and energized critics both within and outside the administration. Nixon's report of his trip concluded that the United States should give "top priority" to the region.

Three additional developments helped to push the Eisenhower administration to alter its policies. First, some U.S. officials became concerned with what they interpreted as a major new Soviet political and economic thrust into the third world. The Soviet Union launched a trade-and-aid offensive in Latin America in 1956 and followed it with an even more impressive effort, beginning in 1959 with the visit of Anastas Mikoyan to several countries, including Cuba. Second, the U.S. recession of 1957–58 precipitated a severe balance-of-payments crisis throughout the region. U.S. officials worried that the region's growing economic problems would inspire even more instability; Latin American political elites played on this concern to demand increased U.S. aid. Third, the chief protagonist of the economic hard line, Treasury Secretary Humphries, left the administration in 1958, and Dulles, his counterpart on questions of politics and security, departed a year later.

Their successors proved to be more in tune with the times, less rigid on economic and ideological issues.

The most noisily proclaimed change in administration policy occurred in 1958 and involved a pronounced rhetorical tilt toward democratic regimes. Henceforth, administration spokesmen explained, the United States would offer increased support and aid for the region's democracies and no more than a "formal handshake" to the dictators. This newfound passion for democracy did not occur until most of the dictators the United States had been courting were driven from power and, in any case, had little impact on the Eisenhower administration's behavior in Central America. The administration responded to free elections in Costa Rica (1958), as well as to fraudulent polls in Guatemala (1958) and Panama (1960), with equal tolerance. And it treated Villeda's tame reformism in Honduras with the same indifference it applied to the continuation of the Somoza family's rule in Nicaragua.

The economic policy changes embraced by the Eisenhower administration in its last years had much more substance. They had been repeatedly urged on U.S. officials by Latin American governments and the region's leading economists, beginning with the Chapultepec conference in 1945. By the mid-1950s, these proposals were reinforced by an impressive body of economic analysis produced by the U.N. Economic Commission for Latin America (ECLA), whose creation the United States had opposed. U.S. officials sharply criticized ECLA's work and labored to prevent most of its recommendations from being adopted by governments in the region. Until the 1954 Caracas meeting on Guatemala, the Eisenhower administration continued the Truman policy of evading Latin American proposals for an inter-American meeting to discuss economic issues. At the Caracas OAS meeting in 1954, however, Dulles finally agreed to such a meeting as one of the concessions needed to secure support for the U.S. resolution against Guatemala.[5]

The economic meeting took place in Rio de Janeiro from 22 November to 2 December 1954. Eisenhower appointed Treasury Secretary Humphries to represent the United States. In meetings within the administration to prepare for the Rio conference, Humphries opposed any U.S. concession to Latin American interests. He had to yield on increased Ex-Im Bank lending because Eisenhower had authorized Dulles to promise it at Caracas, but he won on all other issues. The U.S. delegation opposed the creation of an inter-American bank, refused to consider the resumption of long-term "development" loans by the Ex-Im Bank,[6] opposed export price-stabilization agreements, expressed reservations about regional economic or common market schemes, and abstained from voting on most of the proposals that came before the conference. At a second inter-American economic conference in Buenos Aires in 1957, the United States took essentially the same positions, opposing nearly every Latin American proposal on the grounds that Latin America needed to make itself more attractive to foreign capital, reduce government intervention in economic activity, privatize government enterprises, and reduce tariffs on imports from the United States. Officials within the administration who supported policies more responsive to Latin American demands were ignored or dismissed.

The changes in U.S. foreign economic and aid policies that began in 1958 followed months of discussion and debate within the administration after Nixon's ill-fated Latin American trip in May.[7] Unlike the rhetorical tilt toward democracy, these changes did have consequences for Central America. The first of these changes occurred in August, when the United States suddenly announced that it would support the creation of an inter-American bank to provide public capital for long-term development lending in the region. The announcement was made by the new undersecretary of state, Douglas Dillon, at the third inter-American economic meeting in August, and it was repeated by Eisenhower at the U.N. General Assembly the next day.[8] The initial capitalization of the bank at $1 billion, with the U.S. contributing 45 percent of the capital, fell short of Latin American expectations, but the administration also relaxed its prohibition on Latin American lending by the Development Loan Fund (DLF—part of the U.S. foreign aid agency) in 1959.[9] The Inter-American Development Bank (IADB) did not open for business until October 1960, however, and neither the IADB nor the DLF made any loans to Central America until after Eisenhower left office. Thus the main effects of these changes in U.S. aid policy were not felt until after the Kennedy administration took over in January 1961.

The second major change in economic policy occurred at the end of 1958, when the United States joined inter-American Study Groups looking into ways of stabilizing the prices of coffee, tin, and zinc. Prices for all three commodities had fallen after 1954, when the Korean War ended, and fell even further during the 1957–58 recession. Price-stabilization efforts by coffee-producing countries had already yielded modest results, without U.S. participation. In late 1957 the four Central American coffee producers signed an agreement with Brazil, Mexico, and Colombia to impose export quotas on themselves for a period of six months. Then they negotiated the Latin American Coffee Agreement in 1958, which yielded mixed results. With the United States involved, the International Coffee Agreement, which included African producers, was negotiated and signed in September 1959. This agreement helped to stabilize coffee prices but did not restore them to pre-1954 levels. No serious attempts to stabilize tin and zinc prices were ever made.

The third major change in economic policy occurred in 1959, when the United States endorsed the creation of the Central American Common Market (CACM). As in the case of the coffee agreements, the U.S. changed its position only after it became clear that governments in the region were proceeding anyway. The ECLA had begun working for a common market in Central America in 1952, when it had sponsored the creation of a Committee of Economic Cooperation (CEC), composed of the economic ministers from each of the five countries. In 1958 and 1959 the five Central American countries[10] signed three separate ECLA-endorsed agreements, in which they pledged to eliminate tariffs on a long list of products traded among them, promote integrated regional industrialization, and equalize tariffs on imports from the rest of the world.

The United States played no role in the negotiations that led to these initial CACM agreements but refrained from its usual criticisms of such schemes. Then, shortly after the last of the treaties was signed, the United States announced that it would support the Central American Common Market and offered to provide $10 million to finance the administrative and technical agencies the common market envisioned, on the condition that a new and revised treaty be drafted. The three northern republics responded favorably, and a new Tripartite Treaty embodying the U.S. amendments was signed in February 1960. In the original treaty the commodities to be traded freely were specifically enumerated; in the U.S. version free trade was the norm, and only the exceptions were listed. The United States also succeeded in eliminating any mention of integration industries in the revised treaty. These were industries that were to monopolize the production of particular goods for all the CACM nations, because the market for their products in any single Central American country was too small to sustain efficient and profitable production. In the original treaty the governments had agreed to grant designated integration industries an effective monopoly in the regional market to ensure their success, and to apportion such new industries equitably among the several republics. The United States, however, objected to the idea of politically negotiated industrial monopolies administered by local governments.[11] Eliminating them reduced the CACM's ability to promote industrialization in the region; thus, as Bulmer-Thomas noted, the new treaty "pulled the rug from under [ECLA's] feet."[12]

Eventually, however, in December 1960, a new General Treaty of Central American Economic Integration was signed by four of the Central American states. Costa Rica added its signature in 1963. The final version of the CACM treaty reintroduced the idea of integration industries but kept the freer trade provisions desired by the United States. While the retention of the integration industries idea was a victory for the ECLA, only three such industries were ever created, in large part because U.S. financial support of the CACM gave the United States immense influence in determining the pace and pattern of the CACM's evolution.[13] In sum, the original ECLA scheme envisioned the development of regional planning mechanisms that would have coordinated trade and investment policies among the Central American states to promote balanced industrialization, whereas the revised formula created a free-trade zone without an institutional structure capable of regulating private interests.

As the administration moved on all these fronts, a major new crisis erupted unexpectedly in Panama. On Panamanian Independence Day, 3

November 1959, a group of Panamanian demonstrators marched decorously into the canal zone and planted Panamanian flags. As the group left the zone, some of the student participants turned back. They were met by canal zone (U.S.) police, and one was arrested. This provoked efforts by the other students to rescue their comrade. A small riot developed, and U.S. troops were called out with fixed bayonets to suppress it. The rioting spread as thousands of Panamanians, on hearing of the confrontation, rushed into the streets and attacked U.S. property in Panama City and Colón. The rioters burned U.S. flags, assaulted the U.S. Embassy and U.S. Information Service with rocks and other missiles, overturned and torched cars with U.S. license plates, broke windows and vandalized the offices of U.S. corporations, and engaged in running battles with canal zone police and U.S. soldiers. More than 100 Panamanians were injured, along with several police and soldiers. The rioting continued until Panamanian National Guard units arrived, hours later, to quell the disturbance.

At a press conference the next day President Eisenhower said he was puzzled by the violence, because U.S.-Panamanian relations had been going so smoothly. He attributed the outbreak to "extremists." Nonetheless, with Cuban relations deteriorating rapidly, the president dispatched Undersecretary of State Dillon, the key architect of the new approach to Latin American affairs, to parley with Panamanian leaders. On Dillon's advice the administration announced a series of concessions to Panamanian demands in March and April 1960. On 12 March the United States agreed to implement the provisions of the 1955 memorandum in which it had promised to purchase goods from Panamanian firms whenever they were available at competitive prices.[14] On 19 April the president announced a nine-point program to improve relations between the canal zone and Panama. The program included a commitment to upgrade living conditions and wages of Panamanian employees in the zone and to promote Panamanian employees to supervisory positions, among other measures. Finally, on 17 September, Eisenhower ordered the Panamanian flag to be flown at a single location within the zone, despite opposition from the Pentagon, U.S. employees in the zone, and a number of vociferous conservative congressmen of both parties. The administration also proposed increased economic aid for Panama to Congress.[15]

Despite the Eisenhower administration's remarkable new activism in Latin American affairs, events in the region seemed to spiral out of control in 1960, its last year in office. The revolutionary government of Fidel Castro, which took power in Cuba on 2 January 1959, posed the greatest challenge. Meeting that challenge dominated much of the administration's foreign policy-making activity from late 1959 until Eisenhower left office. The president traveled to Argentina, Brazil, Chile, and Uruguay early in 1960. Though he encountered virtually no support for a U.S. move against Cuba, he issued an order on 17 March 1960 for the CIA to organize a Guatemala-style interven-

tion against the Castro government and plunged into a series of well-orches-
trated confrontations that led to the eventual break in U.S.-Cuban relations
on 3 January 1961.[16] Preparations for what became the Bay of Pigs fiasco
involved four of the Central American republics as well as Panama. On 17
May a CIA transmitter located on Great Swan Island, off the Caribbean
coast of Honduras, began broadcasting anti-Castro propaganda.[17] Later the
station served as the main communications link between the invading
Cuban counterrevolutionaries and their CIA supervisors. Honduran
President Villeda gave permission for the construction of the facility,[18] just
as Gálvez had bowed to U.S. pressure in 1954 to permit Guatemalan exiles
to launch their invasion from Honduras.[19] Nicaraguan President Luis
Somoza contributed logistical support, a training camp on one of his estates,
arms, and equipment, and opened military air strips for training Cuban exile
pilots. Somoza also initiated a series of skirmishes and incidents along the
Costa Rican border, perhaps to remind the Costa Ricans of their military
dependence on the United States, lest they fall victim to another bout of
self-righteousness.[20] The Guatemalan government, which owed its existence
to U.S. covert diplomacy,[21] provided the main training camp for the Cubans
at the private La Helvetia estate near the town of Retalhuleu, where hundreds of Cubans began arriving in July 1960. Finally, U.S. military installations in the Panama Canal Zone provided various kinds of logistical support
and training facilities.

Aside from Costa Rica, the only isthmian country that did not contribute
to the anti-Castro cause was El Salvador. On 26 October 1960 a group of
reformist military officers and their civilian allies toppled the repressive
right-wing government of Colonel José María Lemus. Lemus had come to
power in 1956 in elections tainted by fraud and intimidation. Early in 1960
he confronted student protests with a crackdown that was brutal even by
Salvadoran standards. In May, despite the escalating repression carried out
by his government, Lemus was invited to visit New York and Washington,
where he was feted by administration officials and met with President
Eisenhower. The U.S. administration was not happy with Lemus's ouster. It
had come to view any evidence of instability, especially in the Caribbean, as
potentially helpful to pro-Cuban and left-wing political organizations.
Cooperation with the new government on the project to overthrow Castro
could have backfired; some of the military officers and civilians identified
with the new regime were alleged to harbor "anti-imperialist" views.

The Eisenhower administration reacted to the Salvadoran coup by delay-
ing recognition of the new government. A month later, it dispatched a team
of officials, headed by the director of the State Department's Office of
Central American and Panama Affairs, to San Salvador to investigate
charges (manufactured in Washington) that the Salvadoran junta was permitting Communists and other anti-U.S. elements to infiltrate the new government. U.S. officials leaked word to the press that the administration

viewed the new regime as insensitive to the threat posed by Communists and pro-Cuban agents in Honduras. By the time recognition was extended on 3 December, plans for a counter-coup by right-wing military officers, considered more trustworthy in Washington, were already well advanced. The new coup took place on 25 January 1961, four days after the inauguration of President Kennedy. On 15 February Kennedy announced U.S. recognition and pledged aid to the new government of Colonel Julio Rivera.

Among the Central American countries directly involved in the U.S. preparations to overthrow the Cuban government, Guatemala proved to be the weakest link in the chain. President Ydígoras did not consult the army high command when he gave permission for the CIA to train Cuban exiles in his country. Moreover, he had alienated important sectors of the military and the traditional conservative elite because of the corruption, nepotism, and disorganization that characterized his government. When news of the Cuban training camp leaked, discontent in the officer corps exploded. On 13 November a third of the army's troops, including garrisons in Guatemala City and Zacapa, declared themselves in revolt and demanded that Ydígoras resign. The United States backed Ydígoras to the hilt. Ydígoras was ready to employ the CIA's Cubans to suppress his rebellious troops, but the project was vetoed by U.S. Ambassador John Muccio. The United States did, however, provide crucial covert aid in suppressing rebel forces that had occupied the port city of Puerto Barrios. The CIA loaned Cuban-exile pilots, who flew six B-26 bombers painted with Guatemalan air force markings, to blast rebel positions. The rebellion collapsed in three days, but its effects remained for more than a decade. Two young lieutenants who participated in the defeated revolt, Luis Turcios Lima and Marco Antonio Yon Sosa, returned from exile two years later to become leaders of the two main Guatemalan guerrilla movements of the 1960s.

As the coup collapsed, Ydígoras charged that pro-Castro Cuban agents had been behind it. His charge was seconded by the Nicaraguan government, which claimed that Cuban agents had landed on Nicaragua's coast as well. Both governments lodged complaints with the OAS, charging Cuban interference in their internal affairs. The Cuban government rejected the charges indignantly; the Cuban official radio commentator called Ydígoras a "wicked rat." Guatemala and Nicaragua also sent formal notes to the U.S. government, requesting the protection of the U.S. Navy to prevent Cuba from launching "further attacks" against them. The United States solemnly declared its commitment to defending its sister republics and dispatched the aircraft carrier *Shangri-La* and four destroyers to patrol the Caribbean waters southwest of Cuba, as well as another destroyer to guard the east coast of Guatemala and Nicaragua. Two P-2V patrol bombers were hurriedly flown to Panama for coastal surveillance. Less than a month later, on 7 December, Eisenhower recalled this armada upon receiving assurances from Nicaragua and Guatemala that the "emergency" had passed.

While the administration was escalating its campaign against Cuba, it introduced the last two major changes in its Latin American policy. The first involved a new foreign aid initiative, and the second was the elaboration of a new U.S. security doctrine for the region. On 11 July 1960 Eisenhower proposed to Congress the creation of a Social Progress Trust Fund (SPTF). The fund would lend money to governments in Latin America for investment projects in infrastructure, education, housing, agriculture, and the like. Unlike Ex-Im Bank loans and other foreign aid loans, SPTF loans would be granted at low rates of interest and could be repaid in local currencies. In effect, this was the Eisenhower administration's first real aid program for Latin America.[22] Moreover, the administration proposed that the SPTF be administered by the new Inter-American Development Bank rather than by the U.S. aid agency. This concession to Latin American sensibilities would be balanced by the disproportionate influence the United States exercised over the granting of SPTF loans as the fund's chief source of capital. The United States pledged itself to contribute 45 percent of the fund's initial capital of $500 million.

The change in U.S. strategic doctrine also developed as a response to the Cuban challenge. Congressional committees and other critics had repeatedly pointed out that the Eisenhower administration's reliance on nuclear deterrence for defense against the Soviet Union was useless in the third world. The U.S. nuclear arsenal had little or no effect on local or regional conflicts affecting U.S. interests and influence. This had been clear enough since the Korean War. It became even clearer in 1954, when Vice-President Nixon announced that the United States would consider the use of nuclear weapons to prevent a Communist victory against the French in Indochina. The threat had no effect. It did not even succeed in torpedoing the Geneva Conference, at which the French government ceded the northern half of Vietnam to the Vietminh rebels, recognized the independence of Laos and Cambodia, and agreed to withdraw its armed forces from the region. Nor did the U.S. nuclear arsenal stop the Cubans from defying the United States much closer to home after 1959. Aside from the CIA, whose successes in Iran and Guatemala gave the administration what critics called a false sense of security, the United States did not have at its disposal effective means to confront its enemies in many parts of the globe. In much of the third world, as in Latin America, U.S. strategic doctrine assigned to local military establishments the role of assisting the United States in defense against "external aggression." In practice, however, U.S. military aid programs, particularly those in Central America, tacitly undercut this doctrine by supplying weaponry more suited to maintaining internal order (often to the benefit of local dictators) than to defending against a Soviet attack.

The new Eisenhower doctrine essentially embraced the views of the administration's critics but turned their criticism on its head. The Latin American military should be encouraged to concentrate on internal security, administration spokesmen argued; rather than cut aid because the local military contributed little or nothing to hemispheric defense, the United States should increase aid because the main threat to the hemisphere was no longer external. In August 1960 U.S. military advisers in the Panama Canal Zone welcomed the first group of Latin American military officers to an expanded training program designed to inculcate the new U.S. doctrine. Latin American military officers were to be taught the new doctrine of national security, according to which they were encouraged to see themselves as guardians of their countries' commitments to the free world. In addition to training in techniques of counterinsurgency warfare and intelligence gathering, the officers were encouraged to develop civic action programs (e.g., road building and other useful and constructive projects) to improve the image of the military in their countries. Eisenhower's own preferences were evident in repeated U.S. statements emphasizing the need to keep military spending down in the Latin American countries in order to devote resources to social and economic development. The main effect of the new doctrine, however, was to legitimize and reinforce the propensity of Latin America's armed forces to seize power from civilian politicians whenever, in the opinion of the generals and their U.S. advisers, they failed to take sufficiently effective measures to suppress internal dissent.[23]

These final policy changes of the Eisenhower era were accompanied by a growing impatience with, at times bordering on contempt for, the perceived deficiencies of Latin America's economic and political elites. Many in the administration resented the need to appropriate large sums of money to bail out countries whose "irresponsible" leaders had failed to contain communism by enacting equitable tax systems, paying for decent education and social programs, and co-opting popular organizations before they became captives of radicals and Communists. The SPTF, under U.S. supervision, was created not just to aid Latin America but also to transform it under U.S. supervision. By 1960 the administration was pointing with approval to the achievements of moderate reformist leaders it had once dismissed as too left-wing. For example, Rómulo Betancourt, by then President of Venezuela, was the man Dulles had pressured Figueres to expel from Costa Rica in 1955; now, along with other anticommunist reformers, he was viewed as one of the administration's best friends in the region.

Thus, in its last three years in office, the Eisenhower administration laid the foundations on which its successor built the anticommunist Alliance for Progress. Between 1958 and 1960 the United States reluctantly abandoned the policies of "the cheap backyard," according to which Latin America's subordination to U.S. economic and strategic interests was to be assured at relatively minor cost to the United States. In 1958 and 1959 official U.S. rhetoric and behavior tilted toward the region's democratic governments as pro-U.S. dictators fell from power. Simultaneously, the United States reversed its opposition to the creation of a regional development bank, joined with the Latin American countries to create the IADB, and opened the Ex-Im Bank and the DLF to consider requests for long-term development loans to the region. U.S. foreign economic policy changed to accommodate commodity price-stabilization agreements, though the United States avoided joining any effort apart from the coffee scheme; also, the United States belatedly endorsed the CACM and used its leverage to alter its structure and to secure a permanent influence over its evolution.

These changes occurred before the Cuban revolution became a direct challenge to U.S. dominance in the Caribbean. Though Fidel Castro and his bearded cohorts came to power in January 1959, and although their behavior unsettled U.S. policy makers almost immediately, the Castro regime did not appear to pose a major threat to U.S. interests until late in the year. Once the Cuban revolution had turned to the left, but before the Soviets became committed to the Castro regime, the U.S. administration opted for a policy of hostility and confrontation and sought to mobilize its Latin American allies for an intensified struggle against communism in the Western Hemisphere. To have any chance of success, this policy required a carrot as well as a stick. The carrot was embodied in the creation of a new foreign aid program, the SPTF, designed to increase the economic benefits flowing to countries that remained committed to their alliance with the United States. The new stick included increased aid and training for military establishments on which the United States (and local elites) had to depend more than ever for protection against domestic political and social movements, now that the Cubans were supporting such movements. The Eisenhower administration left office with a new strategy in place, but before the new policies could claim any important results.

The Central American republics were affected by the changes in U.S. policy in the late 1950s but contributed little to inspire them. What leverage they had in relations with the United States diminished after 1954 and did not begin to increase again until the United States needed allies for its effort to overthrow the Cuban government, beginning in 1960. Even then the compliant regimes of the region gained little from their cooperation. The Ydígoras government in Guatemala survived an attempted coup, in part owing to covert U.S. support, but received no other reward. Panama got a new canal agreement with a substantial increase in user fees, and then used anti-U.S. rioting as leverage to pressure the United States into some additional concessions, but the United States retained control of the canal zone, obtained a new lease on the Río Hato military base, and continued to use its Panamanian facilities against Cuba despite local protests. The U.S. decision to support a coffee agreement and to endorse the creation of the CACM, however, were major achievements, in large part because of initiatives already taken by governments in the region. The coffee pact lasted only a few years, however, and U.S. participation in the CACM gave the United States greater influence than it would otherwise have had in shaping the

CACM's development as a free-trade pact rather than the basis for a new state-led push for industrialization in the region.

THE KENNEDY YEARS, 1961–1963

The Alliance for Progress was proclaimed by President Kennedy in Washington at an assembly of Latin American ambassadors to the United States on 16 March 1961, one month before the Bay of Pigs debacle.[24] Kennedy's speech left no doubt that the main goal of the Alliance would be to meet the political challenge posed by the Cuban revolution. The Castro government had managed to extricate Cuba from U.S. dominance by combining domestic reforms that mobilized public support with an effective appeal for aid from an external superpower. Kennedy made it clear that the United States did not accept Cuba's defection and was prepared to act decisively to prevent other nations from following its example.

The U.S. effort to overthrow the Castro regime, authorized by Eisenhower in early 1960, failed completely under Kennedy. After the Bay of Pigs, Kennedy ordered the CIA to assassinate Castro and to continue supporting small-scale terrorist attacks by Cuban exiles on power plants, sugar mills, and other targets on the island. Meanwhile, operational plans were drawn up—though not finally approved—to launch a full-scale U.S. invasion of Cuba. These plans had reached operational status by the fall of 1962, but the Cubans, with their new Soviet allies, had already anticipated a U.S. invasion and taken steps to prevent it.

In October 1962 U.S. reconnaissance flights over Cuba discovered unmistakable signs of Soviet missile emplacements. Kennedy ordered a naval "quarantine" of Cuba and demanded that the Soviet Union remove its missiles. After three tense days in which the threat of nuclear confrontation between the United States and the Soviet Union seemed to grow ever closer, Soviet Prime Minister Nikita Khrushchev agreed to withdraw the missiles in exchange for a U.S. commitment not to invade Cuba and to cease sponsoring terrorist attacks by exile groups. Unable to overthrow Castro, the administration resigned itself to a "long, twilight struggle" against Cuban and Soviet influence through the Alliance for Progress.

The new U.S. administration's rhetorical support for democracy in Central America was not applied in practice. Three military coups d'état occurred in the isthmus during the Kennedy era. The United States approved two of them in advance—in El Salvador on 25 January 1961 (mentioned earlier) and in Guatemala against Ydígoras on 31 March 1963. In each case the Kennedy administration recognized the new regime within a month. The third coup ousted Villeda from the presidency of Honduras on 3 October 1963 and was carried out against the express wishes of U.S. authorities. By this time, however, no one in the region (including the Honduran military) still took the administration's commitment to defending democratic regimes seriously. In addition to having approved the coups in El Salvador and Guatemala, the United States had done nothing to prevent coups, or to punish the military juntas that seized power, in Argentina and Peru in 1962 and in Ecuador and the Dominican Republic (as well as Guatemala) in 1963. From proclaiming a ringing defense of democracy, the Kennedy administration had retreated to the position that as long as new military regimes pledged themselves to hold elections and to restore democracy within a year or so, they could count on U.S. recognition and a resumption of U.S. aid. In the case of Honduras the United States extended recognition on 14 December, barely two months after the coup.

The Salvadoran coup took place less than a week after Kennedy's inauguration. Although the new administration had done nothing to prevent it, the inspiration for the coup had come from officials of the outgoing administration. The new Salvadoran regime promised to work closely with the United States, both to rid the country of Communist influence and to undertake needed reforms. Its first measures included a purge of nationalists and alleged radicals sympathetic to Cuba from government service, the arrest and imprisonment of suspected Communists, and the expulsion of several hundred leftists from the country. The leader of the new regime, Colonel Julio Rivera, endorsed the Alliance for Progress and promised quick elections. With civil and political liberties curtailed, Rivera organized an official party, the Partido de Conciliación Nacional (PCN), and had himself elected constitutional president as its candidate the following March.

Working with U.S. Ambassador Murat Williams, Rivera announced a series of modest reform programs, including the levying of new taxes on income and wealth and an expansion of government services in education, housing, and public health, all supported by the Alliance for Progress. These initiatives were viewed as unnecessary or subversive by many among the country's business elite, who appealed to the U.S. State Department to replace its "pro-communist" ambassador. The State Department ignored their pleas, Ambassador Williams inspired the organization of a pro-Alliance business group to counteract the reactionaries, and the administration allocated more economic aid to El Salvador than to any other Central American country save Guatemala between 1961 and 1963.[25]

For the Kennedy State Department, Rivera turned out to be an ideal leader—absolutely reliable on political and security issues, as demonstrated in his repression of the left, but flexible enough to see the need for moderate reforms. The reforms, however, ran out of steam in the face of continuing opposition from the Salvadoran elite, which saw no reason to make concessions to populist schemes once Rivera had subdued the left. Most of the reform measures, including tax reform, were ultimately reversed. Rivera's cooperation in security and intelligence activity, however, had a lasting effect. With help from the CIA, he created a Salvadoran National Security Agency (ANSESAL) to track down and persecute Salvadoran leftists. Under the leadership of Colonel José Alberto Medrano, ANSESAL founded ORDEN—a nationwide network of informants called *orejas* (ears)—which by 1970 "included one out of every 50 people in the country."[26] Rivera thus made his peace with the oligarchy and was succeeded by a series of PCN presidents, all military officers and all elected by suppressing the opposition, until the events that touched off the Salvadoran civil war in 1979–80.

In Guatemala, Ydígoras's relations with the United States deteriorated rapidly after the Bay of Pigs invasion, along with his already shaky support in the military. In an interview with *New York Times* correspondent Paul Kennedy in October 1962, immediately after the Cuban missile crisis, Ydígoras denounced the United States for its failure to support Guatemalan claims to Belize.[27] He said U.S. officials had promised to help him recover Belize in exchange for permitting the CIA to base its Bay of Pigs preparations in the country. The United States claimed it had not done so, and in fact had pointedly associated itself with British moves to protect Belize from any military threat from Guatemala. Ydígoras said that because of the U.S. betrayal on Belize, he had refused a U.S. request the previous month to use Guatemala as a base for bombing Cuba, and that anti-Castro activity in Guatemala had ceased.

One month later a unit of the Guatemalan air force revolted and strafed buildings in Guatemala City. The revolt was subdued, but the United States did nothing to help Ydígoras and made no public statements defending his government. To compensate for his deteriorating position, Ydígoras launched a wave of repression against opposition parties and organizations after students staged protests in March 1962. To shore up his position he appointed a new cabinet composed mainly of military officers, but his hold on the presidency was fortified mainly by the fact that his term would end in 1963, and because he could not constitutionally succeed himself in office, he was not a candidate in the national elections scheduled for November. The United States and the Guatemalan military looked forward to the end of the Ydígoras administration but did nothing to cut it short until late March 1963, when Juan José Arévalo, Arbenz's exiled predecessor, slipped into Guatemala illegally and proclaimed himself a candidate for the presidency.

Arévalo's announcement electrified the country. His election would have reversed the 1954 counterrevolution, undermined the military's emerging dominance, and called into question the U.S. role in reshaping Guatemala's political and economic life. When one of the legal opposition parties made Arévalo its candidate and the Guatemalan Supreme Court refused to exclude him from the ballot, Ydígoras announced that he would respect the court's decision. President Kennedy then signaled his approval for a coup to the Guatemalan military high command, already poised to save the nation from this new threat. On 31 March General Enrique Peralta Azurdia seized power, claiming that Ydígoras had been conspiring "to return the government to anti-democratic elements that were expelled by the sacrifices of the people of Guatemala" in 1954. The United States recognized the new regime on 17 April, citing Peralta's promise to hold new elections in 1965.

The Honduran coup later that year followed military takeovers in Ecuador in July and the Dominican Republic in September. The Dominican coup ousted President Juan Bosch, the country's first democratically elected president since Trujillo's assassination by CIA agents in 1961. Despite Bosch's impeccably anticommunist credentials and his enthusiasm for the reformist slogans of the Alliance for Progress, the Kennedy administration gave him little aid and did virtually nothing to save his government. Bosch irritated administration officials by refusing to repress Dominican political organizations that openly expressed enthusiasm for the Castro government in Cuba. Kennedy's failure to support democracy in the Dominican Republic convinced the Honduran high command that the United States would not react to a coup in their own country.

Unlike the Bosch regime, however, Villeda's government had cooperated with U.S. efforts to exclude Communists and radicals from Honduran political life and had consistently supported the U.S. campaign against Cuba. Villeda was the first Central American leader invited to Washington after Kennedy's inauguration. When coup rumors reached Washington in late September, Kennedy dispatched Major General Theodore Bogart, U.S. South Atlantic commander, to Tegucigalpa to persuade his Honduran counterparts to permit the October elections to take place and to allow Villeda to serve out his term.[28] The military ignored U.S. efforts to stop them and seized power on 3 October—a week before the national elections, which the candidate of Villeda's Liberal party, Modesto Rodas Alvarado, was expected to win. The Honduran military viewed Rodas as hostile to its interests and likely to favor the new Civil Guard (national police) created by Villeda as a means of diminishing the military's power and authority. The coup itself proved unusually bloody; poorly armed Civil Guards fought a series of losing battles against army units for four days after Villeda was ousted.

On 4 October, the day after the coup, the United States announced that it was cutting off all aid to the Dominican Republic and Honduras and began withdrawing its aid-mission personnel from both countries. The cutoff would not apply to Guatemala or Ecuador, the administration stated, because these two countries were already moving toward new elections and the restoration of democratic rule. The Honduran military got the message; new elections were promised within a year. On 14 December the United States recognized the new government of Honduras and resumed aid to that country shortly thereafter. Fifteen months later Colonel López Arellano had himself named constitutional president by a newly elected congress dominated by his supporters. "Elected" military presidents dominated Honduras for the next 20 years.

U.S. aid to the six isthmian republics increased substantially during the Kennedy years. Though the sums involved remained small, they were large by local standards and in comparison to the trivial sums allocated during most of the Eisenhower years. From an annual average of $37 million during the Eisenhower administration, U.S. aid rose to $95 million per year in 1961–63 (see Table 4.1). Most of the economic aid to the region during the Eisenhower years, however, consisted of grants (outright gifts), whereas most of the aid during the Kennedy years consisted of loans. Grant aid did increase, from an annual average of $22.4 million in 1953–60 to $34.9 million in 1961–63, but in real terms (correcting for inflation) the increase was negligible. Excluding Guatemala, where aid was concentrated between 1954 and 1960, total U.S. assistance (loans and grants) rose from an annual average of $24 million to $70 million. The largest increase went to El Salvador, where aid rose from less than $1 million per year under Eisenhower to $17.4 million per year under Kennedy. At the same time military assistance, which had constituted an average of 1.6 percent of U.S. aid to the region under Eisenhower, increased to 5.3 percent in the Kennedy years—that is, it rose from under $600,000 to over $5 million per year. These figures include Ex-Im Bank long-term loans as well as soft loans from the Social Progress Trust Fund (SPTF) of the Inter-American Development Bank (IADB). In addition, the Central American republics received substantial loans from multilateral agencies, such as the World Bank and the International Monetary Fund (IMF). This support was actually more important in the late 1950s and early 1960s than bilateral aid from the United States and played a crucial role in enabling the region to weather balance-of-payments difficulties between 1958 and 1962.

After the Cuban revolution, security measures and military aid to the region also increased rapidly, first under Eisenhower and then during the Kennedy years. The Kennedy administration dispatched a vastly increased number of intelligence agents, military advisers, police-training missions, and political operatives of all kinds to Central America. The CIA and other U.S. intelligence agencies routinely recruited highly placed military intelligence and interior ministry officials and paid them monthly retainers, a practice begun under Eisenhower and now substantially expanded. Kennedy also stepped up the number and size of joint maneuvers and war games involving Central American and U.S. military units and notably expanded training programs for Latin American (especially Central American) military officers. The Kennedy administration enthusiastically supported programs to improve the image of the local military establishments (civic action) and increase their capability for counterinsurgency (antiguerrilla) operations. Throughout Central America the U.S. Defense Department worked to increase cooperation among military establishments that had long histories of mutual suspicion. Officers from El Salvador, Guatemala, Honduras, Nicaragua, and Panama formed friendships in training programs in the United States and the canal zone, participated in joint maneuvers and war games with increasing frequency, and shared intelligence information on suspected subversives.

Table 4.1. U.S. Economic Assistance to Central America, 1953–1988
(Annual Average in 1982 Dollars)

	Costa Rica	El Salvador	Guatemala	Honduras	Nicaragua	Panama	Totals
1953–57	25.6	3.1	41.9	10.3	9.2	27.2	117.3
1958–61	24.0	6.9	52.9	16.8	23.1	19.0	142.7
1962–64	40.9	58.7	36.0	25.6	27.9	58.9	248.0
1965–69	42.4	30.7	33.4	25.9	47.5	62.5	242.4
1970–77	21.8	14.7	29.4	29.3	31.1	43.6	169.9
1978–81	16.9	56.3	26.6	40.0	27.3	18.4	185.5
1982–88	154.5	343.6	82.5	137.7	-0-	21.2	739.5

Sources: U.S. Agency for International Development, *U.S. Overseas Loans and Grants and Assistance from International Organizations, July 1, 1945–June 30, 1966* (Washington, D.C.: U.S. Government Printing Office, 1967), and subsequent editions published in 1976, 1979, 1982, 1984, and 1989. Data from this source were deflated by the producer price index for total finished goods found in *Economic Report of the President Transmitted to the Congress, February 1991, Together with the Annual Report of the Council of Economic Advisers* (Washington, D.C.: U.S. Government Printing Office, 1991), 357.

In 1964 this cooperation was formalized with the creation of the Central American Defense Council (CONDECA), which brought together the military high commands of El Salvador, Guatemala, Honduras, and Nicaragua (Panama was not a formal member) to coordinate activities and share intelligence.

The nature of the strategic objectives pursued by the Eisenhower and Kennedy administrations did not change as much as the conditions in which they had to be pursued and the policies required to achieve them. Until 1959 the main security objective of U.S. policy was defined as defense of the hemisphere against external aggression, though this objective required continuous vigilance (as in Guatemala) against what were termed the Soviets' local agents. Individuals and organizations opposed to particular U.S. interests or policies were scrutinized for evidence of ties to the Soviet Union and subjected to U.S. pressure. U.S. officials found it useful to blur the distinction between efforts to project U.S. power and defend U.S. economic and political interests on the one hand, and efforts to contain a Soviet strategic threat on the other. This discursive muddle often proved difficult to sustain, especially when U.S. interests were criticized by reliably anticommunist politicians and political organizations or when Communist threats denounced by Washington proved to have little substance. The problems were compounded by U.S. domestic politics; it proved difficult to generate public or congressional support for foreign policy initiatives, including foreign aid, without the stimulus of an imminent threat.

The changes in U.S. policy toward Latin America in 1958 and 1959 had first been proposed during the Truman administration. They were not implemented until a decade later, when evidence of public and even elite hostility toward the United States in the region came to be seen as potentially dangerous to U.S. interests. The Cuban revolution demonstrated that Eisenhower's warnings were not idle. It focused attention on the region and pushed Latin America closer to the top of the U.S. foreign policy agenda. To maintain U.S. dominance and prevent further defections, both Eisenhower and Kennedy found it necessary to increase economic aid and to restructure and intensify overt as well as covert security measures.

The major innovation of the Kennedy aid program was a new emphasis on planning. The Alliance for Progress aid program required recipients to draw up elaborate economic plans with the aid of U.S. and IADB advisers. Governments that failed to specify economic and "social progress" targets consistent with Alliance objectives had their aid cut or postponed until they produced the appropriate document. This innovation formalized the ad hoc procedures of the Eisenhower era and gave the new administration and its successor greater direct leverage over economic policy making throughout Latin America. Much of the economic aid granted by the Alliance, however, actually went to U.S. corporations, which received a major portion of the funds destined for economic-development projects.

The Kennedy administration also increased the size and complexity of activities designed to reduce the influence of left-wing elements in student movements, trade unions, peasant organizations, and both social democratic and Christian democratic political parties. The American Institute for Free Labor Development (AIFLD)—a private, not-for-profit organization run by the AFL-CIO, with a board of directors that included representatives of major U.S. firms with holdings throughout the Americas—was founded with administration support in 1962 and immediately began receiving large contracts from the U.S. aid agency and other bodies, including the CIA, to operate training programs and to support "moderate" anticommunist unions.[29] The AIFLD provided a convenient organizational structure for the collaboration of AFL-CIO leaders and several affiliated unions with the foreign policy and intelligence agencies of the U.S. government. The U.S. Agency for International Development (USAID—Kennedy's new name for the omnibus agency that managed foreign aid programs) sponsored a long list of training programs and seminars for labor, peasant, and political leaders, both in the region and at sites in the United States. Less sinister but no less purposeful was an expanded program of student and academic exchanges, begun under Eisenhower, which the administration saw as a means of reducing hostility toward the United States and occasionally used to recruit friends and agents.

The alterations in U.S. policy between 1958 and 1963 were not directed primarily at Central America. The United States increased economic assistance and endorsed the CACM, but it also increased military aid, joint maneuvers, and covert activity designed to suppress or control domestic opposition. By 1963 none of the Central American regimes displayed much interest in the social or political aims of the Alliance. In Guatemala, with U.S. support, the military turned back the threat of an open electoral contest, which could have restored the pre-1954 reformist coalition to power. In Honduras the United States acquiesced in the restoration of military rule and an end to liberal reformism. In El Salvador the United States encouraged the overthrow of a reformist military-civilian junta committed to social change and open elections; the succeeding regime consolidated military domination of the nation's political system. In Nicaragua the United States and the sons of Anastasio Somoza reached an accommodation after an initial period of strained relations, during which Kennedy fired the U.S. ambassador, Thomas Whelan, a close friend of the Somozas since his appointment to the post in 1951. Luis Somoza agreed to a cosmetic liberalization in exchange for a resumption of cordial relations.[30] In Panama and Costa Rica, relatively open electoral processes gave power to conservatives opposed to the reformist objectives of the Alliance. In Costa Rica, Figueres's party lost the 1958 elections but regained the presidency in 1962 by running Francisco Orlich, leader of the party's most conservative wing. In Panama, Remón's reforms died with him, and the relatively open elections of 1960 restored political power temporarily to the country's discredited oligarchy.

THE JOHNSON ALLIANCE, 1964–1969

By the time of President Kennedy's assassination on 22 November 1963, the Alliance for Progress had already lost much of its initial dynamism. The administration had managed to persuade Congress to appropriate funds for expanded economic and military aid programs, but the initial emphasis on democracy and social progress had begun to fade. The political coalition that supported the Alliance in Congress included many whose primary concern was to meet the Cuban threat, particularly conservatives hostile to the administration's idealistic rhetoric. By 1963 the Cuban challenge had become the main preoccupation of most policy makers within the administration as well. Thus, when the political and strategic objective of countering Cuban influence conflicted with the persistence of democratic regimes, the administration sponsored, or quickly accommodated itself to, military dictatorships—as long as they pledged to restore electoral processes and constitutional rule (always after lengthy periods during which left-wing and nationalist organizations were effectively eliminated from the local political scene). Even in nations where democratic regimes continued to exercise power, the administration insisted that local leaders take steps to repress or disrupt pro-Cuban groups in cooperation with U.S. intelligence agencies.

The Johnson administration quickly moved to bring U.S. rhetoric closer to the realities of policy making. Early in 1964 the new president appointed Thomas Mann as assistant secretary of state for inter-American affairs. To emphasize Mann's authority, Johnson simultaneously appointed him director of the Alliance for Progress and special assistant to the president. Mann did not share the enthusiasm of some of the Kennedy appointees for democratic government in Latin America. At a private meeting for U.S. ambassadors in Latin America on 19 March, within weeks of assuming office, Mann sketched a new, more "pragmatic" policy toward dictatorships in the region. By this time he had already learned of the impending military coup in Brazil; his remarks merely confirmed private assurances of U.S. support already communicated to the plotters. On 31 March 1964, with U.S. warships stationed off Rio de Janeiro in case they were needed to help, the Brazilian military seized power. Although the new regime made no pledge to restore democracy at any time in the future, the United States recognized it immediately and quickly arranged a massive infusion of foreign aid to help the new government restructure its debt. Referring to the "revolution" in Brazil at a news conference on 4 April, Johnson said it had been "a good week for this hemisphere."[31]

The Brazilian coup signaled the final abandonment of the democratic rhetoric of the Alliance for Progress in the face of widespread pressure for social and political change throughout the hemisphere. The short U.S. courtship of democratic reformers came to an abrupt end. So, too, did the nonintervention pledge of the Good Neighbor policy. In 1965, faced with a revolt against the military regime that had taken over the Dominican Republic in 1963, Johnson ordered 22,000 troops to occupy the capital city of Santo Domingo. This move, the first overt U.S. intervention in the Western Hemisphere since the withdrawal of U.S. troops from Nicaragua 30 years before, saved the Dominican military from collapse and prevented a reformist coalition from taking power. The Johnson administration also supported military coups in Bolivia (November 1964), Argentina (June 1966), and Panama (October 1968). An exception to this militarist turn in U.S. policy occurred in Peru, where military officers committed to social reform and nationalist economic policies seized power in October 1968, one week after the Panamanian coup. In response U.S. officials lamented the end of Peruvian democracy and cut off military as well as economic aid. The Johnson administration thus moved back to the policies of the first Eisenhower administration in accepting and even aiding right-wing (although not nationalist or "Nasserist") military coups against democratic governments in Latin America.

The social aims of the Alliance were attenuated in three ways. First, the administration's political and security aims relied on local elites, who opposed agrarian reforms and higher taxes for social programs; Alliance pro-grams were therefore often diverted to other purposes. Second, 40 percent of the aid supplied by the Alliance in its first three years was used to overcome the balance-of-payments deficits that resulted from negative shifts in Latin America's terms of trade in the late 1950s, and much of the rest was chan-neled to U.S. corporations to encourage private investment in the region rather than to repair the region's social ills. Third, the administration viewed many of the political and social organizations most committed to addressing the region's social problems as pro-Cuban and hostile to the United States. Their suppression, with U.S. support, reduced domestic pressures for social change in most of the Latin American countries.

Johnson did, however, honor Kennedy's pledge to provide a higher level of economic aid to Central America than had previous administrations, though Alliance aid to Latin America as a whole declined. As Table 4.1 shows, U.S. economic assistance to Central America in 1982 dollars increased in the last three years of the Eisenhower administration by 21.7 percent over the average of the preceding five years. During the three years of the Kennedy administration, U.S. aid to the region was nearly 74 percent higher than the aid level of Eisenhower's last years. For the next five years, under Johnson, aid remained at roughly the Kennedy levels (see Table 4.1). This was a substantial achievement, given congressional pressures on the administration to cut back as the costs of the Vietnam War escalated, begin-ning in 1965. In part it reflected a shift in the administration's concerns—from South America, where relatively solid military regimes had assumed power in key countries and aid could be reduced if necessary, to the Caribbean, where (as in the Dominican Republic) conditions appeared less secure. In the small countries of Central America, as in Cuba, relatively small guerrilla forces could pose significant threats to the regimes in power. During the Johnson years guerrilla outbreaks occurred in Guatemala, El Salvador, Honduras, Nicaragua, and Panama, though only in Guatemala did the armed opposition escape swift suppression by the retrained and newly reequipped armies of the isthmus.

The Guatemalan insurgency proved the most complicated, because two powerful guerrilla organizations based their appeals for support on popular sympathy for the pre-1954 reforms and on nationalist resentment of the con-tinuing U.S. role in the country. U.S. policy makers persisted for a time in their efforts to persuade the Guatemalan military of the need to preserve a semblance of democratic forms. In December 1965 the U.S. Embassy man-aged to prevent a coup that would have cancelled the national election scheduled for the following March. The embassy threw its support in the electoral contest to Julio Méndez Montenegro, a university professor of mod-erate views who was opposed by a candidate selected by the military high command. Méndez won the March election, but the military was not dis-posed to let him assume office until he signed a pact, approved by the United

States, that ceded executive authority to military commanders in much of the country. The result was a reign of terror in which thousands of civilians, most of them uninvolved with the guerrillas, lost their lives at the hands of the security forces or the death squads, which worked closely with military intelligence. Méndez occupied the presidential palace but never effectively governed. He was succeeded by military presidents elected through massive fraud and intimidation until the 1980s.

It was Panama, however, that posed the most visible and controversial foreign policy problem of the Johnson era in Central America. From 9 to 13 January 1964 anti-U.S. rioting erupted again. The violence began after three days of demonstrations by U.S. high school students and other U.S. residents of the Panama Canal Zone, protesting the implementation of a decision by the late President Kennedy to display the Panamanian flag alongside the flag of the United States at 16 sites in the zone. The decision had gone into effect on 2 January 1964, three months after Kennedy's assassination. The U.S. students, urged on by their parents, insisted on raising the U.S. flag alone in front of the Balboa High School, located just inside the canal zone. Zone authorities and the high school principal took the flag down because it violated the Kennedy agreement; the students raised it again, and it stayed up. When several hundred Panamanian students marched peacefully into the zone to protest the violation of the Kennedy agreement and the absence of the Panamanian flag, canal zone police allowed the group to enter the zone and gave a half dozen representatives of the group permission to plant the Panamanian flag alongside the U.S. flag at the high school. Several hundred U.S. students and residents had also gathered at the school. The police let the two groups come too close to each other. The U.S. demonstrators hurled insults at the Panamanians and tried to prevent them from planting the Panamanian flag. To avoid trouble, the police asked the Panamanians to leave, but it was too late. Fighting broke out as some of the U.S. students went after the Panamanian flag. The flag was seized and trampled. The fighting spread as the police escorted the Panamanians back across the border. Responding to news broadcasts about the incident, as many as 30,000 Panamanians swarmed into the streets, attacking the property of U.S. citizens, businesses, and government agencies and attempting to enter the zone, with flags or without. The canal zone authorities summoned U.S. troops to aid the police. At several points during the first day of rioting, the troops fired into crowds of Panamanians trying to push their way across the border.

The rioting lasted for four days and spread to other cities, including Colón and David. Four U.S. soldiers and 24 Panamanian civilians were killed; 85 U.S. citizens (mostly soldiers) and more than 200 Panamanians were injured or wounded. For at least two days U.S. troops in the zone were fired on by snipers shooting from the windows of buildings located just across the street from the zone's border. The Panamanian National Guard stayed away from the fray and did little to contain the violence until it had already begun to subside on 13 January.[32]

On the morning of 10 January, the second day of the rioting, President Roberto Chiari suspended diplomatic relations with the United States, recalled Panama's ambassador to Washington, and issued a "formal protest for the unmerciful acts of aggression carried out by the armed forces of the United States of America stationed in the Canal Zone against the territorial integrity of the republic and its undefended civil population."[33] Chiari announced that Panama had decided to invoke the Rio Treaty and appealed to the OAS for assistance against the United States. Chiari's anger and defiance, from which he descended as quickly as Panamanian political passions permitted, threw U.S.-Panamanian relations into momentary turmoil.

Once order was restored, the Panamanian and U.S. governments began an elaborate dance around the issues the rioting had raised. Johnson sent Mann, together with Secretary of the Army Cyrus Vance, to talk to Chiari—Mann to threaten him, and Vance to offer him a deal. When the talks failed, Chiari formally broke relations with the United States on 18 January and repeated his request for OAS intervention.[34] Panama's complaint precipitated a crisis in the OAS. It was the first time that the machinery of the organization had ever been invoked against the United States. None of the member states was willing to sacrifice its relations with the United States to engage in costly acts of charity toward Panama. On the other hand, nearly all viewed the U.S. presence in Panama as an anachronism, and none wished to inflame public opinion at home by publicly endorsing the U.S. position. After much anguished diplomatic confabulating, the OAS appointed two commissions—one to investigate Panama's charge of U.S. aggression,[35] the other to mediate between the two countries.

For the next two months the controversy degenerated into a war of diplomatic semantics. Panama insisted that it would not restore full relations with the United States until the U.S. government agreed to renegotiate the 1903 treaty. The Johnson administration, already in the midst of presidential primaries and unwilling to hand its opponents an issue, insisted on full restoration of relations and refused to agree publicly to a new treaty. On 15 January and again on 10 March, the two governments seemed to agree to resume relations and begin formal negotiations. In each case, however, Panama insisted on interpreting the deal as an agreement to renegotiate the 1903 treaty, whereas Washington claimed it had agreed only to talks that would not necessarily lead to a new treaty. At the end of March, after the OAS mediation commission had twice given up its efforts only to be sent back to try again, Johnson announced at a news conference that the United States had found that some "adjustments" in the 1903 treaty would be justified (although, as in the U.S.-Panama accords of 1936 and 1955, these could presumably have been made without scrapping the 1903 treaty). Publicly, Chiari chose to interpret this statement as a victory; privately, he agreed not to insist on a new treaty once relations were restored and the talks were under way. On 4 April diplomatic relations were restored, and negotiators were appointed for the talks to follow.

The approach of Panama's presidential elections, scheduled for 10 May, put negotiations with the United States on hold. Meanwhile, Chiari, with U.S. help, arranged for the election of Marco Robles to succeed him, against a powerful campaign mounted by Arnulfo Arias. Within days of his electoral victory, Robles announced that Panama would adopt a new, more pragmatic approach in its talks with the United States regarding the canal: instead of insisting on a new treaty, Panama would negotiate to increase the canal's economic benefits to the country.[36] In effect, the Robles announcement simply made public the deal Chiari had already made six weeks before. With the pressure of the election campaign over, Robles could afford to defer the emotional issue of sovereignty in favor of what his government sorely needed: economic aid for a deteriorating economy. He also won points in Washington for defusing an election-year issue for Johnson. The Panamanian announcement was not, however, an entirely voluntary act of goodwill. On 17 April Johnson had announced plans for talks with the government of Colombia on a possible route through Colombian territory for a new sea-level canal.[37]

Having thus turned a major foreign policy problem into an election-year triumph for U.S. diplomacy, Johnson could afford to be generous after his landslide electoral victory. On 18 December he announced that the United States had decided to enter negotiations with Panama for a new canal treaty. Simultaneously, he let it be known that the administration was looking at four possible routes for a new sea-level canal: two in Panama, one in Colombia, and another along the border between Costa Rica and Nicaragua. As negotiations opened, the United States insisted that the new treaty leave the Panama Canal under U.S. control until the new canal could be built, include a "new defense facilities agreement" that would allow the United States to retain military bases in the canal zone area, and contain language granting the United States the right to intervene to protect the canal from future threats to its neutrality and efficient operation. The major U.S. concession in the talks was its willingness to yield formal sovereignty over the canal to Panama. These terms were not acceptable to the Panamanians, who insisted on full sovereignty over the canal zone, full control of the canal itself, the cancellation of clauses permitting U.S. intervention, and the closing of U.S. military installations.

The talks dragged on for two and a half years. On 26 June 1967 the two governments announced that they had reached agreement on the drafts of three new treaties. Until the drafts were reviewed by the two presidents, however, the texts would not be released to the public. The first of the three treaties granted the United States the right to construct a new sea-level canal or to modify the existing canal to accommodate more traffic and larger ships. The second concerned the defense and neutrality of the old and new canals. The third specified changes in the operation of the canal. The treaties recognized Panamanian sovereignty over the canal zone and specified that the the United States would turn the canal over to Panama in 1999. After 1999, however, the canal was to be operated by a joint U.S.-Panamanian commission of nine members, five of whom were to be appointed by the United States, thus leaving effective control of the waterway in the hands of the U.S. government. The treaties also granted the United States a new lease on its canal zone military bases; the lease was set to expire in the year 2004, but the treaty made the lease renewable.

With the treaty drafts produced, formal negotiations between Panama and the United States ended. All that remained was for the two presidents to review them, add their signatures, and submit them for legislative ratification. This never happened. Instead, both Johnson and Robles hinted at reservations and the need for additional talks. Months dragged by without a formal signing. The drafts were leaked to the press, initially in bits and pieces and finally in their entirety. The ensuing frenzy of opposition, especially in Panama, made it politically impossible for either president to sign them.

While the treaties languished, Panamanian politics erupted once more. In December 1967 Robles's eight-party coalition split over the presidential succession, with four parties and part of a fifth opting to support the candidacy of Arnulfo Arias. Robles was accused of plotting to rig the May elections in order to impose his handpicked candidate, David Samudio. The National Assembly voted to impeach Robles on 25 March 1968 and named a new president to serve the remainder of his term. Robles held on to the final months of his presidency, however, by calling in the National Guard to close the legislature and to suppress opposition demonstrations. In the elections Robles expected to guarantee an electoral victory for Samudio by employing the power of his office to intimidate voters and to manipulate the vote count, just as Chiari had done to secure his own victory four years earlier. Even the intended victim of Robles's plan, perennial opposition candidate and former president Arnulfo Arias, was the same as four years earlier. But Robles had miscalculated. The vote against the official candidate was so overwhelming that no amount of manipulation could disguise the result. Worse yet, the chief of the National Guard, Brigadier General Bolívar Vallarino, angry that he had not been chosen by Robles as the Liberal party candidate, maintained a semblance of neutrality by refusing to allow the guard to be used to rig the results. Robles appealed to the United States for support—a logical move since most of his political troubles arose from the canal talks and his commitment to such Alliance for Progress goals as tax reform—but his appeals were rebuffed. Arias had already taken steps to reassure both the guard (most of whose officers despised him) and Washington (he even announced that he had forgiven President Roosevelt for engineering the coup that had overthrown him in 1941). Arias was proclaimed the winner and inaugurated as president on 1 October.

Because Arias had convinced Washington of his good intentions, his survival in office now depended on his ability to neutralize opposition in the National Guard. After winning the election, but before his inauguration, Arias struck a deal with the guard. Vallarino, who had served for 16 years as the guard's commander-in-chief, agreed to retire, and Arias promised to respect the guard's chain of command in the reshuffling of positions that would ensue. The new guard chief would be Colonel José M. Pinilla, and other officers would move up according to their rank and seniority. This agreement was crucial to ensuring Arias's inauguration. As soon as he took office, however, Arias broke the agreement, forced Pinilla to step down, appointed opponents in the officer corps to posts as military attachés in Panamanian embassies abroad in order to get them out of the country, and ignored the guard's promotion lists by naming his own candidates to all the important command positions. The guard responded by throwing him out of office only 10 days after his inauguration.

The coup of 11 October 1968 took Washington by surprise. Arias, with eight members of his cabinet and Vallarino, the then-retired guard commander, fled to the Panama Canal Zone. Arias appealed for U.S. troops to restore him to office. His request was rejected, but Arias and his party were provided lodging in the zone while U.S. officials attempted to cut a deal that would restore Arias to the presidency and mollify the guard. When Arias's appeals to the population, issued in leaflets and over clandestine radio broadcasts, failed to bring his supporters into the streets of Panama City (now occupied by guard tanks and soldiers), the United States gave up. The State Department, which had made the dubious claim that Arias was in the zone as a guest of the independent Panama Canal Company, now officially rebuked Arias for trying to incite violence and, after failing to persuade any Latin American country to take him, finally flew him to Washington, where he moved into the Panamanian Embassy and made a nuisance of himself for some weeks thereafter. With the guard firmly in power and with Richard Nixon about to be inaugurated, U.S.-Panamanian relations entered a new era.

CONCLUSIONS

Most works on the Alliance for Progress, both journalistic and academic, have judged it a "noble failure."[38] Although analysts have differed on the timing and the causes of the failure, they generally agree on its dimensions. First, the Alliance did not promote democracy and contributed, in its obsession with security, to the wave of military coups that swept all of Latin America in the 1960s. Second, the Alliance failed to promote social progress and economic reform. The priority given by U.S. policy makers to preserving stability, along with elite resistance (both in Latin America and in the United States), made dead letters of the Alliance's commitment to greater equality through agrarian reform, progressive taxation, and improvements in education, health, housing, and public services. Third, the Alliance failed to improve U.S. relations with Latin America and weakened hemispheric institutions. Many Latin American governments resented being drawn into the U.S. confrontation with Cuba and were appalled by the U.S. intervention in the Dominican Republic. The OAS came to be seen as a mere "tool of U.S. policy"[39] or, as Fidel Castro called it, "the colonial ministry of the U.S. government"—a perception reinforced by the contempt displayed by U.S. officials for OAS mediation efforts during the Panama crisis of January to May 1964.

One dissenting radical evaluation of the Alliance for Progress concluded that "John Kennedy's Alliance worked from the start to strengthen Latin American armies, defend U.S. business, and help native elites stave off basic reform. Given those aims, it didn't do so badly."[40] This view abstracts from the policy debates and decision-making processes of the Alliance era by dismissing entirely all the explicit aims of the Alliance that were not pursued consistently (democracy, reform, etc.). It is nonetheless accurate in its summary of the results of a decade of U.S. foreign policy activism in the region. Latin American military establishments grew in size, capacity, and willingness to assist the United States in achieving its security objectives by suppressing internal opposition. U.S. officials believed that this helped to prevent any further defections to the nation's cold war opponents after Cuba turned to the Soviet Union in 1960–62. Success in meeting its security aims helped the United States to better protect U.S. enterprises with investments and trading interests in the region; indeed, the Alliance provided government funding to subsidize and promote new U.S. private investment in the region. Local elites managed to resist reforms—modest as well as "basic"[41]—in most cases because organizations and individuals advocating reforms suffered persecution at the hands of the local military, and in other cases because the United States failed to provide crucial financial and political support.

Ultimately, however, evaluations of the Alliance have turned largely on judgments about what the course of events in the region might have been if the United States had behaved differently. Many in Congress and in three successive administrations have maintained that the Alliance was needed to save the hemisphere from additional defections to the Soviet Union. On the face of it, this claim is implausible. None of the Latin American countries faced a credible short-term threat of such a defection in the Alliance era. Not one of the 10 military governments that replaced democratic regimes in the region during this period did so to prevent an imminent Communist takeover. Even in the case of the Dominican Republic, to which the United States dispatched an army of occupation in 1965, the U.S. "white paper" purporting to demonstrate that 119 Communists were among the thousands rebelling against the country's military rulers turned out to be full of inaccuracies.

U.S. officials worried less about imminent and explicit threats than they did about the potential for undesirable outcomes inherent in unstable political conditions. Fidel Castro had not become a Communist until after taking power. The lesson of the Cuban Revolution for the United States was that any uncontrolled instability could lead to disaster. The United States implicitly agreed with the Cuban government's conclusion in the early 1960s (which the Cubans later revised) that Latin America was ripe for revolution. Thus the United States and its allies in the region did not confine themselves to suppressing Communist and pro-Cuban organizations. They moved against any organized challenge to the institutional or political status quo whose leaders were not known and trusted in Washington and whose success at the polls or on the battlefield was deemed likely to produce unpredictable consequences.[42] Nonviolent reformist, populist, and, of course, revolutionary movements, as well as innumerable left-wing politicians and nationalist military officers, were considered unreliable by Washington, and their access to power was diminished by U.S. efforts. Highest priority was given to the suppression of guerrilla movements supported by the Cuban regime. Although most such movements were directed against military and personal dictatorships and were usually small and ineffective,[43] their very existence was viewed as dangerous to the United States.

In Central America, where U.S. influence was already pervasive, the resources mobilized in the Alliance era enhanced the power of local military establishments and gave U.S. officials additional direct political leverage. At critical junctures in the history of five of the six countries, the effect of U.S. decisions to give or withhold support had immense long-run consequences. In Guatemala the U.S. intervention in 1954 had already moved the country away from democratic reformism, strengthened the minority right-wing parties, and enhanced the power of the military. Not until the Alliance era, however, did the armed forces attain the degree of institutionalized power and autonomy they have enjoyed since that time. Professional education and internal reorganization, accomplished with the help of U.S. advisers and training programs, along with military aid ranging from new uniforms to tanks and aircraft, transformed the Guatemalan army in less than a decade. The Guatemalan guerrilla war of 1965–70, in which U.S. arms and advisers played an important role, provided a sense of unity in the face of a common enemy, allowed the officer corps free rein to employ the full range of tactics and armaments in actual combat conditions, and justified the military's assumption of civil authority, first in combat areas and then throughout the country. The military's chief supporters in this process consisted of the country's business elite, which had already found anticommunism to be a convenient framework for expressing its resistance to land reform, union organizing, and taxes and regulation of any kind.

Students of the period are divided on how crucial U.S. aid was to the military's success against the guerrillas. By some accounts the insurgents dissipated their strength when they might have seized power, waiting for political turmoil in other countries to reduce the prospects of a U.S. military intervention. Most accounts, however, suggest only that U.S. aid helped the Guatemalan military achieve a swifter and more decisive victory. In either case, absent U.S. aid, pressures to negotiate with the rebels and even to make some concessions to their programmatic demands would certainly have increased. In such circumstances it would have been more difficult, though certainly not impossible, for the military to consolidate the kind of garrison state that Guatemala became in the Alliance era.

This impression is reinforced by examining the direct political role the United States played in facilitating Guatemala's drift toward militarism at two critical points. First, it approved in advance the military coup in late March 1962, which deposed Ydígoras and prevented Arévalo from running for president. Given Ydígoras's weakness and the hostility toward Arévalo in the officer corps, the coup might have gone forward in any case, but U.S. support for an open electoral contest could have strengthened prospects for a future evolution in that direction. Equally significant was U.S. acquiescence to the military's efforts to strip authority from the Méndez Montenegro administration in 1966–68. In part, Méndez had been elected because the United States had pressured the military to put aside its plans to rig the elections in favor of its own candidate.[44] Once elected, however, Méndez was compelled by the military, with U.S. backing, to abandon his plans to conduct negotiations with the guerrillas and to accept military co-rule in most of the country. When he mounted his only major effort to confront the country's most pressing economic needs by proposing a fiscal reform that would have levied modest sales and other taxes on businesses, the United States did nothing to help him resist elite protests against it, despite the importance of tax reform in Alliance rhetoric. The business elite, aided by its military allies, forced Méndez to rescind the tax bill, which had already been approved by the Guatemalan congress.[45] By the time Méndez left office, the Guatemalan military had had enough of civilian politicians and, with the guerrillas nearly gone, no longer needed the facade of civilian rule that had once been helpful in securing U.S. aid. For the next 15 years all the presidents of Guatemala were generals, and none saw any need for reforms.

In El Salvador, Honduras, and Nicaragua the influence of the United States worked in similar ways. In El Salvador the United States actively sabotaged the reformist civil-military junta that took power in October 1960. When more conservative officers seized control early the next year, the new Kennedy administration recognized the new regime immediately and a week later announced an increase in U.S. aid. The reforms promised by the new regime quickly withered away, despite the initial prodding of an unusually energetic and experienced ambassador. Three years later, in October 1963, the United States attempted at the last minute to prevent a coup in Honduras but failed. The Hondurans knew that as in other cases, U.S. disapproval would not be followed by serious efforts to undermine their regime, reverse the coup, and drive them from power. Since the main issue in the canceled elections was precisely the inordinate power of the military establishment, U.S. recognition of the new regime (after barely two months) and the restoration of U.S. aid shortly thereafter confirmed the military's triumph over civilian authority. In Nicaragua, U.S. aid to the Somoza regime never lapsed. No serious effort was made to push the regime toward more than a cosmetic liberalization at the two points at which U.S. leverage would have been most effective: after the assassination of Anastasio Somoza García, the founder of the dynasty, in 1956, and during the period of civil unrest that preceded the fraudulent election of his son, Anastasio Somoza Debayle, to the presidency in 1967. In each of these three cases the U.S. government chose, at critical junctures, to behave in a way that diminished prospects for democratic change and social or economic reform. In each case, though with somewhat different consequences in each country, U.S. action or inaction helped to strengthen militarism and defeat reform.

In Panama the U.S. role was complicated by the canal issue. During the Alliance era the United States increased its aid, as well as Panama's share of canal tolls, substantially. Modest economic and social reforms, begun during the presidency of José Remón (1952–55), were reversed after his assassination, but under pressure from the Alliance, and despite protests from the country's business elite, Marco Robles announced a major reform of the tax system to finance the social and economic development goals of what became known as the "Plan Robles." Tainted by (accurate) charges that his election had been rigged by Chiari and the National Guard, Robles was strengthened considerably by Johnson's unexpected agreement to negotiate a new canal treaty. Robles had a reasonable chance of succeeding in his efforts to modernize public administration within the framework of Panama's imperfect but still functioning democratic constitution. To do so he needed a new canal treaty negotiated quickly, on terms sufficiently responsive to Panamanian sensibilities to win him the public and legislative support required to impose his taxation and development program. Instead the canal negotiations dragged on for two and a half years, the treaty drafts undermined his authority, the tax reform backfired, his political support evaporated, the National Assembly voted to impeach him, and the candidate to succeed him in office (who had been in charge of implementing the tax reform) failed miserably at the polls. The U.S. administration abandoned Robles to his fate and acquiesced to the coup that ousted his successor in October 1968.

In the cases of Guatemala, El Salvador, and Nicaragua, U.S. policy sought fundamentally to avoid instability and its unpredictable consequences—in Guatemala by backing the military against the guerrillas, in El Salvador by substituting a certifiably anticommunist military regime for a more reform-minded and nationalist one, and in Nicaragua by supporting (although at times with well-publicized distaste) the continuation of the Somoza family's rule. In Honduras and Panama, where the military took power not to prevent or to end instability but merely to maintain and assert its independence of civilian authority, the United States initially expressed disapproval of, but then quickly accepted, the new regimes.[46]

Thus U.S. policies in the Alliance era succeeded in raising the costs each society would have to pay to achieve political and social change. While this achievement served U.S. cold war security objectives by contributing to stability in the short run, it also helped to undermine the long-term stability of the affected polities.

chapter 5

IMPERIAL DECAY, 1969–1981

THE END OF THE ALLIANCE

By 1969, the last year of what was to have been Latin America's "decade of development," most of the region's nations, including five of the six isthmian republics, were ruled by repressive governments—ranging from personal or family dictatorships (as in Nicaragua and Paraguay) to highly institutionalized and "modernizing" bureaucratic authoritarian regimes (as in Argentina and Brazil). A decade later only Colombia, Costa Rica, Mexico, and Venezuela had managed to escape the continental descent into militarism. This shift altered the context of U.S. policy making. Because nearly all of the repressive regimes cooperated closely with the U.S. effort to isolate Cuba and suppress internal dissent, Washington's worries about the development of another Cuba diminished. This made it easier for the United States to turn its attention back to the unstable periphery of the "free world," and to Southeast Asia in particular. With Latin America apparently secure, the large-scale economic and military aid programs embodied in the Alliance for Progress became unnecessary at precisely the time when funds were needed to pay for the escalation of the Vietnam War. The Alliance budget, already cut substantially by the end of the Johnson administration, was reduced to a minimum under his Republican successors, Richard M. Nixon (1969–74) and Gerald Ford (1974–77). U.S. military and intelligence assets in the Western Hemisphere, along with aid and diplomatic personnel, were redeployed to Southeast Asia and elsewhere. The United States thus lost some of its capacity to monitor and manipulate events in the region, but since most of the Latin American countries were securely under the control of reliably anticommunist military establishments, the significance of this loss did not become apparent until later.

During the two postwar decades (1945–65) the revival of Western European and, eventually, Japanese economic competition had no significant diplomatic or political consequences. As the United States had foreseen, the creation of the OAS made it possible to contain most Latin American problems within a U.S.-dominated hemispheric organization. The few times that inter-American issues were brought to the United Nations, the United States had sufficient leverage with its allies to persuade or pressure them into referring those issues to the OAS.[1] None had strategic or economic interests independent of the United States in the region that were worth paying much to pursue.[2] The Soviet Union and its allies did, of course, pursue policies opposed to those of the United States, but outside of their role in protecting isolated Cuba, their economic significance and political influence in the region continued to be minimal. The United States thus enjoyed a relatively free hand in the Western Hemisphere; no external power had both the interest and the ability to challenge U.S. predominance.

Two major developments in the 1960s worked to dilute U.S. predominance in the Western Hemisphere and to make Latin America's external environment more competitive. The first was the Cuban Revolution and its consequences. No Western European power, much less the Japanese, responded to the Cuban government's appeals for aid against U.S. pressures and attacks after the revolution—a situation that helped to propel the Cubans toward the Soviet Union.[3] Western European governments had private misgivings about U.S. actions in Cuba, public opinion throughout Western Europe was sympathetic to the Cubans, and many of the Continent's political and cultural figures (nearly all social democrats, socialists, or British laborites) traveled to Cuba to express their support; nevertheless, Cuban appeals to the United Nations and to Western European governments got no response. Western European governments did not criticize the United States or try to meddle, but neither did they break relations with Cuba or join the U.S. trade embargo. The October 1962 missile crisis marked a turning point. Suddenly, a conflict in the Western Hemisphere threatened the globe with nuclear annihilation. However they viewed the Cuban and Soviet regimes, Western European governments and their publics were appalled that the United States had so mismanaged affairs in its own backyard as to put the world at risk.[4] Western European nations were relieved when the crisis ended and did not immediately alter their policies toward the Cuban government, but they would no longer remain aloof from developments in Latin America. This change was subsequently reinforced by Western European public and official misgivings about the wisdom and morality of the escalating U.S. military intervention in Southeast Asia.

The second development was economic. The relative economic decline of the United States vis-à-vis Western Europe and Japan created balance-of-payments problems that forced the Nixon administration to abandon the gold standard in 1971 to avert a financial crisis. The oil shock of 1973, during which petroleum prices quadrupled, undermined the advanced as well as the less-developed economies and, incidentally, highlighted the failures of U.S. diplomacy in the Middle East. The costs of the Vietnam War, which Nixon extended to Cambodia and intensified in Laos, continued to escalate, even after the president announced the first withdrawals of U.S. troops.

The economic dominance of the United States in Latin America, absolute in the immediate aftermath of World War II, eroded irrevocably thereafter. As the European and Japanese economies recovered in the 1950s, prewar trade patterns were restored. By the early 1960s U.S. multinational companies began to be confronted with competition from outside the hemisphere for investment opportunities. The profitability of many ventures depended on tax and regulatory concessions negotiated with national governments, often with the help of diplomats from the companies' home countries. By the early 1970s Western Europe's stake in Latin America had not only recovered from the effects of the depression and World War II but also had begun to overtake that of the United States. Japan had become a major economic actor in Latin America as well.

In 1948 the six isthmian countries sent an average of more than 80 percent of their exports to the United States (see Table 1.2). Exports to United States had fallen to 56.2 percent by 1960 and to 40.6 percent by 1970. The decline in imports from the United States was even sharper—from 77.6 percent in 1948 to 36.2 percent in 1970. The decline continued, though at a slower rate, throughout the 1970s. By 1980 the six isthmian countries sent only 39.2 percent of their exports to the United States and received only 32.8 percent of their imports from this country. The U.S. share of new direct investment in the six countries also declined sharply in the 1970s. While U.S. firms accounted for more than 90 percent of the region's stock of foreign direct investment in 1967, their share had dropped to less than 75 percent by 1978. Similar trends occurred in U.S. trade with, and investment in, nearly all the other Latin American countries. With a growing stake in the region's economy, the countries of Western Europe (and, to a lesser extent, Japan) found additional reasons for formulating their own foreign policies toward Latin America.

The initial signs of this independence could be seen in official assistance to business interests competing with U.S. firms. Most Latin American governments welcomed opportunities to diversify their external economic ties. In addition to the economic advantages of diversification, declining dependence on the United States could reduce constraints on economic policy making. Whereas the United States had a long history of military intervention and political meddling, and often deliberately confused nationalist and reformist efforts at taxation, regulation, and nationalization of U.S. businesses with "Communism," the governments of Western Europe and Japan had no such record. Western Europe and Japan thus managed to exploit the impression that they were more sympathetic to state intervention in the economy than the United States at a time when many governments, authoritarian and democratic alike, were pursuing aggressively interventionist economic programs. To facilitate trade and favorable treatment for their investors, Canada, Western Europe, and Japan (with U.S. encouragement at first) developed new economic aid programs just as the U.S. commitment to the Alliance for Progress was declining. In the six isthmian countries U.S. aid consistently accounted for more than 90 percent of all bilateral assistance to the region from the end of World War II until the beginning of the 1970s. Then U.S. aid fell precipitously, from 94.1 percent in 1970 to a low of 44.7 percent in the last year of the Ford administration. In Central America, West German economic aid consistently rivaled that of the United States; Canadian, French, and Japanese aid programs played important roles as well.[5]

As U.S. power and influence in the hemisphere eroded, the larger Latin American countries moved to emancipate themselves from U.S. constraints on their foreign and economic policy making. This trend, together with the U.S. policy of détente with the Soviet Union and Nixon's recognition of the People's Republic of China, called into question the U.S. policy of isolating Communist Cuba. Despite initial U.S. government opposition, most Latin American governments reestablished economic and diplomatic ties to Cuba, although the United States was able to stifle interest in inviting Cuba to rejoin the OAS. The growing vacuum of power in the region encouraged Mexico, Venezuela, Colombia, and eventually a number of the smaller countries in Central America to formulate and pursue policies independent of the United States (and at times even hostile to U.S. objectives) in regard to a growing list of other issues and problems. Their diplomatic independence was further enhanced by a marked shift in sources of public finance, from U.S. aid and loans from the multilateral lending agencies led by the United States to private credit offered by U.S. and European commercial banks awash in funds deposited by the oil-exporting countries of the Middle East. The United States still had means to discourage independence and make it costly to pursue—especially in the case of its Caribbean and Central American clients—but its capacity to do so had diminished substantially.

The Western Hemisphere, and particularly Central America, stood near the bottom of the list of the Nixon administration's priorities. The Alliance for Progress disappeared from official discourse as soon as Nixon was inaugurated in 1969. In a major policy address early in his administration, Nixon called for a new "realism" in U.S. relations with the region's military rulers. Although this speech was widely interpreted as a departure from previous policy, the Johnson administration had already abandoned even rhetorical condemnation of most of the hemisphere's repressive governments. The major innovation of the Nixon administration was its decision to make large cuts in economic assistance to Latin America. U.S. policy reverted, in effect, to "the cheap backyard" approach of the first six years of the Eisenhower administration—an approach Nixon himself had criticized a decade earlier. The administration reduced aid to the region by nearly half. In Central

America, U.S. aid (in 1982 dollars) fell from $273.8 million in 1968 to $149.0 million in 1973. Eventually, Secretary of State Henry Kissinger responded to critics of the administration's "abandonment" of the region by calling for a "new dialogue" between the United States and Latin America, but since he had little to say, no time to listen, and less and less money to spend, nothing of substance followed.[6]

The first test of the new administration's low-profile approach in Central America occurred when a full-scale war, now known as the Soccer War, broke out between El Salvador and Honduras on 14 July 1969.[7] Rivalry, tensions, hostility, and even open warfare between the two countries had a long history. At issue in 1969 was a small patch of inhospitable terrain (measuring 419 square kilometers) claimed by the two countries, whose borders had been in dispute for more than a century. Tensions erupted in 1968, when the Honduran government, facing a growing trade deficit with El Salvador, imposed a 30 percent surcharge on imports of Salvadoran-manufactured goods and launched a campaign to induce Hondurans to buy Honduran goods.[8] The propaganda accused the Salvadorans of producing shoddy merchandise; eventually the press began labeling all Salvadorans as cheaters and exploiters. A major new source of tensions developed when Honduran President Brigadier General López Arellano responded to mounting pressures for land reform, including a wave of peasant seizures of private lands, by ordering the eviction of thousands of Salvadoran squatters from publicly owned lands near the Salvadoran border. Once cleared of Salvadoran immigrants, the lands were to be distributed to landless Honduran farmers. The Salvadoran government, faced with similar agrarian pressures, feared that the Honduran "land reform" would push thousands of newly landless peasants back into El Salvador, where they would add to existing unrest.

In late June 1969, when the Honduran expulsions began, the Salvadoran government lodged a formal complaint against Honduras before the Inter-American Human Rights Commission of the OAS, accusing Honduras of massive abuses against the 300,000 Salvadoran citizens living there.[9] Newspapers in El Salvador published highly colored accounts of mistreatment of Salvadoran citizens by Honduran authorities. The Honduran press responded by whipping up sentiment against resident Salvadorans, whose presence allegedly retarded the economy and threatened national sovereignty. By early July 17,000 Salvadoran refugees had crossed the border. The press frenzy in El Salvador reached a peak when Honduran crowds in Tegucigalpa rioted and attacked Salvadoran fans after the first of three World Cup elimination soccer matches between the national teams of the two countries.[10] After the second game, held in San Salvador the next week, Salvadoran fans assaulted the Honduran team. When the Honduran media gave emotional accounts of the incident, attacks on Salvadorans occurred in Tegucigalpa and in several Honduran towns along the border. On 27 June, the day after the second game, El Salvador broke off diplomatic relations with Honduras; Honduras broke relations a day later. Both sides sent troops to reinforce their borders, and a series of incidents and shootouts occurred in which each side blamed the other. On 14 July the Salvadoran army launched a full-scale attack across the border, with the stated purpose of protecting Salvadoran citizens in Honduras from further abuse.

The U.S. administration received detailed accounts of these developments. A more active diplomacy could have prevented the war. In May 1969 Nelson Rockefeller had visited both countries as Nixon's special envoy and held detailed discussions with their leaders. U.S. embassies and military missions in Honduras and El Salvador were in a position to provide precise information on the extent and seriousness of preparations for combat.[11] President Nixon and his chief foreign policy advisers, however, were mainly occupied with preparing for their trip to Southeast Asia at the end of the month. The United States made no effort to avert the conflict between Honduras and El Salvador, even after the two countries had severed relations. Once the war began, the administration limited itself to imposing an arms embargo on both nations and initially left diplomatic efforts to end the war to the OAS.

The Salvadoran army, better led and equipped, seized a series of Honduran towns and villages, penetrating well beyond the disputed territory to within 75 miles of the Honduran capital, Tegucigalpa. Disorganized units of the Honduran army were reported to have ceased fighting the Salvadorans to engage in banditry. The Honduran air force, however, used its outdated subsonic *Corsair* jet fighters to inflict heavy damage on the Salvadoran oil refinery at Acajutla (jointly owned by the Shell and Standard Oil companies) and on the Shell storage facilities at El Cutuco. Equally outdated Salvadoran P-51s bombed Honduran border towns in support of their invading troops. The war lasted barely four days, by the end of which time both sides began to run out of ammunition.[12] The OAS efforts to arrange a cease-fire were thus fated to succeed, but U.S. pressure (including the threat of an economic embargo) was required to ensure El Salvador's withdrawal from the 1,600 square kilometers of Honduran territory its troops had occupied. The OAS sent observers to monitor the cease-fire, the withdrawal of Salvadoran troops, and the treatment of Salvadoran citizens living in Honduras.[13]

The Soccer War cost the two countries approximately 2,000 lives (most of them Honduran) and sent more than 100,000 Salvadoran residents of Honduras fleeing across the border into refugee camps in El Salvador. Hondurans blamed the United States for their defeat; they were particularly bitter about the arms embargo, which violated the terms of their military assistance agreement with the United States and prevented them from repelling an invasion of their territory. The Salvadorans, equally bitter, blamed the United States for forcing their army to stop short of a well-deserved victory and for doing nothing about Honduran persecution of Salvadoran citizens. In the United States, congressional critics pointed out that both sides of the conflict fought with weapons supplied entirely by the United States and questioned the wisdom of military aid to military regimes in the Western Hemisphere and other third world countries. Democratic Senator William J. Fulbright of Arkansas, chairman of the Senate Foreign Relations Committee, remarked that "they might have solved [their differences] with fists and feet if we had not furnished them the arms to use instead." His Republican counterpart, Senator Jacob K. Javits of New York, agreed.[14]

The most serious consequence of the Soccer War for Central America as a whole was the damage it did to the CACM. Trade between Honduras and El Salvador, important before the war, was embargoed by Honduras. Already convinced that it had not received its fair share of the CACM's economic benefits (while Salvadoran industry was booming), Honduras withdrew from the CACM. Although the CACM had helped to stimulate import-substituting industries throughout Central America, the "easy stage" of this growth had already reached its limit by the time the war broke out. The next stage, involving the development of intermediate and heavy industries, would have required a strengthening of the integrated-industries provisions of the CACM treaty, which the United States had always opposed. The United States therefore did little to save the CACM, other than to express support for a revival of trade in the region.

The Nixon and Ford administrations took a similarly low-profile approach to relations with Panama. The Nixon administration had no trouble establishing good relations with the military regime that had taken over Panama the previous October. In March 1969, however, when the National Guard commander, Colonel Boris Martínez, announced a sweeping agrarian reform and seemed to encourage a renewal of demonstrations against U.S. control of the canal zone, the U.S. administration supported a new coup, led by Colonel Omar Torrijos. When Torrijos was challenged by other guard officers, who attempted their own coup in December, the United States quietly supported him.[15]

The canal issue arose, nonetheless, to trouble U.S.-Panamanian relations. Torrijos was determined to push the United States toward a new canal treaty—one that would embody more concessions from the United States than the hapless Robles had been able to extract from the Johnson administration. Torrijos's strategy for accomplishing this goal had three parts. First, he moved to consolidate domestic support for his regime by proclaiming modest reforms and by pacifying the student movement that had led anti-U.S. demonstrations in the past. In 1970 he mollified the business elite with banking legislation that turned Panama into a kind of isthmian Switzerland, where regulation was minimal and secret accounts could be opened without threat of disclosure. Second, he sought support for a new canal treaty among his Latin American neighbors. Democratic regimes supported Panamanian claims because local public opinion had long been supportive. As the military leader of a military government, Torrijos managed to persuade most of the generals governing the rest of the region to support him as well; some welcomed the opportunity for a relatively low-cost way of demonstrating their independence of the United States. Third, he sought to enlist the support of external powers through the United Nations. He invited the Security Council to meet in Panama in March 1973, at which time it passed a resolution favoring renegotiation of the 1903 treaty, essentially on Panamanian terms, with only the United States dissenting.[16]

The United States responded to these efforts by agreeing to new negotiations in 1971. But when it appeared that opposition, especially within the Republican party, would either defeat a new treaty in the U.S. Senate or force the president to pay too high a political price to secure its passage, the administration simply stalled, refusing to accede to Panama's main demand: the restoration of full, unimpeded sovereignty over the canal zone, including its military facilities.[17] The talks went nowhere, and Torrijos began to complain. As preparations got under way in Panama City for the U.N. Security Council meeting, the U.S. press reported that members of "the White House 'plumbers' unit, now famous for the Watergate burglary and various other crimes, [had been] assigned by unnamed top administration officials to kill Torrijos"—just as Torrijos was beginning his noisy efforts to push the United States into new talks.[18]

After Nixon's resignation in 1974, the United States appeared to give way. Secretary of State Henry Kissinger agreed to a new agenda for canal talks in a meeting with Panamanian Foreign Minister Juan Tack in February 1974. The eight-point Kissinger-Tack agreement included a provision according to which the canal zone would disappear and Panama would assume full sovereignty at a specific future date to be set in a new round of treaty negotiations. President Ford appointed a new negotiating team, headed by career diplomat Ellsworth Bunker, who had negotiated the 1967 draft treaties. Again, the talks went nowhere, this time because of the U.S. election calendar. Under pressure from conservative senators and their allies in the Defense Department, with whom President Ford appeared to agree, Kissinger stated in September 1975 that the United States "must maintain the right, unilaterally, to defend the Canal for an indefinite future."[19] Torrijos then decided to release confidential records showing that first Kissinger and then Bunker had actually agreed not to insist on any indefinite U.S. role in defending the canal. Torrijos accused the U.S. administration of duplicity. Meanwhile, the 1976 presidential elections were fast approaching. The Panama Canal issue became the subject of repeated attacks on President Ford by California Governor Ronald Reagan in the Republican primaries, beginning in January 1976. Ford responded by emphatically endorsing, and even going beyond, Kissinger's new position on the issue. The talks went on, but without any prospect of agreement.

In the context of their reduced attention to the region as a whole, the Nixon and Ford administrations pursued a somewhat more overtly conservative, pro-military, and pro-business agenda in Central America than their two Democratic predecessors. The sharpest cuts in U.S. aid, for example, were imposed on Costa Rica, the sole remaining democracy on the isthmus, where economic assistance fell from $36.9 million in 1968 to $5.7 million in 1973.[20] The United States had actually increased aid to Costa Rica in 1969 and 1970 in order to inspire goodwill toward the United States and to undercut President José Figueres's frequent criticisms, with the aim of averting his reelection. Nevertheless, Figueres was elected to serve another term in 1970, after which U.S. aid fell precipitously. Figueres's main sins, other than his domestic reformism and his well-known antipathy to the Somozas in Nicaragua, were that he legalized the Costa Rican Communist party and followed other Latin American countries in establishing diplomatic and trade relations with the Soviet Union.[21] For a time the CIA worked actively to undermine the new government and seems to have been involved in a plot to assassinate Figueres. The CIA station chief was recalled by Washington after Figueres exposed the scheme.

In Nicaragua the Nixon administration applied pressure on Conservative party opposition leaders to sign a new "pact" in 1972 with the Somoza regime that virtually guaranteed the election of Anastasio Somoza Debayle in rigged elections two years later. The United States signaled its satisfaction with the accord by restoring aid cuts that had been imposed the year before. In Honduras the United States looked the other way when United Brands—successor to UFCO—bribed leading politicians, including the president, General López Arellano, into authorizing new tax breaks in 1971–72. The U.S. administration actively aided the efforts of U.S. banana companies to undermine a 1974 agreement among producing countries (including Panama, Costa Rica, Guatemala, Honduras, and Colombia) to impose a higher uniform tax on banana exports.[22] In El Salvador, when the military regime refused to accept the results of the 1972 national elections, which had been won by a coalition of Christian Democrats and Social Democrats, the U.S. administration had little to say. The military declared its own candidate the winner and brutally suppressed all protests, including an abortive coup by dissident army officers opposed to the electoral fraud and the ensuing repression. President Nixon did, however, join with the Pope and a number of Latin American leaders in urging the release of José Napoleón Duarte, the coalition's presidential candidate, who had been seized in the Venezuelan Embassy and severely beaten while in military custody. Duarte was then put aboard a plane, bound for exile in Venezuela. In Guatemala the military launched unprecedented repression against the civilian opposition during the presidency of Colonel Carlos Arana Osorio, elected in 1970 by means of massive fraud and intimidation. Though the Guatemalan army had already defeated the guerrillas with U.S. aid and thus had no plausible security grounds for its behavior, Washington actually increased military aid.[23] As long as the military regimes of the region did not harm U.S. business interests and avoided creating embarrassing international incidents, the United States left them free to manage their domestic affairs.

During eight years of Republican foreign policy making, little attention and few resources were focused on the Western Hemisphere. When Washington did formulate and pursue coherent objectives in Central America, it departed from previous policies only in the grim self-righteousness with which it openly supported local ultraconservatives and military establishments. The neglect of the region by the Nixon and Ford administrations left them free to concentrate on other international issues and resulted in no notable or costly foreign policy failures. In the short run, therefore, it proved to be eminently sensible. The conditions that made neglect a viable policy, however, were the product of the more activist foreign policy making of the Kennedy-Johnson years. When Nixon assumed office Cuba was isolated; military regimes had succeeded, with U.S. help, in suppressing guerrilla movements (along with most peaceful dissent); and the United States had increased its economic leverage by tying U.S. and IADB development lending to economic plans approved in Washington. By the time Jimmy Carter was elected in 1976, however, Cuba had diplomatic and trade relations with most of the hemisphere,[24] new opposition movements (including a new generation of guerrillas) were forming, and U.S. aid to Central America had declined to its lowest levels in more than a decade.

THE CARTER STRATEGY: PANAMA AND HUMAN RIGHTS

The presidency of Jimmy Carter (1977–81) marked a modest change in U.S. policy toward Latin America in general and Central America in particular. In its first months in office the new administration developed a coherent strategy to restore the U.S. position in the region. First, the new president decided to negotiate and secure ratification of a new Panama Canal Treaty. On this issue the United States still had the upper hand. The status of the canal was within the power of the United States to decide. Moreover, the United States still had the capacity to exert influence on the Panamanian government's decision-making processes (unlike a number of the larger Latin American countries) and could thus exert sufficient pressure on Torrijos to ensure an agreement, even if it fell short of Panama's aspirations. The authoritarian character of the Torrijos regime insulated it from effective opposition to a treaty that would fall short of nationalist goals. Second, Carter launched a campaign on behalf of human rights, backed by both pressure and legislation, to distance the United States from the most unsavory (and increasingly unstable) of the authoritarian regimes in the region. The administration targeted the Central American dictatorships for U.S. condemnation. Several were egregious human rights violators by any standards, all were small enough to expect that U.S. pressure would have some effect, and U.S. interests in the region were so small that no important

U.S. interest group seemed likely to be discomforted. Third, Carter sought, despite severe budget constraints, to increase U.S. economic aid to the region, both to recover U.S. leverage and to assist U.S. firms in an environment that had become dramatically more competitive. Finally, he took steps to normalize relations with Cuba in order to remove a source of tension and potential support to hostile political forces while the United States was recovering its strength in the region. Carter also believed it was prudent both to recognize the failure of past U.S. efforts to isolate Cuba and to explore the extent to which a step-by-step normalization of relations with the United States might induce the Cuban government to alter policies to which the United States objected. The Carter administration was successful in its Panama and human rights initiatives, achieved modest success in its efforts to increase economic aid, and failed only in its Cuban policy. Despite its achievements, however, the administration's strategy was overwhelmed by an explosion of revolutionary turmoil in Central America that it was powerless to avert and unable to control.

The Central American economies, buoyant during the export boom of the 1960s, suffered major setbacks in the 1970s, while deteriorating social conditions contributed to political polarization throughout the isthmus.[25] High prices for the region's traditional exports—bananas, coffee, cotton, sugar, and beef—briefly raised profits for elite export producers, as did the "green revolution," which favored agriculturalists with the resources to invest in irrigation, fertilizers, and new equipment. Small-scale export producers, along with large numbers of peasants producing food crops for domestic consumption, were increasingly marginalized, and landownership became even more concentrated. The virtual collapse of the CACM after the Soccer War checked the growth of markets for manufactured goods. The oil shock of 1973 also hit Central American industries hard, along with rising prices for other manufacturing inputs that had to be imported. Artisan and small-scale industrial producers suffered most; this intensified the tendency toward proletarianization of the work force and further concentration of output in the hands of the larger companies (many of them foreign-owned), which could better weather the storm. Inflation drove down rural as well as urban real wages throughout the isthmus. To cover the rising cost of imports and to assuage an escalating fiscal crisis, the Central American republics borrowed heavily, more and more from private commercial banks at rising rates of interest, and simultaneously cut back on public spending, particularly on social services. Natural disasters compounded these man-made problems: an earthquake destroyed most of downtown Managua in December 1972, Hurricane Fifi devastated the banana plantations on the north coast of Honduras in September 1974, and a series of earthquakes caused extensive damage in Guatemala in February 1976.

The effect of these developments was to raise organized popular discontent to levels unprecedented in Central American history. Trade unions mobilized in defense of living standards in the cities, while peasant protests led to widespread, though largely uncoordinated, land seizures. Even rural workers and landless peasants—among the most difficult to organize and the most easily intimidated of the region's poor—joined unions, social movements, and political parties in large numbers. Where political authorities attempted to accommodate and co-opt this new militancy—in Costa Rica and, to a lesser extent, in Honduras and Panama—economic policy making became more erratic, but social peace was preserved. In El Salvador, Guatemala, and Nicaragua, where elites resisted fiercely, violence became endemic. Political and social conflict reached a peak during the Carter administration, when the Sandinista National Liberation Front (FSLN) tapped both popular and elite resentment toward the Somoza regime in Nicaragua to lead a revolution that hurled the Somozas from power in July 1979. In El Salvador and Guatemala, where the economic crises of the 1970s had stimulated the development of powerful business and employer associations to coordinate control over government policies, elite resistance to change solidified, official repression of dissent intensified, and full-scale civil wars erupted. With U.S. political and economic resources already weakened by a decade of neglect that no longer seemed benign, the Carter administration failed in its efforts to control events and restore U.S. power in the region.

When the Carter administration took office, none of the president's advisers, not even the intelligence agencies, predicted the turmoil that was to come. The president's strategy called for a speedy solution to the Panama Canal issue, and the administration devoted its initial energies to this objective. Carter reappointed Nixon's chief negotiator, Ellsworth Bunker, along with former OAS ambassador Sol Linowitz, to head the U.S. negotiating team. The talks with Panama took nearly a year because of Torrijos's reluctance to accept the U.S. demand for a role in defending the canal into the indefinite future. On 11 August 1977 the negotiators announced that they had agreed on the texts of two treaties—one covering the period up to the year 2000, when Panama would assume full control of the canal, and the other on the defense of the neutrality of the canal after that date. Carter and Torrijos signed the treaties at a formal ceremony at OAS headquarters in Washington on 7 September 1977.

The treaties were less favorable to Panamanian interests than the Kissinger-Tack agreement of 1974 but less humiliating than the three draft treaties that had cost Robles so dearly in 1967. The United States agreed to permit Panama to assume territorial jurisdiction over the canal zone as soon as the treaties were ratified. After three years the canal zone would cease to exist, and Panama would take over full legal jurisdiction of the area. The United States, however, would retain control of the canal itself and continue to assume primary responsibility for its defense until 1 January 2000. Panama's share of the canal's revenues would rise dramatically right away, from an annuity of $2.3 million to between $40 and $50 million per year. In the year 2000 all revenues from the canal would go to Panama. Panama agreed to allow the U.S. School of the Americas, which trained Latin American military officers, to continue in operation in the zone for at least five more years, while the United States agreed to remove the headquarters of the U.S. Southern Command right after ratification. The United States also agreed to close all remaining U.S. bases in the canal zone by 2000, but the treaty did not forbid the two parties from negotiating new leases extending beyond that date. In addition, the United States conceded to Panama primary responsibility for defense of the canal beginning in 2000. Panama's greatest concession was to give the United States the permanent and unilateral right to defend the canal's neutrality, as well as the right, in case of emergency, to send its ships through the canal ahead of all others.

As Walter Lafeber put it, the Panama Canal treaties constituted a "diplomatic triumph"[26] for the United States. The United States agreed to give up (after another quarter century) a constant irritant in its relations with Panama and Latin America but obtained Panama's agreement to unilateral U.S. intervention in perpetuity. The United States gave up military bases of little importance to its security but retained the right to have its warships and commercial vessels take precedence over all other ships in case of a U.S.-declared emergency.

As expected, Torrijos expeditiously engineered Panama's ratification of the treaty, which required a national referendum. He maintained strict censorship of the media, kept a number of prominent opponents in exile, and controlled the vote count. The Carter administration could not act so quickly. The president, impatient to get on with the rest of his agenda, submitted the treaties to the Senate as soon as they were signed, hoping for quick ratification. Opinion polls showed widespread public ignorance of the treaties' terms, as well as opposition to their passage. The Senate leadership urged delay to give the president time to make his case to the public and to recruit crucial Senate votes. The bruising fight over ratification in the U.S. Senate did not begin until the following spring and lasted an unprecedented three months. The first of the two treaties passed by a vote of 68 to 32 (one vote over the two-thirds necessary for ratification) in March 1978; the second treaty passed by an identical margin four weeks later, on 18 April.[27] Despite these victories, however, the administration had to mount another time-consuming effort to secure passage of the legislation implementing the accords, which did not finally pass the U.S. House of Representatives until 26 September 1979.

In the end, ironically, both Carter and Torrijos emerged weakened by their success. Many in the Senate charged Carter with tactical errors that prolonged the debates. Whether the accusation was true or not, the president had been forced to bargain; in order to find the votes needed to ratify the Panama treaties in the Senate, he had to dispense favors and threats that he could otherwise have applied in securing other legislation. In the course of the Senate debate Carter was compelled to accept modifications to the treaties that embarrassed Torrijos but strengthened the provisions specifying the U.S. right to intervene and to claim precedence for its shipping. The House imposed further modifications, equally embarrassing to Torrijos, that removed the fig leaf of Panamanian participation in controlling canal operations up to the year 2000.[28] The maneuverings, which Carter resisted, led to charges that he had failed to protect U.S. interests in the negotiations adequately and damaged his credibility. In Panama the treaties became less and less popular as the U.S. debates dragged on; the Senate and House modifications were not viewed favorably, and U.S. congressmen made statements that Panamanians considered insulting and demeaning. In the long run the major political effect of the treaties in Panama was to shift the focus of internal discontent away from the United States and onto the Torrijos government. Meanwhile, not only had Torrijos been forced to swallow the treaty modifications (and U.S. congressional rhetoric) without protest; he had also been pushed by the attendant scrutiny of his regime and the pressure of Carter's human rights campaign to relax restrictions on opposition political activity, beginning in the spring of 1978.

Carter's human rights initiative advanced simultaneously with the Panama negotiations and debates. In 1976 Congress had already voted to require the Ford administration to report on the condition of human rights in all countries receiving U.S. military aid. The new administration's efforts included the creation of the office of assistant secretary of state for human rights in the State Department, the withdrawal of military aid from countries with documented human rights abuses, and an active diplomacy to convey U.S. concerns to offending regimes. In 1979, with the administration's support, Congress extended the reporting requirement to include all members of the United Nations and made economic aid partly conditional on human rights performance.

Central America became "one of the primary foci of the Carter human rights policy."[29] In its first year the Carter administration announced that it was cutting off military aid to El Salvador and Guatemala. With a self-confidence nurtured by two decades of U.S. training and weaponry, the military governments of the two countries promptly responded by rejecting U.S. military assistance and denouncing the new policy as an unwarranted intrusion into their internal affairs. The effect of the U.S. move was further mitigated by the administration's decision to continue economic aid, which actually increased in the Carter years, in an effort to avoid punishing needy recipients for the sins of their repressive governments. In El Salvador widespread protests against the elections of 1977, which produced another fraudulent triumph for the candidate of the military high command, were violently suppressed, and the new government of General Carlos Humberto Romero embarked on a campaign of terror against the opposition, making use of death squads to eliminate individuals identified by the ORDEN spy network, which had been set up with U.S. help in the 1960s. The ranks of the small and fractious guerrilla movements founded in the aftermath of the 1972 elections swelled with new recruits convinced of the futility of seeking change by more peaceful means. Full-scale civil war was not long in coming.

In Guatemala conditions deteriorated even more rapidly. Military candidates won the rigged national elections of 1974 (General Kjell Laugerud) and 1978 (General Romeo Lucas García) without major difficulties, but from 1977 on the government faced a new guerrilla insurgency more powerful and more popular than any that had preceded it. As in El Salvador, the guerrilla resurgence coincided with a revival of popular protests and mobilizations that pitted opposition political parties, student groups, trade unions, peasant organizations, and radicalized elements of the Catholic church against the government. The intensity of the repression in Guatemala was compounded by fear on the part of the Ladino[30] elite of a political and social awakening among the country's indigenous people. For the first time, popular organizations as well as the guerrilla movements began to recruit successfully in the highland provinces, which had mainly indigenous populations. By the late 1970s "both the government and military were increasingly hard-pressed to maintain control in large areas of the countryside, and sometimes in the capital itself; the bulk of the 100,000 people estimated to have been killed for political reasons since 1954 lost their lives during this period [1977–83]."[31] The Carter administration voiced its disapproval in the annual human rights reports issued by the State Department but lacked any leverage with which to modify the behavior of the Guatemalan regime. By the time the United States imposed its arms embargo in 1977 it was far too late.

In Honduras, however, the Carter policy produced results. The 1975 removal of General López Arellano for accepting bribes led to a period of collective leadership in which the Superior Council of the Armed Forces (CONSUFFAA) was reorganized and began to function as a representative body of the officer corps. The council named General Juan Alberto Melgar Castro as president; he established an advisory council to prepare an electoral law to return the country to civilian rule. Melgar Castro was ousted in 1978 amid charges that high officials of his regime had engaged in drug smuggling and other crimes. The military was divided on the wisdom of giving up power. Consistent U.S. pressure helped to ensure that the three-man junta that replaced Melgar continued with plans to return the country to civilian rule. The transition began with elections to a constituent assembly in 1980; presidential elections took place in November 1981. The country's first elected civilian president since the overthrow of Villeda Morales in 1963, Liberal party leader Roberto Suazo Córdova took office in January 1982.

The U.S. emphasis on human rights should have encouraged a return to cordial relations between Washington and Costa Rica. Figueres was succeeded by his Partido de Liberación Nacional (PLN) compatriot Daniel Oduber

(1974–78) and by a former PLN leader, Rodrigo Carazo (1978–82). U.S. aid to Costa Rica did increase, though not to pre-1970 levels, but relations remained cool—first because of Oduber's ambitious and underfinanced industrial development program, which the United States considered too nationalist and wasteful, and then despite Carazo's neoliberal correctives, because of his administration's turn toward a more independent and nationalist foreign policy that included support for the Sandinista rebels in Nicaragua. Although the Carter administration kept these two Costa Rican governments at arm's length and found it convenient to punish Carazo's independence by ignoring his appeals for support in the face of the country's economic difficulties, it did not actively conspire to provoke a political crisis in Costa Rica, as the Nixon administration had done during the Figueres years.

The Carter administration's efforts to increase foreign aid to Latin America in general and to Central America in particular yielded mixed results. Congress imposed substantial cuts in the administration's foreign aid requests in every year but 1977. In real terms U.S. aid to Central America in the Carter years averaged 9.2 percent more than during the Nixon-Ford years—too little to restore the aid levels of the Alliance era. Given the dimensions of the economic and social crises engulfing the region, and given the administration's interest in reasserting U.S. power, the aid figures (as low as $2.3 million to Panama in 1980 and no higher than $66.2 million to Honduras in the same year)[32] were woefully inadequate.

CARTER AND THE SANDINISTA REVOLUTION

On 19 July 1979 the Sandinista National Liberation Front seized control of the government of Nicaragua. Founded in 1961, the FSLN had fought for 18 years to end the Somoza family's grip on the country. With U.S. military aid and advisers, Somoza's National Guard defeated FSLN guerrillas in 1962 and again in 1967 and 1972. After 1972, however, the regime's power eroded. The Somoza government responded to the earthquake of 23 December 1972 with such incompetence and corruption that it alienated many who had tolerated, and even some who had supported and benefited from, the Somozas' rule.[33] The regime's response to the earthquake became emblematic of its rapacity: the Somoza family appropriated a major portion of the money and supplies sent to the country for earthquake relief from around the world and awarded cleanup and rebuilding contracts to its own companies. After the earthquake, President Anastasio Somoza Debayle (son of the founder of the dynasty), whose illegitimate half-brother was promoted to the rank of general and given command of the National Guard, broke the family's pact with the Nicaraguan business community, according to which the Somozas had agreed not to use their political power to squeeze out or take over businesses that competed with their own. In March 1974 the country's major business association, COSIP, denounced the government and called on Somoza to resign. At the same time, widespread popular discontent became evident in the growing strength of trade unions in the face of deteriorating real wages, peasant protests against growing landlessness and marginalization, student demonstrations for democracy and social justice, and denunciations of Somoza's rule by the (occasionally censored) opposition newspaper *La Prensa* and by the country's leading intellectuals and opposition political leaders.

The FSLN became identified in the popular imagination as the major force in the struggle against the regime when a small group of guerrillas invaded a private party in honor of departing U.S. Ambassador (and Somoza confidant) Turner Shelton on 27 December 1974. Somoza was forced to release 14 political prisoners, publish an FSLN statement in the official paper, pay a ransom of $1 million, and give the raiders safe conduct to leave the country in order to secure the release of hostages who included high government officials and members of the Somoza family.[34] Aside from small-scale guerrilla actions and clandestine organizing, the FSLN did not mount a coordinated military effort against the regime until October 1977, when it failed to achieve its immediate military objectives or to provoke widespread public demonstrations against the regime. Then, on 10 January 1978, Pedro Joaquín Chamorro, the publisher of *La Prensa* and a longtime foe of the Somozas, was assassinated by unknown assailants in Managua. Most Nicaraguans attributed the murder to Somoza; for many, it symbolized the failure of nonviolent methods to reform the regime or remove the Somozas from power. Two weeks later the first of a series of general strikes was called by a broad coalition of opposition groups, including the FSLN; when COSIP endorsed the strike, it simultaneously became a national lockout. The strike lasted three weeks and paralyzed the nation's economy.

On 21 February 1978, soon after the strike ended, residents of Monimbó (a poor section of the town of Masaya, located 20 kilometers southeast of Managua) took up arms against the National Guard in what became the first of a series of violent confrontations between the regime and the impoverished residents of urban shanty towns and working-class barrios. On 22 August FSLN commandos staged a daring daytime raid, seized the National Palace in Managua, and held the entire Nicaraguan Congress hostage until the government again freed prisoners (this time 50), published another FSLN manifesto, paid $500,000 (the original demand had been for $10 million), and guaranteed the raiders and the freed prisoners safe conduct to leave the country. Enthusiastic crowds cheered the raiders on their way to the airport, where they boarded planes sent by the governments of Venezuela and Panama. The FSLN and its allies called a new general strike three days later. The next month FSLN troops invaded from Honduras and briefly seized the northern town of Estelí. By this time attacks on the National Guard had spread throughout the country. In the fall, during U.S.-supported

OAS mediation efforts, FSLN attacks slowed somewhat, although the regime remained off-balance, constantly plagued by strikes, small-scale attacks on barracks and garrisons, and minor protests and uprisings in the cities.

When the mediation failed at the end of 1978 the FSLN attacks resumed with a vengeance. In April 1979 the FSLN retook Estelí and held it for a week, while other units launched small-scale attacks on other towns and cities. On 2 June the FSLN launched a general offensive throughout the country. León, the country's second largest city, fell on 17 June, Masaya on 24 June. Though most of the National Guard continued to fight until Somoza fled the country on 17 July, it suffered so many disastrous military defeats in the last weeks of the fighting that its collapse became inevitable. Support for the revolution was so widespread among all social classes and political organizations in the country that the survival of the Somoza regime, with or without Somoza at the helm, could not have been guaranteed without a foreign occupation.[35]

When the Carter administration took office in January 1977 the unanimous assessment of the U.S. intelligence community was that Somoza faced no insurmountable difficulties and would retain power indefinitely. In the 30 months it took for the regime to fall, the U.S. administration followed a consistent strategy aimed at securing Somoza's departure from power while simultaneously preventing the FSLN from taking control of the country. U.S. officials pressured Somoza to respect civil liberties and to open the country's political system, confident that free elections would ease him out and allow for a peaceful transition to a moderate, pro-U.S. democratic regime. The initial U.S. efforts to pressure Somoza into reform succeeded within a year. In August 1977 Somoza had a mild heart attack; on returning to Managua in September after treatment in the United States, he lifted the state of siege he had imposed after the FSLN's 1974 "Christmas party raid." Then, after the January 1978 assassination of Chamorro and the general strike that followed, U.S. Ambassador Mauricio Solaún succeeded in persuading Somoza to announce his intention not to run for reelection at the end of his term in 1981. Events had already moved so far, however, that this announcement was seen in Nicaragua as a defiant assertion of Somoza's intention to remain in power for three more years rather than as an opening to a peaceful transition to democratic rule.

As the revolution spread, the United States shifted its efforts to securing Somoza's departure before 1981 in order to ensure an orderly transition that would put moderate opposition leaders in power, exclude or minimize FSLN influence on the new government, and leave the National Guard intact. To secure such an outcome the United States played a double game. On the one hand it recognized that the FSLN and its allies helped to increase the pressure on Somoza to make concessions; on the other it sought to prevent the Somoza regime from collapsing until an acceptably moderate alternative could be found. While the two extremes—Somoza on the right and the

FSLN on the left—were locked in mortal combat, the United States hoped to broker a manageably moderate transition in which the traditional political parties and the business community (organized in COSIP, renamed COSEP in 1978) would play the major role. Somoza's strategy also involved a double game. First, he sought to delay, undermine, or eliminate any moderate alternative in order to confront the United States with a choice between himself and the FSLN. Second, he sought to make sufficient concessions to get the United States to back off without actually giving up his power.

In the months following the January 1978 general strike, as the violence escalated, the United States pressed Somoza for additional reforms but did not explicitly demand that he step down. In June, when Carter was in Panama, he discussed the Nicaraguan situation with General Torrijos, who immediately contacted Somoza to report that the United States was preparing to abandon him unless he made concessions. Two days later, on 19 June 1978, Somoza announced that he would release political prisoners, permit exiled politicians and activists to return to the country, reform the electoral system to make an honest vote count possible, and invite the OAS Human Rights Commission to visit Nicaragua. When Carter responded two weeks later with a letter that congratulated Somoza on his new commitment to respecting human rights and democratic procedures, the moderate opposition as well as the FSLN denounced the U.S. move as an untimely expression of U.S. support for a regime the Nicaraguan people were seeking to overthrow.[36] Worse yet, the Carter letter apparently led Somoza to believe for a time that his strategy was working, that the United States was now on his side, and that he would not have to make any further concessions or consider resigning.

By the time the FSLN seized the National Palace and a second general strike erupted in August 1978, only two months after Carter's letter, the U.S. administration had become convinced that Nicaragua could not be stabilized unless Somoza stepped down. Though apparently still convinced that Somoza could survive the FSLN attacks,[37] the administration began to fear that prolonged violence would so polarize the country that the FSLN would be able to achieve a commanding position in the opposition and thus make it impossible to achieve a moderate transition. This was precisely the trap Somoza's strategy was designed to create. To avoid it the administration took three steps in September 1978. First, it increased the pressure on Somoza by suspending the U.S. military assistance program (though arms already on order continued to flow into the country). Second, it exerted intense pressure on Costa Rica, Panama, and Venezuela to stop providing covert support to the FSLN in order to reduce the tempo of military activity, which tended to increase polarization, and thus buy additional time. Third, it launched a major diplomatic effort to enlist OAS support in mediating a deal between Somoza and the "moderate," non-FSLN opposition.

The U.S. role in the OAS mediation was somewhat constrained by Carter's belief that "he should not ask a sitting president to step down, nor should he try to overthrow him."[38] Predictably, Carter's delicacy was not shared by the leaders and diplomats of the other Latin American countries recruited to join the U.S. effort. Carter thus succeeded in communicating the message while protecting the United States from the stain of interventionism that delivering it directly would have entailed. Somoza, however, was not prepared to believe the United States had abandoned him entirely without hearing it directly. The mediation effort was authorized by a meeting of the OAS foreign ministers in Washington on 21–23 September 1978. For the next three months the OAS mediators (from the United States, Guatemala, and the Dominican Republic) shuttled between Managua and Washington, and between Somoza's "bunker" and meetings with leaders of the Broad United Front (FAO), an umbrella organization that included representatives of most of the Nicaraguan opposition groups, initially including the FSLN. The mediation effort failed. The negotiators quickly settled on a national referendum as a means of permitting the population to express itself for or against the regime. Somoza, however, refused either to resign prior to the vote or to permit OAS supervision of the vote count. Despite repeated U.S. efforts, including numerous conversations between Somoza and White House emissaries, Somoza refused to budge.

By the end of 1978 the OAS mediating commission gave up its efforts. Costa Rica then broke diplomatic relations with Nicaragua; Panama, Venezuela, and Costa Rica resumed aid to the FSLN; and the three factions of the FSLN agreed in Havana to unite under a single political-military command to prepare for a final offensive. The U.S. administration reviewed its position and concluded that Somoza would not cooperate in a brokered transition as long as he felt assured that his military forces could contain the revolution. To achieve its objectives, therefore, the United States would have to play a more dangerous game, waiting until conditions in the country deteriorated to the point that Somoza would be forced by military reversals to negotiate. The United States would then have to work to bring a moderate regime to power, but under far less favorable conditions. The alternative scenario—that the National Guard would fight the FSLN to a standoff—would still weaken Somoza sufficiently to force him to negotiate, because his government would be faced with a shattered economy, an empty treasury, and no prospect of recovery without U.S. aid. On 8 February 1979 the United States formally ended all military and economic aid to the Nicaraguan government, reduced its embassy staff by one-half, and recalled Ambassador Solaún to Washington.

Having washed it hands of Somoza for the moment, the U.S. administration spent the next four months, through early June 1979, doing little more than pressuring other governments to stop providing arms to the combatants.

The Israeli government, which had already become a major weapons supplier to El Salvador and Guatemala after the United States had suspended its military aid to those countries, was persuaded to stop selling arms to Somoza. Israeli weapons and ammunition continued to flow into Nicaragua, however, from the stockpiles of the sympathetic military regimes in El Salvador and Guatemala as well as in Honduras. Venezuela stopped aiding the FSLN when a new administration took over in March. Panama ceased to provide facilities for transshipping Cuban and black-market arms in May, both because Torrijos was persuaded to worry about the passage of canal legislation in the U.S. House of Representatives and because the FSLN organized direct flights into Costa Rica, Honduras, and eventually Nicaragua itself. On 20 April, when Mexico broke diplomatic relations with Nicaragua, the United States mounted a successful effort to persuade other countries in Latin America not to follow Mexico's lead. As late as early June, when the canal legislation finally passed the House Committee, where it had been stalled, U.S. intelligence continued to predict that Somoza would survive, although doubts had been voiced since the FSLN's week-long occupation of Estelí in April.[39]

In early June, as the FSLN offensive spread throughout the country, the United States reassessed its position. By the time León fell on 17 June, the U.S. administration had launched a concerted political and diplomatic effort to secure Somoza's resignation while simultaneously averting a military defeat of the National Guard. The bargaining power the United States had had months before, when it had hoped to deliver Somoza's resignation in exchange for a major voice in the composition of a new government, had all but disappeared. The tide of battle was now turning against the regime, and the opposition—the moderates as well as the FSLN—expected Somoza to fall without U.S. help. The National Guard continued to fight, but it was impossible to know what would happen to discipline and fighting spirit should Somoza step down. When the U.S. military attaché canvassed opinion among the key officers he knew, he found unanimous loyalty to the regime and no support for a coup. Preserving the guard while ousting Somoza would be difficult to manage, but U.S. leverage with the opposition would largely disappear if the guard fell apart.

The new U.S. ambassador to Nicaragua, Lawrence Pezzullo, arrived in Managua in the midst of the most intense fighting of the revolution. He went immediately to talk to Somoza. On 19 June he reported that Somoza had agreed to resign on two conditions: that the OAS take charge of the transition to prevent the "Communists" (the FSLN) from taking power, and that he and his family receive visas that would allow them to live undisturbed in the United States. Pezzullo returned to Washington for consultations. Meanwhile, the United States had arranged for a meeting of the OAS foreign ministers to discuss the Nicaraguan crisis. U.S. Secretary of State Cyrus Vance proposed a resolution calling for the dispatch of an OAS peacekeeping force to Nicaragua to "stop the killing" and permit a negotiated end to the Somoza regime. If it had been passed and implemented, the resolution would have ensured the survival of the National Guard by placing OAS troops between the guard and the FSLN forces. The U.S. maneuver was so transparent, however, that in the end only the Somoza government supported it. The resolution that did pass called on Somoza to step down, denounced interventionism, and demanded the creation of a freely elected government in Nicaragua. Time was growing short.

On 26 June Pezzullo was back in Managua, this time with a new message: the United States wanted Somoza to delay resigning to allow time for negotiations. Now able to use Somoza's resignation as a bargaining chip, the United States set out to negotiate the composition of the post-Somoza government. Its aim, as before, was to ensure that the new regime would be controlled by pro-U.S. moderates, not by the FSLN. On the day Pezzullo returned to Managua, Deputy U.S. Assistant Secretary of State for Inter-American Affairs William P. Bowdler was in Panama, where he became the first U.S. official to meet with representatives of the FSLN. The Nicaraguan opposition had already named a governing Junta (council) of National Reconstruction on 17 June, the day León had fallen. Of the five members of the council, three were members of the FSLN: Daniel Ortega, Sergio Ramírez, and Moïsés Hassan. The two other members were Violeta Chamorro, widow of the slain newspaper publisher, and Alfonso Robelo, a leader of COSEP. Present at the Panama meeting were three of the council members, Chamorro, Robelo, and Ramírez. Bowdler's mission was to change the composition of the council to add enough non-FSLN members to ensure a solid majority of moderates.[40] He failed because the council had already received the support of every anti-Somoza organization in Nicaragua, including COSEP, but negotiations between U.S. officials and the council continued for the next three weeks, as the Somoza government neared collapse.

The United States was determined to enlarge the council and exerted every pressure it could to achieve this aim. The governments of Costa Rica and Venezuela were mobilized to inform the council members that they would cut off the FSLN war supplies unless the U.S. demand was met. The council resisted unanimously but played for time by continuing to negotiate. Talks between Bowdler and the council resumed in Costa Rica. On 11 July Bowdler and Pezzullo met with the Junta in San José and secured a public statement offering to incorporate into the ranks of a new Nicaraguan army all guard officers and troops who would surrender to the FSLN. On 12 July Bowdler brought Costa Rican President Carazo, Torrijos, former Venezuelan President Pérez, and former Costa Rican President Figueres to a meeting with the council and two FSLN commanders. At the end of the discussion the council sent a formal letter to the OAS agreeing to its resolution of 23 June, which called for free elections. Two days later, after more negotiations, the council publicly announced the names of the cabinet ministers it expected to appoint on taking power; the list included a majority of non-FSLN moderates.

Back in Managua, Pezzullo worked to ensure the survival of the guard and an orderly transition. Somoza would resign, to be replaced temporarily by the speaker of the Chamber of Deputies, Francisco Urcuyo Maliaño. The guard would be purged, and its new leaders would negotiate the incorporation of their forces into a new Nicaraguan army. On 15 July Somoza announced the retirement of 100 of the guard's senior officers, including all generals and most colonels and lieutenant colonels. A new commander-in-chief, selected by Pezzullo, was appointed. On the night of 16–17 July, as Estelí was falling to FSLN troops for the last time, Somoza resigned, and a rump session of the Nicaraguan Congress elected Urcuyo to replace him. Somoza left Nicaragua before dawn on 17 July.

Later that day, after a tense meeting with Pezzullo, Urcuyo made a speech in which he indicated that he expected to remain in office, called on the "irregular forces" (the FSLN) to lay down their arms, and ordered the guard to continue fighting. According to the deal Pezzullo had made with Somoza, Urcuyo should have done no more than turn over power to the council on its arrival by plane from Costa Rica. Then, according to the script, the new guard commander would discuss the guard's surrender and the incorporation of its remaining units into a new army with the proper officials of the new government. When Urcuyo balked, the council members flew instead to León, already in rebel hands, where a huge celebration of the Sandinista triumph began immediately. Pezzullo, meanwhile, issued a statement denouncing Urcuyo, gathered up what remained of the U.S. embassy staff, and flew out of Managua. Urcuyo was finally persuaded to give up the next morning, 18 July, by a phone call from Somoza in Miami. Threatened with the loss of his U.S. visa, Somoza pleaded with Urcuyo to leave. Taking belated note of the hopelessness of his position, Urcuyo left Managua that evening but refused to resign and participate in an orderly transfer of power. The council then took the position that Urcuyo's behavior had cancelled the Somoza-Pezzullo agreement; there was no longer any reason to hold talks about incorporating guard units into the new army. Because the guard was already disintegrating, the issue became moot. On 17 and 18 July guard units began surrendering in large numbers; many units simply ceased to exist as guardsmen changed to civilian clothes and went home or fled the country. The new guard commander and the remaining top officers left Managua in the early morning hours of 19 July. The Sandinista revolution had triumphed.

It has been argued that the U.S. government could have prevented this outcome, which it had worked actively to avoid, in any of four ways. First, it could have adopted the practice of most previous U.S. governments, which was to accept Somoza on his own terms. U.S. pressure on the regime to respect human rights and reform the electoral system encouraged the opposition and weakened Somoza's grip on the country—even though this pressure was initially exerted at a time when the regime appeared to be firmly in control. The key policy makers in the Carter administration did not believe, until April 1979 at the earliest, that Somoza would fall. The U.S. strategy, which aimed to divert potentially violent unrest into peaceful electoral channels, could have worked. It was defeated by Somoza's intransigence and by the unexpectedly rapid growth of revolutionary turmoil. Given the dramatic deterioration in economic and social conditions throughout Central America, and particularly in Nicaragua, in the 1970s and the repudiation of the regime by nearly every sector of Nicaraguan society, the Somoza regime would have faced a serious and possibly fatal challenge even if the United States had continued to support it. In any case, Somoza was undermined much more by financial support and arms shipments to the FSLN from other governments than by U.S. efforts to push him toward democracy.[41]

Second, the United States could have exerted effective pressure on the Latin American governments that supported the Sandinistas to cease doing so. In fact, the administration did exert pressure to that end with some success, but support for the FSLN from governments in the region was so great, and U.S. leverage so small, that the costs of an effective embargo against either side in the conflict were higher than the administration was prepared to pay—particularly in the face of intelligence reports indicating that Somoza would be able to hang on without U.S. help. The FSLN received arms and financial support from the governments of Costa Rica, Cuba, Panama, and Venezuela. It received financial and political support from all of these plus (at least) the governments of Mexico, Colombia, and the Federal Republic of Germany. It also received financial support from private citizens and nongovernmental organizations in the United States and most of the Western European countries. The U.S. government did not have the means to prevent most of this aid from reaching the FSLN. It succeeded in halting much of the logistical support and weaponry provided by Panama and Venezuela, and forced the Costa Rican government to scale back its support. It could not prevent the FSLN from purchasing arms on the international black market, nor could it stop arms shipments from Cuba. Efforts to prevent the FSLN from buying weapons on the black market (often from U.S. dealers) would have been costly and, ultimately, futile. In the case of Cuba, U.S. leverage disappeared after the collapse of talks aimed at normalizing relations. Stopping the Cuban arms flow, which was not large until the final weeks of the war, would have required cooperative efforts by the very Central American governments that supported the FSLN. In either case it would have been difficult, if not impossible, to stop weapons from entering northern Costa Rica or southern Honduras, for the same reasons it later proved impossible to stem the flow of illegal narcotics through Central America. The vast area, difficult terrain, and lack of roads or other means of access of the regions bordering Nicaragua made them impossible to police.[42]

Third, the United States could have forced Somoza from office early enough in the conflict to have been able to broker a transition without the participation of the FSLN. It failed to do so, however—not only because of Carter's scruples but also (a) because the U.S. intelligence community consistently (and accurately) reported that the National Guard had not been defeated and showed no signs of defeat or collapse until it was too late for the United States to act effectively, and (b) because in the crucial four months from February to June 1979, when the administration might have acted despite the intelligence reports, Somoza's supporters in the U.S. House of Representatives (particularly Democrat John Murphy of New York, who chaired the crucial Merchant Marine and Fisheries Committee) threatened to sabotage the legislation implementing the Panama Canal treaties if the administration moved against Somoza. To achieve the U.S. objective of a controlled transition excluding or minimizing the FSLN role would have been possible earlier, in the last three months of 1978, when the United States, acting through the OAS mediation commission, had tried and failed to get Somoza out, despite repeated though discreet White House support. Somoza refused to agree to any arrangement that included his resignation, both because he believed his forces were strong enough to defeat the rebels and because his friends in the United States, including members of Congress, had led him to discount U.S. pressures. Nothing short of escalating the pressures to the point of a credible threat of unilateral U.S. intervention— unthinkable, under the circumstances—would have made Somoza succumb.

Fourth, the United States could have dispatched troops to Nicaragua in late June or early July 1979 to prevent an FSLN victory, save the National Guard, and impose a new government. Politically, however, such a move would have been disastrous. Opinion polls showed that the U.S. public was overwhelmingly against the Somoza regime and fearful of a repetition of the Vietnam experience. Unilateral U.S. intervention was opposed by most of the Latin American countries. More important, U.S. intervention would have turned Nicaragua's civil war into a war against the foreign occupier, with the same disastrous results that U.S. intervention in Vietnam produced in the 1960s. Few in Nicaragua other than Somoza would have cooperated with such an effort. The United States could have invaded and occupied Nicaragua, but in doing so it would have destroyed any hope of installing a pro-U.S. regime able to govern without a U.S. army of occupation.

Faced with the inevitable, the Carter administration set out to control the damage.

CIVIL WAR IN EL SALVADOR

As the Carter administration moved to adjust its policies to the Sandinista victory in Nicaragua, its first concern was the danger of contagion. In Guatemala and El Salvador, conditions approaching civil war had already developed. In both cases the U.S. administration feared a repetition of the uncontrolled disintegration that had occurred in Nicaragua. In Guatemala the quarter century of military-dominated governments since the 1954 intervention had succeeded in suppressing or driving underground most of the opposition. As a result the deteriorating economic and social conditions of the 1970s produced widespread support for a renewal of guerrilla warfare. The Lucas García government responded with a new campaign of terror and repression and was impervious to U.S. suggestions that its approach was neither morally satisfying nor politically astute. Until 1982, when the unity of the armed forces cracked in the face of internal pressures and personal rivalries in the officer corps, the United States had little influence on the Guatemalan regime.

In El Salvador the officer corps was rife with personal and political conflicts, and popular political mobilization escalated to unmanageable levels in the late 1970s; thus the United States had greater leverage. Unlike the business elite of Nicaragua, a large majority of which opposed the Somoza regime, the Salvadoran business class tended to be divided according to sectoral interests (i.e., ultraconservative coffee exporters and their allies tended to unite against a minority with manufacturing and other "modern" investments) and did not, therefore, contribute consistently to undermining the regime in power. On the other hand, the Romero regime had come to power in El Salvador in 1977, determined both to close the political system to the opposition (including the moderate Christian Democrats as well as the left) and to resist any push for reforms. The preceding Molino government had twice attempted (in 1973 and again in 1976) to introduce a modest agrarian reform and to evoke peasant support mobilized through the army's spy network, ORDEN, in order to displace the excluded opposition and provide military rule with some semblance of a social base. Molino had been defeated both times by a combination of elite resistance and opposition within the military itself. Romero's designation as the official party's candidate for the 1977 elections signaled the defeat of Molino's reform efforts and ushered in a new wave of repression. With neither a political opening nor any hope for even modest reforms, the country's deepening economic and social crisis produced increasingly violent confrontations.[43]

The Carter administration initially adopted a harshly critical attitude toward the military regime in El Salvador because of its flagrant human rights abuses. From 1977 to mid-1979 its principal objective was to modify the regime's behavior sufficiently to facilitate a transition to democratic rule. As in the case of Nicaragua, however, this effort was predicated on intelligence assessments that indicated that the three small guerrilla organizations founded in the 1970s lacked popular support and posed no challenge to the regime. As the Somoza government in Nicaragua neared collapse, decision-making initiative in the Carter administration passed from the State Department to the National Security Council (NSC). The long-term goal of creating stable democratic regimes was superseded by the short-term objective of preventing a total collapse of the Nicaraguan regime and the National Guard. When the collapse occurred despite U.S. efforts, the administration—led by the NSC, with increasing support from the Pentagon—became primarily committed to avoiding a repetition elsewhere in the region. Thus U.S. support for a transition to democratic rule and moderate reforms in El Salvador quickly took second place to the narrower short-term objective—never explicitly acknowledged—of preserving the institutional integrity of the Salvadoran armed forces. Explicit acknowledgment of this objective would have caused the administration to lose political support from Congress and from the public. It would also have carried the risk of encouraging the Salvadoran military to persist in brutal behavior that undermined support for the administration's policy at home and increased support for the left, and particularly the guerrilla movements, in El Salvador itself.

In addition to being driven by the triumph of the Nicaraguan revolution, the administration's policy shift in El Salvador was also spurred by a series of events that provoked attacks from conservatives in both major political parties. These included the seizure of the U.S. embassy and its staff by Islamic revolutionaries in Teheran, the alleged discovery of a Soviet combat brigade in Cuba,[44] the collapse of congressional support for the Strategic Arms Reduction (START) treaty with the Soviet Union, and the subsequent Soviet intervention in Afghanistan, among other developments. Election-year politics also intervened to push the administration toward a more defensive posture in foreign policy making, as the Republican opposition accused the Carter administration of neglecting U.S. security interests abroad.

Because the mid-1979 shift in U.S. policy could not be made explicit without losing liberal support in Congress and undermining the administration's human rights efforts elsewhere, a certain cognitive dissonance developed within the policy-making community. Success in achieving the administration's primary goals of avoiding "another Nicaragua" and preserving the military came to depend in part on the creation of a reliably pro-U.S. civilian government willing to collaborate with the military but credible enough to maintain the congressional support the administration needed to make the policy work. U.S. policy makers and diplomats continued to emphasize the need for an end to human rights abuses by the Salvadoran military and supported the creation of a civilian-led government. Policy makers also continued to believe that the long-term stability of the country depended on such changes. Whenever improving human rights or enhancing the power of civilian authorities threatened to destabilize the military, however, the United States backed off. Policy makers and diplomats denounced human rights abuses consistently over the four years of the Carter administration, but after mid-1979, as U.S. influence on the day-to-day activities of the Salvadoran regime reached a maximum, the United States began to appear not merely powerless to stop these abuses but complicit in their commission.

General Romero was inaugurated president at the end of June 1977, three months after the United States had suspended its military aid program. The U.S. ambassador had already been recalled to Washington, and U.S. objections were holding up a $90 million loan from the IADB. Romero's initial response to this U.S. pressure was cautious. He lifted the state of siege Molino had imposed after the February elections; suspended the army's violent occupations of rural towns and villages, where it had opened a campaign of terror against peasants occupying private lands; and reduced death-squad activity and political arrests. In September the United States responded by inviting Romero to the ceremony at which the Panama Canal treaties were signed in Washington, appointed a new ambassador, and lifted its objections to the IADB loan. Romero then pursued a double strategy. On the one hand he continued to support human rights in the international arena; he supported an OAS resolution against torture and ratified the Latin American Human Rights Convention, one of Carter's projects. On the other hand, as the opposition moved quickly to fill the political space created by the momentary relaxation of repression, Romero moved to renew it with a vengeance: on 24 November 1977 the Legislative Assembly passed a new "Law for Defense and Guarantee of Public Order," which legalized army and police repression of any political or social movement opposed to the government.

Within days the army and National Guard[45] began a new round of sweeps through rural villages to root out peasant protesters, death squad activity reached new heights, and strikes (many of which had become sit-down strikes or factory occupations) were again violently repressed. Throughout 1978 attacks on Catholic church social workers and priests, deemed allies of the "Communists," resumed; death threats against the Jesuit order were renewed; and the outspoken archbishop of San Salvador, Oscar Romero, became the object of press attacks and death threats.[46] General Romero failed in his effort to suppress the opposition once and for all. He succeeded mainly in turning even the smallest political and social protest into a violent confrontation with the police and army. He also succeeded in renewing U.S. hostility toward his government. The January 1979 State Department annual report on human rights singled out El Salvador for criticism. A month later an OAS Human Rights Commission report added new accusations, including the charge that the Salvadoran government had concealed from the OAS investigating team the existence of torture cells in which political prisoners were systematically brutalized. On 27 February the government succumbed to U.S. pressure and ordered the Legislative Assembly to repeal the Law for Defense and Guarantee of Public Order. But because the government refused to open the political system and because opposition movements continued to grow, the repressive activities of the security forces continued unabated. Moreover, guerrilla attacks on the police and military, as well as kidnappings of prominent businessmen and assassinations of government officials, including the education minister in May 1979, produced a clamor for law and order among the officer corps and the country's conservative businessmen.

Beginning in May 1979 Bowdler made a series of discreet visits to San Salvador, often en route to or from Nicaragua. After the Sandinista triumph in July his visits became more frequent.[47] In August, Romero attempted an about-face. Repression had failed to restore order in the country. Moreover, the refusal of the United States to support Somoza shocked the regime and served as an object lesson. Romero announced a 20 percent wage hike, lifted the state of siege imposed after the assassination of the education minister in May, announced that political exiles would be permitted to return to the country, and promised a reform of the electoral laws to allow the opposition to "compete freely." He was too late. The new moves merely encouraged the opposition without calming the country; they also antagonized Romero's supporters in the army officer corps and the business elite. In September the United States encouraged Romero to resign, an encouragement that soon animated his rivals in the officer corps. On 12 October the Salvadoran air force, with scattered support from army units, moved to stage a coup, the purpose of which was to install a regime that would repeal the August concessions and unleash the armed forces to restore order in the country. Romero suppressed the coup with U.S. support. On 15 October, however, a new coup was proclaimed by a larger number of officers, who secured the support of the U.S. ambassador, Frank Devine. Romero resigned immediately and left the country.

The officers who led the 15 October 1979 coup formed two loose factions within the military. The older, more senior, and more cohesive of the two groups consisted of conservatives (or "moderates"), whose chief aim was to protect the country from a Sandinista-type upheaval and who recognized that U.S. support would be vital to such an effort. Led at the moment by colonels Abdul Gutiérrez and José Guillermo García, this group also included former supporters of President Romero and the bulk of the unit commanders responsible for the repression. The second group consisted of younger and more junior officers, much more loosely organized, some of whom were members of the Military Youth organization led by Colonel Adolfo Majano, among others.[48] This group was inclined toward "modernization," including social reform and democratization, though the attitudes of its members toward the popular movements were decidedly ambivalent and in some cases hostile. This second group of younger officers organized the coup; they contacted Gutiérrez and allowed him to join them only days before the date set for action. On the morning of 15 October junior officers in 37 units arrested their commanders and seized control of troops and bases at key locations in San Salvador and the interior.

The coup leaders proclaimed that the powers of the presidency were to be exercised by a five-man junta composed of two military officers, Gutiérrez and Majano, and three civilians: Guillermo Ungo, leader of the social democratic party known as the MNR[49]; Ramón Mayorga Quiroz, rector of the Jesuit-run Central American University and close to the Christian Democrats; and Mario Andino, without political affiliation, manager of the local Phelps Dodge subsidiary, representing "progressive" business. The junta proclaimed full civil and political liberties and announced its intention to undertake an agrarian reform, reform the banking system, rewrite the tax laws, and take over foreign trade transactions. It ordered the dissolution of ORDEN and promised to fight against extremist organizations that violated human rights. It also proclaimed a general amnesty for exiles and political prisoners, legalized all political parties, promised to respect the right to strike and bargain collectively, and pledged to guarantee the rule of law and to organize free elections. The junta appointed a cabinet that included representatives of the opposition political parties and well-known independents. Colonel García was named minister of defense by Gutiérrez.[50]

From 15 October until the end of the year, the civilians in the junta and the cabinet, backed intermittently by Majano, struggled to consolidate the new government's authority and carry out the promised reforms. Previously outlawed or persecuted political and social groups exploded into new activity. Meetings, strikes, demonstrations, protests, land occupations, and factory seizures erupted throughout the country. While some of these popular outbursts were disruptive and even violent, and a few were organized or supported by the guerrilla movements, most of which denounced the junta as a sham, the vast majority were relatively peaceful expressions of pent-up frustration over falling real wages, declining living conditions, the lack of basic public services, and the abusive behavior of the police and military. As the civilian members of the junta and their ministers struggled to gain control of the corrupt civil bureaucracy, responded to new demands and pressures from militant constituents, and worked on reform decrees, the military and its business allies responded to the new conditions with a wave of brutal attacks on popular organizations, including death-squad kidnappings and executions, that exceeded the worst abuses of the Romero regime. The number of political murders, disappearances, and military and police assaults on peaceful protests escalated. The junta ordered the military to stop the repression and was ignored.

The younger officers allied to Majano were pushed aside by Gutiérrez, García, and the high command. The commanders arrested on the morning of the coup were restored to their commands; Romero's most senior officials were replaced by others with equally bad or worse human rights records. To the senior officers, who maintained their control, reform and repression were two sides of the same coin, both instruments in the fight to save the country from communism. To the civilian members of the junta and the increasingly marginalized reformist officers, repression undermined the government's pledge to respect human rights and to create conditions for democratic elections and peaceful social change. Despite its reform proclamations and the impeccably democratic credentials of the new cabinet, the junta failed either to implement reforms (an agrarian reform decree was blocked for weeks by García) or to create conditions of minimal respect for human rights.

Though it publicly welcomed the coup of 15 October, the U.S. government provided the junta with no new aid and none of the political support that would have helped it to govern effectively. The key policy makers, with the collapse of the Nicaraguan National Guard fresh in their minds, were determined to avoid undermining the military.[51] U.S. Ambassador Frank Devine met repeatedly with Gutiérrez, García, and other military leaders to discuss developments and offer support; his few meetings with the civilian members of the junta and the cabinet were purely ceremonial.[52] If U.S. policy makers had been alarmed by the Romero government's intransigence, which they feared was leading to mass support for a Sandinista-type revolt, they were no less alarmed at the upsurge of political and social agitation that followed the coup. U.S. support for Majano and the civilian members of the junta might have helped to moderate the repression and create sufficient political space for an electoral resolution of the country's political and social conflicts. Instead the United States took what appeared to be the less risky approach—that of backing military officers committed to destroying the guerrillas and the left-wing popular organizations linked to them, so long as they offered at least rhetorical support for the kind of moderate reforms needed to undercut support for the revolutionaries.

The conservatives in the Salvadoran military exploited the change in U.S. policy and, encouraged by news of attacks on Carter's human rights policies within the United States, quickly moved to extricate themselves from the constraints the junta sought to impose on their activities. In early December 1979 Gutiérrez and García provoked a confrontation by sharply escalating the violence against the popular movements; military and National Guard units murdered some 200 people in 10 days. The civilian members of the junta and cabinet responded with a demand that the army obey the law and submit to the authority of the government. The military replied with a statement that affirmed its autonomy in the face of grave threats to public order. On 3 and 4 January 1980 all of the civilian members of the junta and the cabinet resigned, stating that the "historic possibilities for implementing a peaceful and democratic solution" in the country had been exhausted by the behavior of the armed forces.[53]

At U.S. insistence the military then asked the Christian Democratic party (PDC) to serve as the civilian component of a new junta and cabinet. The PDC's decision to abandon its longtime political allies and to replace them in the junta and the cabinet set off an intense internal debate within the party. The decision isolated the PDC from the rest of the opposition as the only historically democratic political organization willing to collaborate with an uncontrolled military. The United States announced its full support for the new junta. On 22 January 1980 between 100,000 and 200,000 demonstrators marched through San Salvador on the forty-eighth anniversary of the fall of the "depression dictator," General Maximiliano Hernández Martínez. Their banners called for the restoration of a government pledged to democracy and social change. The march was attacked by units of the National Guard, firing from windows in the presidential palace, and ended in disorder and violence. The next day in Washington, Bowdler announced a new package of U.S. economic aid for El Salvador. With this announcement the battle lines of the Salvadoran civil war were drawn.

During the final year of the Carter presidency, from January 1980 to January 1981, the U.S. government moved to exercise increasing supervision over the day-to-day activities of the Salvadoran government. The PDC, despised by a major portion of the military and decried as no better than Communists by the major organizations and media of the Salvadoran business elite, depended almost entirely on U.S. support to remain in power. The PDC leaders took nominal control of the government and worked to rebuild the party's shattered political base by decreeing reforms and by developing a network of clients who benefited from various U.S. aid programs. The Salvadoran military, together with ORDEN and its expanding network of death squads, launched a full-scale war of counterinsurgency against all the opposition parties and organizations, including at times the PDC. In the course of these 12 months the security forces killed more than 9,000 people, most of them unarmed civilians. Many of the more conservative military officers sought a quick and bloody pacification in order to free the government of the PDC and U.S. interference. Death squads frequently attacked PDC members and officials to discourage the government and its U.S. supervisors from promulgating reforms and interfering in military affairs. The PDC received active support from the new U.S. ambassador, James Cheek, who arrived just as the first junta collapsed, and from Robert E. White, who replaced Cheek in early March, just as the second junta was falling apart.

In February and again in May 1980, coup attempts by right-wing officers were barely averted by the U.S. ambassador and the high command. On 3 March, after the PDC attorney general was executed by a death squad, one of the two PDC members of the junta, Hector Dada Herezi, resigned, and the party split again. Only its most conservative faction, led by José Napoleón Duarte, was willing to continue in government. Duarte replaced Dada on the junta and succeeded in expelling Dada and his followers from the party. The second junta had just issued the long-awaited Agrarian Reform Law and simultaneously imposed a state of siege, renewed monthly thereafter for the next two years. The army used both decrees as the legal basis for beginning a massive effort to relocate into strategic hamlets peasant villagers suspected of supporting the guerrillas.[54] On 17–18 March the opposition called a two-day general strike to protest repression that paralyzed the country. On 23 March Archbishop Romero denounced the agrarian reform process as "reforms bathed in blood" and appealed to military personnel to disobey orders that were contrary to the law and to their consciences. The next day he was assassinated by a death squad composed of active-duty army officers.[55] At his funeral the army opened fire on thousands of mourners, killing 50 and wounding 600. On 2 April the U.S. government approved a new package of $5.7 million in "nonlethal" military aid for the Salvadoran armed forces. In June, after an army massacre of 600 peasants fleeing into Honduras, another successful general strike lasted three days, provoking the army to occupy the National University, where soldiers killed 50 students and looted classrooms and laboratories. By the summer of 1980 most opposition leaders and organizations had been driven into exile or underground; most of the opposition organizations had suffered repeatedly from assassinations and mass arrests.

Throughout the winter and spring of 1980 the battered opposition fought to preserve enough political space to remain viable. When the PDC, supported by the United States, demonstrated its willingness to govern alone, and the repression reached unprecedented levels, the opposition parties and organizations joined to create an umbrella organization, called the Democratic Revolutionary Front (FDR). Founded on 18 April, the FDR instantly became the largest political movement in the country's history. It included former PDC members, the MNR, most of the left-wing parties, 80 percent of the country's trade unions, and organizations representing professionals, students, peasants, the Catholic and National universities, and Catholic church workers. By late summer the FDR had been driven underground, and its constituent organizations had endorsed armed rebellion as the only solution to the nation's ills. On 28 November the FDR president, four members of the FDR executive committee, and an innocent bystander were seized by the National Guard, taken from the Catholic high school in San Salvador where the committee had been meeting, brutally tortured, and summarily executed. Meanwhile, the five guerrilla movements operating in the country (two of which had formed in the preceding six months) announced the formation of a joint "political-military" command structure and adopted a new name, the Farabundo Martí Front for National Liberation (FMLN). The FDR and FMLN, though distinct organizations, joined forces. The FDR included many organizations that did not officially participate in the armed insurrection against the government, but the execution of its leaders had confirmed the futility of attempting to work for peaceful political and social change.

Ronald Reagan's electoral victory in November 1980 encouraged Salvadoran conservatives to believe that Washington would soon lose its interest in human rights and instead support an all-out war to exterminate their enemies. The result was a new orgy of brutality by the military and its death squads. Thus, in the last weeks of the Carter administration, the contradictions in the U.S. position in El Salvador exploded into public view. In addition to murdering the FDR leaders, military units and death squads kidnapped and assassinated a large number of second-line FDR and opposition figures. U.S. citizens were not immune. On 3 December four U.S. churchwomen, two of them nuns, were taken into custody by National Guardsmen in plain clothes as they left the airport in San Salvador. The women were driven to an isolated area a few miles away, where they were raped and murdered. Criticism of the administration's support for the Salvadoran regime erupted in the media, in Congress, and from a broad spectrum of political, religious, and human rights organizations. The day after the murders the United States suspended all military and economic assistance to El Salvador. In the intense negotiations that ensued between the U.S. embassy, the military, and the PDC, Gutiérrez and García promised to find and punish the perpetrators. They also agreed to the formation of a new, fourth junta, identical to the third except for the elevation of Duarte to the rank of president.[56] On 13 December the United States announced resumption of economic but not military aid, and three days later approved a new $20 million loan for economic assistance. U.S. spokesmen insisted, however, that military aid would not be renewed until the Salvadoran military took additional steps to demonstrate improvement in its respect for human rights. Within a month the U.S. administration reversed itself.

The resumption of U.S. military aid came in response to a "final offensive," launched on 11 January by the FMLN with the hope of seizing power (or coming too close to be stopped) prior to the inauguration of President-elect Reagan on 20 January 1981. Urgent appeals from the Salvadoran Defense Ministry, which had done nothing to implement its latest human rights promises,[57] produced immediate results. The United States resumed military aid on 14 January, including "lethal" weaponry for the first time since 1977, and dispatched six military advisers to join others who had quietly entered the country during 1980. On 17 and 18 January the United States announced a total of $10 million in additional emergency military aid for El Salvador and the deployment of three more teams of military advisers.

The FMLN offensive failed to reach its objective. The insurgents could not match the firepower of the U.S.-equipped Salvadoran armed forces, their supporters in San Salvador and the towns in the interior had few arms, the five separate guerrilla organizations had only recently begun to coordinate their actions, and the scale of the repression against the popular movements during the preceding year had left many of them in a shambles, too weak to spark the kind of urban insurrections that had accompanied the offensives of the Sandinista National Liberation Front (FSLN) in Nicaragua in 1978 and 1979. The army succeeded in limiting the effectiveness of the general strike called by the rebels through massive deployments of troops in the major cities. As Ronald Reagan took the oath of office, rebels units were retreating from the towns to recover their strength in remote areas of the countryside.

By the time Jimmy Carter left office his administration had achieved its two main objectives in El Salvador. First, it had avoided the collapse of the Salvadoran armed forces. Second, it had secured the installation of reliably pro-U.S. civilian authorities (drawn mainly from the PDC), who had helped to preserve U.S. domestic support for the administration's efforts by proclaiming their commitment to democracy and enacting moderate reforms deemed essential to undercutting popular backing for the guerrillas. These successes for U.S. policy pushed El Salvador into full-scale civil war.

The extent to which U.S. support saved the Salvadoran military from collapse cannot be measured with precision, though the U.S. contribution was probably smaller than U.S. policy makers believed. At the time of the 15 October 1979 coup, the military faced two challenges. The smaller of these emanated from three small guerrilla organizations, large enough to carry out small-scale actions such as kidnappings and assassinations but far too small to worry, let alone defeat, the Salvadoran armed forces. Even in January 1981, 15 months later, when the military's crude brutality and indiscriminate terrorism had created massive popular support for a much larger and now unified guerrilla movement, the Salvadoran armed forces managed to defeat the FMLN's "final offensive" long before U.S. military aid (announced as the guerrillas were already retreating) had reached the country in quantities large enough to make a difference.

The major challenge to the integrity of the military as an institution came from internal divisions and rivalries. In this matter the United States did make a difference by siding with the high command of senior officers in their effort to turn aside the loose grouping of junior officers who had led the 15 October coup. U.S. support for the junior officers and the first junta might have resulted in an effort to purge the most egregiously repressive and corrupt officers, and could easily have led to violent clashes and even to new coup attempts by officers threatened with retirement or prosecution. In such an unstable context the popular movements and even the guerrillas might well have played a key role, moving the junta to the left and threatening the United States with a "new Nicaragua." This risk the United States sought to avoid at any cost—even the cost of providing significant political support for the same officers whose crude methods had produced the Salvadoran crisis in the first place.

Because of its primary commitment to preserving the military, the United States allowed to pass two other major opportunities, and a number of less promising ones, to move the country toward a less violent resolution of its internal conflicts. The first opportunity came in early January 1980, when the first junta collapsed. The United States could have demanded a reversal of the military's declaration of independence from civilian control and an end to the new escalation of repression that had provoked the junta's collapse and insisted on the restoration of a broadly representative junta. Instead the United States worked mainly to persuade the conservative wing of the PDC to break with the rest of the opposition and join the junta alone; from the military the United States demanded little more than promises. The last major opportunity occurred in March 1980, when the second junta collapsed. The United States sought a face-saving solution to the political crisis through the addition of Duarte to the junta but made no significant demands for reform of the military as a condition for U.S. support.

In December 1980, after the murder of the U.S. churchwomen, the Carter administration had another opportunity to alter course, albeit a less propitious one, though its bargaining position had been effectively undercut by the election of Ronald Reagan the previous month. Nonetheless, the U.S. administration could have maintained the cutoff in economic aid, and particularly in military aid, and refrained from efforts to solve the political crisis the murders provoked.[58] Instead the United States acquiesced to what amounted to a silent coup. The military consolidated its autonomy from civilian control in exchange for elevating Duarte to a presidency explicitly stripped of its right to intervene in military affairs.

CARTER AND THE SANDINISTAS IN POWER

U.S. relations with Nicaragua after the Sandinista victory on 19 July 1979 and until the end of the Carter administration reflected the contradictory objectives of the two governments. The U.S. administration sought to exert its influence in the regime through the "moderates" in the junta and the cabinet, while Pezzullo met regularly with FSLN leaders. The Carter administration recognized that its direct leverage was limited but sought a quid pro quo: the United States would maintain cordial relations with Nicaragua, provide aid and encourage allies to do likewise, facilitate loans to Nicaragua from such multilateral sources as the IMF and the IADB, and encourage private investment. In exchange, U.S. officials expected that the new authorities in Nicaragua would avoid attacks on U.S. interests, both within Nicaragua and throughout Central America. Mindful of the history of the Cuban debacle of 1959–62, when U.S. hostility helped to push the Cuban revolutionaries toward economic and military reliance on the Soviet Union, the Carter administration sought to avoid confrontation and antagonism in the expectation that domestic political pressures and geopolitical realities would eventually lead the FSLN toward accommodation with the United States. In August U.S. officials began drafting an aid package to present to Congress. The State Department sent the administration's proposal to Congress on 27 November, but emergency aid was already being disbursed by the embassy, and CIA covert funding for various political and business groups had already begun.

The FSLN, meanwhile, had a quite different and somewhat contradictory agenda. Its chief priority was to consolidate its authority as the dominant political force in the country. This objective conflicted with the U.S. goal, which was to preserve and strengthen the non-FSLN elements in the country. The tug-of-war between the FSLN and the United States, which had begun before 19 July, thus continued after the Sandinista victory. To consolidate its authority the FSLN set out to accomplish three essential tasks with great speed. First, it worked to transform its immense popularity into solid political organization capable of mobilizing support for the regime. Second, it moved immediately to transform its guerrilla forces into a military and police apparatus capable of defending the regime from potential enemies, both internal and external. Third, it sought to limit U.S. influence by developing ties with other countries, both in Latin America and outside the region.

For more than a year after coming to power, the FSLN and the Carter administration pursued their contradictory objectives without major conflicts. The results were not promising for the United States. The Sandinistas succeeded in all three of their objectives. On the political front the FSLN used its popularity to great effect, spawning a series of mass organizations that mobilized a major portion of the population. This success enabled them in December 1979 to reorganize the cabinet agreed to in San José, by dropping several ministers favored by the United States and replacing them with Sandinistas. The most important change occurred in the Defense Ministry, where FSLN commander-in-chief Humberto Ortega replaced Bernadino Larios, a former National Guard officer well known in Washington, who had broken with Somoza in time to be named to his post by the junta in San José. With increasing confidence the nine comandantes in the FSLN National Directorate asserted their informal but decisive control over policy making at the expense of the San José junta, which held nominal executive power in the country. In April the two non-FSLN members of the junta, Chamorro and Robelo, resigned, though they were replaced by two individuals highly regarded by the U.S. embassy.[59] When the membership of the appointed legislative body called the Council of State was announced as planned on 4 May the FSLN had succeeded in increasing its size to ensure a solid FSLN majority. In August FSLN leaders announced that elections would not be held until 1985. In November the six representatives of COSEP and two independent labor federations walked out of the Council of State. By the end of 1980 FSLN dominance of the Nicaraguan government was virtually complete.

In security matters the FSLN moved even more quickly. It received assistance in organizing the new army and national police from several countries, including Panama and France, but Cuban advisers were more numerous and influential than any others by early 1980. Military aid and training were offered by the United States, but the FSLN declined (although it never formally rejected the offer). No U.S. military aid was ever provided. Though the Sandinistas carefully avoided offending the United States, they clearly felt more secure with a new security apparatus free of U.S. influence.[60]

Finally, in foreign policy, the Sandinista government moved with equal speed to end Nicaragua's special relationship with the United States by successfully appealing for aid and establishing closer ties with a large number of countries, some of them traditional enemies of the United States. In the first year of the revolution Nicaragua received $580 million in foreign aid, of which only $62.6 million came from the United States. In Latin America the governments of Colombia, Cuba, Mexico, Panama, and Venezuela mounted impressive efforts, sending money, oil (from Mexico and Venezuela), doctors, technicians, and school teachers; groups of volunteers arrived from several other countries as well. From outside the hemisphere, Nicaragua received significant amounts of aid from most of the Western and Eastern European nations, including France, the Netherlands, the Soviet Union, and West Germany.

The successes of the new regime on all three fronts combined to reduce U.S. influence in Nicaragua to its lowest level in nearly a century. Nonetheless, aside from minor and mostly symbolic irritations,[61] neither side provoked a major confrontation and on many issues the U.S. embassy and the regime cooperated in an almost routine fashion. The United States avoided blatant interference in Nicaraguan domestic affairs, made no noisy threats, and pressed no imperious demands. The FSLN, meanwhile, did not victimize any U.S. citizens or nationalize any U.S. property, forged no formal military alliances with external powers, and refrained from meddling elsewhere in the region, except for expressing sympathy for the FSLN-like guerrilla movements in El Salvador and Guatemala.

This mutual forbearance began to diminish as the U.S. election campaign heated up in 1980. The United States was irritated by a number of the guests invited to the first anniversary of the Sandinista triumph in July, including Fidel Castro, Yasir Arafat, and representatives of the Guatemalan and Salvadoran guerrilla movements. In October a more serious issue arose: the United States claimed to have evidence of Nicaraguan support for the Salvadoran rebels, who had just announced the formation of the FMLN. The Nicaraguans had just signed the long-delayed U.S. aid agreement, which included a stipulation inserted by Congress that the aid would be cut off if the Nicaraguan government was found to be assisting insurgencies in other countries. Nicaraguan officials had said that they had no problem with that proviso or any of the other conditions.[62] They denied the U.S. suggestion that the government was involved in aiding the FMLN. The United States accepted the Nicaraguan denial because it did not yet have clear evidence to the contrary.[63]

By the time the FMLN's "final offensive" erupted in early January 1981, the United States claimed to have irrefutable evidence of Nicaraguan official involvement, including arms shipments and other support for the guerrillas. Some of these charges were probably true, though the scale of Nicaraguan support was undoubtedly small and its effect on the FMLN offensive negligible. The Nicaraguans apparently shipped "bullets, medical supplies, maybe some rifles" in the three months leading up to the offensive, but almost certainly shipped no heavy weapons.[64] The charge by Salvadoran Defense Minister García on 13 January that five boats carrying 100 invaders from Nicaragua had landed on the Salvadoran coast was clearly false.[65] Journalists in El Salvador at the time, including those who later spent weeks travelling with guerrilla units, reported that the guerrillas were not well armed. The few heavy weapons in their arsenal had been captured from Salvadoran army units, as had most of their modern rifles. While the U.S. administration repeated its charges of Nicaraguan aid to the FMLN, it did not cut off aid to Nicaragua and left the issue to be handled by the incoming Reagan team.

CONCLUSIONS

The dominance of pro-U.S. authoritarian regimes in Latin America in the 1970s concealed a substantial erosion of U.S. power and influence during the Nixon and Ford administrations. The major perceived threat to U.S. interests in the region came from Chile, where a multiparty coalition, headed by Socialist party candidate Salvador Allende and including the Chilean Communist party, succeeded in winning the 1970 elections. Allende's victory was due in part to the Nixon administration's decision to withdraw U.S. support, including lavish electoral campaign subsidies, from Chile's Christian Democratic party in favor of the right-wing National party. When Allende won unexpectedly, Nixon moved to bring down his government by cutting off U.S. aid, blocking multilateral assistance, freezing Chilean government assets in the United States, launching a major CIA effort to destabilize the regime, and encouraging the Chilean military to take power. The Allende government fell to a military junta headed by General Augusto Pinochet in September 1973. This success, and others like it, resulted from an intensification of internal conflicts in the region, which made it possible for the United States to influence significant political outcomes at relatively low cost by tipping the balance of forces already in play rather than reversing major trends.

The Nixon and Ford administrations found no compelling reasons to invest much time or resources in Central America. Deteriorating economic and social conditions there did not affect U.S. interests significantly. The corrosive Panama Canal dispute did attract their attention, but neither president proved willing to pay the domestic political costs that a new canal treaty would have entailed. Aside from making occasional efforts to assist U.S. businesses in Central America, administering a drastically scaled-back aid program, and adopting a friendlier tone in relations with the military rulers of five of the six isthmian countries, both administrations virtually ignored the region.

The Carter administration did not initially recognize the depth of the social and political turmoil emerging in the hemisphere, especially in Central America, but did understand that the U.S. position had become much weaker in political as well as economic terms. Its efforts to reassert U.S. preeminence included two successful initiatives: the Panama Canal treaties and the human rights campaign. The Panama Canal treaties removed a source of constant turmoil and uncertainty in U.S.-Panamanian relations and helped to restore credibility to U.S. diplomacy in the region as a whole. The human rights campaign provided the ideological basis for a renewed projection of U.S. influence in the domestic political arrangements of countries throughout the area. The policy was also successful in the sense that U.S. officials at times secured the release of political prisoners and effected the diminution of political abuses, including torture. In Honduras the efforts of the Carter administration helped to sustain the military's decision to hold elections and yield high offices to civilian authorities.

The rapid growth of revolutionary social and political turmoil in Nicaragua in 1978–79 and in El Salvador in 1979–80 forced the Carter administration to downgrade its human rights efforts. Part of a broader political strategy, the human rights campaign served to facilitate the projection of U.S. power in countries where viable, pro-U.S., "moderate" political parties and movements retained sufficient legitimacy and popular support to challenge authoritarian governments. By providing support for democratic alternatives, the Carter administration acquired political resources within the Latin American polities that enhanced its leverage in dealings with the authoritarian regimes. The administration also managed to position the United States to deflect criticism over earlier U.S. support of military takeovers. In so doing, it not only strengthened pro-U.S. elements in the democratic opposition but also helped to reduce the prospect that democratic regimes, when they returned to the region, would see the United States as a threat and thus turn to competing political and economic powers for support. Though this strategy produced tensions between the United States and a number of the Latin American military regimes and did not always produce quick results, either in achieving greater short-term leverage or in ameliorating repressive conditions, it succeeded, probably beyond the administration's expectations, in all of the major Latin American countries. Unfortunately for Carter, the major successes did not occur until after his administration had been voted out of office.

In Nicaragua and El Salvador, however, Carter's political strategy failed. In Nicaragua the failure occurred for three main reasons. First, the deterioration of economic and social conditions had already provoked an unprecedented wave of organized popular discontent throughout Central America by the time the Carter administration took office. Second, the historic identification of the United States with the Somoza dynasty could not be overcome in the short time between Carter's inauguration and the onset of the

Sandinista revolution. Nicaraguan popular nationalism, a powerful unifying force in the opposition to Somoza's rule, was historically "anti-yanqui" and could not have been otherwise. This gave the FSLN a powerful edge in its efforts to take charge of the opposition movements against more moderate, pro-U.S. opponents of the regime. Third, the intransigence of the Somoza regime, coupled with the nearly universal support for Somoza's ouster, even among the country's business elite, made it impossible for the United States to organize a managed transition that would have limited or excluded FSLN participation. Thus, in Nicaragua, the United States did not succeed in promoting U.S. power and influence in the transition to democratic rule. Moreover, the administration's efforts to pressure the FSLN into conceding more power to moderate elements in the opposition before the Sandinista triumph, and its efforts to preserve and strengthen their role thereafter, were as intrusive as they proved to be counterproductive.

In El Salvador the Carter administration's strategy failed because it was abandoned prematurely. As in Nicaragua, the Salvadoran opposition exploded into activity in the 1970s. Unlike the FSLN, however, the small Salvadoran guerrilla movements enjoyed limited popular support; the main opposition parties were congenial, if not always subservient, to U.S. interests; the popular movements were largely preoccupied with domestic enemies, whom they did not identify with the United States; and most of the business elite, whether with distaste or enthusiasm, supported the military regime in power. Moreover, in El Salvador the military was rent with personal rivalries and political discord, whereas in Nicaragua the coherence of the regime depended mainly on a single individual. These conditions, which existed throughout 1979 and into 1980, suggest that a consistent application of the Carter political strategy would have had good prospects for success. It was abandoned, however, at just the moment when it was most likely to succeed, in the weeks following the 15 October 1979 coup.

The Sandinista victory, together with other foreign policy failures and the impending presidential election campaign, induced the Carter administration to adopt a strategy that relied less on skillful political management and reduced the risk of unfavorable outcomes. The United States chose to give top priority to preserving the integrity of the Salvadoran military, which it viewed as its last line of defense against a left-wing or guerrilla takeover, at a time when the risk of such a takeover was small. This shift in U.S. policy had a decisive impact on Salvadoran political life. The military high command successfully resisted reform, marginalized dissent within the officer corps, and emancipated itself from the threat of civilian control. The collapse of the first junta in January 1980 in the face of the military's savage repression pushed the moderate opposition, with the exception of the conservative wing of the PDC, into support for armed rebellion and provoked the creation of two new guerrilla organizations. While the Carter strategy failed in Nicaragua, where it had little chance for success, its abandonment in El Salvador, where it could have succeeded, led straight to civil war.

chapter 6

DESTRUCTION AND DISARRAY, 1981–1989

THE REAGAN COUNTERREVOLUTION

The Reagan administration took office on 20 January 1981, with most of its key foreign policy officials echoing campaign charges against the failures of its predecessor. The security of the United States had been endangered, they argued, by the "loss" of important allies to unfriendly or even hostile governments in large areas of the globe. The list included Afghanistan, Angola, Ethiopia, Iran, Mozambique, and Nicaragua. Moreover, they warned, a number of "friendly autocracies,"[1] such as Argentina, El Salvador, Guatemala, the Philippines, and even South Africa, were threatened by domestic insurgencies allied to the Soviet Union. In addition to closing a dangerous "window of vulnerability" in the nuclear arms race, the new Reagan administration thus committed itself to repairing the deteriorating U.S. position throughout the third world. In the new president's view this deterioration did not stem from objective factors, such as the relative decline of the U.S. economy (in comparison with the economies of Western Europe and Japan) or the high cost and limited utility of deploying U.S. military power to contain or suppress third-world revolutions. Instead, he argued, the U.S. decline had a fundamentally subjective cause the ideological or psychological inhibitions that had prevented his predecessors from making full use of the nation's vast economic resources and undiminished military might. Henceforth, President Reagan pledged, the United States would not hesitate to reward friends and, especially, to punish enemies. The decidedly more aggressive tone of the new administration's statements on foreign policy issues formed an important part of its efforts to shift national priorities toward greater military preparedness and away from what the president deemed an excessive preoccupation with domestic social programs. The Reagan administration committed itself to greater military preparedness to meet external challenges and to less government intervention at home, except in areas of traditional conservative concern, such as the prosecution of criminals, the prohibition of abortion, and the reintroduction of religious practices into public institutions.

In Latin America the administration set out to repair relations with the region's military rulers and to adopt a more actively hostile stance toward revolutionary and reformist regimes and movements deemed unfriendly to U.S. interests. Central America, and the Caribbean region more generally, became the primary focus of its first efforts to "roll back" what the president and many of his supporters viewed as Communist advances in the third world. For the first time since the 1920s the U.S. administration developed a sharp and explicit distinction between the policies applied to the small states of the Caribbean and Central America and those pursued in the rest of Latin America. It did so by reviving security doctrines that emphasized the importance of the Caribbean for the defense of the United States and its allies.[2] Because this region was "vital" to U.S. national security, revolutionary upheavals in the area posed a particularly significant threat. President Reagan announced the economic component of this new approach in a speech to the OAS on 24 January 1982. Called the Caribbean Basin Initiative, the economic program offered aid, as well as lower tariffs on exports to the United States, to Caribbean Basin countries that undertook market-oriented economic reforms. To the rest of Latin America, still governed mainly by apparently stable pro-U.S. military regimes, the president offered nothing comparable.

The main objective of the new administration in Central America—to restore U.S. predominance—did not differ radically from that of its predecessor, but the president and his advisers translated it into policy goals that in some cases involved dramatic changes in U.S. relations with the region. This was particularly true in the case of Nicaragua, where the Reagan administration shifted from efforts to modify the Sandinista government to a policy of implacable hostility designed to subvert and eventually overthrow it. In El Salvador the Reagan policy went well beyond preserving the integrity of the military establishment, which under Carter had allowed room for criticism of human rights abuses and had not excluded a negotiated end to the civil strife, to a policy of all-out "low-intensity warfare" aimed at defeating the insurgents. In Honduras the Reagan administration supported the transition to civilian rule, as had the Carter administration, but also sought to use Honduras as a base for the activities of Nicaraguan counterrevolutionaries, for training an expanded Salvadoran military, and for an eventual U.S. military intervention in Nicaragua or El Salvador. In Guatemala the administration sought initially to establish closer ties with the dominant military but, after the defeat of local insurgents (in which the U.S. played a negligible role), shifted back to the Carter policy of support for a transition to democratic rule. Seeking support against Nicaragua and the Salvadoran insurgents, the administration provided substantial economic aid to Costa Rica and Panama.

The Reagan administration achieved none of its goals in Central America, though it mobilized vast resources and invested a great deal of political capital in pursuing them. By the time Reagan left office in early 1989 the Sandinista government still ruled Nicaragua, the FMLN insurgents in El Salvador had developed into the most effective guerrilla army in the region's history, the Honduran government was actively seeking a graceful end to its role as the U.S. "aircraft carrier" on the isthmus, a Costa Rica peace plan opposed by the United States had been signed by all the Central American governments and backed by the OAS and the United Nations, Guatemala's first civilian president in 16 years was proving incapable of curbing the excesses of the country's military or ending the insurgency, and the leader of the Panamanian National Guard, who had been receiving a CIA retainer of $200,000 per year as late as 1986, was defying U.S. efforts to dislodge him from power. For the first time since the United States had set out to dominate the isthmus late in the nineteenth century, the power of the U.S. government to shape the region's politics and dominate its diplomacy seemed to have all but disappeared.

The extraordinary reverses that U.S. policy suffered in Central America, particularly in the last two years of the Reagan administration, contrasted sharply with increases in the traditional sources of U.S. dominance. Deteriorating economic conditions throughout the region provoked a more rapid decline in trade and investment flows from outside the hemisphere than from the United States, reversing post–World War II trends for the first time. The recession of 1981–82 provoked a severe financial crisis that brought all of the isthmian countries but Nicaragua (which the United States excluded from its aid programs) to increase sharply their dependence on U.S. financial assistance—a dependence that continued throughout the decade. U.S. economic advisers became permanent fixtures in finance and economics ministries throughout most of the region. At the same time U.S. military aid (again, except to Nicaragua) increased to unprecedented levels, as did the numbers of U.S. soldiers and naval units permanently stationed in the region. Military advisers, U.S. Agency for International Development (USAID) personnel and contractors, intelligence agents, diplomats, and officials flooded the region. The gap between the diminished capacity of the U.S. government to control events and the sharp increase in the traditional sources of U.S. power in Central America by the end of the 1980s was a measure of the multiple failures of the policy-making process of the Reagan administration.

Although the Reagan policy makers failed to achieve their major objectives, their policies had an immense impact on Central America. The 1980s witnessed an extraordinary mobilization of the region's human and material resources for or against U.S. objectives. Military expenditures consumed ever-rising proportions of the diminishing tax revenues of the region (excluding Panama), increasing from $140 million to $600 million; the number of military personnel employed by governments in the region rose from 48,000 to 207,000.[3] In the three most affected countries—El Salvador, Guatemala, and Nicaragua—at least 200,000 people[4] died in political violence during the decade, and more than two million people became refugees or emigrated to other countries, including the United States.[5] This carnage and dislocation, together with a prolonged economic crisis compounded by warfare in El Salvador and Nicaragua, had profound effects on Central American society, politics, and culture, as well as on the region's relations with the United States. Though the Reagan administration failed to achieve its main policy objectives, the effects of its attempts to manage the political destinies of the region would be felt for generations.

The Reagan administration confronted three major obstacles to achieving its goals in Central America. The first involved public and congressional resistance to increases in defense and foreign aid expenditures, which the new administration initially proposed to finance through cuts in popular domestic entitlement programs.[6] Overcoming this obstacle was made more difficult by the "Vietnam syndrome"—the public distaste for foreign military intervention that followed the warfare in Southeast Asia. This problem was compounded by public and congressional opposition to aspects of the administration's policies in Central America and by repeated and occasionally successful lobbying efforts by Central American governments and political movements. The second obstacle consisted of the growing political and economic competitiveness of the international environment in Latin America. Despite the increased economic and financial dependence of the region after 1982 and the U.S. commitment of large-scale resources to achieve its goals in Central America, the administration was unable to put an end to independent initiatives, which at times made it possible even for U.S. clients to pursue policies opposed by the United States. The last and perhaps greatest obstacle, which no one in the new administration took seriously at first, turned out to be the Central Americans themselves. Most policy makers in the new administration believed that Central American realities could be readily bent to Washington's wishes. This led them to underestimate both the time it would take and the political and economic price of achieving their goals.

To achieve his defense-spending objectives, the president committed himself and his administration to mobilizing public support. He warned repeatedly, as did key administration officials, of new and growing dangers posed by the Soviet Union and its allies. The temptation to indulge in what one security expert has termed "threat inflation"[7] was irresistible, because the public's opinion of the country's defense requirements remained below that of the new administration. Moreover, opinion polls tended to suggest that the public was more impressed by actions than rhetoric; each time the administration successfully undertook a major military action abroad, public support for the president and for increased defense spending went up temporarily. The policy-making dynamics of the Reagan administration thus tended at times to conflate symbolism with security and, in so doing, provided an unusual degree of leverage to policy makers of determined ideological conviction. This was particularly true in regard to places where U.S. security and economic interests were only marginally engaged, because the risks of failure could be kept low, and the deleterious consequences of imprudence in such regions were also marginal. U.S. policy toward Central America fell victim to this dynamic. Top policy makers kept their attention focused mainly on regions where powerful domestic interest groups and significant U.S. economic and security interests were actually at stake and left Central American policy making to lower-level political enthusiasts for long periods of time. The risks this practice entailed were enhanced at the outset of the administration by a purge of State Department personnel, who were experts in Central American affairs, and the appointment of new officials who knew little about the region.[8] The risks were compounded by an unusual degree of indiscipline and turnover in the ranks of policy-making and diplomatic personnel in the Reagan government.[9]

Skepticism and outright opposition in Congress toward the administration's policies in Central America produced continuous conflicts, particularly between the administration and the Democrat-controlled House of Representatives. Congress repeatedly cut the administration's military aid requests for El Salvador, for example, and imposed conditions for approving what aid it did provide. The administration failed to secure unconditional approval for a Salvadoran aid proposal until after the election of José Napoleón Duarte to the presidency in June 1984. Faced with congressional obstruction, Reagan evaded congressional limits and conditions through the use of unilateral executive authority. As much as 60 percent of all U.S. military aid to El Salvador from 1981 to 1983 was not approved by Congress but instead taken from presidential discretionary funds intended for use in "emergencies."[10] In the case of Nicaragua the House repeatedly attempted to cut off U.S. financing for the contras (CIA-organized anti-Sandinista guerrillas), first through its intelligence oversight committee and then by voting to prohibit all funding. When the Senate finally concurred and Congress suspended contra aid completely in 1984, the administration responded by soliciting private donations and contributions from other governments and then used profits from the illegal sale of weapons to Iran to buy arms for the contras through a secret network of former military and intelligence officers directed from the White House. Not until 1986 did the administration manage to secure congressional approval for military aid to the contras. Military aid requests for Guatemala and Honduras encountered similar difficulties.

Congress was more cooperative, however, in providing economic aid to Central America, portions of which actually went to cover budget deficits incurred as a result of increased military expenditures, especially in El Salvador. The administration managed to increase U.S. economic aid to the six isthmian countries from an annual average (in 1982 dollars) of $185.5 million during the Carter administration to $739.5 million during the eight years of the Reagan presidency—an astounding 345 percent rise (see Table 4.1). The largest increase was made in the case of El Salvador—up from an annual average of $56.3 million under Carter to $343.6 million during the Reagan years. Aid to Costa Rica rose from $16.9 million per year to $154.5 million, while aid to Honduras went from $40 million to $137.7 million, and aid to Guatemala from $26.6 million to $82.5 million. Only Nicaragua, which got no aid, and Panama, whose aid dropped off sharply in the last three years of the administration, did not share in the Reagan-era bonanza.

While the Reagan administration struggled with Congress, it also faced international pressures to modify its policies. Three sets of countries had come to play important roles in Central America by the time the new administration took office. These included several Western European states and, at times, the European Community as a whole; an increasing number of Latin American countries, led at different times by Mexico, Colombia, or Costa Rica; and the Soviet Union and its allies, including Cuba. All three groups provided significant economic aid to Nicaragua and opposed U.S. policy in El Salvador to one degree or another. The Soviet Union and its allies also provided security assistance to Nicaragua[11] and, together with some Western European and Latin American countries, gave both moral support and small quantities of material aid to the Salvadoran insurgents. All three sets of countries also engaged in efforts to broker peaceful settlements to the conflicts in the region, which would have had two negative consequences for administration policy if they had been successful. First, all of the proposed settlements would have required the United States to abandon one or more of its main policy goals, because none would have guaranteed the overthrow of the Sandinista regime in Nicaragua or a victory for the Salvadoran armed forces over the FMLN. Second, all of these international efforts would have removed political and diplomatic initiative in the region from the hands of the United States, an outcome incompatible with the reassertion of U.S. dominance. The United States therefore sought to discourage such efforts and worked to undermine those it could not deflect.

The Reagan administration sought to end Western European aid to Nicaragua, and to enlist support from Western European states for its efforts in El Salvador, with varying degrees of success. Opposing the United States in Central America, though popular with Western European publics, served no security interest for Western Europe and was only indirectly related to that region's economic interests, which were important elsewhere in Latin America but miniscule on the isthmus itself. Most Western European countries reduced their activities in Central America in the face of determined U.S. hostility. The electoral defeat of West Germany's Social Democratic government in 1982 proved to be especially helpful to the Reagan administration; the new Christian Democratic government cut aid to Nicaragua and ended the West German government's interest in mediating regional conflicts. Although various Western European governments and political organizations continued to be active in Central America, they played a decidedly secondary role.

Latin American involvement in Central America also varied over time. The Reagan administration found sympathy for its policies in the military regimes with which it initially sought closer relations. However, domestic political opposition, encouraged by the Carter administration, together with the financial and economic crisis that struck the region in 1982, produced a decided trend toward redemocratization throughout Latin America.[12] While the U.S. administration lost friends in the region, it did not gain many enemies. The Carter human rights strategy had succeeded in deflecting criticism of the United States for its past support of dictatorships. The economic crisis made the new democratic governments more dependent than they would otherwise have been on Washington's financial assistance. Initially, none of the newly elected governments in the region indulged in criticism of U.S. policies in Central America, although by the end of the decade most had come to support the Contadora Group and Arias peace proposals, which the United States opposed. The major regional actors—Mexico, Colombia, and Venezuela among them—had not experienced military rule in the 1960s and 1970s and did not feel threatened by their military establishments. They did, however, suffer from the effects of the economic crisis and increased dependence on the United States. The United States applied pressure to reduce peace efforts in Central America, particularly on Mexico. This pressure was counterbalanced, however, by security concerns. All three nations perceived the fighting in the region as potentially threatening and, to one degree or another, opposed U.S. policies, which tended to intensify the conflicts. Latin American diplomatic initiatives challenged U.S. policy most effectively during periods when the U.S. administration was weakened by domestic political preoccupations—that is, during the 1984 presidential election year and after the November 1986 elections, which returned control of the U.S. Senate to the Democrats and were followed by the Iran-contra scandal.

The problems the administration faced in Central America proved to be the most difficult of all. Allies in the region proved less reliable and effective than anticipated and enemies refused to surrender.

THE SALVADORAN CIVIL WAR

The new administration first gave priority attention to El Salvador, where intelligence estimates indicated that popular support for the

FDR-FMLN, together with the corresponding lack of support and weak authority of the governing junta and the savagery, corruption, and sheer incompetence of the Salvadoran military, threatened an insurgent victory. Though the January 1981 FMLN "final offensive" had failed by the time the new president was inaugurated, the insurgents had demonstrated an alarming capacity to fight effectively in the face of superior numbers and firepower. The administration thus set out to secure additional military aid right away and ordered the Pentagon to devise a long-term strategy for the military defeat of the guerrillas. Military aid to El Salvador rose from only $5.9 million in 1980 to a peak of $196.6 million in 1984. In addition, most of the Economic Support Funds (ESF), classified as economic aid, went to cover budget deficits incurred by the Salvadoran government for war-related expenses; ESF funding reached a high point of $285 million in 1985. Nearly all of the U.S. military (as well as economic) aid to El Salvador during the Reagan administration consisted of outright grants. Economic aid to shore up the country's battered economy increased dramatically.

Increases in military and economic aid required congressional approval, but continuing reports of human rights violations by the Salvadoran armed forces and the death squads linked to them made many in Congress reluctant to support the president's military aid proposals. Few in Congress opposed the administration's goal of defeating the insurgents. Congressional opponents and skeptics claimed, however, that this goal could not be achieved unless the Salvadoran government and military made themselves more attractive to the Salvadoran population by ending human rights abuses, creating democratic institutions, and implementing social reforms, particularly agrarian reform. Members of Congress also argued that the Salvadoran government should negotiate with the noncombatant political opposition, the FDR, as well as the FMLN insurgents, to explore prospects for ending the civil war through a political settlement rather than through further bloodshed.

The administration's initial response was to ignore the human rights question and to sidestep the other issues by claiming that the Salvadoran guerrillas were part of a Soviet-Cuban-Nicaraguan plot aimed at the United States. It escalated the Carter administration's accusations against Nicaragua by claiming that Soviet-bloc countries were sending large quantities of arms and equipment to the FMLN through Nicaragua. On 23 February 1981 the administration issued a white paper based on captured FMLN documents that, it claimed, provided clear evidence to support its charges. In fact, after the January offensive, the Nicaraguan authorities had reduced what aid they had been providing to the Salvadoran rebels in an effort to placate the new administration in Washington, and the administration had no evidence in hand to indicate Soviet-bloc aid to the rebels. Once the captured FMLN documents on which the white paper was based were released to the press, reporters discovered they actually contradicted most of the administration's claims. Congress cut the administration's first aid proposal in April and approved a smaller aid package on the condition that the president certify every six months that El Salvador was making progress in human rights.[13]

Congressional pressure thus forced the administration to reconsider its initial inclination to give the Salvadoran military a free hand to suppress the insurgency without the constraints that a serious human rights effort might have imposed. In a major speech on 16 July 1981 the new assistant secretary of state for inter-American affairs, Thomas Enders, pledged the administration to pursue goals virtually identical to those of the Carter administration: human rights, democracy, agrarian reform, and a negotiated end to the civil war. The speech was intended to assure Congress that the conditions it had imposed in April had become administration policy and thus to facilitate approval of the administration's escalating aid requests. In practice, however, the administration treated these objectives as decidedly secondary to the prosecution of the war. U.S. Ambassador White, whose denunciations of military and death-squad atrocities were deemed excessive, had been fired on 1 February; his successor, Dean Hinton, was reassigned on 28 May 1983, after having been reprimanded for publicly criticizing the military's failure to improve its record in a speech he had made the previous fall.[14] The administration secured the long-promised resignation of Defense Minister General García in April 1983, but he was replaced by General Carlos Eugenio Vides Casanova, whose human rights record was no better. Moreover, the principal motive for ousting García was the army's failure to fight effectively against the FMLN and the conviction in Washington that an effective counterinsurgency effort required new leadership. With Congress threatening to cut off aid altogether, Vice-President George Bush flew into San Salvador for a six-hour visit on 11 December 1983 with a "hit list" of army officers the United States wanted cashiered or transferred away from command positions. The Salvadoran army made most of the changes Bush demanded, but its human rights record initially improved largely because the army ran out of easy targets. Death-squad and military executions began to decline once the civilian death toll approached 40,000 and hundreds of thousands of Salvadorans had fled to neighboring countries or to the United States to escape persecution. Continuing pressure on the administration—mostly by Congress—began to yield some positive results by the mid-1980s. Congress continued to reduce military aid requests and require presidential certification until José Napoleón Duarte won election as president in May 1984.

In addition to belated efforts to improve the human rights performance of the military, the administration also sought to improve the army's performance in the field. As Congress balked at military aid requests in 1982 and 1983, intelligence reports indicated that the FMLN was winning the war. By the end of 1983 the guerrillas controlled "roughly one-third" of the national territory.[15] With García gone as defense minister, the United States persuaded the high command to adopt long-standing U.S. tactical prescriptions and to abandon conventional warfare, with its cumbersome, large-scale sweeps through guerrilla territory, which caught few guerrillas but resulted in massive human rights abuses and occasional massacres of civilian populations. The army began to downsize its units and make them more mobile. The more enthusiastic officers stopped retiring to San Salvador for weekends. The use of air power increased; fixed-wing craft bombed guerrilla-held territory, while helicopter units were used on a larger scale to respond to guerrilla attacks and sitings more quickly. These innovations, together with an increase in the size of the armed forces from 12,000 to more than 50,000, began to produce results in 1984. The FMLN was forced to reorganize its battalions into smaller forces and to disperse them more widely. In 1985 and 1986 the Salvadoran army managed to retake territory formerly held by the FMLN, though in most cases an FMLN infrastructure continued to govern these areas and the guerrillas returned as soon as the Salvadoran army units withdrew. The army's new tactics required a civic-action counterpart; instead of terrorizing rural populations into submission, the army was now expected to engage in "counterinsurgent political warfare"[16] to improve relations with the civilian population and thus reduce the guerrillas' base of support. By late 1986 the guerrillas had completed their adjustment to the army's new tactics and were once again capable of launching major battalion-sized assaults, as well as coordinated offensives, throughout the country.

U.S. political debates and the fortunes of war had a major impact on Salvadoran politics and society. One month after Congress cut aid to El Salvador and imposed the certification requirement on the president in April 1981, the Reagan administration sought to recover political initiative. On 10 May, at the urging of the United States, junta president Duarte announced that elections would be held the following year to create a constituent assembly empowered to elect an interim president, serve as a temporary legislature, and draft a new constitution. The U.S. administration hoped that these elections would dampen congressional criticism of its policy; it also sought to "deflect strong pressures for a negotiated settlement" with the FMLN.[17] Coming in the midst of a civil war in which civil liberties scarcely existed, and organized at the behest of the dominant superpower, the 1982 poll was a classic demonstration election, whose purpose was mainly to legitimate the Salvadoran government in the eyes of the U.S. public and Congress.[18]

The FDR parties and organizations, representing the entire political spectrum to the left of the PDC, did not participate in the election, because to do so would have risked the lives of their candidates and supporters in an environment characterized by continuous repression. By law, however, Salvadoran citizens were required to vote. National identity cards were stamped when votes were cast; citizens whose cards were not marked risked harassment, arrest, or worse. Once having marked their ballots, voters placed them in transparent vote boxes in full view of election judges (an innovation designed to make traditional ballot-box stuffing more difficult). Fewer than 400 polling places were established for the country's more than one million eligible voters, guaranteeing long lines of apparently eager voters for the army of reporters and television cameras that descended on the country to witness the voting on 28 May 1982. Despite its limitations, the election was a public relations triumph for the Reagan administration, made all the more impressive by threats against voters issued by one of the FMLN guerrilla organizations and by sporadic attacks on military installations located near polling places in several localities.

The Constituent Assembly elections gave a plurality to the Christian Democratic party (PDC). Two right-wing parties emerged with a majority of the vote and control of the assembly, however. These were the Partido de Conciliación Nacional (PCN), the party controlled by the military and the civil bureaucracy, which had always backed military candidates for the presidency, and the Alianza Republicana Nacional (ARENA), a new party of the extreme right, led by the former deputy chief of military intelligence, Roberto D'Aubuisson, who was linked to the death squads and implicated in the March 1980 assassination of Archbishop Romero. The PCN-ARENA coalition would have elected D'Aubuisson as interim president of the republic had the U.S. embassy not intervened. Eventually, the military high command chose Alvaro Magaña from a list of five names presented to it by Ambassador Hinton, and the assembly voted him into office. D'Aubuisson was elected president of the constituent assembly, which promptly set about reversing the 1981 agrarian reform decree to prevent further distributions of land to landless peasants and tenants. These developments produced discomfort in Washington, particularly when it became evident that President Magaña, himself a former officer and head of a state bank that made unsecured loans to many members of the officer corps, would be less than energetic in pressing for an end to human rights violations. After an initially positive response, which enabled the administration to obtain twice as much aid for El Salvador in 1982 as in 1981, congressional resistance to administration proposals reemerged as the human rights situation failed to improve and the constituent assembly gutted the agrarian reform.

The constituent assembly adopted the new constitution in 1983. It called for presidential elections the following year. With Congress again restive, the Reagan administration recognized that a PDC electoral victory was indispensable to securing the military aid needed to defeat the FMLN. With covert support from the CIA and other U.S. agencies, PDC candidate Duarte won a plurality of the votes in March and defeated ARENA candidate D'Aubuisson in the runoff between the top two vote-getters on 6 May 1984. The PDC followed this success by unexpectedly winning an absolute majority (33 of 60 seats) in the legislative elections held a year later on 31 March 1985.[19] Because of Duarte's reputation as a democrat and reformer, his election served to cement congressional support for the administration's military aid requests. In 1984 Congress approved the Reagan administration's proposal for major increases in military and economic aid and deleted the certification requirement for the first time. Though congressional misgivings resurfaced in subsequent years, the PDC victory produced a broad congressional consensus that guaranteed the passage of aid bills throughout President Reagan's second term, though not always at the levels the administration proposed. Duarte himself traveled to Washington frequently and proved to be an effective lobbyist on behalf of the administration's aid proposals.

Although the 1984 and 1985 elections had many of the hallmarks of demonstration elections, Terry Karl has argued persuasively that the PDC victories were more than mere shows for U.S. consumption because they produced important consequences for the Salvadoran political system.[20] The PDC could not have won without genuine campaigning in which it promised to curb the abuses of the security forces, reactivate the agrarian reform, restore trade union rights, and negotiate an end to the war. The PDC victories thus served to open political space for at least moderate opposition to the status quo and encouraged a cautious renewal of the social movements the army had violently suppressed in 1981 through 1983. The armed forces, which had become steadily more dependent on U.S. aid as guerrilla successes mounted, accepted the PDC victory for the same reason that the U.S. administration had promoted it: it was the price they had to pay to raise the funds needed to prosecute the war.

Duarte, however, lacked the authority to reform the military, and with at best ambivalent support in Washington, his pledges to do so went largely unfulfilled. Death-squad killings and other indicators of human rights abuses declined, but no institutional means were created to exercise effective control over the military. None of the perpetrators of past massacres and abuses was brought to trial, except in the two cases involving U.S. citizens (the four churchwomen raped and murdered in December 1980 and the two AIFLD employees gunned down in January 1981). Duarte's efforts to build the PDC organization relied on traditional patronage, in which the beneficiaries of the government's reforms were to become a permanent electoral base. Despite the PDC's control of the constituent assembly, however, Duarte did little to reactivate and extend the agrarian reform and was unable to arrest a continuing decline in living standards. The PDC peasant organization eventually broke with the party, even though it lost U.S. government aid money channeled through its AIFLD advisers. Similarly, the PDC attempted, initially with some success, to replace the decimated left-wing parties at the head of the labor movement, but economic conditions continued to deteriorate, the government broke strikes, and the PDC lost ground again. U.S. aid became a major source of clients for the regime, but well-documented charges of corruption by PDC officials and organizers turned this source of support against the PDC by the end of the Duarte administration.

Nor did Duarte fulfill his promises to end the civil war through negotiations, since neither the military nor the Reagan administration was prepared to abandon its goal of a military victory over the insurgents. Duarte did exploit a momentary lapse in the usual belligerence of the U.S. posture to offer negotiations in a speech he delivered to the U.N. General Assembly in September 1984, despite last-minute efforts by U.S. Ambassador Thomas Pickering to dissuade him. The U.S. administration, unwilling to appear intransigent in the final weeks of the campaign to reelect President Reagan, expressed warm public support for the initiative. The FDR-FMLN accepted Duarte's offer immediately. On 15 October 1984 Duarte traveled to the small town of La Palma to meet with a delegation led by FDR President Guillermo Ungo (his 1972 running mate). The talks created a sensation in El Salvador, but after President Reagan's reelection on 6 November, Duarte was forced to abandon the effort. The two sides met again at Ayagualo on 30 November, as agreed to at La Palma, with neither Duarte nor Ungo present. The government negotiators had no proposals to make and, after denouncing FMLN intransigence, Duarte suspended the talks. The next time Duarte communicated with the guerrillas, it was to negotiate the release of his daughter, whom the FMLN kidnapped on 10 September 1985 in order to secure the release of political prisoners held by the security forces; she was released unharmed on 24 October. Contacts were resumed following an FDR-FMLN peace initiative in 1986, but nothing resulted from them; the FMLN canceled a meeting both sides had agreed to hold in Sesori when the army occupied the town. In August 1987 Duarte, along with the four other Central American presidents, signed the Esquipulas II accords, which committed the signatories to negotiate a political settlement with armed insurgents, but only Nicaragua complied fully with its terms. Duarte left office in 1989 with the civil war still raging.

The major achievement of the Duarte presidency was, as Karl has suggested, "unanticipated" by the military, by the United States, or even by Duarte and the PDC. Salvadoran "democracy," which had begun as a convenient facade for prosecuting the war, evolved into a complex, hybrid regime. It was not democratic in any conventional sense; its survival depended on the largesse of a foreign power, its electoral results and political decision making were largely subject to decisions made in Washington, and it did not even directly control its own military establishment. But neither was it a continuation of the pre-1979 regime, in which the military ruled in alliance with a narrow sector of the business elite. Criticism of the government, particularly by the right-wing parties and their business allies, became commonplace. The PDC government and its followers criticized the oligarchy and, rhetorically at least, championed democracy and reform. Moreover, Duarte's peace initiatives proved immensely popular[21] and, though stifled by the United States and the military and criticized by the right-wing opposition, served nonetheless to broaden the limits of political dialogue in the country. Turmoil in the Reagan administration after the Iran-contra scandal broke in November 1986, together with the peace process initiated by Costa Rican

President Oscar Arias in January 1987, had similar effects. Small numbers of FDR militants and politicians returned to El Salvador during 1986 and 1987. Some managed to reestablish contact with grass-roots movements through the Church or PDC-affiliated organizations. Toward the end of 1987 Ungo and the FDR Vice-President Rubén Zamora returned to El Salvador to test the limits of the country's shaky tolerance for political debate and dissent. They survived.

Duarte's failure to end the war, the drop in living standards, the disillusionment of many PDC supporters with the slow pace of reform, splits in the party, and the widespread impression of persistent corruption among PDC officials weakened the Duarte government and, in the absence of the left, produced an electoral swing to the right. In the 20 March 1988 municipal and legislative elections the PDC lost control of the National Assembly to the right-wing coalition of ARENA (13 seats), the PCN (12 seats) and two minor parties (one seat each). The PDC remained the largest party in the assembly, with 29 seats, but lost 200 of the 262 municipal governments (the exact ratio of its electoral victory in 1985). On 19 March 1989 ARENA won the presidential elections as well. FDR candidates did not run in the 1988 elections, which the FMLN opposed, but after long negotiations the FMLN agreed to respect the FDR's decision to run candidates for president and vice-president in 1989. Though beset by death threats and actual assaults and unable to campaign effectively outside San Salvador, the FDR candidates managed to test the limits of the new and more open political system the Reagan administration had inadvertently created for the country.

Meanwhile, the civil war had reached a stalemate. The army could not defeat the guerrillas, but the guerrillas had little prospect of defeating the army and taking control of the country. By the end of the Reagan administration the death toll had passed 70,000, with no end in sight.

REAGAN AND THE SANDINISTAS

While U.S. policy toward Nicaragua never wavered from its goal of overthrowing the Sandinista regime, domestic and international pressures on the administration varied over time. Policy making fell roughly into four periods. From 20 January 1981 until late November or early December 1983 the administration orchestrated a dramatic escalation in tensions in U.S. relations with Nicaragua. This escalation included the organization and financing of irregular military forces, led mainly by former officers of Somoza's National Guard (eventually referred to as contras),[22] to conduct terrorist attacks from the territory of Honduras and, for a time, from Costa Rica. The administration rejected Nicaraguan concessions and appeals for negotiations, turned aside offers to mediate from Western European and Latin American countries, employed CIA agents (initially under contra cover) to attack targets and mine harbors inside the country, carried out a series of large-scale military exercises from newly constructed bases in Honduras, ordered the Pentagon to study the feasibility of direct U.S. military intervention, and fired policy-level and diplomatic personnel whose enthusiasm for negotiations or mediation it deemed excessive. The economic component of this escalation included the suspension of the economic aid program initiated by the Carter administration, a successful effort to push the Western European countries to scale back their aid programs, pressure on multilateral lending institutions to reject new loan applications from Nicaragua, and a 90 percent reduction in the Nicaraguan sugar quota. This phase ended late in 1983, when the president was persuaded to deescalate the conflict temporarily in order to avoid making Central America an issue in the presidential primaries and general election in 1984.

The second phase lasted from late 1983 to 6 November 1984, the date of the U.S. presidential election. During this period of somewhat less than one year, the United States opened diplomatic negotiations with Nicaragua, accommodated itself publicly to a congressional ban on contra aid (while initiating secret efforts to circumvent it), expressed support for third-party mediation efforts (notably that of the Contadora Group, which consisted of Colombia, Mexico, Panama, and Venezuela), and barely managed to turn aside both domestic and international pressures for a peace settlement when the Nicaraguan government unexpectedly agreed to sign a Contadora draft treaty that embodied nearly all of the U.S. security concerns. The main problem the administration faced in this period stemmed from its own rhetoric, which created the impression that it could be persuaded to reach an agreement with the Sandinista regime. This gave a certain unwanted momentum to peace efforts by Mexico and its Contadora partners, as well as to various Western European initiatives. Resisting these intrusions without creating a campaign issue for the Democrats complicated the work of various administration policy makers. This phase ended with President Reagan's landslide reelection victory.

The third phase ran from 6 November 1984 to November 1986. During this two-year period the administration rapidly reescalated the conflict with Nicaragua. It suspended the negotiations with Nicaragua begun the year before, imposed a full-scale economic embargo, refused to recognize decisions of the International Court of Justice (the World Court) on matters pertaining to Central America, persuaded Congress to vote military aid to the contras for the first time, successfully sidelined the Contadora and all other mediation efforts, forced Mexico to end subsidized oil shipments to Nicaragua as a condition for new lending from the International Monetary Fund (IMF), pushed the Soviet Union to reduce economic and military aid, and stepped up military exercises in Honduras. The administration did not, however, reach the point at which direct U.S. military intervention would have become politically feasible. In the 4 November 1986 mid-term elections the president's party lost control of the Senate. Two weeks later the administration fell into confusion and turmoil as the Iran-contra scandal erupted.

In the fourth and final phase, from November 1986 to the inauguration of President George Bush in January 1989, the administration effectively lost control of events in Central America. The Arias peace plan, opposed by the United States, was launched in January 1987 and signed in August by all five Central American presidents supported by the Contadora Group, four South American democracies, and the Soviet bloc. Congress supported the agreement, turned aside new requests for contra military aid, and approved only humanitarian assistance until the Arias plan could take effect. By January 1989, with the peace process in full swing, the contras politically isolated, and the Nicaraguan government preparing for elections it felt confident of winning,[23] U.S. policy toward Nicaragua had virtually collapsed.

As soon as it took office, the Reagan administration expressed the view that Nicaragua was becoming, or had already become, a Marxist-Leninist instrument of Soviet designs upon the United States. While initial statements about Nicaragua complained chiefly about Nicaraguan arms aid to the Salvadoran insurgents, the president soon made it clear that he objected to the Sandinista regime as much for what it was as for what it did. Nicaragua had become a "Soviet beachhead" on the American mainland and "a totalitarian dungeon." Nicaragua, in short, had either become or was fast becoming "another Cuba."

The evidence for such characterizations was surprisingly thin. The FSLN never abandoned its public commitment to "pluralist democracy and a mixed economy." It did not carry out a large-scale program of nationalizing privately owned productive property (apart from expropriating Somoza family assets), nor did it impose a single-party monopoly on political power. The Sandinistas did, however, consolidate their authority as the country's dominant political party, mobilize domestic support through a diverse array of mass organizations, create a new security apparatus impervious to U.S. influence, and seek closer relations, including economic and military aid, from a wide range of foreign governments. Left to its own devices, the Sandinista regime would probably have evolved into a populist variant of the Mexican model, with a relatively open political system and regular elections to serve as a kind of plebiscite on the dominant party's rule as well as a means for the regime to take stock and alter course as needed to maintain popular support. In economic policy the regime would probably have attempted to pursue a state-centered development model with private investors, both domestic and foreign, subject to a greater degree of supervision and regulation than the United States, particularly during a conservative administration, would have preferred. Given internal resource constraints as well as external limitations on the country's trade-dependent economy, however, the Sandinistas would have had to modify some of their more ambitious plans for public-sector development over time, as in fact they did after 1985. Given the high level of domestic and international support the FSLN attracted in its early years, and its capacity to resist extraordinary U.S. pressure for most of the 10 years it held power, FSLN rule might well have proved as durable as that of the Mexican Partido Revolucionario Institucional (PRI).[24]

The FSLN's endorsement of democratic institutions and a mixed economy was consistent with the domestic as well as the international constraints the Sandinistas faced on taking power. Unlike the Cuban revolutionaries two decades earlier, the Sandinistas confronted a large and well-organized business elite whose active participation through its own organizations in the struggle to overthrow the dictator led it to demand a prominent role in the new regime. Moreover, the Nicaraguan private sector controlled nearly all of the country's export-producing capacity, which the Sandinistas not only refrained from nationalizing but actually subsidized heavily in order to generate foreign-exchange earnings. Unlike the Cuban business class, which fled the island en masse in 1960–61 in the expectation that the United States would depose Castro, most of Nicaragua's capitalists (except those closely linked to the Somoza regime) stayed in the country.

Also, the "popular" classes in Nicaragua were structured and organized differently from those in Cuba. Unlike Cuba's large proletariat, with its well-organized trade union movement, in which the country's large Communist party played an important role, the Nicaraguan working class was relatively small, largely unorganized, and, until the Sandinista revolution, politically demoralized. The Nicaraguan Communist party, important in the populist phase of the first Somoza's regime in the 1940s, was no more than a shadow of its former self by 1979, after decades of repression. Moreover, the Cuban countryside in 1959, with its huge sugar *centrales* that employed hundreds of unionized cane cutters and mill workers and its relatively small class of independent and tenant farmers, bore little resemblance to the Nicaraguan *campo* of 1979, with its huge class of land-hungry squatters, tenants, and independent farmers. In short, the social base and potential political support for a socialist transition along Cuban lines did not exist in Nicaragua, and the FSLN prudently refrained from launching the country onto such a path.

The Cuban and Nicaraguan revolutions differed in yet another important way. From 1959 to 1962, when the Castro government sought external support in the face of actual and anticipated U.S. hostility, only the Soviet Union and its bloc allies responded. Twenty years later the Sandinistas received aid not only from the Soviet bloc but from Latin America and Western Europe as well. The Mexican government mounted an impressive aid program and, together with Venezuela, initially provided a major portion of Nicaragua's oil imports on credit at low rates of interest. A number of Western European countries also implemented large aid efforts, as did Canada and Japan. The economic crisis that struck Latin America in 1982, together with U.S. pressures, reduced aid from Latin America, while several Western European countries, along with Japan, later scaled back their programs for various reasons (including U.S. pressure) in 1981–82 and again in 1985. Many, however, continued to offer diplomatic support (or at least diplomatic opposition to U.S. policy) throughout the 1980s. Nicaragua thus faced a far more competitive international environment than Cuba had encountered in the early 1960s. Even at its highest levels, however, foreign aid to Nicaragua never reached the levels of what Cuba had received from the Soviet Union. The Sandinistas were never free to ignore the United States; to the contrary, they were under constant pressure to negotiate and compromise. Moreover, the advice Nicaraguan leaders received from Cuba and the Soviet bloc tended to agree with what they heard from Latin American and Western European governments. None urged them to follow the Cuban model of socialist transition, one-party rule, and alignment with the Soviet Union.

Sandinista foreign policy was generally nonaligned, although it had a decided tilt away from the United States.[25] While initially cautious about relations with the United States and circumspect about exporting its revolution, the regime provided some aid to the Salvadoran FMLN in the fall of 1980 and in early 1981 in the hope of confronting the new Reagan administration with a second revolutionary government on the isthmus and thus deflecting some of the hostility that incoming officials, including the president-elect, had already expressed toward it. But, aside from small quantities of material aid, which could have slipped through to El Salvador undetected, and financial support, which could easily have been concealed, there was little evidence of continuing Sandinista support for the FMLN after April 1981. In October 1983 Salvadoran exiles, including leaders of the FDR and FMLN, departed Managua, where they had been residing or taking occasional furloughs from combat, in order to avoid further complicating Nicaragua's relations with the United States. While FSLN leaders made no secret of their sympathy for the Salvadoran revolutionaries, they did not engage in a major effort to export their revolution.[26]

With both domestic and international pressures pushing them toward compliance with their explicit commitments to political democracy and a mixed economy, the Sandinistas gave no evidence of any intention to alter the course of their regime. In the process of consolidating their power within Nicaragua, the Sandinistas initially moved with some caution. They abolished the death penalty, freed many of the National Guard soldiers they had captured, and avoided confrontations with the business elite or the U.S. embassy. They refrained from criticizing the efforts of U.S. Ambassador Pezzullo, from 1979 until his departure in late 1981, to strengthen political and civic organizations opposed to or competitive with the FSLN—even though they ran contrary to the Sandinistas' desire to emancipate the country from U.S. tutelage and conflicted directly with their own efforts to consolidate their dominance of the country's new political institutions. By the time Pezzullo's replacement, Anthony Quainton, arrived in March 1982, however, U.S. policy had shifted decisively away from the Carter-Pezzullo strategy. The contras, rather than the moderate businessmen and politicians of Managua, had become the preferred instruments of U.S. policy in Nicaragua. While this tended to free the regime from immediate concerns about U.S. reaction to its treatment of the domestic opposition, it was not until the first major contra attack, on 14 March 1982, that the government decreed a state of emergency, imposed press censorship, and restricted civil liberties.[27]

Thereafter the U.S. government and the FSLN leadership engaged in an elaborate tug-of-war, in which U.S. officials cited Sandinista wartime restrictions on the press and civil liberties as additional evidence of their totalitarian bent, while the Nicaraguan government occasionally lifted or modified such restrictions to preserve its democratic credentials in Nicaragua as well as in the United States, Western Europe, and Latin America. The Sandinistas also sought to signal to the Reagan administration their willingness to return to the Carter-Pezzullo game plan, in which pro-U.S. parties, politicians, and media could operate more or less freely, if the United States would call off the contras. The United States was thus forced to choose between the contras and the moderates. It was an easy choice for Washington. Committed to ousting the FSLN from power by military means, the Reagan administration had little use for the nonviolent opposition in Nicaragua, except for propaganda purposes, until after the Sandinistas were gone. Nonetheless, the administration continued the Carter policy of subsidizing the internal opposition, including the Catholic church, the opposition newspaper *La Prensa*, COSEP (the anti-Sandinista business association), and various political parties, trade unions, and other organizations. The total expended on these subsidies, however, was far less than the administration devoted to the contras and, unlike contra aid, evoked no controversy in Congress.

Despite the contra war, the Sandinista regime did not engage in systematic repression of the opposition. The state of emergency imposed in 1982 was lifted during the period of the national election campaign in the summer and fall of 1984, but reimposed in October 1985.[28] Opposition political parties and civic organizations were occasionally harassed but never proscribed (except for the contras, who were offered amnesty if they surrendered voluntarily). Opposition parties ran candidates in the 1984 elections and participated actively in the drafting of the country's new constitution.[29] The government censored the main opposition newspaper, *La Prensa*, and closed it down from July 1986, after the U.S. Congress voted to approve military aid to the contras (which *La Prensa* had endorsed), until October 1987, when it was permitted to resume publishing in compliance with the peace accord signed in August. The Sandinistas also closed the Catholic church radio station on 1 January 1986, ostensibly because it had refused to broadcast President Daniel Ortega's New Year's message. That station resumed broadcasting in October 1987, as did several other radio news programs that had been ordered off the air during the state of emergency. The regime made no effort to jam radio and television broadcasts from neighboring countries (which reached most of the Nicaraguan population), never imposed controls on travel into the country, issued exit visas routinely to Nicaraguans who wished to travel abroad (except for draft-age men and individuals who owed back taxes), and allowed unrestricted travel within the country, except in the war zones. Nicaraguan wartime restrictions on civil liberties were not accompanied by human rights abuses comparable to those committed in El Salvador, Guatemala, or pre-Sandinista Nicaragua; security personnel accused of abuses were usually brought to trial quickly and were frequently convicted and sentenced to prison.

The contras began as disorganized bands of former National Guardsmen who took to raiding towns and attacking government outposts in the remote mountainous region along Nicaragua's border with Honduras soon after the Sandinistas took power. They were encouraged by the chief of the Honduran national police, General Gustavo Alvarez Martínez, and initially aided by Argentine military officers, who provided training and some light arms, beginning in the spring of 1981 at the request of Alvarez, the CIA, and several prominent anti-Sandinista politicians.[30] In March the administration informed the intelligence committee of the Senate that it had decided to organize a paramilitary force of some 500 men to help stem the flow of arms from Nicaragua to the Salvadoran guerrillas. Some $19.5 million, the committee was told, would be devoted to various projects in Central America, including the organization of this force and the provision of subsidies to various Nicaraguan opposition groups. In August 1981 the CIA put together a political organization called the Nicaraguan Democratic Front (FDN), which was to take nominal charge of the contra forces. On 17 November President Reagan signed National Security Directive 17, which authorized an initial expenditure of $19.95 million to cover the costs of organizing, training, and supplying the contras. By this time the Argentine officers were already training contra units in Honduras; other training camps were set up in Florida, Texas, and California. Contras eventually received training from U.S. military personnel at the Laterique base near Tegucigalpa and, beginning in 1986, at Elgin Air Force Base in Florida.

The contra forces grew in number until they reached a peak of approximately 15,000 in the late 1980s.[31] While the contra officer corps was composed mainly of former National Guardsmen, the contras expanded their initial base of former guard soldiers by recruiting backwoods peasants in the mountains, where they were most active. In addition, the United States provided initial support for a southern front of some 2,000 fighters, organized by former FSLN leader Eden Pastora from Costa Rica, and for irregular forces of anti-Sandinista Indians, numbering up to 3,000, that operated in the lowlands along the Honduran border to the east of the FDN, near the Atlantic coast. The southern front collapsed by late 1984, and when Pastora refused to subordinate his forces to the FDN, the CIA ended its support. Most of the leaders of the Indian irregulars made a separate peace with the Nicaraguan government shortly thereafter. For most of the war the contras were synonymous with the FDN.

As a fighting force, the contras' fortunes depended primarily on arms and supplies provided by the U.S. government, either directly or through various intermediaries. U.S. funding was channeled through the CIA from early 1981 through the fiscal year ending in October 1983. Support also came from the Defense Department, which provided training, equipment, and transport facilities and constructed FDN command centers in northern Honduras. Beginning in fiscal year 1983–84, contra funding became overt and subject to congressional appropriation. In that year Congress voted openly to provide $24 million for the contras. During the campaign year of 1984 revelations that the CIA had mined Nicaraguan harbors and carried out other terrorist acts, along with charges of contra corruption, human rights abuses, alleged connections to drug traffickers, and political isolation, persuaded Congress to cut off contra aid entirely for fiscal year 1984–85. After President Reagan's reelection in 1984, however, Congress reversed itself and approved $27 million in "nonlethal" aid to the contras for fiscal year 1985–86. The administration's greatest congressional victory came in 1986, when Congress approved an administration request for $100 million for fiscal year 1986–87, of which $30 million could be spent on arms. Then came the Senate losses in November 1986, followed by the Iran-contra scandal and the Arias peace plan. After voting down funding for fiscal year 1987–88, Congress approved "nonlethal" or humanitarian aid for 1988–89. Throughout the Reagan years contra aid appropriations depended mainly on votes in the House of Representatives, where fewer than 30 legislators, mainly Democrats, determined the outcome. The administration's margin of victory in the 25 June 1986 House vote to approve the $100 million for 1986–87 was only 12 votes (221 to 209).

The administration's difficulties in securing congressional support for contra funding were compounded by various restrictions on what aid it did get (except in 1986). In December 1982 Congress approved the first of two Boland amendments (named for their sponsor, Representative Edward Boland) that forbade any expenditure for the purpose of overthrowing the government of Nicaragua. The administration claimed that the contras' purpose was to interdict supplies to the Salvadoran FMLN and ignored the restriction. The following year, when Congress openly voted for aid, it imposed the same condition and further specified that the administration could not supplement the funds approved by Congress with money from the CIA's secret budget. The administration ignored this restriction as well. When contra funding for fiscal 1984–85 was voted down, Congress passed a second Boland amendment forbidding any intelligence agency of the government from providing assistance to the contras. The administration evaded this restriction by organizing an elaborate aid effort, managed by Colonel Oliver North, a White House aide employed by the National Security Council, with the cooperation of policy-level personnel at the CIA and the Department of State. This effort provided the contras with more than $50 million in supplies, including arms, from 1984 through late 1986.

In addition to private donations solicited directly by Colonel North and other officials, assistance came from the governments of Brunei, Costa Rica, El Salvador, Guatemala, Honduras, Israel, Panama, Saudi Arabia, and Taiwan.[32] U.S. officials also approached the governments of Chile, China, Great Britain, Singapore, South Africa, and Venezuela for help. Funds were channeled through a private network organized by North and operated by former U.S. military and intelligence officials as a private "enterprise." The most spectacular of the White House efforts involved the sale of U.S. weaponry (mainly antitank missiles) to the government of Iran. In exchange for these weapons, the Iranians agreed to secure the release of U.S. hostages held by terrorists in Lebanon. Profits from the sales were diverted to Swiss bank accounts and used to purchase weapons for the contras. This scheme provided the contras with another $10 million to $30 million for arms purchases. All of these contra aid efforts violated congressional restrictions as well as other federal laws. When they were revealed, beginning in November 1986, congressional support for the administration's policies toward Nicaragua evaporated.

With or without congressional approval, the administration managed to keep the contras in arms and well supplied for most of the period from mid-1981 until it left office. Supply difficulties occurred in the summer of 1981, late in 1984, and again in the fall of 1985, in the latter instance because the Honduran government refused to permit contra supplies to be shipped through its installations outside Tegucigalpa for several months. From 1986 until well after the Reagan administration left office, the contras had sufficient arms and supplies to mount widespread attacks inside Nicaragua.

The contras failed, however, to come close to their objective of overthrowing the Sandinista regime, for two main reasons. First, their battlefield performance left much to be desired. Between 1984 and late 1985 the Nicaraguan army managed to inflict a strategic defeat on the contras, imposing severe losses that forced the contras to abandon attacks on military targets and to concentrate on poorly defended civilian farms and villages. This shift in tactics allowed the contras to continue to inflict economic losses on the Nicaraguan regime—both directly, through damage to crops and installations, and indirectly, by forcing the government to impose an unpopular military draft and devote more than half of its budget to military expenditures. At no time after late 1984, however, did the contras pose a serious military threat to the Sandinista regime. Despite urgings from their CIA supervisors, the contras never managed to seize and defend any territory. Second, the contras' military incapacity reinforced their political weaknesses. In part because their officer corps was dominated by former National Guard officers, the contras failed to develop a credible political identity. After repeated charges of human rights abuses, in part the result of the tactical shift to civilian targets, the CIA (and later the NSC) attempted various reforms of the contra leadership, mainly to impress Congress. But the FDN (renamed the United Nicaraguan Opposition—or UNO—in one of its U.S.-engineered reforms) never developed much of a following within Nicaragua.

In response to congressional and public criticism, the administration repeatedly expressed its willingness to reach a negotiated diplomatic resolution of its conflict with the Sandinista regime but made no serious attempt to do so. Assistant Secretary of State Enders made several trips to Managua in the summer of 1981, met with Nicaraguan leaders, and suggested that the United States would be willing to tolerate the FSLN regime in exchange for a Nicaraguan agreement to end all aid to the FMLN and reduce the size of its armed forces. Back in Washington, however, Enders encountered problems within the administration. In letters to the Nicaragua authorities detailing his proposals, his position hardened. The United States insisted that Nicaragua limit its army to 15,000 to 17,000 and halt acquisition of "armed or unarmed helicopters and aircraft, armored personnel carriers, howitzers, and armed vehicles."[33] Nicaragua would also have to "recrate its newly acquired Soviet tanks and ship them back to countries of origin."[34] The Nicaraguans, who had been willing to stop aiding the FMLN and to accept some arms limits, responded by demanding that the United States enforce its own laws, shut down camps at which contras were already training in the United States, and take steps to reduce tensions in the region—a reference to Nicaraguan discomfort at large-scale U.S. military maneuvers in Honduras. Enders did not pursue the matter further, and U.S.-Nicaraguan negotiations came to an end until 1984.[35]

The United States reopened negotiations as Congress moved toward cutting off aid in early 1984 and the presidential election campaign began to heat up. In June 1984 Secretary of State George Shultz, on a visit to El Salvador to attend the inauguration of President Duarte, stopped in Managua on the way home and met for two and a half hours with FSLN leader Daniel Ortega. Shultz "reaffirmed the usual four points of concern about the Sandinistas' foreign military advisers, support for the Salvadoran insurgents, the military build-up, and finally the 'failure to fulfill their 1979 promises of pluralism, democracy and elections.'"[36] Ortega replied that Nicaragua was not prepared to negotiate about Nicaragua's internal politics, but the two agreed to send representatives to what would become a series of talks in the Mexican resort town of Manzanillo. The talks were conducted by U.S. Special Envoy in Charge of Central American Negotiations Harry Shlaudeman and Nicaraguan Deputy Foreign Minister Victor Hugo Tinoco. The Nicaraguans had requested that a Mexican official attend the talks, but the United States resisted. Instead officials of the Mexican foreign ministry stayed nearby and consulted regularly with their Nicaragua counterparts. Though the talks began in late June, the U.S. side did not even present a written proposal until 5 September. The document called for a series of Nicaraguan steps, including the withdrawal of foreign advisers, the expulsion of FMLN personnel from the country, an agreement to limit arms acquisitions, cease-fire negotiations with the contras, and internationally supervised elections. The proposal offered little in exchange for these steps, and the Nicaraguans did not take it seriously. The Nicaraguan counterproposal, submitted in late October, responded to the security issues raised by the United States—foreign advisers, support for for FMLN, and arms limits—but did not refer to internal politics. On the security issues, the Nicaraguans referred to the text of the Contadora draft treaty, which they had unexpectedly agreed to sign on 21 September. Within days of the Nicaraguan proposal at Manzanillo, President Reagan was reelected. The U.S. administration suspended the talks on 18 January 1985.[37]

After January 1985 the administration made no further effort to negotiate with the Nicaraguan government. In April of that year, in an effort to persuade Congress to resume contra aid, the president did offer a peace plan, secure in the knowledge that its terms would be unacceptable to the Nicaraguans. The Sandinista foreign minister, Miguel D'Escoto, reacted in less than a day: "What President Reagan has said is: 'You drop dead or I will kill you.'"[38] While proposing terms the Nicaraguans would not accept, the administration worked hard to deflect other proposals the Nicaraguans might have accepted; this policy continued until the administration left office in January 1989. When a negotiated peace was actually achieved in August 1987 the U.S. administration did not participate directly in designing it, sought to undermine its implementation, and left office blaming Congress for failing to provide adequate support for its policies.[39]

The U.S. administration was aware of the contras' military and political limitations, as internal documents released during the Iran-contra scandal amply demonstrated. Since the contras could not have been expected to achieve the objective for which they were created—the overthrow of the Sandinista regime—commentators have offered diverse hypotheses to explain the administration's unswerving support of them. The hypotheses fall into three broad categories. The first, best articulated by reporter Roy Gutman, offers "bureaucratic politics" as an explanation. His work stresses the peculiar decision-making style of President Reagan, which "invited indiscipline and competition"[40] and thus made it difficult for the administration to develop a coherent set of diplomatic objectives. Lack of direction and indecision favored the hard-line contra supporters, who used the president's uninstructed but decidedly anticommunist sentiments to block any serious efforts to reach an accommodation with the Sandinista regime. A second hypothesis emphasizes the domestic political constraints on the administration. The contras could not be abandoned without alienating the right wing of the Republican party, whose votes the president needed in Congress and whose rank-and-file supporters provided the most enthusiastic volunteers on election days. The hard right got what amounted to a veto on Central American policy, which helped the administration retain its support for more pragmatic foreign policies toward other regions where more important U.S. interests were at stake. While each of these hypotheses rests on well-known facts, both imply that U.S. support for the contras was irrational as a policy. In a narrow sense this implication is certainly true. As William LeoGrande suggested, however, the administration's persistent efforts to secure congressional support for the contras may also be seen as part of a larger strategy of escalation, "aimed less at the immediate goal of securing a few million dollars for the contras than at the longer term goal of breaking the back of the domestic political opposition to Reagan's aggressive use of military force to overthrow the government of Nicaragua."[41] In this third view, support for the contras did make sense as policy, but only as part of an effort to create the political support necessary for a direct U.S. military intervention.

The contras also made policy sense in a larger regional and international context, given the administration's more general objectives. First, to abandon the contras would have left the administration no alternative but to revert to the Carter policy of accepting Nicaragua's independence of U.S. dominance and attempting to exert influence in unfavorable circumstances. Such a policy would certainly have produced results in the long run, but it could also have encouraged the insurgent movements elsewhere in the region, particularly in El Salvador and possibly in Guatemala as well. Even a verifiable prohibition on Nicaraguan aid to the Salvadoran rebels, to which the Sandinistas were willing to agree, would have called into question the U.S. objective of defeating the FMLN in El Salvador by implying that the United States was willing to tolerate a regime run by like-minded leftists. Second, the contras had the salutary effect of punishing the Sandinistas, forcing them to divert immense resources from social and economic development and undermining their domestic support as a result. Ravaging Nicaragua would thus discourage others, policy makers believed, from confronting the United States. Third, U.S. aid to the contras helped to deflect the efforts of other governments to push the United States into agreements that would have left the Sandinistas in power. On several occasions, when peace pressures developed, the administration managed to deflate them by insisting that the Sandinistas negotiate directly with the contras. Until 1987 the Nicaraguan government predictably responded in the negative, preferring to negotiate directly with the contras' "employer."

No one in the Reagan administration ever publicly proposed that the United States deploy its overwhelming military force to overthrow the Sandinista government. On the other hand the administration never ruled out this option. Many in the United States, Nicaragua, and elsewhere believed that the United States was preparing to invade in 1983 or early in 1984. In July 1983 the president ordered the Defense Department to step up its aid to the contras.[42] The contra offensive, broken off in June 1983, resumed in October and November. By fall some 15,000 contras in three CIA-supported forces were active: the FDN in the mountainous northwest (capable of striking within an hour's drive of Managua), the Miskito Indian irregulars on the Atlantic coast, and Pastora's men in the south. In October the CIA official in charge of contra operations, Duane Clarridge, urged the FDN leadership to organize its forces to "seize territory" by January 1984 in preparation for a U.S. intervention. Attacks carried out by CIA Unilaterally Controlled Latino Assets (UCLAs)—that is, Spanish-speaking CIA employees—also escalated in September and October, with major sabotage operations. UCLAs blew up oil storage tanks in Corinto on 11 October and an oil pipeline in Puerto Sandino three days later. Between September 1983 and April 1984 the CIA "carried out at least twenty-two attacks on vital installations."[43] Honduran armed forces chief General Alvarez, who had put his forces on "red alert" in the summer of 1982, was impatient for a U.S. invasion and ready to support it. He took the initiative, supported by the United States, to revive the Central American Defense Council (CONDECA), which "could provide a legal fig leaf for a U.S. intervention."[44] CONDECA's rebirth was announced after a meeting of the defense ministers of El Salvador, Guatemala, and Honduras on 1 October 1983. U.S. military exercises in Honduras that fall eventually involved 10,000 U.S. troops and three naval groups including 19 ships; additional exercises were scheduled for January 1984.

Back in Washington, 1983 began with a major escalation of verbal attacks on the Sandinista regime that culminated in President Reagan's speech to a joint session of Congress on 27 April. The next month Assistant Secretary of State Enders was fired, after the White House leaked a memo he had written urging negotiations to end the Salvadoran civil war and suggesting that the United States accept an offer from Spanish President Felipe González to act as an intermediary. Enders had also attempted to tone down the administration's anti-Sandinista rhetoric.[45] U.S. ambassadors in El Salvador and Costa Rica were also summarily fired in May and July, respectively. On 10 May President Reagan cut Nicaragua's sugar quota by 90 percent—an act that cost the country 5 percent of its export earnings for the year. In June he ordered the closing of all six Nicaraguan consulates in the United States the day after Nicaragua expelled three U.S. embassy employees for spying. In July he announced new military exercises in Honduras and named former Secretary of State Henry Kissinger to head a bipartisan commission to report on U.S. policy in Central America. Throughout the summer and fall of 1983 rumors of an invasion, fed by leaks from the administration, were denied in a perfunctory manner that made them seem increasingly plausible. Late in the year detailed plans for an invasion in early 1984, called Operation Pegasus, circulated in Washington. Finally, in a move the president linked explicitly to the Nicaraguan "threat," the United States invaded and occupied the island nation of Grenada on 23 October.

Despite all these preparations, the United States did not invade Nicaragua in late 1983 or early 1984. In December 1983 the military exercises planned for the following month in Honduras were scaled back. CIA emissaries to the contras countermanded Clarridge's urgings with orders to pull back for the coming year. The president and his advisers toned down their rhetoric and began to emphasize the need for a peaceful solution to conflicts in the region. The circumstances that led the administration to pull back from the brink included polls showing that a large majority of the public still opposed any U.S. military involvement in Central America. Opposition dipped only slightly after the Grenada triumph in October 1983, enough to help secure congressional approval of contra aid. Much less aid was approved than the administration wanted, however, and only after the House had voted twice to cut it off altogether.

Although many U.S. officials, probably including the president, would have welcomed an opportunity to invade Nicaragua, and although some worked actively to create the appropriate conditions, senior officials (including Defense Secretary Caspar Weinberger and Secretary of State Shultz) never advocated it. Opposition was also voiced discreetly by the uniformed military. Though the Pentagon was confident that U.S. forces could occupy Nicaragua's major cities and reduce the Sandinista army to small-scale guerrilla attacks within 90 days, it also understood that no post-Sandinista regime installed by the United States would be likely to survive without a U.S. army of occupation. The prospect of a prolonged conflict, opposed by the U.S. public, in a country where U.S. forces would have to support a weak local government and find themselves surrounded by a hostile population supporting armed insurgents sounded too much like Vietnam for many in the military. In the Restricted Inter-Agency Group, created to manage Central American policy in June 1983, only Vice-Admiral Arthur Moreau, Jr., representing the Joint Chiefs of Staff, consistently opposed proposals to have the contras create a "liberated zone" in preparation for U.S. recognition and a military intervention.[46]

Problems at home were compounded by events abroad. The Contadora Group had been launched in January and had achieved some initial diplomatic successes. On 9 September 1983 it issued its initial "21 Points," a statement of the principles on which a Central American peace agreement could be achieved. Two weeks later Nicaragua announced its support of the Contadora declaration. Then the Nicaraguan government, worried that the United States might invade after the U.S. occupation of Grenada, took a series of unilateral steps designed to convince Congress and the public of its good intentions. In November it persuaded FDR-FMLN leaders to depart

Managua, sent 1,000 Cubans home, and relaxed the state of emergency. In December it announced that the national elections, originally scheduled for 1985, would be moved up to November 1984. A U.S. National Intelligence Estimate in January 1983 had indicated that the Sandinistas still enjoyed the support of most Nicaraguans; nothing had happened by the end of the year to alter that conclusion. Nor had the rapid escalation of U.S. pressure in 1982–83 produced any discernible cracks in the regime, as had occurred in Grenada on the eve of the U.S. invasion.

After the reelection of President Reagan in 1984, the reescalation of U.S. hostility toward Nicaragua in 1985 and 1986, accompanied by congressional approval for aid to the contras in both years, created a more favorable climate for U.S. military action. The administration also made some headway in discouraging Western European and Latin American aid to Nicaragua and, by late 1985, in turning aside the Contadora mediation effort. Intelligence estimates showed increasing alarm and opposition within Nicaragua as contra attacks continued, military conscription proved unpopular, and the Nicaraguan economy was strained by depression and inflation. Public hostility in the United States to military intervention, the contras' problematical reputation and military setbacks, Pentagon reservations, and other difficulties could have been overcome, but the 1986 congressional election losses and the eruption of the Iran-contra scandal two weeks later put an end to the administration's capacity to pursue its goal of overthrowing the government of Nicaragua.

MOBILIZING CLIENTS

In its relations with Costa Rica, Guatemala, Honduras, and Panama, the Reagan administration sought primarily to mobilize support for the Salvadoran government and the Nicaraguan contras. From 1981 to 1983 its efforts succeeded in Honduras and Panama, achieved some gains in Costa Rica, and failed in the case of Guatemala. In the U.S. presidential election year of 1984 the administration successfully mobilized Costa Rica, El Salvador, and Honduras to block the Contadora mediation effort (though Honduran enthusiasm for the contras diminished). Panama aided the contras but continued its membership in the Contadora Group, while Guatemala extended its neutral stance to include support for Contadora. As tensions reescalated in 1985–86, U.S. efforts encountered increasing difficulties. Honduran President Suazo became truculent when the U.S. administration refused to support his anticonstitutional grab for a second term, Guatemala's newly elected civilian government began promoting peace talks, Costa Ricans unexpectedly elected a peace candidate opposed by the United States, and Panamanian military chief Manuel Antonio Noriega, a major CIA asset, balked at U.S. requests for additional contra aid and refused U.S. demands that he resign when his drug trafficking, human rights violations, and other frailties were exposed by the U.S. media. When the Reagan administration weakened in late 1986, support for U.S. policy toward Nicaragua in the region quickly evaporated.

Honduran collaboration with U.S. policy included the virtual surrender of control over territory along its border with Nicaragua to the contras, as well as the nominal participation of its armed forces in joint military exercises with U.S. forces. The inauguration of President Suazo on 27 January 1982 cemented this relationship. Suazo's election owed much to the Carter administration's pressure on the Honduran military to permit a transition to civilian rule. The Reagan administration capitalized on Suazo's dependence when it persuaded him to appoint General Alvarez as armed forces chief on assuming office. Alvarez provided enthusiastic support for the contras and lobbied for a direct U.S. military intervention in Nicaragua. In exchange for Honduran support, the Reagan administration pushed Congress to approve substantial increases in U.S. economic and military aid.

Guatemala proved more complicated. Preoccupied with internal turmoil and divided by internal rivalries, the country's military establishment was in no position to offer much help to Washington. Moreover, the administration could not persuade Congress to renew military aid,[47] despite evidence that the Guatemalan guerrilla movements posed a serious threat to the regime. The administration's initial efforts to improve relations thus produced no tangible results for policy goals elsewhere in the region, but the U.S. administration and Guatemalan military leaders agreed that priority should be given to defeating the insurgents. By 1981 three guerrilla armies were fielding 6,000 armed combatants against the 17,000 men in the Guatemalan army. The largest of the guerrilla movements "was active on seven fronts nominally covering two-thirds of the country's territory."[48] Guerrillas had already "occupied about forty important settlements, including one provincial capital."[49] Meanwhile, the government's political resources had reached a low point. After years of repression, the government had little active support to match the growing popularity of the guerrillas, especially in the Indian highlands. A major army offensive in Chimaltenango province in November 1981 made some headway, but most of the guerrillas in the area escaped unharmed. The president, General Romeo Lucas García, sought to impose his own candidate as president in blatantly fraudulent elections on 9 March 1982 and sent troops into the streets of Guatemala City to suppress protests. The international reaction to these events threatened to isolate Guatemala still further from potential sources of external aid, including the United States, just as its economy turned sharply downward. On 23 March dissident army units staged a coup, arrested and exiled Lucas García, and named former General Efraín Ríos Montt to head a new governing junta.[50]

The Ríos Montt regime set out to implement the army's counterinsurgency plan with a vengeance. Between 1982 and the end of 1983 the army destroyed some 400 towns, villages, and hamlets; herded 20,000 people into strategic hamlets (called "poles of development"); killed as many as 50,000 to 75,000 people; forcibly recruited 800,000 peasants into poorly armed but tightly supervised "civil patrols"; displaced one million people from their homes (150,000 of whom fled into Mexico); and dealt the guerrilla movements a major defeat.[51] President Reagan praised the Ríos Montt regime on a visit to Guatemala City in December 1982, after ordering a resumption of economic aid in October. In January 1983 he lifted the arms embargo and dispatched $6.3 million in helicopter spare parts and other equipment. But because Guatemala's costly counterinsurgency effort did not depend critically on U.S. aid, the new regime felt free to adopt a neutral stance on conflicts elsewhere in the region.[52]

Ríos Montt set out to match the success of the army's counterinsurgency program with a "moralization" campaign against government corruption and major fiscal and economic reforms. In doing so, and in outspokenly supporting evangelical protestantism, to which he had converted some years earlier, he managed to alienate every major source of support for his regime: civil and military officials, accustomed to supplementing their meager salaries through public business and bribery; the country's business elite, incensed at his imposition of a value-added tax, price controls, a new labor code, and a promised agrarian reform; and the Catholic church. Ríos Montt fell from power when the army turned against him. The counterinsurgency effort was succeeding, but the carnage had increased Guatemala's international isolation, and Ríos Montt had lost the support of key elements of the country's traditional rulers. A new coup took place on 8 August 1983, headed by armed forces chief General Oscar Mejía Victores, who rescinded the Ríos Montt reforms and pledged to return the country to civilian rule. Mejía Victores also reaffirmed Guatemala's neutrality in relation to the bloodshed elsewhere in Central America. His foreign minister declared a year later that "the Guatemalan government has rejected pressures to become involved in the Central American conflict,"[53] and Mejía Victores himself went as far as to declare that "the countries of the isthmus could coexist with a Communist Nicaragua."[54] In November 1983, after the military killed two Guatemalan USAID employees, the United States suspended economic aid again.

The Reagan administration welcomed the election of Luis Alberto Monge as president of Costa Rica in 1982. Monge, leader of the most conservative wing of the PLN, had worked for many years to eliminate Communist influence in the Costa Rican labor movement, often cooperating with the American Institute for Free Labor Development (AIFLD) and the Inter-American Regional Organization of Workers (ORIT). His predecessor, President Carazo, was not popular with the U.S. administration because of his support for the Sandinista revolution and his reluctance to impose austerity measures when the Costa Rican economy turned sour. After his inauguration in May 1982 Monge found himself faced with an economic and financial crisis that required large doses of U.S. aid to resolve.

Simultaneously, he faced pressures from Washington both to assist the contras and to accept unwanted military assistance. Though he feared being drawn into the growing regional conflict and resisted militarization, Monge had little choice but to "rent part of his country to the Contras' fledgling southern front as a base and supply route in exchange for aid to cushion Costa Rica's steep economic slide."[55] Monge also denounced Sandinista restrictions on civil liberties and organized a "Peace and Democracy Forum" with El Salvador and Honduras, which met in San José in October 1982 and contributed to isolating the Nicaraguan regime diplomatically. Nonetheless, he resisted U.S. pressure to become more actively involved in the war against Nicaragua, which would have required succumbing to U.S. pressures to reverse the country's 1948 decision to abolish its military. His efforts were complicated when Frank McNeil, a sympathetic career diplomat appointed ambassador by Carter, was fired in July 1983. McNeil was replaced by a political appointee, Curtin Windsor, Jr., "an ultra-right-wing former West Virginia coal magnate" who criticized the country's social welfare system and "was not subtle about making the link between the interests of the Contras and the still expanding U.S. aid project in Costa Rica."[56]

Monge could not, however, ignore opposition within his own party and cabinet to the contra war. When death squads linked to the contras murdered six residents of a town near the Nicaraguan border, anticontra ministers pushed Monge to change course. Beginning in August 1983, cabinet crises provoked the resignation of 16 ministers and vice-ministers. In November 1983, after firing his pro-contra foreign minister, Monge organized a ceremonial declaration of Costa Rica's neutrality. But the contras operating from Costa Rican territory were not disturbed. Unlike the FDN in Honduras, the contras operating on the southern front (northern Costa Rica) were smaller in number and never managed to take over any Costa Rican territory. By the end of 1984 they had suffered a series of military setbacks, and the following year, after refusing to unite with the FDN, they lost their CIA funding.

In Panama the Torrijos government was troubled by the new administration. President Reagan and most of his Latin American advisers had opposed the Panama Canal treaties; their Republican allies in Congress had repeatedly denounced the Torrijos regime for its aid to the Sandinista revolution, alleged corruption, and authoritarian methods. Torrijos died in a plane crash on 31 July 1981 and was succeeded by the National Guard's intelligence chief, General Manuel Antonio Noriega, who had been under contract to the CIA since 1966 or 1967. Although he had been cut from the CIA payroll during the Carter administration, his annual $100,000 retainer had later been restored by Reagan's CIA director, William Casey. By the time Noriega was cut off again after June 1987, his fee had doubled. Initially, Noriega accommodated himself to the administration's objectives, passing on valuable information about the Sandinista regime and the FMLN and raising no objections to the use of U.S. military bases to support the contras and the Salvadoran government, despite provisions of the canal treaty strictly limiting the U.S. military presence to activities directly related to the defense of the canal.

During 1984, as the U.S. deescalated, the seeds of future troubles were sown. On 31 March 1984 the Honduran officer corps forced General Alvarez to resign and leave the country. His replacement, General Walter López, proved a more circumspect ally, unwilling to endorse U.S. military intervention in Nicaragua and more concerned with the potential danger to Honduras posed by the contras, particularly after Congress voted to cut off funding. Though Honduras continued to cooperate with U.S. military exercises and rejected the Contadora treaty, the price of cooperation rose. In Guatemala, Mejía Victores announced plans for a transition to civilian rule and scheduled elections for a constituent assembly for 1 July 1984. The United States resumed economic aid in September, but the Guatemalan regime—having dealt with the guerrillas without much U.S. help and confident that its international respectability and domestic legitimacy were on the mend as a result of the elections—could not be pressured to ally itself with the United States against Nicaragua. Guatemala announced that it was ready to sign the September 1983 Contadora draft treaty and refused to join Costa Rica, El Salvador, and Honduras in rejecting the treaty proposal after Nicaragua endorsed it.

The Monge administration in Costa Rica, on the other hand, shifted back during 1984 to a more firmly pro-U.S. stance, and even requested an increase in military aid for the country's civil guard. Within weeks of Monge's declaring Costa Rica's neutrality in November 1984, a dispute over the arrest by Sandinista police of a draft dodger sheltered in the Costa Rican embassy in Managua allowed the Costa Rican president to withdraw his ambassador and effectively cut off relations with Nicaragua. Monge's maneuvers did not satisfy Washington, which pushed for a stronger commitment to its aims in the region, or the contending factions of his own party, a majority of which had become increasingly worried, along with the Costa Rican public, about the country's drift away from its traditional neutrality and toward a potentially dangerous confrontation with Nicaragua.

On 6 May 1984 in Panama, General Noriega presided over fraudulent elections in which the government party's presidential candidate, Nicolás Barletta, was declared the winner by 1,713 of the 650,000 votes cast. Although the U.S. embassy estimated that opposition candidate Arnulfo Arias had actually won by as many as 30,000 votes, Secretary of State Shultz attended Barletta's inauguration in October. Noriega continued to be helpful to U.S. policy makers, but domestic opposition mounted in reaction to the electoral fraud and then to a new economic austerity program Barletta imposed after taking office.

Major problems for U.S. policy makers emerged during the 1985–86 reescalation of the U.S. conflict with Nicaragua. Honduran President Suazo, irritated that the United States would not support his reelection, demanded a major increase in U.S. aid. In October 1985 the Honduran military seized a contra supply plane and refused to permit further flights until after Suazo left office the following January. Incoming President José Azcona Hoyos allowed the flights to resume,[57] but resisted U.S. pressures to declare an emergency and mobilize the armed forces when Nicaraguan troops crossed into Honduran territory in March 1986 in pursuit of retreating contras. The Honduran and Nicaraguan military commands had worked quietly to create effective communications between them. When the United States chose to call the incursion an invasion, in part to impress Congress, Azcona declined the U.S. suggestion that he send an urgent appeal for $20 million in "emergency" military aid and calmly prepared for a holiday weekend at the beach. U.S. ambassador Jack Ferth finally pushed him into requesting the $20 million on orders from Washington; he also persuaded Azcona to request U.S. military helicopters to transport Honduran troops to the border area, but the Honduran command saw to it that its soldiers were dropped far from the fighting.

In Guatemala the December 1985 presidential runoff election produced a victory for Christian Democratic candidate Vinicio Cerezo, the first civilian president in 16 years.[58] The military severely limited Cerezo's power and retained its nearly total independence of civil authority. After his inauguration on 14 January 1986 Cerezo sought to increase his domestic leverage by enhancing his international standing through a foreign policy of "active neutrality."[59] He supported the Contadora mediation, as had his predecessors, but intervened more actively to promote negotiations. His ability to pursue this policy was limited, however, by economic difficulties that increased the country's need for external aid. Though Cerezo managed to secure some economic aid in Western Europe, Guatemala's dependence on the United States, and with it the constraints on Cerezo's foreign policy activism, increased.

As Guatemala's voice dimmed, that of Costa Rica changed in tone and grew louder. During the last year of the Monge administration the president's ability to keep his balance diminished. He managed to get U.S. Ambassador Windsor fired, but the replacement, Lewis Tambs, arrived with orders from Washington to revive the southern front. Having withdrawn his ambassador from Managua in December 1984, Monge overreacted to border skirmishes in May 1985 and, in November, acceded to Tambs's request that Costa Rica secretly turn over the small Santa Elena air strip near the Nicaraguan border for contra operations. In the end Monge provoked such a reaction in his own party that, against his wishes, it nominated Oscar Arias, an anticontra "peace" candidate, to succeed him. The United States reacted by supporting the opposition in the 2 February 1986 elections. Arias's unexpected victory created new problems for Washington. Two weeks after his election, Arias traveled to Washington, where he publicly condemned U.S. aid to the contras. In September, when he learned of the contras' use of the Santa Elena airstrip, he ordered it closed despite appeals from Washington.

Panama also defected during the 1985–86 reescalation. Initially, Noriega continued to cooperate fully with the United States. In March 1985 he sent a sabotage team to Managua, and it managed to blow up a major military installation and hospital. In June he met with Colonel North and agreed to allow contras to train in Panama and to meet publicly with the FDN leadership. U.S. operations against Nicaragua continued at full tilt from bases in the former canal zone. In September, however, a major crisis erupted. When opposition activist Hugo Spadafora was brutally murdered, apparently on Noriega's orders, President Barletta felt compelled to order an investigation. Noriega removed him from office and installed his vice-president, Eric Delvalle, in his place. Although a meeting in Washington in November with CIA Director Casey went well enough (Noriega was still on the payroll), Noriega infuriated the national security director, Admiral John Poindexter, by refusing to meet a new list of U.S. demands that Poindexter brought to Panama in December. Complaints about Noriega's alleged ties to drug trafficking and illegal gun running were already circulating in Washington. In April 1986 the *Wall Street Journal* ran a story by its Central American correspondent, Clifford Krauss, charging that the administration was covering up Noriega's illicit activities.[60] In June the *New York Times* published an exposé by Seymour Hersh.[61] Noriega attempted to deflect the scandal by offering to increase aid to the contras and to carry out sabotage and assassination missions in Nicaragua, but to no avail. When the Iran-contra scandal broke in November 1986 Noriega lost his main supporters in the U.S. administration. Colonel North, whom he had met with in London to discuss operations in Nicaragua only two months earlier, was fired outright. CIA Director Casey fell victim to a stroke on 15 December and died soon after.

By the end of 1986 only Honduras and El Salvador continued to cooperate more or less fully with the U.S. effort to dislodge the Sandinistas. This, together with the disarray in Washington, the defection of Costa Rica and Panama, and the steady though less active neutrality of Guatemala, helped to doom the Reagan campaign to overthrow the government of Nicaragua.

THE PEACE PROCESS

The Reagan administration's policies in Central America inspired numerous efforts by one or more of the isthmian countries, several Latin American nations, a number of Western European countries, and various international organizations to search for diplomatic and political formulas that could succeed in reducing conflict in the region, particularly in El

Salvador and Nicaragua. Efforts to mediate the Salvadoran conflict subsided, however, with the election of President Duarte in 1984. Christian Democratic governments in Venezuela, West Germany, and elsewhere supported his government. Moreover, the pro-Duarte consensus in the U.S. Congress after 1984 reduced the likelihood that attempts at conflict mediation in El Salvador would prove fruitful. International initiatives to promote peace in the region thenceforth focused primarily on the U.S.-Nicaraguan conflict. The two most important were the effort undertaken by the Contadora Group, led by Mexico, which attempted to exploit the 1984 U.S. deescalation to mediate an agreement among the five Central American countries, and the 1987 Arias Plan, supported by the Contadora Group, which succeeded in forging a peace agreement the year after the U.S. administration fell victim to the Iran-contra scandal.

The Contadora Group had been founded at a meeting of the foreign ministers of Colombia, Mexico, Panama, and Venezuela, held on Panama's Contadora Island on 8 January 1983. The meeting was called by Mexican Foreign Minister Bernardo Sepúlveda, whose aim was to promote negotiations among the Central American countries that could lead to a deescalation of the conflicts in the region. Sepúlveda's other aim was to reduce tensions between Mexico and the United States by placing Mexico's opposition to U.S. policy in Central America in a multilateral context—one in which others might be induced to play a leading role.[62] The strategy worked; Colombian President Belisario Betancur Cuartas initially assumed informal leadership of the group and managed to persuade all five of the Central American governments to begin talks under the Contadora Group's auspices. In September 1983, after extensive consultations, the Contadora foreign ministers issued a Document of Objectives, which all the parties, including the United States, endorsed. By June 1984, just before the Manzanillo talks began, the Contadora Group produced the first draft of a treaty; after further meetings, a revised Contadora treaty was presented to the Central American governments on 7 September.[63] Although the treaty required all five governments to make commitments to internal democracy, it focused primarily on security issues. The draft treaty would have required Nicaragua to cease all aid to the FMLN, send home all Cuban and Soviet-bloc military advisers, pledge itself never to allow foreign military bases in its territory, limit the size of its army, and permit intrusive verification of its compliance with the treaty. U.S. policy makers initially responded positively to the treaty, certain that Nicaragua would not sign.[64]

On 21 September 1984, however, President Daniel Ortega announced that Nicaragua accepted the treaty "in its totality, immediately, and without modifications."[65] Honduran officials had already expressed some reservations after talks with U.S. envoy Shlaudeman on 19 September. After the Nicaraguan announcement the United States moved quickly to ensure that its other clients would reject the treaty draft. On 24 September the State Department formally announced its own objections to the Contadora draft, stressing the lack of adequate verification and the absence of precise language requiring Nicaragua to democratize its political system. The Costa Rican and Salvadoran governments had already made statements indicating they would sign. By early October both had joined Honduras in demanding adjustments to the draft and refused to sign by the Contadora deadline of 15 October. On the eve of the U.S. election, the National Security Council (NSC) staff reported, "We have trumped the latest Nicaraguan/Mexican efforts to rush signature of an unsatisfactory Contadora agreement."[66] With the reelection of President Reagan, all hope for a peace agreement disappeared. The Contadora Group made several efforts to restart the negotiations, enlisting the support of other Latin American countries as well as the United Nations, but the U.S. reescalation of tensions with Nicaragua and the congressional approval of contra aid in 1985 and 1986 doomed these efforts to failure.

Just as prospects for peace in Central America seemed to have disappeared, a new round of peace talks began that eventually led the Central American countries to sign the Esquipulas II accord on 7 August 1987 (also called the Arias Plan, after Costa Rican President Oscar Arias). The negotiations actually began at a meeting of the five Central American presidents, convened by newly elected Guatemalan President Cerezo on 24–25 May 1986 in the small Guatemalan town of Esquipulas. The five presidents did not agree to sign a new Contadora draft treaty, which incorporated many of the adjustments demanded by Costa Rica, El Salvador, and Honduras, but did sign a statement of principles and agreed to send their foreign ministers to future meetings.[67] At the subsequent 6 June foreign ministers' meeting, Costa Rica, El Salvador, and Honduras again refused to sign. Three weeks later the U.S. House of Representatives approved the Reagan request for $100 million in contra aid. After another Contadora effort to reopen talks failed in January 1987, President Arias called a new Central American summit meeting for February in San José, which pointedly excluded Nicaragua. The United States was pleased at Nicaragua's apparent isolation; the Nicaraguans reacted harshly.

When the four Central American presidents met on 15 February 1987, Arias unexpectedly presented them with a new peace plan. Like the Contadora drafts, the plan addressed all of the security issues raised by the United States, which the Nicaraguans had already conceded, and required the United States to end contra aid. Unlike the Contadora drafts, however, it bound the signatories to undertake specific steps toward democratization, including negotiations with armed insurgents, which the Nicaraguans had repeatedly rejected. The Contadora Group, and Mexico in particular, had sought to avoid making internal matters subject to international agreement and supervision. The Contadora drafts had all contained language committing the signatories to democratic practices and procedures but had tried to preserve the principle of the sovereignty of independent states to govern their domestic affairs without foreign interference. The Arias plan abandoned the sovereignty principle to placate the United States and thus opened the way to a negotiated settlement of the contra war. While the plan did not single out Nicaragua and theoretically required identical commitments to democratization by all the governments of the region, in fact it was aimed primarily at settling the U.S.-Nicaraguan conflict. At the February meeting the four Central American presidents endorsed the plan in general terms but refused to agree to its specific provisions. According to the Arias plan, El Salvador and Guatemala, like Nicaragua, would agree to open negotiations with the guerrillas operating in their territories, while Honduras would pledge itself to close the contra camps.[68]

Arias was not discouraged. He immediately launched an effort to convince the Nicaraguan and U.S. governments to support the plan. With the Iran-contra hearings already under way, Arias's efforts had already had an impact on Congress. On 17 March 1987 the Senate passed a nonbinding resolution endorsing the Arias Plan by a vote of 97 to 1. In April the Contadora Group endorsed the plan and pledged to round up additional diplomatic support in Latin America. Meanwhile, the Nicaraguan government had opened its own channels of communication with Congress. Convinced that the contras would actually be cut off, even over the administration's objections, if they signed the Arias treaty, the Sandinista leaders had come to view Arias's efforts in a more positive light. The U.S. administration, however, was hostile; Arias was summoned to a meeting at the White House on 17 June to hear lengthy objections voiced by President Reagan and his advisers.[69] Predictably, El Salvador and Honduras held back, but finally agreed after much delay to a summit meeting in Tegucigalpa in August, to be preceded by an agenda-setting session attended by the foreign ministers.

The Reagan administration's policy toward Nicaragua finally collapsed in the first week of August 1987. On 5 August, just as the Central American foreign ministers were meeting to review a revised version of the Arias Plan, Representative James Wright, speaker of the House of Representatives, reached an agreement with the administration on the text of a statement that committed the United States to abandon its effort to overthrow the government of Nicaragua in exchange for specific Nicaraguan concessions. The Reagan-Wright agreement called for the contras and the Nicaraguan government to negotiate a cease-fire, after which the United States would end military aid to the contras and the Soviet bloc would halt arms shipments to Nicaragua. Humanitarian aid would be permitted in both cases. Nicaragua would lift the state of emergency, restore full civil liberties, create a multiparty electoral commission, and set a timetable for new elections. Foreign military advisers "in excess of normal and legitimate needs" would be withdrawn from Nicaragua and Honduras. The United States would suspend military exercises in Honduras once the cease-fire took effect. The plan also called for regional negotiations to reduce the size of standing armies, verifiable commitments by the United States and the five Central American republics not to support insurgents in other countries, and an end to humanitarian aid to the contras once the Nicaraguan government declared an amnesty, allowed the contras to participate in political activity, and downsized its armed forces. The administration agreed to the plan "in the full expectation that Nicaragua would reject it."[70] Wright, however, knew that these terms overlapped with those of the Arias Plan and had consulted with Nicaraguan Ambassador Carlos Tunnerman to be sure that the Nicaraguans would not reject them out of hand.

The news of the Wright-Reagan agreement broke just as the Central American presidents gathered in Tegucigalpa. Rather than divert them from the Arias proposals, however, it had the opposite effect of helping to convince reluctant Honduran President Azcona to abandon his misgivings and join the others in signing the document. The modified Arias Plan, thereafter known as Esquipulas II and formally titled "Procedure for the Establishment of a Firm and Lasting Peace in Central America," had three main parts. The first, based largely on Arias's proposals, concerned internal conflicts and specified the steps each state was to take to reach a negotiated political settlement with armed opposition groups. The second part was drawn largely from the last of the Contadora drafts. The Contadora foreign ministers, led by Mexico's Sepúlveda, participated in the agenda-setting session. They took notes on the reservations expressed by the Central Americans and, at the suggestion of D'Escoto, incorporated most of them in the new draft presented to the presidents the following day. The third part concerned "International Verification and Follow-up." On 7 August 1987, at a ceremony in Guatemala's presidential palace, the five presidents signed the peace accord.

The signing of the Esquipulas II accord was facilitated not only by the disarray in the administration (which included the miscalculation that produced the Wright-Reagan agreement) but also by Arias's tireless efforts; the long preparatory work on security issues undertaken by Mexico and the Contadora Group; the endorsement of the Contadora "support group," consisting of four of Latin America's new democratic regimes (Argentina, Brazil, Peru, and Uruguay); the diplomatic support provided by Western European nations and the Soviet bloc, as well as by the U.N. and OAS secretaries general; the political support of many in the U.S. Congress; and the diverse estimates of national interest made by each of the Central American governments. Crucial to the signing was the priority Arias gave to settling the Nicaraguan conflict, which made it possible for the Guatemalan, Honduran, and Salvadoran governments to calculate (correctly) that Arias would hold Nicaragua to a higher standard of compliance than they would be expected to meet.[71] The Cerezo government in Guatemala, which supported the peace process from the beginning, hoped to use the accord as leverage in dealings with its own military, but did not expect to be able to comply fully with the accord. Salvadoran president Duarte, facing the same constraints, was under stronger pressure to sign. His party had suffered political reverses and was to face difficult legislative and municipal elections the following March; the Esquipulas II accord represented Duarte's last chance to salvage the PDC from certain defeat. The most difficult to convince was Honduran President Azcona, who feared irritating the Reagan administration while 15,000 armed contras, all on the U.S. payroll, occupied a portion of his territory. Both Duarte and Azcona, however, recognized that their countries' fate depended as much on the U.S. Congress as on the executive branch; with power rapidly draining from the White House, signing the Esquipulas II accord became far easier.

The most difficult decision was that of Nicaragua, though the decision had been taken prior to President Ortega's arrival in San José and thus produced no last-minute drama at the meeting. For six years the Sandinista regime had sought to defend the country's sovereignty and independence from external intervention. The Esquipulas II accord, by subjecting Nicaragua's internal political arrangements to an agreement negotiated with foreign countries, represented an abandonment of one of the core values of the Sandinista revolution. Worse yet, the accord called for negotiations with the contras, which the regime had consistently refused to do. The Nicaraguan armed forces had successfully contained the contra forces with major offensives during 1984 and 1985, after the threat of a U.S. invasion diminished, and the army was redeployed to assist the militias, which had been assigned to deal with the contras until then.[72] Moreover, the contras had never posed a political threat to the regime and had little support in the country. The accord therefore represented something of a triumph for the United States, whose hirelings the regime would now have to dignify by inviting them to formal negotiations. Moreover, Nicaraguan President Ortega knew that his government would have to comply with the accord, while others would not find themselves under similar pressure.

The principal reason for the Nicaraguan decision to sign, despite these considerations, was economic. The contra war, the U.S. embargo, declining levels of international aid, and the Sandinistas' own miscalculations had plunged the Nicaraguan economy into a profound depression. Per capita gross domestic product (GDP) fell to 50 percent of its prerevolutionary level, while per capita consumption declined by some 70 percent. The Sandinista government had been forced to abandon all of its economic reconstruction goals and most of its social progress objectives. Despite this disaster, however, the regime had suffered no major defections, experienced no popular uprisings as living conditions plummeted, and maintained a high level of public support. Thus the Sandinista leaders took a calculated risk: they traded sovereignty for peace, with the expectation that internationally supervised elections would, in the end, confirm the FSLN in power.

In the remaining year and a half of the Reagan administration, the peace process moved forward despite U.S. efforts to undermine it. Incredibly, Secretary of State Shultz proposed in September 1987 that Congress approve $270 million in contra aid, including weaponry. A month later Arias won the Nobel Peace Prize and Shultz withdrew the administration's request. The House of Representatives voted down a scaled-back proposal from Speaker Wright for humanitarian aid to the contras on 3 February 1988. Left adrift by Washington, the contras finally signed a cease-fire agreement with the Nicaraguan government on 21 March after two days of talks in the Nicaraguan border town of Sapoá. The House then voted to approve $47 million in humanitarian aid, conditioned on contra respect for the terms of the Esquipulas II accord and the cease-fire. Further talks between the contras and the government of Nicaragua proved fruitless; the contras escalated their demands after each Sandinista concession, hoping to convince Congress that Sandinista intransigence justified a renewal of military aid and an end to congressional limitations that prohibited them from launching new attacks. Meanwhile, Arias pushed Ortega to make a series of concessions, including substantial revisions of Nicaragua's electoral laws and procedures, to ensure the participation of all opposition parties, including those that supported the contras. By the time the new U.S. president was inaugurated on 20 January 1989, the Nicaraguans had complied fully with the peace accord and were preparing to announce at the next Central American summit, scheduled for the following month, that they would move up the date of national elections to 25 February 1990. The Sandinistas expected to win these elections and resume the tasks of repairing the country's ravaged economy and diminished sovereignty the next day.

Having failed to overthrow the government of Nicaragua, the Reagan administration turned its attention to Panama. In Reagan's last two years in office, the effort to dislodge General Noriega was supervised by Assistant Secretary of State Elliot Abrams, who, with Colonel North in the White House, had managed U.S. policy toward Nicaragua. Abrams was no more successful in Panama than he had been in Nicaragua. Negotiations with Noriega misfired and proved fruitless. By June 1987 the CIA had cut Noriega from its payroll (though the agency sent him a Christmas present that year— a beanbag with a picture of a frog, Noriega's favorite animal). In July the United States suspended economic aid. When negotiations failed, Panama's sugar quota was eliminated in December. Noriega replied by granting landing rights to the Soviet airline and agreed to permit Soviet fishing vessels to dock in Panama. He also appealed to the Libyan government for money to weather the U.S. pressure. On 4 February 1988 Noriega was indicted by federal grand juries in Florida for drug smuggling and other offenses. Shortly thereafter, on urgings from Washington, President Delvalle tried to fire him from his post as head of the Panamanian military, whereupon Noriega had Delvalle ousted by the compliant National Assembly. The United States continued to recognize Delvalle as chief of state and thus cut off diplomatic relations with Panama. Delvalle hid out in a U.S. safe house in the former canal zone for several months. On 2 March the United States froze $50 million in Panamanian government assets in U.S. banks, causing a financial panic in Panama, which resulted in the closing of most of the country's banks the following day. Two weeks later, on 16 March, Noriega crushed a coup attempt. In May Noriega turned aside an offer to quash the indictments in exchange for his resignation.[73] Another coup effort was aborted on 3 October, when the United States failed to block loyal units from suppressing it. When President Reagan left office the following January, Noriega celebrated his departure from the safety of his military command headquarters.

CONCLUSIONS

No U.S. government has ever devoted as much of its own political capital and the nation's resources to Central America as did the Reagan administration between 1981 and 1989. None had such profoundly traumatic effects on the region. None left office with so little control over events in the region.

The administration's objectives in Central America did not stray from tradition; they were to preserve, extend, or restore U.S. dominance; to avert or remove regional and extraregional obstacles to that end; and to maintain or impose stable pro-U.S. regimes, making them democratic if that was feasible. Previous U.S. administrations had found it possible to achieve these goals at a cost proportional to U.S. interests in the region; the Reagan administration did not. At no time in the twentieth century had the U.S. economic and security stake in Central America been as small as it was in the 1980s, yet it was in this decade that the United States devoted the greatest attention and the largest quantity of resources to the region. Administration policy makers, as well as the Kissinger commission, argued that the Sandinista regime in Nicaragua and the guerrilla movement in El Salvador (as well as the Guatemalan insurgents) constituted sufficient threats to U.S. security as to justify the attention and resources the administration was devoting to remove them. When pressed for detail, the president and his lieutenants proved less than convincing. No serious appraisal of the possible consequences of the survival of the Sandinista government in Nicaragua or of guerrilla success in the other Central American countries ever reached the heights attained by the president's rhetoric.

In Nicaragua the administration consistently rejected alternative policies that would have been less costly and would have served better to advance its objectives. The Nicaraguan government repeatedly signaled its willingness to negotiate on security issues and to accede to virtually all of the U.S. demands. The response of Nicaraguan leaders to Assistant Secretary of State Enders's demands in August 1982, their discussions with U.S. Special Envoy

Richard Stone and their unilateral steps after the Grenada invasion in the fall of 1983, their decision to sign the Contadora treaty in September 1984, and their almost continuous statements on security issues between late 1984 and their signing of the Esquipulas II accord in August 1987 were ample evidence of this. Had the United States wished merely to stop aid to the Salvadoran rebels, reduce the size and weaponry of the Sandinista army, obtain assurances that the Sandinistas would not permit foreign military bases on Nicaraguan territory, and secure the departure of Cuban and Soviet-bloc military advisers, it could have achieved these security goals as early as late 1982 or 1983.

Internal political issues would have taken longer to resolve, but the relatively open election conducted by the regime in November 1984 constituted a significant precedent. With an agreement on security issues in hand, it would have been relatively easy for the United States to reinsert its friends and allies into the Nicaraguan political process (although not into the presidential palace).

A militarily neutral Nicaragua with a political system more open than those of most of its neighbors and endowed with a stable, legitimate, and popular government was not, however, the objective of U.S. policy. If it had been, the contras could have been used as a bargaining chip to secure such an outcome early in the Reagan administration.

In the case of El Salvador the United States faced two less costly alternatives. The first, never seriously considered, would have left the Salvadoran armed forces to face possible defeat at the hands of the FMLN insurgents. Such an outcome was judged likely by U.S. military analysts in 1982–83. The United States would then have confronted a regime rather similar to that of Nicaragua and posing many of the same difficult but ultimately negotiable issues. Occasionally, for rhetorical purposes, U.S. officials accused congressional opponents of favoring a guerrilla takeover and rejected this scenario explicitly on the grounds that a victory for the Salvadoran guerrillas would plunge the country into a "bloodbath." Without massive external aid, however, the FDR-FMLN would have found it impossible to match the bloody record of the Salvadoran armed forces. The second alternative would have involved a U.S. threat to abandon the Salvadoran armed forces in order to force them to acquiesce to serious negotiations between the Salvadoran government and the opposition. U.S. officials argued that the demands of the FMLN and its civilian allies made a negotiated political settlement impossible. The FMLN insisted on "power sharing"—that is, the appointment of its leaders to key posts in a transition government empowered to purge the army and supervise elections. U.S. officials denounced such demands as efforts by the insurgents "to shoot their way into power" against the will of the Salvadoran people. In fact, the FDR-FMLN proposals, made as early as February 1982, sought mainly to ensure that the opposition's return to peaceful political contention would not result in its physical extermination. Guarantees for the physical safety and civil liberties of the opposition could not have been made credible to the FDR-FMLN without a purge of the Salvadoran military and its subsequent transformation. In any case, after the war reached a stalemate in 1985, serious negotiations with the FDR-FMLN could have produced an agreement to end the war. U.S. policy did not seek, however, to create the conditions for a negotiated end to the Salvadoran civil war. It sought instead to provide sufficient aid and advice to the Salvadoran army to enable it to win a military victory over the insurgents.

On the rest of the isthmus the U.S. policy eventually became hostage to its goals in Nicaragua and El Salvador. In Honduras the United States sought a platform from which to launch the contras, and perhaps eventually its own armed forces, against the Sandinista regime. Aside from the nearly 250 dead and "disappeared" Hondurans, whom contra and Honduran military death squads executed in 1981–83 (until the officer corps replaced the armed forces chief Alvarez), the principal casualties were the country's already compromised sovereignty and the loss of control over territory along its northern border with Nicaragua. In Guatemala, U.S. support was not required to carry out the scorched-earth policies that temporarily defeated the guerrillas in 1982–84, and need not have been provided. U.S. support did encourage the military to permit the election of a civilian regime in 1986, but the Cerezo administration had even less leverage with its military establishment than did successive Salvadoran governments, whose armed forces depended on U.S. aid. In Costa Rica, U.S. pressure on the Monge administration on behalf of the southern contras produced turmoil in the ruling party and compromised the country's "unarmed neutrality," though the large economic aid program of 1981–84, which reinforced the pressure, proved helpful to the government in confronting the country's economic crisis. The decline in aid after Arias's election in 1986, the delay in sending aid already approved by Congress, and other multiple pressures exerted to discourage the new president from pursuing his peace efforts not only harmed Costa Rica but also failed to achieve U.S. goals. In Panama evidence of General Noriega's drug dealing and gun running as far back as 1971 had led the Carter CIA to remove him from the U.S. payroll. Nothing other than his usefulness to the contra effort and his occasional contributions to intelligence gathering on Cuba, Nicaragua, and the Salvadoran opposition led the Reagan administration to rehire him and endorse the blatant electoral fraud of 1984. Worse yet were the bungled efforts to remove him in 1987–88.

The U.S. failure to achieve its policy goals in Central America during the Reagan administration had no impact whatever on significant U.S. security or economic interests, since the region was of marginal importance to these interests. In the process of assigning disproportionate priority to the attainment of unachievable goals, however, the Reagan administration did have an impact on the U.S. domestic political process. Administration officials systematically engaged in blatantly illegal activities forbidden by federal statute and congressional legislation. Their illegal activities included perjured testimony before congressional committees, violations of neutrality acts and treaty obligations, the use of humanitarian aid to the contras for arms purchases, the sale of weapons to Iran and use of the profits to purchase contra arms, the solicitation of contributions to the contras from individuals and foreign governments, and a host of smaller infractions. At least as unsettling to Congress were the bitter internal debates over policy, the lack of discipline that enabled some officials to leak sensitive information and attack their colleagues in the press, the frequent firing of policy-making and diplomatic staff, and the apparent incompetence of a number of the officials charged with implementing the president's goals in the region. Had the administration pursued policies in Central America that were less costly or less radical, particularly in Nicaragua and in Panama after 1986, these failings would not have had so great an effect on congressional and public trust in the country's leaders.

chapter 7

CENTRAL AMERICA AFTER THE COLD WAR

PEACE WITHOUT VICTORY

The four years of the presidency of George Bush (1989–93) witnessed an epochal transformation of the international arena. Between 1989 and 1991 the Soviet Union unilaterally divested itself of its Eastern European client states and then disintegrated into its constituent republics. The cold war ended abruptly, leaving the United States as the only nation capable of projecting military power on a global scale and terminating more than four decades of bipolar political, economic, and cultural competition between the two superpowers. The end of the cold war had three important consequences for U.S. policy in Latin America.

First, it helped to reduce the competitiveness of the international environment in the region. This was true not only because the Soviet Union no longer existed and thus could not be used to balance against the United States but also because the attention of the Western European nations and Japan turned from Latin America (and elsewhere in the third world) to Eastern Europe and the new states that emerged from the wreckage of the Soviet Union, which represented new opportunities for economic and political gain. The end of the cold war thus threatened to divert badly needed capital from the south to the east while simultaneously eliminating the competition that provided the main incentive for U.S. and other Western aid. In Latin America, U.S. economic and political leverage increased in proportion to the Soviet decline and the distraction of friendly economic competitors. The post–cold war world thus looked far less promising to the less developed countries than it did to the triumphant policy-making establishments of the developed world. In response most of the Latin American countries intensified their efforts to diversify their external diplomatic and economic relations, particularly with Western Europe, while simultaneously rushing to seek free-trade agreements and the other benefits to be derived from closer economic and political relations with the United States.

Second, the putative security threat to the United States posed by the Soviet Union and its allies in Central America disappeared. This momentous change altered the U.S. domestic political debate over Central America by undermining the principal argument in favor of U.S. efforts to preserve its traditionally exclusive dominance in the region. No significant U.S. security interests had been at stake on the isthmus in the 1980s; the region's importance for U.S. policy had rested largely on the issue of the credibility of the U.S. commitment to the East-West conflict.[1] When that conflict disappeared, Central America lost much of its importance for U.S foreign policy. In the short run, however, U.S. policy in Central America continued to have considerable symbolic importance in U.S. domestic politics, and though the security issue evaporated, other U.S. interests—often confused with, or concealed behind, a rhetoric of containment—gave new life to interventionist sentiments: economic interests, narcotics trafficking, immigration, and the like. Meanwhile, as the Bush administration quickly discovered, the collapse of the Soviet Union reduced both the costs and the risks of U.S. military intervention throughout the third world, including the isthmus.

Third, within Latin America the Soviet collapse tended to discourage or alter left-wing and populist political parties, social movements, and ideological currents, which the United States traditionally viewed as hostile to its interests. At the same time, however, it undermined right-wing and conservative political organizations, military establishments, and governments whose power derived in part from their extreme anticommunism and the tacit or active support of the United States. The end of the cold war also reduced the incentive for the United States to support local political contenders in the third world as Soviet-bloc aid disappeared. As ideological contention narrowed and external sources of polarization declined, the preexisting trend toward democratization gained strength. Since the poverty and inequality afflicting most of the region had always provided the left with a much larger potential social base than that of the more conservative groups, the long-term consequences of these changes favored the emergence of powerful new forces for social reform.

Independent of the Soviet collapse, the economic boom of the Reagan years had succeeded in stabilizing the U.S. share of the global economy, though this achievement was purchased with capital borrowed mainly from Western Europe and Japan to fund both private investment and a growing federal budget deficit. In Latin America, the economic crisis that began in 1982 blocked economic growth, but the U.S. share of trade and investment in the stagnant economies of the region increased during the decade. The influence of the United States on economic policy making in Latin America increased even faster than its share in the region's economies, as the U.S. government and the multilateral lending institutions linked to it conditioned badly needed aid on the adoption of programs to restructure local economies by reducing government spending and regulation, abandoning protectionism, and privatizing publicly owned companies. The potential for conflict between demands for social progress and pressures to restructure economic policy making was left unresolved by most of the Latin American governments.

The Bush administration responded to these new conditions with a mix of policies that ranged from continuity with Reagan initiatives to relatively abrupt alterations. Continuity was most evident in economic policy toward Latin America. To the Caribbean Basin Initiative of the Reagan era President Bush added a new Free Enterprise Initiative for the Americas in a major address in June 1990. The Bush initiative pledged to increase U.S. aid (though by relatively small amounts) and to negotiate free-trade agreements with countries that restructured their economic policies. The new administration also lent the good offices of the U.S. treasury to promote debt renegotiation, which enabled several Latin American countries to reduce somewhat the financial burdens of servicing their huge external debts, though at the cost of imposing austerity programs and restructurings that adhered to U.S. economic policy preferences. Relations with Mexico, which had deteriorated during the Reagan administration (in part due to Mexico's Contadora leadership), improved rapidly as a result of Bush initiatives and of decisions taken by the new Mexican president, Carlos Salinas de Gortari. In 1992 Mexico and the United States, together with Canada, signed the North American Free Trade Agreement (NAFTA), intended to institutionalize closer political and economic ties between the three nations. While economic growth had resumed in much of Latin America by 1989, the U.S. recession that began in 1991 and the European and Japanese downturns that commenced in 1992 reduced prospects for a rapid recovery of the economic dynamism the region had enjoyed between the 1950s and the early 1980s.

In Central America the new administration pursued two major objectives. The first was to eliminate the region as an issue in domestic politics and as a cause of political contention between the White House and Congress. The second was to reduce the region's importance in U.S. foreign policy in general and as a recipient of U.S. aid in particular. To accomplish these objectives the administration intensified U.S. efforts, begun under Reagan in 1987, to dispose of the Noriega government in Panama—a goal for which bipartisan congressional support had emerged toward the end of the Reagan administration because of Noriega's alleged participation in drug trafficking. On the rest of the isthmus, however, the new administration adopted policy goals that reflected a more pragmatic assessment of U.S. interests and capabilities. The Reagan administration had reinforced U.S. power in the region but had failed to capitalize on its efforts. Led by Secretary of State James Baker, the

Bush administration succeeded in developing bipartsan support for policies that included rhetorical endorsement of the peace process in Nicaragua while continuing to provide "nonlethal" aid to the contras (which the Esquipulas II accord prohibited) and maintaining high levels of economic and military aid to the Salvadoran government (which reduced its incentive to negotiate with the rebels, as Esquipulas II required).

Although he had served as vice-president for eight years under Reagan, George Bush had managed to distance himself from the Iran-contra scandal and the Reagan administration's conflicts with Congress. The new administration assigned a high priority to avoiding a repetition of the confrontations that had nearly paralyzed policy making in the last two years of the Reagan government and set about restoring confidence in the credibility and competence of policy-making personnel in foreign affairs and national security. It did so in part by appointing officials untainted by direct association with the scandals of the outgoing administration. Strengthened by its mending of political fences with Congress and then by the end of the cold war, the Bush administration moved to translate U.S. power into a restoration of the country's traditional dominance in Central America while simultaneously moving to reduce the time and resources devoted to the region. In Panama this strategy succeeded. In Nicaragua and El Salvador, however, the Bush administration had little choice but to abandon the Reagan goal of achieving military victories. By the time President Bush lost his bid for reelection four years later, the three major conflicts afflicting the Central American isthmus when he assumed office had ended with outcomes favorable to traditional U.S. policy objectives.[2]

First, the conflict between the United States and Panama ended when U.S. military forces invaded Panama on 23 December 1989, took chief of state General Manuel Antonio Noriega prisoner, and installed a new government. The Reagan administration had contemplated just such an option, but was so weakened politically in its last months in office that it refrained from military action. The U.S. invaders dispensed with the Panama Defense Forces in a matter of days. A week after the invasion Noriega surrendered to U.S. authorities, who carried him off to a federal detention center in Miami, where in 1992 he was tried and convicted on narcotics-trafficking charges and sentenced to a long prison term. The invasion of Panama was not undertaken to defend traditional U.S. economic or security interests but rather in response to U.S. domestic political circumstances: Noriega's complicity in drug smuggling and his defiance of U.S. efforts to dislodge him threatened to undermine the Bush administration's relations with Congress and its credibility in foreign affairs.

Second, the conflict between the United States and Nicaragua ended when Violeta Chamorro—the presidential candidate of a U.S.-supported coalition of 14 Nicaraguan opposition parties, called the United National Opposition (UNO)[3]—won a majority of the votes in an internationally supervised election on 25 February 1990, held according to the terms of the Esquipulas II accord. Chamorro unexpectedly defeated President Daniel Ortega, the FSLN nominee, and UNO candidates won a majority of the seats in the National Assembly. The U.S. government did not assent to the disarming of the contras until after the elections. Throughout 1989 the contras launched new attacks with weaponry provided by the United States during fiscal year 1986–87 and stockpiled for future use. The Sandinistas' electoral defeat stemmed in large part from the widespread belief in Nicaragua that the United States would respond to an opposition victory by finally ending the contra war and providing economic aid to revive the country's shattered economy. The invasion of Panama may also have convinced many voters that Nicaragua would be next if the FSLN were returned to power.[4]

Third, the conflict between the United States and the Salvadoran insurgents ended when the government of El Salvador and the FMLN guerrillas concluded a peace agreement at U.N. headquarters in New York on 31 December 1991; the agreement was signed at a ceremony in Mexico City on 16 January 1992. According to its terms, the guerrillas were to disarm in stages over the next two years, in exchange for which the Salvadoran government was to purge and downsize its armed forces and take other measures to guarantee the human and political rights of insurgents who laid down their arms to participate in peaceful political activity. The Bush administration, unlike its predecessor, belatedly supported the negotiation process that led to the accords and welcomed provisions that called for international supervision of the process.[5]

In all three of these cases the need for massive economic aid to restore devastated economies seemed to ensure that the United States would again enjoy all the prerogatives of dominance that General Noriega, the Sandinistas, and the FMLN had once attempted to deny it. The promised U.S. aid never materialized, however. As these three major conflicts came to an end, relations between the United States and the other Central American countries drifted back into patterns reminiscent of earlier eras. While the structure of the international system changed forever during the Bush presidency, U.S. relations with Central America seemed merely to have resumed their familiar shape. But appearances were at least partially deceptive.

In the case of Panama the United States resorted to unilateral military intervention in December 1989, in direct opposition to OAS resolutions and in violation of international law. In the case of Nicaragua, however, the administration chose not to continue the Reagan efforts to undermine the Esquipulas II accords directly. While it refused to disarm the contras (despite U.N. and Latin American calls to do so), it did not launch an all-out effort to undermine the peace process, nor did it challenge the presence of the United Nations, the OAS, or other foreign governments in supervising its implementation. By late 1991, nearly two years later, tolerance had become a warm embrace. With the Sandinistas out of power in Nicaragua and the cold war over, the Bush administration supported the Salvadoran government's decision to sign an agreement that gave the United Nations and OAS secretaries general, together with several foreign governments, crucial roles to play in its implementation. For the first time in the twentieth century the United States actively promoted an arrangement that encouraged other international actors to become involved without direct U.S. leadership or supervision in the internal political affairs of a Central American nation.

PEACE VERSUS SOVEREIGNTY

The peace that came to Central America during the Bush administration was purchased at the cost of each conflicted nation's sovereignty, but the consequences were not unambiguously favorable to the traditional U.S. objective of exclusive dominance. In the larger historical sense, the ways in which the region's major conflicts were resolved led to outcomes that foreclosed others that might have ensued if the United States had failed to secure its objectives, adopted different goals, or merely ceased to take an interest in the region. In the narrower, technical sense, the sovereignty of each of the three countries was diminished by the subjection of its internal political processes to external supervision. In all three cases submission to external supervision had profound (but not identical) effects on the legitimacy and durability of the political order established or modified as a result.

In Panama the Reagan embargo on trade had provoked a financial panic and a disastrous drop in foreign trade and economic activity, beginning in 1987. The economic crisis and clear indications of U.S. support encouraged opposition to the regime, yet the Noriega government did not fall until U.S. troops invaded. Had the United States refrained from invading, the fall of the Noriega regime would have had to wait until Panamanians proved willing and able to accomplish it. The government that would have resulted from a continuation of the Noriega regime or from a successful popular revolt against it would have looked quite different from the government installed by U.S. troops in December 1989.

The new Panamanian government was headed by the apparent winners of the May 1989 elections, which Noriega had set aside—essentially, a coalition of political parties dominated by the white economic elite that had misgoverned the country prior to the Torrijos coup of 1968. The new president, Guillermo Endara, assumed office in a ceremony at a U.S. military base in the former canal zone while U.S. forces were occupying his country. The Panama Defense Forces (PDF) were dissolved and replaced by a new national police force staffed by former PDF officers but subject to U.S. influence. Drug smuggling through Panama increased dramatically as the new government proved less capable of controlling it than Noriega, who had used the PDF to suppress trafficking from which he received no benefit. The dubious legitimacy of the Endara government, its inability to redress the nation's glaring social and economic problems, the occasionally frivolous behavior of the president, and rampant corruption, together with the failure of the United States to provide as much economic aid as it had promised, all contributed to the popular repudiation of the regime in a national referendum on constitutional reforms, defeated by an overwhelming vote in December 1992. The United States had succeeded in replacing the Noriega regime with a government it preferred, but that government's lack of popular support appeared to presage a major realignment of Panamanian political life, in which demands for social change and popular nationalism, targeted at U.S. control of the Panama Canal until the 1978 treaties, were likely to reemerge.

In Nicaragua the 1990 elections were mandated by the Sandinista constitution and would have been held without the contra war. Both the conduct of the elections and the outcome, however, would have been different without the contra war and the Esquipulas II agreement. In the months leading up to the elections, when the United States and Honduras openly violated the agreement by refusing to disarm the contras and dismantle their bases, the Sandinistas gambled on an election victory to legitimate their rule, to turn international and U.S. opinion in their favor, and to persuade the U.S. Congress (if not the Bush administration) to stop the war. For the same reasons the Sandinistas also agreed to major changes in the country's electoral laws, demanded by the opposition parties, which virtually eliminated all the advantages of incumbency. An election sullied by the opposition's refusal to run candidates would not have succeeded in ending the war. The concessions went so far as to permit the U.S. government to provide substantial financial support to the UNO coalition during the electoral campaign in late 1989 and early 1990.[6] U.S. government officials also helped to push the 14 weak and divided opposition parties to unite behind the Chamorro candidacy. The elections were monitored by the International Commission of Verification and Follow-up, created by Esquipulas II and composed of representatives of the U.N. and OAS secretaries general and a group of eight Latin American countries. Additional monitoring was undertaken by nongovernmental organizations, including the U.S. Latin American Studies Association and the Council of Freely Elected Heads of Government (the latter led by former U.S. President Jimmy Carter). Without the contra war, the Esquipulas II accord, U.S. funding for UNO, and opposition unity, the FSLN would probably have won the 1990 elections, with important consequences for the country's future.

Had the Reagan administration succeeded, either through an improbable contra victory or through a U.S. invasion in support of a contra government, the new post-Sandinista regime would have moved quickly to extirpate all vestiges of the Sandinista revolution. Since the Nicaraguan transition occurred through elections, however, the FSLN not only remained intact but also emerged, despite its defeat, as the country's largest political party. The Cha- morro government was thus constrained to seek political compromises with the FSLN, which helped to assure a peaceful and orderly transfer of power with a minimum of reprisals. Eventually the contras agreed to disarm, under U.N. supervision, in exchange for government guarantees of their safety and promises of land grants to the contra soldiery under the terms of the Sandinista agrarian reform legislation. The Chamorro government's policy of national reconciliation was opposed by former contra supporters, both in the UNO coalition and in the U.S. Congress, who agitated for a harsher (and thus an inevitably repressive) transition. U.S. aid to the Chamorro government was less than promised, and the economy failed to recover as anticipated.[7]

When the UNO coalition collapsed in late 1992, President Chamorro turned to the FSLN. In January 1993, deserted by the bulk of the UNO deputies in the National Assembly, who called for her resignation, Chamorro reached an accord with the FSLN in which the Sandinistas agreed to support her government in the National Assembly and revised the government's economic plan to incorporate increases in social spending. Thus the Chamorro government, which came to power largely as a result of circumstances that sharply reduced Nicaragua's independence, found in its principal electoral antagonist both a counterweight to the social conservatism of its former political allies and a means to balance against destabilizing U.S. intrusions. The future of the Chamorro government's policies of reconciliation, and thus of Nicaraguan democracy, may be determined in large part by the success or failure of this strategy.

In El Salvador, U.S. military and economic aid succeeded in denying victory to the insurgents at a cost of more than 75,000 lives and severe economic dislocation, but the peace agreement of 1992 would have been impossible had the guerrillas not succeeded in fighting the Salvadoran army to a stalemate. In November 1989 the FMLN launched a nationwide offensive that was repulsed by the armed forces only after the guerrillas had succeeded in seizing a number of important towns and military installations, including part of the capital. As the fighting raged, the armed forces reverted to traditional brutalities. A senior military official ordered a unit of the U.S.-trained Atlacatl batallion to execute six Jesuit priests, all professors (including the rector and vice-rector) at the Church-run Central American University in San Salvador.[8] This atrocity revived opposition to U.S. aid to the Salvadoran regime in the U.S. Congress. In October 1990 Congress cut military aid by 50 percent and threatened to eliminate the rest unless the perpetrators of the Jesuit murders were brought to justice. After the Bush administration restored the funds, Congress voted in August 1991 to impose new conditions that could have ended all aid to El Salvador, with or without the administration's concurrence. With sufficient U.S. aid the Salvadoran armed forces could have continued to deny victory to the insurgents. Without U.S. aid the prospects for an eventual guerrilla victory would have increased dramatically.

The Bush administration's belated support for the negotiations that ended the war represented an important change in the U.S. position. In the face of congressional resistance to further aid, the administration's rhetorical support for the Esquipulas II accord turned into real pressure on the Salvadoran military and the ARENA government of President Alfredo Cristiani in the final stages of the negotiations at the United Nations in New York in late 1991. Though the administration had initially viewed the U.N. role in Nicaragua with some suspicion, the favorable outcome of the Nicaraguan elections reduced its resistance to a U.N. role in El Salvador. The agreement called for the U.N. and OAS secretaries general and a number of Western European and Latin American governments to become involved in its implementation to assure the guerrillas that their physical saftey and human rights would not be jeopardized as they disarmed. The agreement also called for U.N. supervision of the demobilization of the guerrillas and a major portion of the Salvadoran armed forces (including all of their U.S.-trained special counterinsurgency batallions, the National Guard, the national police, and the treasury police), as well as U.N. monitoring of the human rights situation to ensure protection for former guerrillas. In addition, the "Group of Friends" of the agreement, which included Colombia, Mexico, Spain, and Venezuela, took on monitoring and mediating tasks during the implementation of the accord.

This external supervision of the Salvadoran peace process, which included frequent mediation of frictions and disagreements between the government and the FMLN, helped to keep the peace process on track and to certify its fairness. On 15 December 1992 the demobilization of the guerrillas and most of the force reductions in the Salvadoran army had been completed. The purge of the officer corps was completed by mid-1993, by which time the FMLN had already begun its transformation from armed force to political party in preparation for internationally monitored national elections in 1994.

While resolution of all three of the major Central American conflicts involved an attenuation of sovereignty for the countries involved, the United States was the sole external actor only in the case of Panama. In both Nicaragua and El Salvador, the United States had allied itself with one of the major contenders for power and had thus eliminated itself as a potential mediator and peacemaker.[9] If the U.S. administration wanted peace, it had no choice but to accommodate itself to the presence of other international actors. The limited direct role played by the United States in shaping the agreements under which peace was restored tended further to diminish the power of the United States to control the political outcomes that resulted, at least in the short run. Moreover, the failure to provide the amount of economic aid promised to Panama and Nicaragua, along with declining levels of assistance to El Salvador and the remaining countries on the isthmus, reinforced this downward trend in U.S. influence.

CONCLUSIONS: THE FUTURE OF U.S.–CENTRAL AMERICAN RELATIONS

The two main interpretations of the Central American upheavals of the past half-century have failed to explain why a region so closely tied to the United States should have become the site of so much bloodshed and brutality. The first of these interpretations, embraced by the U.S. government and its allies in Central America, has emphasized the role of "outside agitators," agents of foreign powers such as the former Soviet Union, intent on exploiting popular discontent to undermine democracy, destroy private enterprise, and threaten the security of the United States. This interpretation, repeated endlessly and carried at times to ludicrous extremes, is scarcely credible. It fails to explain how popular discontent arose in the first place, exaggerates the extent and impact of external aid to left-wing parties and insurgencies, and inflates the potential security threat that the success of such movements could have posed to the United States.

The second interpretation, in contrast, has insisted that social and political upheaval in the region has stemmed mainly from internal causes. Popular discontent may have been championed and even materially abetted by external powers from time to time, but the root causes of revolutionary upheaval are to be found in the widespread poverty and inequality that afflict Central American societies. This interpretation has the advantage of a more measured assessment of the role of external powers because its proponents have generally downplayed or ignored it. The weakness of this interpretation lies in its failure to offer a convincing alternative analysis of the impact of the external environment on Central America's internal development.

Poverty and inequality do not, by themselves, cause political and social turmoil. The past half-century's major internal upheavals in Central America were the result of political breakdowns, in which local economic and political elites failed to accommodate to the clamorings of diverse interest groups and social strata for changes in political institutions and public policies. Economic and social problems have affected the pattern and timing of the region's political upheavals, as in the late 1970s and 1980s, when conditions deteriorated throughout the isthmus. However, the recurrence of violent polarization, even during periods of relatively rapid economic growth and measurable improvement in living conditions, as in the 1950s and 1960s, suggests a deeply rooted political dynamic.

The extraordinarily high levels of political and social turmoil that have characterized the recent history of Central America are the result, in large part, of excessively close and subordinate ties to the United States. The subordination of the Central American republics as client states of the United States helps to explain both the extraordinary intransigence of local elites and the unusual intensity and persistence of opposition movements. U.S. dominance of the region simultaneously shaped the development of political elites and made it difficult, at times impossible, for the governments over which they have presided to pursue policies that conflicted with those of the United States. Subordination deprived governments of legitimacy, especially when significant domestic interests had to be sacrificed (or appeared to be sacrificed) to maintain good relations with Washington. Because U.S. policies and the interests of Central America (however defined) often conflicted, subordination aroused opposition across the political spectrum, from groups—not necessarily on the left—whose interests or policy preferences suffered. Nationalist sentiments that arose in the region in the twentieth century inevitably targeted the United States as the enemy "Other," particularly in the two countries where the United States was the direct cause of great national humiliations: Nicaragua and Panama. As in other client-state systems in the modern world, relatively brittle and narrowly based regimes predominated in most of Central America for most of the past century.

The cold war led U.S. policy makers to institutionalize mutually beneficial relations with narrow strata of the region's economic and political elites. This process of institutionalization had two components: a more continuous and intrusive manipulation of local politics in favor of reliably pro-U.S. political forces and, especially after the Cuban Revolution, a more direct and supportive link to local military establishments. During the cold-war era U.S. policy makers successfully imposed a new and narrower standard of political loyalty on governing elites and political leaders and simultaneously pushed to diminish or eliminate the power and influence of political movements and personalities deemed insufficiently attached to U.S. policies. As in the era before the Good Neighbor policy of the 1930s, U.S. officials routinely meddled in local politics, providing support for favored groups and individuals while pressuring for and aiding more effective efforts to discourage or suppress local "Communists." U.S. officials repeatedly played decisive roles in overthrowing or preserving governments, selecting presidents and presidential candidates, scheduling or setting aside elections, naming key military and cabinet officers, shaping economic and social policies, and influencing the leadership and politics of political parties, trade unions, peasant organizations, and other private associations (including the mass media). The United States did not always succeed, but its efforts were always consequential.

These efforts did not require a major commitment of U.S. resources (until the 1980s, when less costly alternatives were at hand). Relatively small—even insignificant—efforts by the United States could have major effects on the tiny polities of Central America. The effects of many U.S. activities, such as the more or less continuous monitoring and manipulation of political organizations, were felt mainly at the margin, in tipping the balance of political forces already in play. The cumulative impact of these U.S. efforts shaped Central American politics decisively. With some notable exceptions, the Central American political actors who benefited most—whether or not this was the United States' intention—came from the conservative to right-wing of the political spectrum. The political actors that suffered were the less reliably pro-U.S. nationalist and left-wing organizations and movements, whose real or merely potential ties or ideological affinities to Moscow or Havana made them anathema to U.S. policy makers. Central American political systems thus became less flexible and accommodating and Central American governments more resistant to change than they would otherwise have been. When pressures for change accumulating beneath the surface of political life finally erupted, the United States usually responded by escalating its efforts to preserve or restore stability and block major changes. At key turning points in the political history of five of the six Central American states between 1954 and 1981, the U.S. government played a direct role in turning aside challenges to the status quo.

The prominence of military establishments in Central American political life is often attributed to local traditions that antedate the United States' twentieth-century dominance in the region. In the nineteenth century, however, the Central American militaries operated with antiquated weaponry, little training, and, except for a few officers, frequently without uniforms. Even as late as the 1930s the military establishments of the depression dictators were little more than glorified police forces. During the cold war the Central American militaries were strengthened and professionalized with U.S. aid (except in the case of Costa Rica, which abolished its army in 1948). The objective of U.S. military aid programs, made explicit by the early 1960s, was to maintain reliably pro-U.S. governments (as perceived in Washington) against internal opposition. The Central American militaries fulfilled this mission during the cold-war era by taking or retaining power for extended periods of time in El Salvador, Guatemala, Honduras, and Panama, and by remaining loyal to the Somoza regime in Nicaragua. Without the supportive environment of their alliance with the United States, however, the Central American military establishments would have found it much more difficult to rule and repress. In fact, four of the six Central American military establishments were either defeated on the battlefield by insurgents (Costa Rica in 1948, Nicaragua in 1979) or might have been defeated without U.S. aid (Guatemala in the 1960s and El Salvador in the 1980s).

Policy makers in the United States have often preferred Central American regimes that are reliably pro-U.S. and democratic. Most Central American governments, however, have not managed to combine both of these qualities at the same time for more than brief periods of time. Forced to choose between adherence to U.S. political norms and the maintenance of more open political regimes, local political and economic elites nearly always opted for the former with U.S. support. From time to time, U.S. governments have attempted to distance themselves from the extreme brutality of the more repressive Central American governments. Efforts by U.S. officials to promote democracy inevitably suffered from two debilitating limitations. First, U.S. support for democracy never implied a willingness to tolerate governments unwilling to subordinate their policies to U.S. security, political, and economic interests, no matter how democratic they might be.[10] The United States has sought democratic clients, which in most cases turned out to be a contradiction in terms. The political dynamics of most client states, in Central America as elsewhere, have seldom proved compatible with durable, democratic regimes. Second, at any time since about 1910, the characteristics and relative power of key political actors—including political parties, interest groups, social and civic organizations, and such major institutions as the military and the judiciary—have reflected the cumulative effects of each country's subordinate relationship with the United States. Within that larger context, however, each of these Central American actors and institutions has pursued its own needs and interests. In a number of cases pressures exerted by the U.S. government for democratization have encountered resistance from "monsters" created in large part by the United States itself.

With the end of the U.S.-Soviet confrontation, U.S.–Central American relations, like U.S. relations with many other countries, have became less predictable. As Abraham Lowenthal wrote recently,

> It is not yet clear how the Central American nations and Panama will relate to the United States in the [rest of the] 1990s. It may be that the intense U.S. involvement of the 1980s (and the 1920s before them) will continue, at least for a while, albeit in modulated tones. But it is equally possible that the United States will disengage, finding cosmetic devices to cover a substantial reduction of U.S. military and economic programs, as was the case in the late 1920s, the 1930s and the 1970s. The rapidity with which Washington has in practice diminished its announced commitments to economic reconstruction in Nicaragua and Panama is sobering. Ambivalence and contradiction, not a clear cut policy, are probable in the U.S. relationship with Central America.[11]

The U.S. security interest in Central America virtually disappeared with the cold war, and U.S. trade and investment in the area remain marginal. The new structure of international relations suggests that the United States will revert willy-nilly, as Lowenthal suggests, to a policy of disengagement—"the cheap backyard" policy of the early cold war and the Nixon-Ford era in the 1970s—reducing economic and military aid along with the quantity and quality of its diplomatic personnel and intelligence assets.

At the same time, however, the potential costs and risks of U.S. military intervention have declined, the disproportionate symbolic importance that Central America acquired in U.S. political discourse during the 1980s has not entirely disappeared, and a full agenda of other U.S. interests remains.

The list of potential offenses capable of inspiring a reassertion of U.S. dominance in Central America now lacks the urgency that once invested the struggle against communism, but the invasion of Panama—the first of the U.S. post–cold war military interventions—took place without reference to the Communist menace. Central American governments that fail to respond to U.S. concerns on a wide variety of issues may have no more reason to feel secure in the future than they have in the past.

The Bush administration's behavior in El Salvador, however, provides a glimpse of a somewhat different future. In that case the United States welcomed the participation of other international actors in order to make credible its willingness, and that of the Salvadoran government, to accept the guerrillas as a legitimate and "representative political force" in Salvadoran political life.[12] The U.S. government took this position, however, only after it had spent 10 years and $6 billion in a failed effort to defeat the guerrillas and keep other actors out. Had the cold war not ended and the Sandinistas not lost the 1990 elections in Nicaragua, congressional pressure to reduce U.S. aid to El Salvador would probably have been less insistent, and the administration's desire to extricate itself much weaker. It is impossible, therefore, to know whether the Salvadoran peace agreement actually set an important precedent or merely marked a temporary detour.

The chief attraction of the Salvadoran model is that it suggests an alternative that could prove, in the long run, less costly for the United States and less destabilizing for Central America (and the Caribbean) than the policy of unilateral dominance pursued by the United States for most of the past century. Emancipation of the Central American states from the constraints that have bound them as clients to the United States is not likely to occur, however, unless both parties act in ways that translate their long-term interests into realistic short-term policy goals that alter the structure of their historic relationship. This would be particularly difficult for the United States because it would imply a conscious effort by policy makers to insulate Central American policy making from U.S. domestic political debate and controversy, to break the historic ties that have linked the United States to pro-U.S. political organizations and institutions (including military establishments) in the region, to accommodate to political developments that may at times appear unfavorable or even hostile to U.S. interests, to tolerate occasional instability and disorder as local political systems adjust to these changes in U.S. policy, and to respect the constraints imposed by international law and opinion despite the relatively low cost of ignoring them. It would also require that the United States cease its historic efforts to exclude other international actors from acquiring influence in the region and accept responsibility for providing economic assistance without always expecting or extracting much short-term political leverage.

Changes of this magnitude in U.S. policy toward Central America may be impossible to achieve and hence unrealistic to contemplate. On the other hand the U.S. security interest virtually disappeared with the end of the cold war, the U.S. economic stake has never been significant, many other U.S. interests (drugs, immigration, terrorism, environment) may better be served at less cost to both sides by dignified cooperation than by enforced subordination, and U.S. domestic public opinion has usually opposed U.S. military interventions in the area.[13] Geographic proximity, economic dependence, cultural and ideological affinities, and inevitable asymmetries in power and resources will continue to make the Central American nations attentive to U.S. concerns, even under conditions of greater autonomy. Moreover, U.S. post–cold war foreign policy may be moving toward placing greater emphasis on the role of international institutions (such as the United Nations) and on respect for international legal norms in order to reduce conflict and insulate the United States from the costs of unilateral action. In short, the basis for a gradual evolution of U.S. policy toward self-interested restraint, international burden-sharing (and thus power-sharing), and even a certain tolerance for political and social pluralism in Central America has already begun to emerge.

The Central Americans themselves could contribute to such an evolution in U.S. policy by creating or strengthening democratic institutions and exploiting the opportunities they provide for mobilizing domestic political resources, by maximizing their efforts to attract economic aid and political support from the industrial giants of Western Europe and East Asia, by working together to create regional (Latin American) and subregional (Central American or Caribbean) economic and political institutions with a higher degree of autonomy than in the past, by making full use of international organizations and legal norms to defend their interests and sovereignty (rather than limiting their efforts to the OAS, for example), and by pursuing means to insert their concerns in the U.S. political process. For the first time in the twentieth century, there is at least a chance that such efforts could bear fruit.

CHRONOLOGY

1821   Five provinces of the Central American isthmus (Guatemala, Honduras, El Salvador, Nicaragua, and Costa Rica) gain independence from Spain, briefly join Mexico, and then form the Central American Federation.

1823   U.S. Secretary of State John Quincy Adams formulates (and President James Monroe proclaims) the Monroe Doctrine, which commits the United States to opposing the reimposition of colonial rule over the newly independent states of Latin America.

1838   The Central American Federation dissolves into five independent states.

1846   The United States and Colombia sign the Mallarino-Bidlack Treaty, in which the United States agrees to defend Colombian sovereignty over Panama in exchange for free transit of goods across the isthmus and access to a future canal.

1846–1848   Mexican War; California Gold Rush begins.

1849   U.S. entrepreneurs secure contracts from the Colombian and Nicaraguan governments to develop transportation systems linking Atlantic and Pacific coast ports.

1850   The Clayton-Bulwer Treaty provides for joint U.S.–British development of any future canal across Central America.

1855	William Walker arrives in Nicaraguan during civil war with force of private mercenaries and seizes power.
1856	In June Walker stages fraudulent elections, has himself inaugurated president of Nicaragua, legalizes slavery, and proclaims English as an official language of the country.
1856	Military forces from Costa Rica are joined in the fight against the Walker regime by Nicaraguan opponents, as well as by troops from Guatemala, El Salvador, and Honduras.
1857	Walker flees after defeat by Nicaraguan opponents and armies from Costa Rica, El Salvador, Guatemala, and Honduras. On his second attempt to regain power in 1860, he is captured and executed in Honduras.
1861–1865	U.S. Civil War.
1894	Great Britain yields control of Mosquito Coast to Nicaragua under U.S. pressure.
1898	Spanish-American War; United States seizes Cuba, Puerto Rico, and the Philippines.
1899	United Fruit Company (UFCO) is formed by merger of two major U.S. banana companies controlling most Central American plantations; UFCO eventually dominates the region's rail network and steamship connections with the United States.
1903	Panama declares independence from Colombia with U.S. help; United States negotiates a treaty that guarantees Panamanian independence in exchange for the right to build a canal and to control the Panama Canal Zone. U.S. troops are stationed in Panama until 1914.
1904	In the Roosevelt Corollary to the Monroe Doctrine, President Theodore Roosevelt announces that henceforth the United States will police the Caribbean to ensure that foreign debts are paid.
1907	In Washington, D.C., five Central American states and the United States sign treaties for political and economic cooperation and create the Central American Court of Justice.

1909	U.S.-backed conservative revolt removes Nicaragua's liberal dictator, General José Santos Zelaya, from power.
1910–1917	Mexican revolution.
1912–1925	U.S. troops occupy Nicaragua to protect conservative Nicaraguan government from liberal opponents, supervise elections, and maintain order.
1914–1918	World War I.
1921	Second Washington, D.C., conference of five Central American nations; participants pledge nonrecognition of unconstitutional regimes.
1926–1934	U.S. Marines resume occupation of Nicaragua to protect the government from liberals led by Augusto César Sandino, supervise elections, and create new Nicaraguan army called the National Guard. Anastasio Somoza is selected as National Guard commander by U.S. authorities.
1933	At the Seventh Pan-American Conference (Montevideo, Uruguay) in December, U.S. Secretary of State Cordell Hull pledges the United States to a policy of nonintervention, initiating President Franklin D. Roosevelt's Good Neighbor policy for the Western Hemisphere.
1934	First major strike by banana workers on UFCO plantations in Costa Rica; labor movement with Communist leaders becomes a major actor in country's political life.
1936	Panama and the United States sign the Hull-Alfaro Treaty, by which the United States withdraws its guarantee of Panamanian sovereignty and gives up its right to intervene in Panama with military force. Anastasio Somoza imposes himself as president of Nicaragua.
1939	World War II begins in September.
1940	Rafael Calderón Guardia is elected president of Costa Rica and enlists Communist support for reforms.
1941	United States secures overthrow of Panamanian president Arnulfo Arias by U.S.-trained National Guard when he refuses to turn over land for U.S. military bases outside the canal zone. United States enters the war in December.

1944   Two "depression dictators" fall. In April a mass movement culminating in a general strike persuades the Salvadoran armed forces to eject General Maximiliano Hernández Martínez, who had seized power in 1931. In July Guatemalan dictator Jorge Ubico, also in power since 1931, flees the country amid mass protests and strikes; Juan José Arévalo is elected president of Guatemala the following year. Teodoro Picado is elected president of Costa Rica and continues reforms with labor and Communist support.

1945   In January an inter-American meeting (United States and Latin American countries) is assembled at Chapultepec Castle in Mexico City. War in Europe ends in May. At a meeting in San Francisco in June Latin American nations support U.S. proposals that result in the inclusion of Articles 51–53 in the U.N. Charter. War in the Pacific ends in August.

1947   The Inter-American Treaty of Mutual Assistance (the "Rio Treaty") is signed in Rio de Janeiro; it binds the United States and the Latin American republics to a military alliance in which each nation agrees to come to the aid of any other that might be threatened by external aggression. In Nicaragua, Somoza steps down from the presidency and engineers election of Leonardo Argüello.

1948   In Costa Rica, José Figueres leads "National Revolution," supported by Arévalo's Guatemalan government, that ousts President Picado in April. Figueres outlaws the Communist party, enacts new social legislation, and abolishes the army. In Nicaragua, Somoza ousts President Argüello and opposes Figueres's seizure of power in Costa Rica. In late April the Organization of American States (OAS) is created at an inter-American meeting in Bogotá, Colombia. Figueres arms Nicaraguan exiles opposed to Somoza. When Nicaragua backs an invasion of Costa Rica by opponents of Figueres in December, Figueres appeals to the OAS. With U.S. support, the OAS brokers an agreement in which Nicaragua ends the invasion and Costa Rica disarms Nicaraguan exiles plotting against Somoza. In Honduras, strongman Tiburcio Carías, in power since 1932, resigns under pressure; he is replaced by his defense minister, and the political atmosphere improves.

1950   Korean War begins on 25 June; Jacobo Arbenz is elected president of Guatemala.

1952   Guatemala issues agrarian reform decree 900 and legalizes the Community party.

1953   Guatemala expropriates idle UFCO lands for distribution to landless peasants. U.S. President Dwight D. Eisenhower orders the CIA to overthrow Guatemalan government. Korean War ends in July.

1954   At the Tenth Inter-American Conference (Caracas, Venezuela) in March the United States insists that the delegates approve a strongly worded declaration aimed at Guatemala (but without mentioning any specific country) that condemns the spread of communism to the Western Hemisphere. Nicaragua sponsors a new invasion of Costa Rica. The United States aids the government of Costa Rica after President Figueres supports U.S. position on Guatemala. A major strike against UFCO erupts in Honduras. In June the Arbenz government is overthrown by the CIA, and an armed force of exiles is organized and financed by the United States. The United States agrees to talks with Panama on a new canal accord.

1956   Nicaraguan President Anastasio Somoza is assassinated in September and is succeeded by his sons Luis and Anastasio. In October the Honduran military seizes power but promises open elections in a year.

1957   Reform-minded Ramón Villeda Morales becomes president after Liberals win Honduran elections.

1958   In May Vice-President Richard M. Nixon is greeted in Caracas, Venezuela, by angry protesters who attack his motorcade and nearly kill him. The United States announces support for creation of an inter-American development bank.

1959   Revolutionary government of Fidel Castro takes power in Cuba on 2 January. In November violent protests against the United States erupt in Panama.

1960   In the spring the CIA begins training Cuban exiles in Guatemala for planned invasion of Cuba. In October the repressive right-wing government of Colonel José María Lemus in El Salvador is ousted by military and replaced by reformist civil-military junta; the United States pressures the new junta to suppress pro-Castro elements. In December the Central American Economic Common Market is born with a new General Treaty of Central American Integration, signed by Nicaragua, El Salvador, Honduras, and Guatemala (Costa Rica joins in 1963).

1961   United States breaks diplomatic relations with Cuba on 3 January. A 25 January military coup in El Salvador ousts the reformist junta; the United States recognizes and pledges aid to the new government of Colonel Julio Rivera. In April the U.S.-sponsored Bay of Pigs invasion of Cuba proves disastrous. In August, at the Inter-American Economic and Social Council meeting in Punta del Este, Uruguay, the charter for the Alliance for Progress is formulated. In November the United States supports Guatemalan President Miguel Ydígoras Fuentes against an attempted coup.

1962   October: Cuban missile crisis.

1963   In late March the Guatemalan military stages a coup (approved by the United States) that deposes Ydígoras and prevents Juan José Arévalo from running for president. In October a coup by the Honduran military ousts the reformist government of President Ramón Villeda Morales.

1965   United States dispatches army to the Dominican Republic.

1965–1970   Guatemalan guerrilla war.

1965–1973   Vietnam War.

1967   Through fraud, Anastasio Somoza Debayle is elected president of Nicaragua. U.S. and Panamanian negotiators finally agree on new canal treaties; controversy erupts in both countries, and the treaties are never signed.

1968   In March the Panamanian National Assembly votes to impeach Marco Robles; former president Arnulfo Arias is proclaimed winner of Panamanian election, inaugurated as president 1 October, and deposed in a coup on 11 October.

1969   In March U.S. administration supports a new coup in Panama, led by Colonel Omar Torrijos. "Soccer War" breaks out between El Salvador and Honduras in July.

1972   Major earthquake in Nicaragua destroys most of the capital city of Managua.

1973   International oil crisis.

1975   In Honduras General López Arellano is removed from office for accepting bribes.

1977   In September President Torrijos and President Jimmy Carter sign Panama Canal treaties. Fraudulent elections in El Salvador install the repressive government of General Carlos Humberto Romero. Military regime in Guatemala stiffens repression in response to guerrilla resurgence. The United States imposes an arms embargo on El Salvador and Guatemala owing to human rights abuses in both countries.

1978   United States pressures Somoza of Nicaragua to end repression and negotiate a transition to democratic rule as Sandinista Revolution heats up; OAS mediation team fails. U.S. Senate passes Panama Canal treaties by slim margin.

1979   In June the Sandinista National Liberation Front launches final offensive; Somoza flees to Miami on 17 July; Sandinistas take power on 19 July. In September U.S. Congress passes legislation implementing the Panama Canal treaties. On 15 October in El Salvador, General Romero is ousted in a coup that brings reformist, civilian-military junta to power; repression escalates.

1980   In January the Salvadoran junta resigns en masse, charging uncontrolled human rights abuses by the military. Ten-year civil war begins. The United States brokers the creation of a new junta from the Christian Democratic party alone. Archbishop Oscar Romero is assassinated by military death squad in March; in November the Farabundo Martí National Liberation Front (FMLN) unites five guerrilla factions. In December Salvadoran soldiers kill four U.S. churchwomen, and the United States briefly suspends military and economic aid.

1981   In January the "Final Offensive" by the FMLN in El Salvador fails as the United States resumes military aid and accuses Nicaragua of supplying weapons to insurgents. Panamanian President Torrijos is killed in a plane crash in July; control of the National Guard passes to intelligence chief and CIA asset General Manuel Antonio Noriega. The new U.S. administration cuts off economic aid to Nicaragua and organizes "contra" forces. It also begins major new aid effort in El Salvador, where the governing junta announces reforms to undercut guerrilla support.

1982   In Honduras Liberal Roberto Suazo Córdova takes office in January, that country's first elected civilian president since 1963. Also in January President Ronald Reagan announces the Caribbean Basin Initiative, offering aid to countries that undertake market reforms. In March the Guatemalan army ousts General Romeo Lucas García, installs General Efraín Ríos Montt to head a new governing junta, and launches a bloody counterinsurgency campaign in Indian highlands. Elections staged in El Salvador bring right-wing coalition to power; reforms are stopped.

1983   The Contadora Group (Colombia, Mexico, Panama, and Venezuela) is launched in January to mediate Central American conflicts. In August a coup headed by General Oscar Mejía Victores ousts the Ríos Montt regime in Guatemala and promises elections. Contra and CIA attacks on Nicaragua are widespread. In October the United States occupies the Caribbean island nation of Grenada

1984   United States adopts a more moderate tone on Central America. In March the Honduran officer corps forces General Gustavo Alvarez Martínez to resign and leave the country; he is replaced by General Walter López. In May José Napoleón Duarte is elected president of El Salvador with U.S. help; in the same month General Noriega engineers fraudulent elections of Nicolás Barletta as president of Panama. U.S. Congress votes down aid to contras. U.S. and Nicaraguan negotiators begin meeting in June. Nicaragua accepts Contadora draft treaty in September; Costa Rica, El Salvador, and Honduras reject it after U.S. criticism. On 15 October Salvadoran president Duarte meets with delegation representing the Democratic Revolutionary Front (FDR— the nonviolent opposition) and the FMLN at La Palma for talks but suspends negotiations on 15 November. On 4 November the Sandinistas win national elections in Nicaragua; Daniel Ortega is elected President. U.S.- Nicaraguan talks end.

1985 Christian Democrats sweep municipal and national assembly elections in March. United States imposes economic embargo on Nicaragua on 1 May. In Guatemala, Vinicio Cerezo is elected first civilian president in 16 years in December.

1986 In February Oscar Arias is elected president of Costa Rica despite U.S. backing for opponent; two weeks later, on a visit to Washington, he opposes U.S. aid to the Nicaraguan contras. U.S. Congress approves $100 million for Nicaraguan contras in June. In 4 November U.S. elections the Democrats recapture control of the Senate; Iran-contra scandal breaks out three weeks later.

1987 Costa Rican President Arias initiates peace process in January. U.S. Senate endorses Arias plan in March. After press reports of his involvement in drug trafficking, General Noriega of Panama loses his CIA retainer. In August five Central American presidents sign the Esquipulas II accord, despite U.S. opposition. The accord calls for the United States to cease aid to the contras in Nicaragua and for that country to negotiate a cease-fire with the contras and hold internationally supervised elections. Terms of the accord also call for government-insurgent negotiations in El Salvador and Guatemala. President Arias wins Nobel Peace Prize in October.

1988 In February General Noriega is indicted by federal grand juries in Florida for drug smuggling and other offenses; the United States imposes economic embargo. Also in February, the U.S. Congress ends military aid to the contras; in March Sandinista government and contras sign cease-fire agreement. Christian Democrats in El Salvador are crushed in March municipal and national-assembly elections by right-wing parties.

1989 On 19 March El Salvador's right-wing ARENA party candidate, Alfredo Cristiani, wins presidential election. U.S. military forces invade Panama on 23 December, capture Noriega as prisoner, and install a new government. Guillermo Endara is sworn in as the country's new president on a U.S. military base in the former canal zone.

1990 In Nicaragua Violeta Chamorro—the presidential candidate of a U.S.-supported coalition of 14 Nicaraguan opposition parties (the United National Opposition)—wins a majority of the votes in an internationally supervised election on 25 February. The contras agree to disarm under U.N. supervision.

1991   The government of El Salvador and the FMLN guerrillas conclude a peace agreement at U.N. headquarters in New York on 31 December.

1992   Mexico, the United States, and Canada sign the North American Free Trade Agreement. General Noriega is tried and convicted on narcotics-trafficking charges in Miami and sentenced to a long prison term. The demobilization of FMLN guerrillas and most of the force reductions in the Salvadoran army are completed by 15 December.

1993   In January President Chamorro, under pressure from the United States and right-wing parties in the UNO coalition, reaches legislative accord with the FSLN. By mid-year the Salvadoran officer corps is purged of human rights violators in preparation for internationally supervised elections in 1994.

NOTES AND REFERENCES

CHAPTER 1

1. Throughout this book, therefore, the terms *Central America* or *Central American* will refer to these six countries (the five republics of historic Central America plus Panama) unless otherwise stated in the text.

2. The United States did, of course, apply to British Honduras the same security doctrines that governed its relations with the other Britsh colonies as well as the independent states of the region. In the face of political developments it deemed unacceptable, the United States intervened decisively in British Guyana in the early 1950s and in Granada in 1983. In the early 1990s, as conflicts in El Salvador and Nicaragua came to an end and Guatemala set aside its territorial claims, Belize opted to pursue closer relations with its Central American neighbors.

3. Central American states have virtually no influence on the strategic balance in the Caribbean region, where the United States is dominant. One or another of them has managed to alter the subregional balance of military might within Central America, but throughout the twentieth century direct or indirect U.S. intervention has, in every case, proved decisive to the outcome of military conflicts on the isthmus.

4. See James R. Kurth, "Economic Change and State Development," in *Dominant Powers and Subordinate States: The United States in Latin America and the Soviet Union in Eastern Europe*, ed. Jan F. Triska (Durham: Duke University Press, 1986), 85–101. Kurth uses the term *hegemonic system* to describe the United States' relationship with Latin America as whole. The tighter U.S. dominance in the Caribbean is closer to the Soviet relationship (until 1989) with Eastern Europe. Kurth also applies this term to the looser hegemony of "France in sub-Saharan Africa from the 1960s to the present" (86).

5. Both Cuba and Panama were reduced to formal protectorates of the United States for extended periods of time. The 1905 Roosevelt Corollary to the Monroe Doctrine constituted a unilateral U.S. proclamation of protectorate status for all the states in the Caribbean.

6.   Constitutionally, Guadeloupe, Martinique, and French Guiana are not colonies but overseas departments, which elect representatives to the French parliament, as do the mainland departments in France.

7.   For example, see the influential work of Alfred Thayer Mahan, *The Interest of America in Sea Power* (1897; Boston: Little, Brown, 1918). Mahan advocated construction of a Central American canal and the acquisition of naval bases to defend it. For a summary of U.S. and other plans and schemes to build a trans-isthmian canal, see Thomas M. Leonard, *Central America and the United States: The Search for Stability* (Athens: University of Georgia Press, 1991), chap. 3.

8.   See Ernest R. May, *Imperial Democracy: The Emergence of America as a Great Power* (New York: Harcourt, Brace & World, 1961); Walter Lafeber, *The New Empire: A Interpretation of American Expansion, 1860–1898* (Ithaca, N.Y.: Cornell University Press, 1963); and William Appleman Williams, *The Roots of the Modern American Empire* (New York: Random House, 1969).

9.   Robert Olds, "Confidential Memorandum on the Nicaraguan Situation," January 1927, National Archives, p. 2.

10.   International-relations theorists refer to this behavior as "balancing." See Stephen M. Walt, *The Origins of Alliances* (Ithaca, N.Y.: Cornell University Press, 1987), 18–19.

11.   Walt refers to this as "bandwagonning" (19–21) and concludes that weak states will prefer to balance against the state that most threatens them. Walt's conclusion is not confirmed by the behavior of the Central American states, in part because the United States has usually managed to prevent governments capable of formulating foreign policies resembling those of fully sovereign states from coming to power or to eliminate them on the few occasions when they appeared.

12.   The Esquipulas II agreement of 1987 marked an important exception to this general rule.

13.   For a theoretical discussion that combines the notions of "critical junctures" (or turning points) and "path-dependent" development, see Ruth Berins Collier and David Collier, *Shaping the Political Arena: Critical Junctures, Trade Unions, and the State in Latin America* (Princeton, N.J.: Princeton University Press, 1990), chap. 1

14.   The only significant exception to this rule occurred in 1954, when France and Great Britain voiced objections to the U.S.-backed overthrow of the Guatemalan government. The Eisenhower policy establishment was furious. See Stephen Rabe, *Eisenhower and Latin America: The Foreign Policy of Anticommunism* (Chapel Hill: University of North Carolina Press), 60.

CHAPTER 2

1.   William Walker, *The War in Nicaragua* (Mobile, Ala.: S. H. Goetzel, 1860), cited in Karl Bermann, *Under the Big Stick: Nicaragua and the United States since 1948* (Boston: South End Press, 1986), 73.

2.   For example, Thomas Mann, assistant secretary of state for inter-American affairs under President Lyndon Johnson: "I know my Latins. They understand only two things—a buck in the pocket and a kick in the ass" (cited by George Black, *The Good Neighbor: How the United States Wrote the History of Central America and the Caribbean* [New York: Pantheon Books, 1988], 115).

3. In Guatemala and elsewhere in Central America, Europeans, mestizos, and those Indians who have adopted European dress, speech, and customs are referred to collectively as *Ladinos*.

4. See Kenneth J. Grieb, *Guatemalan Caudillo: The Regime of Jorge Ubico* (Athens: Ohio University Press, 1979).

5. See Thomas P. Anderson, *Matanza: El Salvador's Communist Revolt of 1932* (Lincoln: University of Nebraska Press, 1971). The Salvadoran Communist party—whose leader, Farabundo Martí, was captured and executed on the eve of the revolt—led urban protests against the newly installed military dictatorship of General Maximiliano Hernández Martínez but apparently had little to do with the indigenous movement in the countryside.

6. For most of the twentieth century, Honduran presidents and other key officials allied themselves with the banana companies, mainly the United Fruit Company (UFCO), in exchange for various favors. As recently as 1972, UFCO bribed the country's president to receive favorable tax treatment. Honduran leaders who provoked UFCO seldom lasted long.

7. The Pan-American Union was founded at the fourth International Conference of American States, held in Buenos Aires in 1910. The first such conference had been convened by the United States in Washington in late 1889 and early 1890. The Pan-American Union was replaced by the Organization of American States (OAS) at the ninth conference, held in Bogotá in 1948. See G. Pope Atkins, *Latin America in the International Political System* (Boulder, Colo.: Westview, 1989), 205–7.

8. The U.S. Customs receivership in the Dominican Republic did not end until 1940, however.

9. Victor Bulmer-Thomas, *The Political Economy of Central America since 1920* (Cambridge: Cambridge University Press, 1987), 78.

10. Ibid., 79.

11. Jacobo Schifter, *Las alianzas conflictivas: Las relaciones de Costa Rica y Estados Unidos de la segunda guerra mundial a los inicios de la guerra civil* (San José, Costa Rica: Libro Libre, 1986), chap. 2.

12. Ibid., chaps. 2–3.

13. The rubber agreement also specified that the entire output of rubber from each country would be sent to the United States, a provision that virtually stripped the region of rubber tires for most of the war. See Schifter, *Alianzas conflictivas*, chap. 3.

CHAPTER 3

1. Argentina later did declare war on the Axis powers, in March 1945. The United States then insisted, against considerable opposition, that Argentina be invited to attend the San Francisco conference and to join the United Nations.

2. See, for example, the 1947 exchange between Secretary of State Dean Acheson and Secretary of War Robert P. Petterson in *Foreign Relations of the United States: 1947* 8: 105–12.

3. "Inter-American Treaty of Reciprocal Assistance," in U.S. Department of State, *Treaties and Other International Acts Series 1838* (Washington, D.C.: U.S. Government Printing Office, 1949), 25.

4. Alain Rouquié, *The Military and the State in Latin America*, trans. Paul E. Sigmund (Berkeley: University of California Press, 1987), 24.

5. Ibid., 23.

6. U.S. Department of State, *United States Treaties and Other International Agreements* (Washington, D.C.: U.S. Government Printing Office, 1952), 2419.

7. President Truman's address before the final session of the Rio Treaty meeting made clear the U.S. view that economic aid was appropriate for war-ravaged Europe but was not justified in Latin America, where private enterprise could satisfy the need for economic development. The speech is published in U.S. Department of State, *Bulletin* 17, no. 428 (14 September 1947), 498–501.

8. Quoted in David Green, *The Containment of Latin America* (Chicago: University of Chicago Press, 1971), 262.

9. See the *New York Times* report (13 January 1927, 1) of testimony by Secretary of State Frank B. Kellogg before the Senate Foreign Relations Committee. The text of his statement, "Bolshevik Aims and Intentions in Mexico and Nicaragua," is in Green, *Containment of Latin America*, 2.

10. See Schifter, *Alianzas conflictivas*, chap. 6, on the role of U.S. Ambassador Scotten.

11. See Ronald Radosh, *American Labor and United States Foreign Policy* (New York: Random House, 1969), chaps. 11–12. The CIO remained an affiliate of CTAL until 1948. It did not join the anticommunist crusade in Latin America until the Taft-Hartley Act initiated a purge of Communists within its ranks.

12. Lawrence Duggan, *The Americas: The Search for Hemispheric Security* (New York: Henry Holt, 1949), 171.

13. The Costa Rican national revolution of 1948 and the Guatemalan coup of 1954 are discussed in detail below.

14. Bulmer-Thomas, *Political Economy of Central America*, 130.

15. See Richard Immerman, *The CIA in Guatemala: The Foreign Policy of Intervention* (Austin: University of Texas Press, 1982), chap. 1.

16. Ibid.

17. These include Piero Gleijeses, *Shattered Hope: The Guatemalan Revolution and the United States, 1944–54* (Princeton, N.J.: Princeton University Press, 1991); Immerman, *CIA in Guatemala*; Stephen Kinzer and Stephen Schlesinger, *Bitter Fruit: The Untold Story of the American Coup in Guatemala* (Garden City, N.Y.: Anchor Books, 1983).

18. Cole Blasier, *The Hovering Giant: U.S. Responses to Revolutionary Change in Latin America* (Pittsburgh: University of Pittsburgh Press, 1976), 155.

19. Patterson left Guatemala on 6 April 1950; he was replaced by Rudolf Schoenfeld nearly a year later. Schoenfeld, judged "too cautious" by CIA and State Department officials planning Arbenz's ouster, was reassigned as ambassador to Colombia in April 1953. John Peurifoy, the "activist" ambassador sought by the plotters, was selected for the post in August and arrived in Guatemala City on 29 October 1953. See Immerman, *CIA in Guatemala*, 134–35.

20. Arévalo announced that Araña had been killed by "reactionaries" and made a speech mourning the nation's loss. Few believed it, and most historians have concluded that Arbenz had Araña killed to ensure his own election. Gleijeses's account (*Shattered Hope*, chap. 3) is the first to detail the circumstances of this event.

21. Gleijeses, *Shattered Hope*, 195.

22. Of the 350 positions in the Departamento Agrario Nacional, no more that 26 were filled by Communists. See James Dunkerley, *Power in the Isthmus: A Political History of Modern Central America* (London: Verso, 1988), 149.

23. Gleijeses, *Shattered Hope*, 362.

24. Ibid., 147.

25. Cited in Schlesinger and Kinser, *Bitter Fruit*, 158.

26. The information on this early plotting was discovered by Immerman, *CIA in Guatemala*, 120–21. See also Gleijeses, *Shattered Hope*, 228–31.

27. Guatemalan foreign policies were as moderate as its domestic reforms in the Arévalo-Arbenz era. For example, although Guatemala and the Soviet Union had agreed to mutual recognition in 1945, neither nation took steps to put the agreement into practice. Arévalo and Arbenz declined to appoint an ambassador to Moscow. Guatemala did refuse to sign the Rio Treaty unless it could append language mentioning its claim to Belize, but this option was rejected at the insistence of the United States. After the 1954 coup Guatemala signed the Rio Treaty with the appended statement on Belize, the United States having dropped its objection in the meantime.

28. Immerman, *CIA in Guatemala*, 132; Gleijeses, *Shattered Hope*, 243.

29. The first nine conferences were called Pan-American conferences, but the term fell into disfavor in Latin America because it was perceived to have a connotation of U.S. dominance. The phrasing was changed to "Inter-American" in the 1948 OAS Charter. See Immerman, *CIA in Guatemala*, 145.

30. In May 1954 the U.S. administration considered calling an OAS meeting to condemn Guatemala by name after the discovery of the Czech arms shipment, but it decided against the action on realizing that it would not have the two-thirds majority vote needed to approve collective action. The only elected governments that would have supported the United States were Bolivia and Costa Rica. Bolivia, in the midst of economic turmoil following its 1952 national revolution, had become dependent on U.S. aid. Costa Rica had been induced by threats from Nicaragua to appeal for military assistance from the United States. On the Caracas meeting see Rabe, *Eisenhower and Latin America*, 49–53; on the Costa Rican conflict with Nicaragua see below.

31. The best account of the circumstances surrounding Arbenz's resignation is in Gleijeses, *Shattered Hope*, chap. 14.

32. "The American Republics," *Foreign Relations of the United States: 1952–1954* 4: 385.

33. In both elections the United States covertly supported candidates more closely associated with the Guatemalan military high command. Castillo Armas's party, the Movimiento Democrático Nacional (MDN), ran Interior Minister Miguel Ortíz Passarrelli in October; in the January poll it ran Colonel José Luis Cruz Salazar. Ydígoras helped his cause by organizing street demonstrations to protest the October fraud and threatened to call on his friends in the officer corps to organize a coup unless a new election were held. In the second electoral campaign the CIA contributed to the Cruz campaign, hoping to prevent Ydígoras from winning. Ydígoras, however, increased his vote by appealing obliquely to Arbenz supporters with "calls for an end to persecution and a new period of reconciliation—as well as . . . greater distance from the US" (Dunkerley, *Power in the Isthmus*, 439). In office Ydígoras proved corrupt, incompetent, and at least as repressive as Castillo Armas, but he abandoned his anti-U.S. rhetoric for a time and conformed to U.S. requirements until the last days of his regime.

34. The United States failed to honor its treaty commitment to Honduras when the Salvadoran army invaded Honduras to seize disputed territory in the 1969 "Soccer War." The United States insisted that Honduras take its complaint to the OAS and refused to send any aid.

35. "Honduras," *Foreign Relations of the United States: 1955–1957* 7: 104.

36. Ibid., 109.

37. Bulmer-Thomas, *The Political Economy of Central America*, 166–67.

38. "Costa Rica," *Foreign Relations of the United States: 1955–1957* 7: 4.

39. Ibid., 2–18.

40. "The American Republics," *Foreign Relations of the United States: 1952–1954* 4: 378.

41. U.S. employees would "continue to receive a 'differential' of 15 percent for serving overseas, as well as leave benefits and income tax allowances" (Walter Lafeber, *The Panama Canal: The Crisis in Historical Perspective*, upd. ed. [Oxford: Oxford University Press, 1989], 120).

42. Figueres would not have outlawed the Costa Rican Communist party, a measure to which he was pushed by his conservative allies and the U.S. embassy. On resuming the presidency two decades later, Figueres granted legal status to the party (though he had refrained from doing so during his term as president in the 1950s).

43. "Nowhere in Central America or the Caribbean," concludes Gleijeses, "has U.S. intervention been so decisive and so baneful in shaping the future of a country" (*Shattered Hope*, 381).

44. This unidentified U.S. official is quoted in Marlise Simons, "Guatemala: The Coming Danger," *Foreign Policy* 43 (Summer 1981): 103; also cited by Immerman, *CIA in Guatemala*, 197.

45. The Figueres government nationalized domestic banking in 1949; thereafter banking remained a government monopoly. The National Revolutionary Movement (MNR) government in Bolivia nationalized the major tin-mining companies. The Arbenz regime intervened when some enterprises were involved in labor disputes but did not nationalize any private enterprises. The MNR sanctioned the seizure of private lands, even those that were in production and highly productive. Arbenz's agrarian reform expropriated only unused private lands.

46. Blasier notes that by early 1953, in the conflict between UFCO and the Guatemalan government over the agrarian reform law, "the Department of State . . . entered directly into the controversy as a spokesman for the company, representing the company's position to the government of Guatemala on virtually all major aspects of the dispute" (*Hovering Giant*, 89).

47. Blasier, *Hovering Giant*, 59–60, 64.

48. "The American Republics," *Foreign Relations of the United States: 1952–1954* 4: 192. The report that prompted this decision was drafted at the State Department and revised by staff at the National Security Council. The report also claimed that prosecution of UFCO would also encourage nationalization of UFCO and other U.S. assets throughout the region and jeopardize U.S. security, because U.S. access to transportation facilities and raw materials in times of war "could not be counted on with the same security as in direct control of American citizens" (193).

49. Quoted in Gleijeses, *Shattered Hope*, 366.

50. Ibid.

CHAPTER 4

1. Haiti, Nicaragua, and Peru (1956), Guatemala (1957), Argentina, Colombia, and Venezuela (1958), Cuba (1959), and El Salvador (1960). The victims of assassination were Anastasio Somoza of Nicaragua and Carlos Castillo Armas of Guatemala.

2. On welcoming the new Venezuelan ambassador to the United States, Eisenhower in effect announced the new policy by denouncing "authoritarianism and autocracy of whatever form." As Rabe points out, "Eisenhower's statement marked the first time a high administration official had openly and unequivocally recommended representative government for Latin America" (*Eisenhower and Latin America*, 105).

3. Cuba was an exception to this rule. To avoid a repetition of the criticisms leveled at the United States in other such cases, and under intense public and congressional pressure, the administration officially suspended military aid to the government of General Fulgencio Batista several months before it fell to Castro's guerrilla army.

4. Eisenhower had, among other gestures of support, given Pérez Jiménez the Legion of Merit—the highest award the United States could bestow on a foreign leader. See Rabe, *Eisenhower and Latin America*, 86.

5. The Caracas declaration condemned communism but did not mention Guatemala by name.

6. During the Truman administration the Ex-Im Bank had begun to extend long-term loans to a number of Latin American countries for various development projects. Eisenhower stopped the practice, and the bank went back to providing mainly short-term commercial loans to finance exports of U.S. products.

7. See Rabe, *Eisenhower and Latin America*, chap. 7.

8. This sudden change in the U.S. position owed in part to Eisenhower's desire to offer something positive in the portion of his U.N. speech dealing with the Middle East. His advisers suggested calling for the creation of a Middle Eastern development bank, to which the United States would contribute a major portion of the capital. When the text was evaluated in the State Department, officials warned that the president might have difficulty explaining his willingness to create a Middle Eastern bank, in light of the administration's long-standing rejection of similar proposals from Latin America. The inconsistency was eliminated at the last minute by adding a development bank for Latin America. The Middle Eastern project never got off the ground (and was not expected to, in any case, because of U.S. reluctance to include all the Arab states and because of rivalries among them), but the IADB project moved forward quickly.

9. The administration also relaxed its prohibition on long-term lending by the Ex-Im Bank, from which Panama and the five Central American countries had received small loans by the end of 1960.

10. Panama, not technically a Central American country, did not participate in the CEC or in the CACM negotiations.

11. Through this provision the ECLA sought to promote import-substituting industries with markets large enough to allow them to take advantage of economies of scale. To the United States, this threatened to reduce demand for U.S. exports to the region. Moreover, since the decision to grant monopolies (actually, effective tariff

protection) to particular companies was to be made by agreement among the CACM governments, the U.S. government also worried that U.S. firms might be excluded.

12. Bulmer-Thomas, *Political Economy of Central America*, 174.

13. Ibid., 178–79.

14. Despite official reminders and protests, the United States had failed to implement the 1955 agreement.

15. See Lafeber, *The Panama Canal*, chap. 4. The administration simultaneously responded to Pentagon and right-wing worries by authorizing a series of highly publicized military deployments to the zone, including an additional 1,000 infantry troops and two Hawk missile units in July 1960; these deployments and the highly visible maneuvers of U.S. military units in the zone were usually described as measures to meet the Cuban-Soviet threat. Many Panamanians interpreted them as crude attempts to intimidate opponents of the canal zone status quo.

16. The CIA had actually been recruiting, training, and financing anti-Castro Cuban terrorists on a smaller scale for several months before Eisenhower's 17 March Executive Order.

17. The radio also broadcast attacks on the dictator of the Dominican Republic, General Rafael Leónidas Trujillo. The occasion for U.S. hostility toward Trujillo arose when Dominican agents twice attempted unsuccessfully to assassinate President Rómulo Betancourt of Venezuela, an old enemy of the Trujillo regime. The vehemence of the U.S. campaign against Trujillo was motivated by the desire for rhetorical balance in its defense of democracy (against Cuba on the left and Trujillo on the right) and by the conviction in Washington that Trujillo's arbitrary rule could make him the Caribbean's next Batista. Nothing came of the effort, though it set the stage for Trujillo's assassination in 1963 by agents of the CIA.

18. This move was decidedly unpopular in Honduras. The United States had claimed sovereignty over the Swan Islands since 1863. The CIA transmitting post was nearly compromised in 1961, when a group of Honduran students landed on the beach and insisted on raising the national flag. The CIA operative in charge of the station plied the students with cold beer and other refreshments, allowed them to raise the flag and lay cement lettering claiming the island for Honduras, and sent them on their way unaware of the transmitter and its purpose. In 1972 the United States ceded its claims to Great Swan and the other islands in the Swan group to Honduras. See David Wise and Thomas R. Ross, *The Invisible Government* (New York: Random House, 1964), 328–37, and David Atlee Phillips, *The Night Watch* (New York: Atheneum, 1977).

19. Villeda's long cooperation with CIA projects in Honduras and with U.S. officials did not prevent him from playing his own game. The Great Swan Island gesture was in part penance for his support of a plot, "masterminded by Che Guevara," to overthrow the government of President Luis Somoza of Nicaragua in June 1959 (Bulmer-Thomas, *Political Economy of Central America*, 166–67.

20. By this time Figueres had left office, and the conservative opposition party was firmly in power. The new Costa Rican president, Francisco Orlich, elected in 1958 with covert U.S. support, endorsed the U.S. campaign against Cuba. His party included many of the anti-Figueres Calderonistas who had launched attacks from Nicaragua in 1948 and 1955. The border incidents with Nicaragua ceased by the end of 1960.

21. This was true in two senses. First, the 1954 overthrow of Arbenz put the nation's political system on a new trajectory by eliminating the left and elevating the

army to the role of ultimate domestic arbiter of the nation's political life. Second, President Ydígoras owed his "election" to U.S. pressure, which forced the army to set aside the fraudulent elections of 1957, order new elections in early 1958, and recognize Ydígoras's victory.

22. Until the creation of the SPTF, U.S. "aid" consisted mainly of U.S. government loans at commercial rates of interest, with relatively short amortization schedules and repayment required in dollars. The 1958–59 concessions made long-term loans available through the Ex-Im Bank and the Development Loan Fund (DLF), but again at commercial interest rates, with repayment required in dollars. The administration did provide grant aid (gifts) in small amounts, mainly in the form of "technical assistance" (larger grants were confined to Bolivia and Guatemala). With the exception of grant aid, therefore, U.S. foreign "aid" did nothing more than supplement private lending, and usually specified terms similar to those offered by private commercial banks. The SPTF was the first U.S. program that offered loans on terms much better than those available from private sources, to finance social as well as directly economic spending in the region.

23. As Rabe has pointed out, Eisenhower's "new direction in military policy violated U.S. law"—that is, "the stricture that internal security requirements could not normally be the basis for military assistance to Latin America" (*Eisenhower and Latin America*, 148). The Democrats in Congress who imposed this constraint were not, however, prepared to enforce it, for fear they might be accused of being "soft on communism"; also, some found the concept of military "civic action" congenial.

24. On 17 April 1961 some 1,400 well-armed Cuban counterrevolutionaries—organized, trained, and equipped by the CIA—landed at Girón Beach on the Bay of Pigs, located on the southern coast of Cuba. The expedition failed; all of its members were killed or captured by Cuba's Revolutionary Armed Forces within three days. After first ordering U.S. officials, including U.N. Ambassador Adlai Stevenson, to deny any U.S. involvement, President Kennedy eventually took responsibility for the disaster. See Peter Wyden, *Bay of Pigs: The Untold Story* (New York: Simon & Schuster, 1979), for a well-researched and highly readable account.

25. See the *New York Times*, 26 January 1962, 14, and 14 October 1962, 34.

26. Clifford Krauss, *Inside Central America: Its People, Politics, and History* (New York: Summit Books, 1991), 66.

27. *New York Times*, 14 October 1962, 1ff.

28. This unusual deployment of a ranking U.S. military commander was motivated by the administration's fear that the Honduran military would not take seriously the importunings of U.S. Ambassador Charles R. Burrows. In the Dominican Republic the U.S. ambassador's last-minute efforts to forestall a coup "had to attempt to overcome the influence of certain key members of United States military missions there" (*New York Times*, 5 October 1963, 5).

29. AFL activity on behalf of U.S. foreign policy objectives has a long history in Latin America. After the AFL merged with the CIO in 1955, this activity continued under AFL-CIO auspices. In Central America AFL-CIO influence reached its high point in Honduras after the banana strike of 1954.

30. Luis Somoza assumed the presidency of Nicaragua after a fraudulent election in 1957. In 1963 he ceded the office to a handpicked successor, René Schick, whose election was equally fraudulent. Luis and his brother Anastasio retained their posts as heads of the Liberal party and the National Guard.

31. For the text of this news conference and accompanying stories, see the *New York Times*, 5 April 1964, 1ff. Johnson's comment also referred to an agreement with Panama to begin talks on the status of the canal.

32. Panamanian authorities later acknowledged that the National Guard's absence was deliberate. The government wanted to avoid a confrontation between the guard and U.S. troops, and the guard's officers did not wish to be seen attacking defenders of the national flag. See the *New York Times*, 11 March 1964, 17.

33. For Chiari's statement, see the *New York Times*, 11 January 1964, 4.

34. Panama also took its case the the U.N. Security Council, which solemnly urged both sides to compose their differences. Chiari withdrew his request for a full meeting of the Security Council in order to make use of the OAS machinery.

35. This commission issued its report on 16 February. It concluded that the United States had not engaged in acts of aggression against Panama. Contrary to U.S. assertions, however, it found little evidence of Communist involvement in the rioting and stated that U.S. troops had used excessive force and failed to show proper restraint and discipline in responding to Panamanian protesters.

36. *New York Times*, 4 May 1964, 1ff.

37. *New York Times*, 18 April 1964, 1.

38. Joseph S. Tulchin, "The United States and Latin America in the 1960s," *Journal of Inter-American Studies and World Affairs* 30, no. 1 (Spring 1988): 1–36. Tulchin's phrase summarizes the judgments of "most scholars." For a standard account by journalists, see Jerome Levinson and Juan de Onis, *The Alliance That Lost Its Way: A Critical Report on the Alliance for Progress* (Chicago: Quadrangle Books, 1970).

39. Tulchin, "United States and Latin America in the 1960s," 28.

40. Steve Weissman, "An Alliance for Stability," in *The Trojan Horse: A Radical Look at Foreign Aid*, ed. Steve Weissman (San Francisco: Ramparts Press, 1974), 73.

41. Peru after the military coup of 1968 was an exception to this rule, but the United States opposed the new regime and cut off most aid.

42. The most forceful and persuasive critique of the U.S. abhorrence of instability in the cold war era is by Lars Schoultz, *National Security and United States Policy toward Latin America* (Princeton, N.J.: Princeton University Press, 1987).

43. Venezuela was the major exception. U.S. aid was not critical to the Betancourt government's victory over a Cuban-supported insurgency in the early 1960s. The Betancourt regime's legitimacy as an elected government proved an insurmountable obstacle to guerrilla success, despite repeated states of siege in which individual rights were suspended.

44. While Arévalo, like all candidates with left-wing or populist leanings, was excluded from participating in the 1966 elections, Méndez had received electoral support from many former partisans of the pre-1954 regime. He promised mild reforms and was elected on 6 March 1966, after the United States had interceded with the military to prevent a coup that would have canceled the elections. On the U.S. role, see the *New York Times*, 23 February 1966, 22.

45. *New York Times*, 22 January 1968, 14.

46. To do otherwise, U.S. officials explained, could have precipitated the very instability the United States sought to avoid.

CHAPTER 5

1. See Chapter 3, on the Guatemalan issue in 1954.

2. Occasionally, playing for small political gains at home, European politicians made comments that irked the State Department, but these were relatively minor irritations.

3. The Cubans did receive considerable diplomatic support, but virtually no aid, from sympathetic members of the nonaligned movement.

4. Many European governments and public figures were also incensed that the United States had incurred such a risk without consulting them in advance, because the NATO alliance ensured that they would be drawn into any war between the United States and the Soviet Union.

5. Western European governments also made a point of providing help to political exiles from Latin America and managed to convey growing dismay at the brutality of the region's military rulers.

6. For Nixon's speech, see "Action for Progress for the Americas," *State Department Bulletin* 61, no. 1586 (17 November 1969). Kissinger's promise of a "new dialogue" was made off the cuff at a meeting in New York in October 1972 with the U.N. ambassadors of a number of Latin American countries. The Latin Americans saw to it that the statement received much publicity; Kissinger, however, never intended it to be taken so seriously. See Michael J. Francis, "United States Policy toward Latin America during the Kissinger Years," in *United States Policy in Latin America: A Quarter Century of Crisis and Challenge, 1961–1986*, ed. John D. Martz (Lincoln: University of Nebraska Press, 1988), 41. Later, in September 1974, Kissinger spoke of a "new partnership" but left the term undefined and did not follow it with any new policies.

7. For an account of the war, its causes, and its aftermath, see Thomas P. Anderson, *The War of the Dispossessed: Honduras and El Salvador, 1969* (Lincoln: University of Nebraska Press, 1981).

8. The right to impose such a tax had been granted by the CACM after Honduras and Nicaragua complained that they had reaped few of the benefits of free trade and needed to protect their markets in order to avoid accumulating unmanageable trade deficits. Nicaragua imposed a similar tax on all manufactured imports from the rest of Central America but eliminated it a year later.

9. The commission's report was submitted to the OAS two weeks after the war had ended. It concluded that Honduran authorities had committed acts of "aggression and unrestrained violence" against Salvadorans residing in Honduras.

10. Each of the teams won the game it played on its home turf. The last of the three games was moved to Mexico City, where on 28 June the Salvadoran team won by a score of 3 to 2 in overtime. Players on the two teams shook hands and embraced when the game ended.

11. The Nixon administration, however, had not managed to appoint a U.S. ambassador to Honduras by the time the war broke out. During the war the embassy in Tegucigalpa was virtually useless. The deputy chief of mission fell ill, and communications with Washington "were dependent primarily on amateur radio operators because of a shortage of personnel at the embassy" (*New York Times*, 19 July 1969, 3).

12. Nicaragua apparently dispatched military supplies to Honduras at the

height of the conflict, but the help had no discernible effect on the Honduran army's miserable performance, and Nicaragua denied having provided it.

13. The territorial dispute, which had festered since 1863, was resolved in 1992 by a decision of the World Court in the Hague. The two countries had agreed to refer the case to the World Court in a treaty brokered by the United States late in the Nixon administration. The World Court awarded two-thirds of the disputed territory to Honduras, including sovereignty over two islands in the Gulf of Fonseca, which guaranteed its access to the Pacific Ocean (*El País* [Madrid], 12 September 1992, 6).

14. *New York Times*, 24 July 1969, 5.

15. Somoza helped Torrijos by supplying him with a private plane that got him back to Panama from Mexico City in time to suppress the coup attempt (Lafeber, *Panama Canal*, 127).

16. The vote was 13 in favor, one (Great Britain) abstaining, and one opposed. This was only the third U.S. veto in U.N. history (ibid., 143).

17. The best account of the Nixon-Ford Panama negotiations is found in William J. Jordan, *Panama Odyssey* (Austin: University of Texas Press, 1984). Jordan was the National Security Council staff member who became U.S. ambassador to Panama during the period in which the talks took place.

18. Jordan, *Panama Odyssey*, 141. The "plumbers" were allegedly called back from Mexico City on their way to do the deed.

19. Ibid., 147–48.

20. See sources cited in Table 1.2.

21. These two initiatives were linked. Figueres arranged to sell Costa Rican coffee to the Soviet Union through a local Communist leader and financed his election campaign with the proceeds. Once elected, he rewarded the Soviets with recognition and the Communist party with legalization.

22. See Bulmer-Thomas, *Political Economy of Central America*, 202–4.

23. See James Dunkerley, "Guatemala since 1930," in *Central America since Independence*, ed. Leslie Bethel (Cambridge: Cambridge University Press, 1991): "Arana imposed a state of siege for the first year of his regime, during which more than seven hundred politically motivated killings took place, exiles both official and voluntary abounded, the university was intervened" (143). Arana had been in charge of the antiguerrilla campaign between 1965 and 1970: "Combining a scorched earth policy of generalized repression with a U.S.-backed 'civic action' programme whereby certain communities were politically and economically favored by the army, Arana's campaign resulted in the death of some ten thousand people in the space of five years . . . and the establishment of 'military commissioners' in the villages laid the basis for the death squads of the 1970s and the civil patrols of the 1980s" (141–42). Washington's confidence in the new Guatemalan president was in part due to this earlier success.

24. The Ford administration, responding to Latin American pressures in July 1975, had shifted its position to one that favored continued U.S. sanctions, but no longer sought to impose them on the other members of the OAS. The OAS then voted to lift the sanctions. Had the United States not changed its position, however, the OAS would have voted to lift the sanctions anyway.

25. This paragraph largely summarizes the insightful analysis of Bulmer-Thomas, *Political Economy of Central America*, chap. 10.

26. Lafeber, *Panama Canal*, 161.

27. Carter and Torrijos met again on 16 and 17 June 1978 in Panama City to exchange the "instruments of ratification."

28. Canal operations, according to the treaty, were to be controlled by a nine-member commission of five U.S. and four Panamanian citizens. The House kept control over the canal budget, stripped the commission of its power and independence, and gave the U.S. secretary of defense the power to name all nine commissioners (ibid., 185–86).

29. Schoultz, *National Security and United States Policy*, 40.

30. In Guatemala, *Ladino* refers to the "non-Indian" population, which consists of a small elite of mainly European extraction, a large number of mestizos (persons of mixed indigenous and European ancestry), and an indeterminate number of Indians who have adopted the language, dress, and behavioral norms of the dominant Ladino culture. The Ladino elite's traditional fear of the Indian masses—inherited from the Spanish conquest and the colonial era—reached nearly pathological dimensions in the Arbenz era (1951–54); in the late 1970s and 1980s it got worse.

31. Dunkerley, "Guatemala since 1930," 148.

32. Figures in 1982 dollars.

33. At the Somoza government's request, the United States sent a contingent of U.S. military police from the Panama Canal Zone to help maintain order in the city when units of the National Guard were too busy looting to do so.

34. Ambassador Shelton had left the party a half hour before the raid and was not among the FSLN hostages.

35. This is precisely what the United States proposed to the OAS in late June 1979, as discussed later in this chapter.

36. The Carter letter, now recognized as a major tactical error, was drafted by NSC staff member Robert Pastor at Carter's request, which was communicated through National Security Adviser Zbigniew Brzezinski. The human rights and Latin American staffs in the State Department opposed sending it. See Pastor's account in *Condemned to Repetition*, 66–71; see also Shirley Christian, *Nicaragua: Revolution in the Family* (New York: Vintage, 1986), 66–67.

37. See Robert Pastor, "The Carter Administration and Latin America: A Test of Principle," in *United States Policy in Latin America*, 82.

38. See Pastor's account in "Carter Administration and Latin America."

39. See Pastor, *Condemned to Repetition*, chap. 7.

40. The FSLN had already "rejected a so-called Brzezinski plan calling for Somoza to resign in favor of his handpicked Senate leader, Pablo Rener, who would turn the country over to an unnamed 'council of notables' in which the rebels would have only a nominal role" (Bernard Diederich, *Somoza and the Legacy of U.S. Involvement in Central America* [Maplewood, N.J.: Waterfront Press, 1989], 286). Diederich presumably refers to an administration effort to create an executive committee of moderates as "an alternative governing structure with an independent power base that would negotiate with the Junta"—a scheme that failed almost as soon as it was set in motion by the administration on 25 June. See Pastor, *Condemned to Repetition*, 151–59.

41. It is possible, however, that with full U.S. backing from the outset, and with aid on the multibillion-dollar scale of the U.S. program in El Salvador during the Reagan administration in the 1980s, the Somoza regime could have been saved. This alternative was not politically feasible for two reasons. First, neither the U.S.

public nor the Congress would have approved a massive aid program to keep Somoza in power. Second, such a program would have been opposed by most of the Latin American governments and would have subverted the administration's efforts to recover U.S. initiative and credibility in the region. The alternative the administration actually pursued—that of seeking a moderate transition—was both more feasible and more attractive.

42. The United States could have pressured Costa Rica and Honduras to patrol their skies and land borders aggressively to interdict weapons supplies. Costa Rica had no army to perform such duties, however, and it supported the FSLN. The Honduran military regime, which was cautiously supportive of Somoza, had neither the troops nor the equipment to undertake an effective effort. Moreover, it had no interest whatever in making its own army an open ally of the Somoza regime at a delicate moment in the process of returning the country to civilian rule. Only a major U.S. commitment of ground and air forces could have stopped the flow of arms to the FSLN.

43. For the best concise account of the development of the Salvadoran political and social crisis of the 1970s, see Sara Gordon, *Crisis política y guerra en El Salvador* (Mexico: Siglo XXI, 1989). This and subsequent paragraphs draw heavily on Gordon's analysis.

44. This nonevent was precipitated by Senator Frank Church, who sought to improve his reelection prospects among Idaho's conservative voters by denouncing Soviet perfidy. In fact, no new Soviet troop deployments to Cuba had occurred. Church lost his bid for reelection but helped to damage the prospects for the ratification of the START arms control treaty with the Soviet Union; the administration withdrew the treaty from consideration by the Senate that fall.

45. The National Guard, "a 3,500 man rural constabulary, created in the 1920s, on the model of the Spanish *Guardia Civil*," was controlled by the Ministry of Defense and commanded by regular army officers. Its primary role was to help landowners resist labor unions and peasant squatters. See Richard Millett, "Praetorians or Patriots: The Central American Military," in *Central America: Anatomy of Conflict*, ed. Robert S. Leiken (New York: Pergamon Press, 1984), 73.

46. Assistant Secretary of State for Inter-American Affairs Terrence Todman, whose support for the administration's human rights efforts was seldom wholehearted, expressed concern for the safety of the archbishop, as well as U.S. support for the archbishop's criticism of the military, by pointedly seeking him out on a visit to San Salvador in 1978 (Gordon, *Crisis política*, 253).

47. Ibid., 273.

48. The most important of the leaders of the younger officers was Colonel René Guerra y Guerra, shunted aside by adroit maneuvering on the part of Gutiérrez and his allies as the coup unfolded. Guerra y Guerra was committed to restructuring the government as well as the armed forces. Gutiérrez, who ended up on the new governing junta, was not.

49. Ungo had been the vice-presidential running mate of Christian Democratic presidential candidate José Napoleón Duarte in a coalition of opposition parties, including the Communist party, in 1972.

50. García appointed close associates to take command of the National Guard and the National Police, both noted conservatives known for their crude methods.

51. The single consistent exception was Patricia Derian, assistant secretary of state for human rights, whose objections were ignored.

52. See Cynthia Aronson, *El Salvador: A Revolution Confronts the United States* (Washington, D.C.: Institute for Policy Studies, 1982), 45. Aronson notes that the only new aid provided by the United States to El Salvador in the fall of 1979 was a small loan for the acquisition of riot-control equipment.

53. Gordon, *Crisis política*, 291–92.

54. The term *strategic hamlet*, used during the Vietnam War, was scrupulously avoided by U.S. and Salvadoran authorities in the 1980s.

55. The organizer of the assassination was the former deputy chief of army intelligence, Roberto D'Aubuisson, who became president of the National Assembly in 1982.

56. Duarte only became president of the junta, however, not president of the country. Gutiérrez remained commander-in-chief of the nation's armed forces, while Defense Minister García, who promised to step down, later refused to do so.

57. Salvadoran military leaders believed that the incoming Reagan administration would be more sympathetic to their views and unlikely to press them to comply with the commitments they were pushed into making in late 1980.

58. Because the murder of the U.S. churchwomen was followed on 5 January—prior to the "final offensive" and the subsequent resumption of military aid—by the execution of two more U.S. citizens, the circumstances could have justified such a position. The victims were two American Institute for Free Labor Development (AIFLD) advisers to the Salvadoran Agrarian Reform agency, at least one of whom also worked for the CIA. They were gunned down in the restaurant of the Sheraton Hotel, along with the president of the Salvadoran Institute for Agrarian Transformation, by two soldiers in civilian clothes acting on orders from superior officers.

59. The two were Arturo Cruz, well known in Washington from his years at the World Bank and a friend of U.S. Ambassador Pezzullo, and Rafael Córdova Rivas, a former Supreme Court justice under Somoza. Pezzullo, working behind the scenes to keep moderates in positions of influence, had a hand in their selection for appointment to the junta. See Christian, *Revolution in the Family*, 186.

60. See Pastor, *Condemned to Repetition*, 205.

61. For example, the Sandinista anthem, sung at most major public gatherings, referred to "yanquis" as "enemies of mankind." Similarly, the U.S. Congress imposed a series of amendments to the administration's aid bill, which annoyed the Sandinistas. During the debate on the measure, the speeches by U.S. congressmen—some of whom were former supporters of Somoza—made vivid reading in the Nicaraguan press.

62. Additional conditions required that aid be terminated on evidence of human rights violations, restrictions on labor unions, or the presence of Soviet, Cuban, or other foreign combat troops. Congress also forbade that any aid be given to any Nicaraguan educational institution that housed, employed, or was made available to Cuban personnel; required that 60 percent of the aid go to the private sector; and stipulated that all loan funds be spent in the United States. In addition, Congress required that 1 percent of the aid be used to publicize the fact that the United States was providing the other 99 percent. See Schoultz, *National Security and United States Policy*, 47n.

63. Pastor, *Condemned to Repetition*, chap. 11.

64. Raymond Bonner, *Weakness and Deceit: U.S. Policy and El Salvador* (New York: New York Times Books, 1984), 227.

65. Ibid., 225–26.

CHAPTER 6

1. The term is taken from Jean Kirkpatrick, "Dictatorships and Double Standards," *Commentary* 68, no. 5 (November 1979): 34–45.

2. See the discussion in Michael C. Desch, "Turning the Caribbean Flank: Sea-Lane Vulnerability during a European War," *Survival* 29, no. 6 (November–December 1987): 528–51. For a different view see Schoultz, *National Security and United States Policy*, 48–67.

3. The figures are for the period 1977 to 1985; see the International Commission for Central American Recovery and Development, *Poverty, Conflict, and Hope: A Turning Point in Central America* (Durham, N.C.: Duke University Press, 1989), 23.

4. Of this number, roughly 100,000 were Guatemalans, 70,000 Salvadorans, and 30,000 Nicaraguans. Most of the Guatemalan and Salvadoran dead were unarmed civilians killed by local security forces and the death squads they sponsored. In Nicaragua nearly all the civilian casualties were inflicted by the U.S.-backed contra rebels. A small number of Hondurans and Panamanians also died as a result of political violence during the decade.

5. Patricia Weiss Fagen estimated the total number of refugees and displaced persons in 1987 at between 1,877,785 and 2,893,985. Salvadorans accounted for the largest numbers (between 1.2 and 1.6 million). Guatemalans numbered between 250,000 and 600,000; Nicaraguans, 350,000 to 500,000; and Hondurans, 85,000 to 135,000. See her essay "Central American Refugees and U.S. Policy," in *Crisis in Central America: Regional Dynamics and U.S. Policy in the 1980s*, ed. Nora Hamilton, Jeffrey A. Frieden, Linda Fuller, and Manuel Pastor, Jr. (Boulder, Colo.: Westview Press, 1988), 76–77.

6. Entitlement programs provide benefits to which citizens are automatically "entitled" under specified conditions, such as Social Security pensions, medical care for the elderly and indigent, unemployment compensation, and the like. The administration overcame the resistance to increases in defense and foreign aid expenditures by financing many of them with foreign loans to cover rising budget deficits.

7. See Robert H. Johnson, "Exaggerating America's Stakes in Third World Conflicts," *International Security* 10 (Winter 1985–86): 32–68.

8. Roy Gutman, *Banana Diplomacy: The Making of American Policy in Nicaragua, 1981–87* (New York: Simon & Schuster, 1989), 26.

9. As Roy Gutman's account emphasizes, the Reagan decision-making "style" gave subordinates great latitude in formulating and implementing policy. Differences of opinion and occasionally bitter conflicts among his staff were common (ibid., 23–24). George P. Shultz, Reagan's secretary of state from 16 July 1982 to the end of Reagan's term, discusses some of these internal conflicts in *Turmoil and Triumph: My Years as Secretary of State* (New York: Charles Scribner's Sons, 1993). On Central American disputes, see chaps. 23 and 45 of Shultz's book.

10. Cynthia Aronson, "The Reagan Administration, Congress, and Central America," 37.

11. France and Panama also provided limited and "nonlethal" military aid in the early 1980s.

12. Elected governments replaced military regimes in Argentina, Bolivia, Chile, Ecuador, Paraguay, Peru, and Uruguay during the Reagan administration.

13. The president was also required to certify that the government of El Salvador was making progress in implementing political and economic reforms and in seeking a negotiated end to the civil war (see Aronson, "The Reagan Administration, Congress, and Central America," 40). The president's first certification was issued on 28 January 1982, less than three weeks after the Salvadoran army massacred nearly 1,000 unarmed civilians in and near the town of Mozote. U.S. and Salvadoran officials denied any massacre had taken place. Two months later, on 17 March, Salvadoran and Honduran troops caught civilians attempting to flee from the fighting by crossing the Lempa River into Honduras and massacred hundreds of them. The two governments denied reports of the incident. Congress continued to insist on regular certification, but the administration reduced the requirement to a mere formality, regularly issuing certifications of progress that cables from its own embassy in San Salvador frequently contradicted.

14. Hinton gave his speech, to the Salvadoran Chamber of Commerce, only three days after the under secretary of defense, Fred Iklé, had appeared in San Salvador with a similar message, which he had delivered directly to the Salvadoran high command. Iklé was not reprimanded.

15. See Deborah Barry, Raúl Vergara, and José Rodolfo Castro, "'Low Intensity Warfare': The Counterinsurgency Strategy for Central America," in *Crisis in Central America*, 87.

16. Ibid.

17. Terry Karl, "Exporting Democracy: The Unanticipated Effects of U.S. Electoral Policy in El Salvador," in *Crisis in Central America*, 174. The following account of the Salvadoran elections and their consequences draws heavily upon Karl's excellent analysis. The pressures for a political settlement, initially supported by Duarte, resulted from FDR-FMLN statements that expressed their readiness to negotiate, as well as from diplomatic initiatives launched by Mexico and the Socialist International. The Mexican efforts culminated in a joint declaration issued by France and Mexico on 28 August 1981, in which the two countries recognized the Salvadoran opposition as a "representative political force" and called for negotiations to end the civil war.

18. Edward S. Herman and Frank Brodhead, *Demonstration Elections: U.S.-Staged Elections in the Dominican Republic, Vietnam, and El Salvador* (Boston: South End Press, 1984).

19. The PDC also won 200 of the 262 municipal government elections held on the same day. For a survey of Salvadoran elections from 1948 to 1988, see José Z. García, "El Salvador: Recent Elections in Historical Perspective," in *Elections and Democracy in Central America*, ed. John A. Booth and Mitchell A. Seligson (Chapel Hill: University of North Carolina Press, 1989), 60–92.

20. See Karl, "Exporting Democracy," 187–88.

21. Karl has observed that Duarte's peace efforts "followed political rhythms that moved in tandem with the country's electoral cycle" (ibid., 183).

22. The name comes from the Spanish word *contrarevolucionario* (counter-revolutionary), the term the Sandinistas used to describe the U.S.-sponsored forces.

23. The FSLN lost the February 1990 elections to an unlikely coalition of opposition parties, headed by presidential candidate Violeta Chamorro. See Chapter 7.

24. The PRI has governed Mexico continuously since its founding in 1928.

25. In the United Nations, for example, Nicaragua often voted against the

United States and with the Soviet Union. This pattern, however, did not distinguish its voting record from that of many third-world countries. Nicaragua's votes coincided with Mexico's more often than with the Soviet Union's. See Mary D. Vanderlaan, *Revolution and Foreign Policy in Nicaragua* (Boulder, Colo.: Westview, 1986), 322.

26. Whether Nicaragua would have maintained this posture without U.S. pressure, however, is subject to question. A victory for the Salvadoran FMLN was as much in Nicaragua's interest after January 1981 as it was before. The analytical issue is whether Nicaraguan forbearance could have been assured by the Reagan administration through negotiations with the Sandinistas (an option not seriously explored) rather than attempts to overthrow them.

27. This attack, which involved the dynamiting of the two highway bridges that linked Nicaragua with Honduras, "was carried out by the FDN at express U.S. request," according to the contra's military chief (quoted in Gutman, *Banana Diplomacy*, 104). Aside from small-scale operations, the first major contra offensive did not begin until a year later.

28. When the state of emergency was reimposed, "many opposition politicians joined the Right in condemning the decree and temporarily withdrew from the National Assembly. The Supreme Court, including the FSLN-allied justices, unanimously condemned the decree. Within days, the FSLN softened its terms, and many of its harshest provisions were never enforced" (Eric Weaver and William Barnes, "Opposition Parties and Coalitions," in *Revolution and Counterrevolution in Nicaragua*, ed. Thomas W. Walker [Boulder, Colo.: Westview, 1991], 131).

29. The United States promoted Arturo Cruz, former head of the central bank and Nicaraguan ambassador in Washington, as a candidate for the presidency. Cruz broke with the Sandinista regime in 1983 and went on the CIA payroll shortly thereafter. The Nicaraguan government initially agreed to a series of conditions Cruz set down for running, but broke off negotiations brokered by officials of the Socialist International when Cruz escalated his demands to include Nicaraguan negotiations with the contras. Most observers expressed doubt that Cruz would have agreed to run under any circumstances. Without Cruz in the running, Daniel Ortega won the presidency with nearly two-thirds of the popular vote in the 4 November 1984 elections, which were deemed fair and open by international observers. See Gutman, *Banana Diplomacy*, 235–55.

30. After the Falklands War, which began in April 1982, the contras' Argentine advisers were replaced by U.S. government personnel, though the departure of the Argentines was delayed for nearly a year.

31. Some estimates of the contras' peak strength run as high as 20,000. This number may have been reached in 1990, when the contras moved into camps in Nicaragua under the terms of the peace accord signed in August 1988 and began recruiting new members. The population of the contra bases in Honduras also included more than 50,000 members of the families of the contra soldiers by the time the war ended.

32. The sheik of Brunei gave $10 million, but his contribution was deposited in the wrong Swiss bank account because of a clerical error in transcribing the account number at the NSC. Costa Rican assistance was reluctant and limited to permitting use of its territory for contra activities during the Monge administration. The main Salvadoran air force base at Ilopango was used as a transshipment facility for contra aid. The Salvadoran armed forces also provided small quantities of arms. In addition to

arms, the Guatemalan government issued false "end-user certificates" that facilitated the purchase of weapons from the governments of China and Portugal. (End-user certificates state that the purchaser will be the "end user"—that is, will not resell the weapons to others. Governments that acquire U.S. weapons must agree not to resell them to third parties without such certificates, to ensure that the weapons do not fall into the hands of terrorists.) Honduran aid included use of its territory for bases and resupply operations and the rental of such equipment as helicopters to transport supplies, as well as some training and arms aid. Israel provided financial assistance and acted as intermediary in the arms sales to Iran. Panama provided facilities for contra training and resupply operations, as well as financial contributions, some arms, and political support. Saudi Arabia provided over $31 million in financial assistance, used mainly for arms purchases, from 1984 to 1986. Taiwan also gave money. See Gutman, *Banana Diplomacy*, passim, and William I. Robinson and Kent Norsworthy, *David and Goliath: The U.S. War against Nicaragua* (New York: Monthly Review Press, 1987), 87.

33. Gutman, *Banana Diplomacy*, 75.

34. Ibid., 74.

35. U.S. Ambassador Anthony Quainton submitted an eight-point proposal to the Nicaraguan government on 8 April 1982, but its chief purpose was to impress Congress, which was then debating contra aid. The Nicaraguans rejected it because, in addition to including demands on security issues, it elevated "Nicaraguan internal affairs to the status of 'essential elements' in future relations with the United States" (William Goodfellow and James Morrell, "From Contadora to Esquipulas to Sapoá and Beyond," in *Revolution and Counterrevolution in Nicaragua*, 371)—a position the Nicaraguans had already rejected.

36. Ibid., 211. The Nicaraguan government, however, had already scheduled national elections for the following November. For Shultz's account of the meeting, see *Turmoil and Triumph*, 410–11.

37. The Manzanillo talks were opposed by the NSC, the CIA, and the Department of Defense from the beginning and were nearly called off before they could begin. See Shultz, *Turmoil and Triumph*, 411–15.

38. Quoted in Joel Brinkley, "Reagan Offer: A Way to Help the Contras," *New York Times*, 6 August 1987, 14.

39. For a quite different account of the U.S. attitude toward Contadora, see Shultz, *Turmoil and Triumph*, chaps. 23 and 45. The former secretary of state's account contains a retrospectively positive "spin" on his own attitude toward Contadora, which was not reflected in U.S. policy.

40. Brinkley, "A Way to Help the Contras," 14. An English translation was published in the *New York Times* on 12 August 1987. The official translation, which varies somewhat from the *Times* version, was published as an appendix to the International Commission for Central American Recovery and Development, *Poverty, Conflict, and Hope*, 121–26.

41. William M. LeoGrande, "The Contras and Congress," in *Reagan versus the Sandinistas: The Undeclared War on Nicaragua*, ed. Thomas W. Walker (Boulder: Westview, 1987), 223.

42. Defense Department assistance included the acquisition of PLO arms captured by the Israelis in Lebanon for shipment to the contras and the donation of surplus aircraft to the CIA for transfer to the FDN. See Peter Kornbluh, "The U.S. Role in the Counterrevolution," in *Revolution and Counterrevolution in Nicaragua*, 327.

43. Peter Kornbluh, "The Covert War," in *Reagan versus the Sandinistas*, 29.

44. Gutman, *Banana Diplomacy*, 177. CONDECA was founded in 1963 "at the behest of the U.S. Southern Command in Panama" to improve coordination of anti-Castro counterinsurgency efforts in El Salvador, Guatemala, Honduras, and Nicaragua (*Banana Diplomacy*, 176). General Alvarez, former head of the national police and a strong supporter of the contras, was named chief of the armed forces with Washington's support in January 1982 after the inauguration that month of President Roberto Suazo Córdova.

45. Enders was subsequently appointed U.S. ambassador to Spain in what may have been the sole demonstration of elegance in handling personnel matters in the history of U.S. diplomacy in the Reagan era. For an account of the circumstances surrounding Enders's departure, see Gutman, *Banana Diplomacy*, 129–41.

46. Gutman, *Banana Diplomacy*, 177. Senior military officers, as well as Defense Secretary Caspar Weinberger, consistently favored supporting the contras as an alternative to a U.S. invasion. Doubts about the military capacity of the contras to seize territory created uncertainty about the feasibility of this scheme, though the Hondurans and the CIA would probably have been able to provide enough help to make the plan work.

47. Despite the official cutoff in 1977, deliveries of U.S. military equipment valued at $2 million to $3 million per year continued. Military aid was resumed in 1984. Economic aid was never cut off. See Lars Schoultz, "Guatemala: Social Change and Political Conflict," in *Trouble in Our Backyard: Central America and the United States in the 1980s*, ed. Martin Diskin (New York: Pantheon, 1983), 187–89.

48. Gabriel Aguilera Peralta, "The Hidden War: Guatemala's Counterinsurgency Campaign," in *Crisis in Central America*, 155.

49. Ibid., 156.

50. Ríos Montt had been the Christian Democratic presidential candidate in 1974. His election victory was set aside by the military, who declared their own candidate the winner. Ríos Montt was therefore viewed as a reformer in the United States, though he had previously served as army chief of staff under President Arana Osorio (1970–74) during a period of severe repression. After "losing" the 1974 election, Ríos Montt converted to evangelical protestantism.

51. Aguilera Peralta, "The Hidden War," 160.

52. See Floria Castro, "La política exterior de Guatemala: 1982–1986," *Estudios Sociales Centroamericanos* 43 (January–April 1987): 65.

53. Cited in ibid.

54. Ibid.

55. Krauss, *Inside Central America*, 224. The southern front, however, collapsed by the end of 1984.

56. Ibid., 226.

57. Azcona's decision was presumably made on the recommendation of Armed Forces Chief López, who on 10 January 1986 received a payment of $450,000 from the U.S. Nicaraguan Humanitarian Assistance Office (NHAO), the State Department agency created to provide "nonlethal" aid to the contras when Congress forbade further CIA involvement in 1985. See Kornbluh, "The Covert War," 34.

58. As usual in Guatemala, left-wing parties could not participate in the election because of the threat of repression.

59. See Castro, "La política exterior de Guatemala," 68–69.

60. *Wall Street Journal*, 26 April 1986, 1ff.

61. *New York Times*, 12 June 1986, 1ff.

62. Mexican-U.S. relations suffered during the Reagan administration at a time when Mexico's economic crisis made that nation particularly vulnerable to U.S. pressure.

63. By mid-1984 the Contadora presidents had convened once, and their foreign ministers had met 17 times alone and seven times with the Central American foreign ministers. The Contadora's "technical group" and "working commissions" had met even more frequently. See Mario Ojeda, "México: Su ascenso a protagonista regional," in *Las relaciones de México con los países de América Central*, ed. Mario Ojeda (Mexico City: El Colegio de México, 1985), 29.

64. The original draft treaty would have applied to all of Central America, and thus required the closing of U.S. military bases in Honduras (but not in Panama, because Panama was not a party to the treaty), the departure of U.S. military advisers, an end to U.S. military exercises in the region, and a cutoff of all aid to the contras. The revised draft softened some of these provisions but maintained the contra aid prohibition.

65. Cited in Goodfellow and Morrell, "From Contadora," 322.

66. U.S. National Security Council internal memorandum, 20 October 1984 (cited in ibid., 372).

67. On the eve of the 24–25 May summit the United States again signaled its opposition to a negotiated solution to the Nicaraguan conflict and to the efforts of the Contadora Group. It did so by repudiating a letter to Congress from Philip Habib, who had replaced Shlaudeman as the administration's Central American special envoy. The Habib letter, dated 11 April 1986, was intended to summarize the administration's policies (and promote support for contra aid) and had been cleared by the White House. The letter stated that the administration would be willing to cut off aid to the contras if Nicaragua were to sign a verifiable Contadora treaty. The White House repudiated the Habib letter on 23 May.

68. Salvadoran President Duarte is reported to have said, "If I sign this plan, you might as well shoot me here, because I will be shot when I return [home to El Salvador]" (quoted in Goodfellow and Morrell, "From Contadora to Esquipulas," 176).

69. The talk was not idle. The administration was already putting pressure on Arias. It held up badly needed economic aid and launched a campaign of vilification in the main Costa Rican news media, subsidized by the CIA. Former Secretary of State Shultz did not mention this encounter nor any of the U.S. pressures applied to Arias; his memoirs (*Turmoil and Triumph*, chap. 45) claim that he held a generally positive view of the Arias plan.

70. Brinkley, "A Way to Help the Contras," 14. For Shultz's account of the Reagan-Wright agreement, which he helped to negotiate, see *Turmoil and Triumph*, 957–60.

71. In this sense historian Alejandro Bendaña, secretary general of the Nicaraguan Foreign Ministry in the Sandinista government, was right when he observed two years after the elections that "the 'independence' assumed by the four [other Central American] leaders in relation to the United States, was relative. . . . The Central Americans, along with the Contadora countries and the Support Group years before, had the premise that, in the face of the irrationality and increasing lack

of viability of the Reagan policy, Latin America was called upon to assume the rational defense of U.S. ideological and security interests with respect to Nicaragua and then the Salvadoran opposition" ("El proceso negociador de Esquipulas: Orígenes y perspectivas," *Boletín-CEI* [Centro de Estudios Internacionales, Managua] 2, [Primer Semestre, 1992]: 2).

72. In early 1987, however, "ten thousand [contra] troops marched south into Nicaragua," equipped with new uniforms, weapons, radios, and supplies from the $100 million approved by Congress in 1986. Even in such numbers, and carrying new *Redeye* antiaircraft missiles for use against the Nicaraguan army's Soviet-made helicopters, the contras were forced to operate in platoon-size units dispersed throughout the country and avoided attacking army units in favor of mainly civilian targets. The contras were supplied by illegal CIA-run air drops. See Sam Dillon, *Comandos: The CIA and Nicaragua's Contra Rebels* (New York: Henry Holt, 1991), 180–84.

73. For an inside account of this offer and the negotiations that nearly succeeded, see Shultz, *Turmoil and Triumph*, chap. 48.

CHAPTER 7

1. See the Kissinger commission report, *Report of the National Bipartisan Commission on Central America* (Washington, D.C.: U.S. Government Printing Office, 1984), chap. 1. The commission also advanced a version of the domino theory but discreetly avoided naming Mexico as its main concern. The prospect of Red hordes on the Rio Grande did not prove compelling in the post-Vietnam era.

2. A fourth major conflict, between the guerrillas and the armed forces in Guatemala, did not end, though negotiations occurred, because the Guatemalan government failed to convince the insurgents that adequate conditions for the exercise of their political and human rights would be created once they laid down their arms. The United States supported the negotiations and made constructive comments on human rights and democracy, but because the guerrillas had been contained by the scorched-earth policies of the Guatemalan army in the early 1980s and were no longer threatening to take power, the United States assigned a low priority to the peace process in Guatemala. With no incentive to negotiate, the Guatemalan government refused to do so. The U.S. administration, which provided little military aid and had not played an important role in the Guatemalan military's campaign against the insurgents, could not have influenced the behavior of the Guatemalan army without investing more effort and resources than it deemed appropriate under these circumstances. The Guatemalan government did agree to permit the return of some 45,000 refugees from camps in southern Mexico, where they had fled in the early 1980s. The first group of some 2,500 refugees crossed the border in January 1993. See *El País* (Madrid), 25 January 1993.

3. Not to be confused with the United Nicaraguan Opposition (also known as UNO), the name taken by the contra leadership organization when it was reorganized in 1985 by the CIA to blunt criticism in the U.S. Congress.

4. For an account of the electoral campaign and the conditions surrounding it, see Latin American Studies Association (LASA), *Electoral Democracy under International Pressure: The Report of the Latin American Studies Association Commission to Observe the 1990 Nicaraguan Election* (Pittsburgh: LASA, 1990), and the Council

of Freely Elected Heads of Government, Special Report No. 1: *Observing Nicaragua's Elections, 1989–1990* (Atlanta: Carter Center of Emory University, 1990).

5. For an excellent account of the peace agreement and its initial implementation, see Terry Karl, "El Salvador's Negotiated Revolution," *Foreign Affairs* 71, no. 2 (Spring 1992): 147–64.

6. The full amount of U.S. government support for UNO and its affiliated organizations may never be known. The U.S. Congress appropriated $9 million while the CIA was reported to be sending another $5 million. UNO's statement to the multiparty electoral commission reported that the coalition had received only $3.7 million by election day. This, together with at least $1.5 million to a UNO-dominated organization involved in voter education, registration, poll watching, and other activities would bring the overt total alone to $5.2 million. This is roughly (in U.S. dollars) $3.50 per voter, or nearly $7.00 per UNO vote. See Latin American Studies Association, *Electoral Democracy under International Pressure*, chap 8.

7. In 1992 U.S. Senator Jesse Helms managed to delay a portion of the economic aid the administration did secure from Congress to pressure the Chamorro government into dismissing the Sandinista chiefs of the armed forces and national police, whose cooperation had been vital to ensuring a peaceful transition for the new government.

8. The soldiers also murdered the priests' cook and her daughter, who witnessed the massacre. Terry Karl has referred to the November 1989 offensive as "El Salvador's Tet" and a "turning point on the road to negotiations" ("El Salvador's Negotiated Revolution," 151).

9. This was precisely the trap that the Carter administration adroitly avoided during the Nicaraguan revolution but fell into in El Salvador immediately after the Sandinista triumph in 1979.

10. U.S. policy toward Nicaragua from July 1979 until January 1981 constituted, arguably, an important exception to this rule.

11. Abraham F. Lowenthal, "The United States and Latin America in a New World," *North South: The Magazine of the Americas* 2, no. 1 (June–July 1992): 7.

12. The phrase "representative political force" was used in the Franco-Mexican Declaration of August 1981. The declaration urged a negotiated political settlement of the Salvadoran civil war. Infuriated Reagan administration officials rejected it immediately and exerted pressure on Latin American governments to follow suit.

13. Important exceptions were the 1954 intervention in Guatemala and the 1990 invasion of Panama.

BIBLIOGRAPHIC ESSAY

What Fidel Castro did for Cuban studies and the study of U.S.-Cuban relations, the Sandinista revolutionaries (and their cohorts in El Salvador and Guatemala) accomplished a generation later for the study of Central America. Since the Sandinista revolution of 1979, the number of historical and social-scientific works on Central America has increased exponentially. This brief essay mentions some of those I have found most useful, but many fine studies could not be included.

For information on Central America up to the mid-1950s, the published volumes of U.S. diplomatic correspondence are an invaluable primary source, despite the exclusion of still-classified materials for the cold war years. These volumes are published annually in Washington, D.C., under the title *Foreign Relations of the United States* (usually abbreviated *FRUS*, followed by a reference to the year and the volume cited). Additional materials are available in the National Archives and in presidential libraries (especially the Roosevelt, Truman, Eisenhower, Kennedy, Johnson, and Carter collections) and in the numerous volumes of memoirs published by former presidents, secretaries of state, national security advisers, and their aides, some of which are mentioned below. Until the Carter administration, however, the memoirs of presidents and key policy makers devoted little attention to Central America, except for the Guatemala episode of 1954 and the Panama Canal issue.

General histories of U.S. relations with Central America include Walter Lafeber's lively survey *Inevitable Revolutions: The United States in Central America* (New York: Norton, 1983) and Thomas M. Leonard's more sedate *Central America and the United States: The Search for Stability* (Athens: University of Georgia Press, 1991). Surveys of the larger context of U.S.-Latin American relations include Samuel Flagg Bemis's still-useful *Latin American Policy of the United States* (New York: Harcourt Brace, 1943);

Harold Molineu's recent work, which contains a helpful review of competing perspectives, *U.S. Policy Toward Latin America: From Regionalism to Globalism* (Boulder, Colo.: Westview, 1990); and an excellent institutional history of the region's international affairs by G. Pope Atkins, *Latin America in the International System* (Boulder, Colo.: Westview, 1989). Of the many volumes on the origins of the Monroe Doctrine, the best is Ernest R. May's *The Making of the Monroe Doctrine* (Cambridge: Harvard University Press, 1975).

Comparative and theoretical issues are discussed in an important anthology, *Dominant Powers and Subordinate States: The United States in Latin America and the Soviet Union in Eastern Europe*, edited by Jan F. Triska (Durham, N.C.: Duke University Press, 1986). For a superb analysis of U.S. concerns about security and instability in Latin America, with much attention to Central American issues, see Lars Schoultz, *National Security and United States Policy toward Latin America* (Princeton, N.J.: Princeton University Press, 1987). Valuable general works on the United States in Latin America include Cole Blasier, *The Hovering Giant: U.S. Responses to Revolutionary Change in Latin America, 1910–1985* (Pittsburgh: University of Pittsburgh Press, 1985); Abraham Lowenthal, *Partners in Conflict: The United States and Latin America* (Baltimore: Johns Hopkins University Press, 1987); and a number of useful edited volumes, including Kevin J. Middlebrook and Carlos Rico, eds., *The United States and Latin America in the 1980s* (Pittsburgh: University of Pittsburgh Press, 1986), and John D. Martz, ed., *United States Policy in Latin America: A Quarter Century of Crisis and Challenge, 1961–1986* (Lincoln: University of Nebraska Press, 1988).

The best general survey of Central American history from the colonial era (excluding Panama, as most do), is still Ralph Lee Woodward's *Central America: A Nation Divided*, 2d ed. (Oxford: Oxford University Press, 1985). Leslie Bethel has brought together the Central American chapters of the *Cambridge History of Latin America* in a single volume titled *Central America since Independence* (Cambridge: Cambridge University Press, 1991). An excellent summary emphasizing social and economic history is Hector Pérez Brignoli, *Breve historia de Centroamérica* (Mexico: Alianza Editorial Mexicana, 1985). The best history of twentieth-century economic affairs and economic policy making in the region is Victor Bulmer-Thomas's superb *The Political Economy of Central America since 1920* (Cambridge: Cambridge University Press, 1987). James Dunkerley's *Power in the Isthmus: A Political History of Modern Central America* (London: Verso, 1988) is a masterful and detailed survey of politics and social movements. An excellent survey of contemporary conflicts, sensitive to historical and theoretical issues, is John A. Booth and Thomas W. Walker, *Understanding Central America* (Boulder, Colo.: Westview, 1989). On Panama see Andrew Zimbalist and John Weeks, *Panama at the Crossroads: Economic and Political Change in the Twentieth Century* (Berkeley: University of California Press, 1991). Walter Lafeber's readable survey of twentieth-century Panamanian relations with the United States, first written at the time of the 1978 debate over the Panama Canal treaties, was updated and republished, by coincidence, at the time of the U.S. invasion of December 1989: *The Panama Canal: The Crisis in Historical Perspective* (Oxford: Oxford University Press, 1989).

Works on Central American relations with the United States in the nineteenth century and the first four decades of the twentieth century focus primarily on U.S.-British rivalries, the Walker affair in Nicaragua, the development of U.S. banana companies and other enterprises, the history of the Panama Canal, U.S. interventions in the era of "dollar diplomacy," and the shift to the Good Neighbor policy in the 1930s. For general works that cover the whole Caribbean see David Healy, *Drive to Hegemony: The United States in the Caribbean, 1898–1917* (Madison: University of Wisconsin Press, 1988), and Lester D. Langley, *The Struggle for the American Mediterranean: United States–European Rivalry, 1776–1904* (Athens: University of Georgia Press, 1976); see also Langley's *The United States and the Caribbean, 1900–1970* (Athens: University of Georgia Press, 1980). On the Panama Canal see David McCullough's thorough and engaging *Path between the Seas: The Creation of the Panama Canal, 1870–1914* (New York: Simon & Schuster, 1977). On "dollar diplomacy," see Lester D. Langley's *The Banana Wars: An Inner History of American Empire, 1900–1943* (Lexington: University of Kentucky Press, 1983). For a more benign view of U.S. behavior consult the usefully detailed volumes by former State Department official Dana G. Munro, *Intervention and Dollar Diplomacy in the Caribbean, 1900–1921* (Princeton, N.J.: Princeton University Press, 1964), and *The United States and the Caribbean Republics, 1921–1933* (Princeton, N.J.: Princeton University Press, 1974).

The Good Neighbor era in U.S.–Latin American relations is treated in Bryce Wood's classic, *The Making of the Good Neighbor Policy* (New York: Columbia University Press, 1961). More critical surveys of U.S.–Central American relations in the Good Neighbor era are found in David Green, *The Containment of Latin America: A History of the Myths and Realities of the Good Neighbor Policy* (Chicago: Quadrangle Books, 1971), and George Black, *The Good Neighbor: How the United States Wrote the History of Central America and the Caribbean* (New York: Pantheon Books, 1988). For Bryce Wood's later critique of U.S.–Latin American policies, see *The Dismantling of the Good Neighbor Policy* (Austin: University of Texas Press, 1985).

Historical works on each of the Central American republics prior to 1945 have appeared with increasing frequency in recent years. On Costa Rica see Mitchel Seligson, *Peasants of Costa Rica and the Development of Agrarian Capitalism* (Madison: University of Wisconsin Press, 1980). The massacre that inaugurated the military's dominance of Salvadoran political life is the subject of Thomas P. Anderson, *Matanza: El Salvador's Communist Revolt of 1932* (Lincoln: University of Nebraska Press, 1971). On the fall of the

Hernández Martínez dictatorship see Patricia Parkman, *Nonviolent Insurrection in El Salvador: The Fall of Maximiliano Hernández* Martínez (Tucson: University of Arizona Press, 1988). On Guatemala in the 1930s see Kenneth J. Grieb, *Guatemalan Caudillo: The Regime of Jorge Ubico* (Athens: Ohio University Press, 1979). On Nicaragua see Neill Macaulay's *The Sandino Affair* (Chicago: Quadrangle Books, 1967) and Richard Millett's useful history of the National Guard, *Guardians of the Dynasty: A History of the U.S.-Created Guardia Nacional de Nicaragua and the Somoza Family* (Maryknoll, N.Y.: Orbis Books, 1977). The best social history of modern Nicaragua is by Jeffrey L. Gould, *To Lead as Equals: Rural Protest and Political Consciousness in Chinandega, Nicaragua (1912–1979)* (Chapel Hill: University of North Carolina Press, 1990).

General works on the foreign policy and diplomatic history of the Truman and Eisenhower administrations abound, but most of them focus—as did the policy makers of the two administrations—on relations with the Soviet Union, Western Europe, and China, as well as on the Korean War. On the Truman era see Roger R. Trask, "The Impact of the Cold War on United States–Latin American Relations," *Diplomatic History* 1 (Summer 1977): 271–84. For the 1950s, Stephen Rabe's excellent survey fills an important gap: *Eisenhower and Latin America: The Foreign Policy of Anticommunism* (Chapel Hill: University of North Carolina Press, 1988). The collaboration of the AFL and AFL-CIO with the anticommunist crusades of the era, particularly in Latin America, is documented in Ronald Radosh, *American Labor and United States Foreign Policy* (New York: Random House, 1969). On the political history of the region after 1945 see Charles D. Ameringer, *Democratic Left in Exile* (Coral Gables, Fla.: University of Miami Press, 1974) and the surveys cited above.

Studies of individual countries and their foreign relations between 1945 and 1960 have accumulated impressively over the past two decades. For an excellent study of U.S. relations with Costa Rica in the decade leading up to the 1948 national revolution, see Jacobo Schifter, *Las alianzas conflictivas: Las relaciones de Costa Rica y Estados Unidos de la segunda guerra mundial a los inicios de la guerra civil* (San José, Costa Rica: Libro Libre, 1986). A useful biography of José Figueres is Charles D. Ameringer's *Don Pepe* (Albuquerque: University of New Mexico Press, 1978). On U.S. relations with Somoza during the high cold war, see the early chapters of Karl Bermann's excellent *Under the Big Stick: Nicaragua and the United States since 1948* (Boston: South End Press, 1986). On Panama see Larry LaRae Pippin, *The Remón Era: An Analysis of a Decade of Events in Panama, 1947–1957* (Stanford, Calif.: Institute of Hispanic American and Luso-Brazilian Studies, Stanford University, 1964).

The three major works on the U.S. intervention in Guatemala in 1954 are Richard Immerman, *The CIA in Guatemala: The Foreign Policy of Intervention* (Austin: University of Texas Press, 1982); Stephen Kinzer and

Stephen Schlesinger, *Bitter Fruit: The Untold Story of the American Coup in Guatemala* (Garden City, N.Y.: Anchor Books, 1983); and Piero Gleijeses, *Shattered Hope: The Guatemalan Revolution and the United States, 1944–54* (Princeton, N.J.: Princeton University Press, 1991). Gleijeses's powerful book focuses primarily on Guatemala and is the best source on the Arbenz regime. For an influential analysis of the consequences of the 1954 intervention see Richard Adams, *Crucifixion by Power: Essays on Guatemalan National Social Structure, 1944–1966* (Austin: University of Texas Press, 1970). Guatemalan president Juan José Arévalo (1945–50) was a prolific writer; see his *The Shark and the Sardines* (New York: Lyle Stuart, 1963).

On the Alliance for Progress in Latin America, the best survey is still the work of two journalists, Jerome Levinson and Juan de Onis, *The Alliance That Lost Its Way: A Critical Report on the Alliance for Progress* (Chicago: Quadrangle Books, 1970). For reviews of more recent opinions, see Joseph S. Tulchin, "The United States and Latin America in the 1960s," *Journal of Inter-American Studies and World Affairs* 30, no. 1 (Spring 1988): 1–36; and Abraham F. Lowenthal, "'Liberal,' 'Radical,' and 'Bureaucratic Perspectives' on U.S.-Latin American Policy: The Alliance for Progress in Retrospect," in *Latin America and the United States: The Changing Political Realities*, edited by Julio Cotler and Richard Fagen (Stanford, Calif.: Stanford University Press, 1974). For a critical view see Simon G. Hansen, *Five Years of the Alliance for Progress: An Appraisal* (Washington, D.C.: Inter-American Affairs Press, 1967). Hansen edited the journal *Inter-American Economic Affairs* in the 1960s; his criticisms of Alliance programs appeared frequently in its pages. On the impact of the Cuban revolution, the guerrilla movements, and the official terror of the 1960s in Guatemala, see John A. Booth, "A Guatemalan Nightmare: Levels of Political Violence, 1966–1972," *Journal of Inter-American Studies and World Affairs* 22 (May 1980): 195–225.

The origins of the political and social upheavals that engulfed the isthmus by the late 1970s are analyzed in detail in books that deal with individual countries. An important exception is Bulmer-Thomas's *Political Economy* (cited earlier), which compares economic and social developments in all five countries (excluding Panama). Also helpful are John Weeks, *The Economies of Central America* (New York: Holmes & Meier, 1985), and Robert G. Williams, *Export Agriculture and the Crisis in Central America* (Chapel Hill: University of North Carolina Press, 1986). On the 1969 "Soccer War" between El Salvador and Honduras see Thomas P. Anderson, *The War of the Dispossessed: Honduras and El Salvador, 1969* (Lincoln: University of Nebraska Press, 1981).

On the coming of the Sandinista revolution see the works by Bulmer-Thomas, Diederich, Dunkerley, and Bermann (cited earlier); see also Shirley Christian, *Nicaragua: Revolution in the Family* (New York: Vintage, 1986).

Regarding El Salvador, Sara Gordon offers an insightful historical analysis of the political and social conflict that led to the outbreak of full-scale civil war in *Crisis política y guerra en El Salvador* (Mexico: Siglo XXI, 1989). See also Enrique Baylora's important *El Salvador in Transition* (Chapel Hill: University of North Carolina Press, 1982); Cynthia Aronson, *El Salvador: A Revolution Confronts the United States* (Washington, D.C.: Institute for Policy Studies, 1982); James Dunkerley, *The Long War: Dictatorship and Revolution in El Salvador* (London: Junction Books, 1982); and Robert Armstrong and Janet Schenk, *El Salvador: The Face of Revolution* (Boston: South End Press, 1982). For a compendium of important documents and data, see Marvin Gettleman, Patrick Lacefield, Louis Menashe, David Mermelstein, and Ronald Radosh, eds., *El Salvador: Central America in the New Cold War*, rev. ed. (New York: Grove Press, 1986).

On Guatemala in the 1970s and early 1980s see the volume edited by Jonathan L. Fried, Marvin Gettleman, Deborah Levinson, and Nancy Pechenham: *Guatemala in Rebellion: Unfinished History* (New York: Grove Press, 1983); Edelberto Torres-Rivas, "Guatemala—Crisis and Political Violence," *NACLA Report on the Americas* 14, no. 1 (January–February 1980); Gabriel Aguilera Peralta, Romero Imery, et al., *Dialéctica del terror en Guatemala* (San José, Costa Rica: Editorial Universitaria Centroamericana, 1981); and George Black, *Garrison Guatemala* (New York: Monthly Review Press, 1984).

An excellent volume on modern Honduras is Mark B. Rosenberg and Philip L. Shepherd, eds., *Honduras Confronts Its Future: Contending Perspectives on Critical Issues* (Boulder, Colo.: Lynne Rienner, 1986).

The annual reports on human rights published by the U.S. State Department, together with the reports of nongovernmental organizations (NGOs) such as Amnesty International, Americas Watch, and the Washington Office on Latin America, are invaluable sources for understanding political conditions in Central America during the 1970s and 1980s. Also invaluable is Lars Schoultz's analysis of the impact of human rights organizations and other NGOs on policy making in the 1970s, *Human Rights and United States Policy toward Latin America* (Princeton, N.J.: Princeton University Press, 1981).

The Carter administration's efforts to cope with the Sandinista revolution are chronicled and analyzed in Robert Pastor's remarkable *Condemned to Repetition: The United States and Nicaragua* (Princeton, N.J.: Princeton University Press, 1987); Pastor was in charge of Latin American affairs at the National Security Council. Concerning El Salvador, Raymond Bonner, the *New York Times* correspondent in that country, wrote the best-researched and most insightful (and critical) account of U.S. policy in his *Weakness and Deceit: U.S. Policy and El Salvador* (New York: New York Times Books, 1984). On Costa Rica see Mitchell A. Seligson and Edward Muller, "Democracy, Stability, and Economic Crisis: Costa Rica, 1978–1983," *International Studies Quarterly* 31 (September 1987).

The conflicts of the Reagan era inspired a mass of valuable work on the United States and Central America. An important contribution is that by leading Central American historian and intellectual Edelberto Torres-Rivas, *Repression and Resistance: The Struggle for Democracy in Central America* (Boulder, Colo.: Westview, 1989). A number of edited volumes produced in the 1980s contain essays on current developments by leading scholars: Mary Jo Blachman, William M. LeoGrande, and Kenneth E. Sharpe, eds., *Confronting Revolution: Security through Diplomacy in Central America* (New York: Pantheon, 1986); Martin Diskin, ed., *Trouble in Our Backyard: Central America and the United States in the 1980s* (New York: Pantheon, 1983); Nora Hamilton, Jeffrey A. Frieden, Linda Fuller, and Manuel Pastor, Jr., eds., *Crisis in Central America: Regional Dynamics and U.S. Policy in the 1980s* (Boulder, Colo.: Westview, 1988); Robert S. Leiken, ed., *Central America: Anatomy of Conflict* (New York: Pergamon Press, 1984). An excellent source of information—especially for its detailed information on U.S. economic interests in the region—is Tom Barry and Deb Preusch, *The Central America Fact Book* (New York: Grove Press, 1986). See also the Kissinger commission's *Report of the President's National Bipartisan Commission on Central America* (Washington, D.C.: U.S. Government Printing Office, 1984). A useful summary of the U.S. political debates that emphasizes the post-Vietnam "breakdown of consensus" in Washington is Dario Moreno, *U.S. Policy in Central America: The Endless Debate* (Miami: Florida International University Press, 1990). On the Reagan administration's troubles with Congress, an invaluable book is Cynthia Aronson's *Crossroads: Congress, the Reagan Administration, and Central America* (New York: Pantheon, 1989). The memoirs of George P. Shultz, Reagan's secretary of state from 16 July 1982 to the end of Reagan's term, is useful for its description of the administration's chaotic foreign policy decision-making processes: *Turmoil and Triumph: My Years as Secretary of State* (New York: Charles Scribner's Sons, 1993). On Central America, the book contains only brief and largely self-serving narratives on the author's episodic attention to the region.

U.S. relations with Nicaragua, along with the contra war, received the most attention from scholars and journalists during the 1980s. For an excellent account of administration decision making (up to 1987) by a well-informed journalist, see Roy Gutman's *Banana Diplomacy: The Making of American Policy in Nicaragua, 1981–87* (New York: Simon & Schuster, 1989). Some of the best scholarly work was published in anthologies, especially those edited by Thomas W. Walker: *Reagan versus the Sandinistas: The Undeclared War on Nicaragua* (Boulder, Colo.: Westview, 1987) and *Revolution and Counterrevolution in Nicaragua* (Boulder, Colo.: Westview, 1991). For U.S. policy in El Salvador, Terry Karl's work is outstanding for its sophistication and rigor; see especially "Exporting Democracy: The Unanticipated Effects of U.S. Electoral Policy in El Salvador," in *Crisis in*

Central America, edited by Nora Hamilton et al. (cited earlier), and "El Salvador's Negotiated Revolution," *Foreign Affairs* 71, no. 2 (Spring 1992): 147–64. On the confrontation with the Noriega government in Panama that led to the U.S. invasion in 1989, see the updated edition of Lafeber's *Panama Canal* and John Dinges's *Our Man in Panama* (New York: Random House, 1991).

INDEX

Abrams, Elliot, 202
Acheson, Dean, 72
Adams, John Quincy, 36, 223
Afghanistan, 148, 163
AFL-CIO, 76, 108, 241n29
aid. *See* Economic aid
Alianza Republicana Nacional
(ARENA), 173, 175, 215
Allende, Salvador, 160
Alliance for Progress: development of
policy under, 90–91; Eisenhower
administration and, 90–102; end
of, 122–31; failure of, 116–17;
Johnson administration and,
109–16; Kennedy administration
and, 102–9, 117; main components
of, 90; U.S. corporations and,
108
Alvarez Martínez, Gustavo, 182, 188,
191, 194, 205, 230
American Federation of Labor (AFL),
40, 53–56, 241n29
American Institute for Free Labor
Development (AIFLD), 108, 174,
192
Andino, Mario, 151
anticommunism: cold war and, 66–67;

Costa Rican revolution (1948) and,
58, 59–65; democratization and
authoritarian regimes and, 56–58;
labor movement and, 54–56; U.S.
policy and, 56–57, 107
Arafat, Yasir, 159
Araña, Francisco Javier, 69, 236n20
Arana Osorio, Carlos, 130, 228, 244n23
Arbenz, Jacobo, 58, 75, 76, 77, 78, 82,
84–85, 86, 88, 227; overthrow of,
71–74, 240n21; U.S. military intervention (1954) and, 67, 69–71
Arévalo, Juan José, 57, 59–60, 62, 63,
64, 67, 68, 69, 82, 88, 104, 119,
226, 228, 236n20
Argentina, 49, 72, 91, 96, 103, 110, 122,
163, 182, 200, 235n1
Argüello, Leonardo, 62
Arias, Arnulfo, 45, 80, 114, 115–16, 194,
225, 228
Arias, Oscar, 176, 195–96, 198, 200,
202, 230
Arias, Ricardo, 81
Arias peace plan, 178, 183, 197, 198–99,
200
Arms sales, 51, 52, 61, 142, 145, 237n30
Azcona Hoyos, José, 195, 200, 201

THE AUTHOR

John H. Coatsworth is the Monroe Gutman Professor of Latin American Affairs in the History Department at Harvard University and chairs Harvard's Committee on Latin American and Iberian Studies. He received his Ph.D. in economic history from the University of Wisconsin, Madison, and has taught at the University of Chicago, as well as universities and research institutes in Mexico, Argentina, and Spain. He is the author of two books on Mexican economic history and articles on Latin America social and international history. He is president-elect of the American Historical Association.